THE DISCIPLINE OF HISTORY AND THE HISTORY OF THOUGHT

Should historians be story-tellers? How do we know what someone thought? How do we explain it?

Although much has been written on the nature of history and its disciplinary problems, less attention has been paid to the history of thought. M. C. Lemon's rigorously philosophical work first re-asserts the discipline of history in general as narrative based, before pursuing the methodological implications for the history of thought.

The appeal of M. C. Lemon's approach lies in its direct treatment of questions such as the logic of narrative explanation, issues which other philosophers of history have neglected or, in his view, misunderstood. Rather than 'ideas', M. C. Lemon focuses on the activity of thinking and the centrality of method. He then analyses the communication of thought, based partly on the observation that not all that is thought is said, and not all that is said is the product of thinking.

M. C. Lemon concludes by raising questions regarding the status as real historical phenomena of intellectual movements such as the Renaissance and the Enlightenment.

This original work of scholarship will raise the level of argument in philosophy of history and provoke debate among historians, philosophers, and political theorists.

M. C. Lemon is Lecturer in History at the University of Ulster at Coleraine.

THE DISCIPLINE OF HISTORY AND THE HISTORY OF THOUGHT

M. C. Lemon

London and New York

First published 1995
by Routledge
11 New Fetter Lane, London EC4P 4EE

Simultaneously published in the USA and Canada
by Routledge
29 West 35th Street, New York, NY 10001

Reprinted in 1996

© 1995 M. C. Lemon

Phototypeset in Bembo by
Intype Ltd, London

Printed and bound in Great Britain by
Antony Rowe Ltd, Chippenham, Wiltshire

British Library Cataloguing in Publication Data
A catalogue record for this book is available from the British Library

Library of Congress Cataloguing in Publication Data
Lemon, M. C. (Michael C.)
The discipline of history and the history of thought/M. C. Lemon.
p. cm.
Includes bibliographical references (p.) and index.
1. History–Methodology. 2. History–Philosophy. I. Title.
D16.L54 1995
901–dc20 94–41276

ISBN 0–415–12346–1

CONTENTS

PREFACE

The notion of attempting a theoretical study into methodology in the history of thought was put to me by Henry Tudor, of the Politics Department in the University of Durham. His encouragement, but more especially, his stature as inspiring tutor and meticulous intellect, has sustained my efforts long after geography has distanced contact. In what follows, there are thus doubtless some ideas, arguments, and approaches which were directly generated in our early discussions, and any virtues this book might display may safely be attributed to him. What mistakes, misperceptions, and dubious arguments might be found are, of course, entirely my responsibility.

My thanks go to John Springhall for directing my attention to relevant writings about social history, and to the remainder of my colleagues in History at the University of Ulster at Coleraine for being unwitting objects of study from time to time! I am also grateful to Joanne Taggart for her patient and generous technical assistance.

A word about the Notes and references, and the Bibliography, particularly since I devote considerable discussion to the issue of explaining what individuals both think and write (or say), partly in terms of what was on their minds; approximately one third of the Notes and references, and one half of the items in the Bibliography (including all the additional references in the selective reading section), were added after the text was completed, better to locate the reader in some of the relevant literature of the past three decades. The notes and references in question are: all to Chapter One except 3, 6, and parts of 7, 8, and 9; 1, 4, 5, 10, 12, 13, to Chapter Two; 11, 12, 17, 18, to Chapter Three; 1, 2, 15, 19, 20, 21, 24, 25, 26, 28, 34, to Chapter Four; 1, 2, 4, 5, 6, 8, 9, 16, 17, 18, 19, 23, 31, 59, to Chapter Five.

M. C. Lemon
University of Ulster at Coleraine

INTRODUCTION

This book stems from reflections on methodology in the study and writing of history, especially the history of political thought. In thinking about what are, and ought to be, the characteristics of these activities, it has seemed necessary to my mind to enquire closely into the nature of the phenomena they deal with – provisionally, for example, past events, present evidence, and human activity in relation to history generally; and ideas, thinking, and arguments in relation to the history of thought. Rather than omit them, I have chosen to present these considerations (in the form of organised arguments) as preparatory to the principal conclusions I advance regarding the topic of historical methodology, and it is their inclusion which warrants this book's description as, in part, a contribution to the analytic philosophy of history. Further, to the extent there are lines of consistency between the different areas treated, the book as a whole is indicative of a more general philosophical position under which its content is subsumed. Where addressing theorists, then, it is unreasonable to expect the general run of historians (with the exception of historians of thought, much of whose material is itself theoretical), to take any special interest in much of what follows despite its being centred on the methodology of their discipline. They might, however, be interested in the conclusions which analytic theorists of history reach, and the more so the more prescriptive these conclusions are regarding what is after all their, the historians', activity. Yet it is understandable that ultimately such interest remain, for historians, merely 'academic'; rightly, examples are of far more immediate relevance to practitioners than a list of prescriptions from theorists. Insofar as this is a book of theory, then, the instruction it contains is poles apart from telling historians what they ought to do. Rather, it tells philosophers what historians, in the main, *actually* do; further, it tells them that this is also what they *ought* to do in any event. In so doing it contains far more instruction for philosophers than for historians.

Consequently in this book I do not enumerate all the prescriptions its arguments might imply. Rather, I am concerned to elaborate a framework for the study and writing of history which serves to identify the discipline as having a distinct rationale or coherence. In so doing the task here is that of exploring the nature of things (in this case, those intellectual activities associated under the notoriously broad term, 'history'), and as such the purpose of the book is explanatory rather than prescriptive. Yet as must always be the case, to single out, characterise, and explain the nature of something is to straddle the actual and the ideal world. We can say what those known as historians actually do and find that different historians do things so diverse that we cannot identify, from the real world, a specific single activity called 'history'. Or we may find all historians do roughly the same thing but that it is such a combination of otherwise discrete activities that again we cannot identify, from the real world, a singular activity specified in terms of its internal coherence. In either case one is at liberty to conclude that all 'doing history' means is that which is actually done by historians, and that it happens to have no singular coherence.

On the other hand the very posing of the question, 'what is history?', seems to invite an answer identifying a particular discipline in terms of its having specific boundaries the historian should not step outside of if he is to remain an historian rather than become, for instance, a philosopher or a social scientist. These parameters might be more or less generous, for example embracing economic, social, and intellectual history, and the history of art, science, and warfare. But this only highlights the notion that there are indeed boundaries; and to the extent they are conceptual rather than merely empirical or conventional, we seem to be entering an ideal world where we run the risk of appearing to discover, or invent, an activity perfectly coherent in its internal logic but which has never been achieved in reality, and which may never even have been attempted. In itself this would seem odd enough; such an idea of what history 'is' might be a curiosity and no more. Yet as an 'ideal type' such an idea cannot but be prescriptive – it purports to exemplify what actual history ought to be – and thereby excites controversy rather than mere curiosity. Whether actual historians think and write about Joseph Stalin being a good or bad individual is an empirical question answered by historiography. Alternatively, whether historians *should* think and write about Stalin in moral terms is a philosophical question to which different ideal conceptions of history supply different answers. But just as we might find alternative ideal conceptions of history more or less satisfactory to the extent they relate more closely or distantly to what historians actually do, so we might find different historical writings more or less satisfactory to the extent they succeed or fail in relating to some ideal conception of the discipline.

In short, philosophy of history should be realistic and historiography should be critical, so that we can look forward to a productive marriage of the ideal and actual world rather than an uncomfortable straddling of the two. No one who wishes to understand and possibly engage in the activity of gardening would find it sufficient to be shown, uncritically, a few gardens, for they may be poor examples; neither, however, would it suffice to present them with this or that 'theory' of gardening derived from philosophical elaborations upon its dictionary definition. This is where the plain man would take his stand with respect to gardening and I suggest it is where the intellectual should stand with respect to doing history. Only to the extent that the theory and the practice of 'doing history' interpenetrate can we expect historians to attend seriously to analytic theorists of history and the latter in their turn to produce worth-while ideas.

Chapter One, 'What is history?', revisits familiar territory, but in focusing on what most historians actually do, leads to the following chapter's analysis of an 'unfashionable' phenomenon amongst many philosophers of history, namely, narrative. Chapter Three identifies and addresses problems the practising historian encounters in fulfilling the demands implied by those principles of narrative explanation and construction theorised in Chapter Two – for instance, agency, continuity, intelligibility, selection, relevance, origins, consequences, and subject-areas. In the light of those principles thus teased out as underpinning history as a coherent discipline, Chapter Four assesses different *esoterica* in analytic and speculative philosophies of history, as a way of distinguishing, clarifying, and summarising this book's arguments regarding the distinctness, rationale, and coherence of history as an intellectual activity. Chapter Five then seeks to exemplify the general principles arrived at by demonstrating their literal application to what is otherwise often regarded and treated as a separate kind of study, namely, the 'history of thought'. In the course of this I introduce actual examples drawn principally from well-known thinkers and other phenomena in the history of political thought.

1

WHAT IS HISTORY?

THE DIVERSITY OF HISTORY

When we think of the term 'history' we recognise it with an easy familiarity and are likely to be impressed rather than bewildered by the massive variety of subject-matter it encompasses. Its immense scope does not discourage us from nevertheless regarding it as a distinct, singular subject, and in this respect it is similar to 'literature' and 'science'. Unlike subjects such as music and theology which seem intrinsically well-defined in scope, 'history', 'literature', and 'science' are still easily recognised as distinct subjects despite the diverse abundance of topics and approaches they respectively embrace. This is a statement of fact, of course, not a philosophical point – and yet we might take encouragement from a possible perception it offers; namely, that despite the huge difficulties philosophy encounters in trying to extract the 'essence' of history as a discipline from the vast field of historical studies, the common wisdom of language, at least, promises that such efforts can be rewarded.

What, on the face of it, are these difficulties? If we ask what the subject-matter of history is we can begin by suggesting the layman will often respond by saying countries are the subject of history – 'history' is about the history of, for example, England, France, or Japan. And what he is likely to mean by a country's history is primarily its *political* history; for instance, which monarch was in power, what problems beset his reign, what wars he fought, who succeeded, and how – and in more modern times, what constitutional changes occurred, which parties gained power, and why they were ousted. In recounting such a political history it is clearly necessary to refer to religion, trade, warfare; maybe even to science and the arts, depending upon the particular problems and influences relevant to a given period. Yet these other subjects are not central. They crop up as factors influencing what *is* essential, namely, the political history of a country. In this 'mainline' version of what history is, politics assumes its Aristotelian role of 'the master science'; the 'history' of a country is equated with its political history.

4

Whatever we might say about this view of history as a subject, maybe to discard it as the 'unscientific' popular conception or to locate it as an illusion of merely liberal historiography, it nevertheless implies certain distinctions which introduce us to some of the difficulties in 'pinning down' its subject-matter. Firstly it suggests the history of a country should be looked at through political lenses, so to speak. It would seem absurd to look at the history of a country through, for instance, artistic, scientific, or even religious lenses. More generously, others might say we should trace a country's history through political, economic, and maybe even 'social' lenses – but they would still discount tracing it through, for example, its music, philosophy, or technology. What, however, is not discounted is the notion of looking at, for instance, the history of art or philosophy *in* a country, or even such histories outside national limits. Such histories, then, do not have 'a country' as their subject-matter (and survey it through political or economic lenses). They have art, science, philosophy, or religion as their subject-matter and appear to need no separate 'lens' with which to survey them. At most, just as 'mainline' political history might need as the occasion arises to pay attention to religious topics, so might the historian of art, for example, need to pay attention to political matters.

This gives rise to a second suggestion which points to added difficulties in 'pinning down' what history is, for if we can distinguish between 'mainline' history construed as the political history of a country and 'sideline' history construed as, for instance, the history of art *in* a country, then why should we not conceive of the history of politics *in* a country, and hold that distinct from the political history *of* a country? In other words, for example, would not the political history of France differ from the history of politics in France? Further, why should we not conceive of a history of politics released from national boundaries, and what would be the relation between such a history and national histories looked at 'through political lenses'? In the former case politics is the subject matter of the history, whereas in the latter case 'the country' is the subject-matter (dealt with in political terms), and it is clear the two histories would differ because of their differing subject-matters.

In short, then, histories differ to the extent their subject-matters differ. History has to be the history of something, and what that thing is must, at least in part, determine the approach of the historian. If an art historian, he will be writing about art and must needs know a considerable amount about it; likewise, respectively, with the history of religion, science, philosophy, and architecture. If a 'mainline' historian he presumably needs to know about, although perhaps not master, many different subjects. Are, then, the demands made upon the historian's approach to his subject-matter *from* that subject-matter so diverse (either as specialised, or as jack-

5

of-all-trades) as to persuade us there simply is no such thing as 'history' understood as a unitary, common discipline?

Let us not underestimate the issue. In terms of subject-matter we talk of 'mainline' history, often of a country, or of certain topics such as the history of the Peloponnesian Wars, the French Revolution, British imperialism, or Arab nationalism. Distinct from such mainline history we talk of economic history, social history, international history, the history of thought, art, and leisure; and there seems nothing intrinsically wrong with the history of wine-making, or of aviation, for example. There is even the history of history, of course – namely, historiography. Given their respective subject-matters, what does the historian of the Irish language do that is the same as the historian of the First World War, and what do they both do that is the same as the historian of Roman architecture? What this amounts to is to ask again, in a highlighted way, what it is that 'the historian' does to identify him as an historian rather than as, for instance, an expert on the Peloponnesian Wars, the Irish language, or Roman architecture. His discipline, if it exists at all, seems impervious to its subject-matter to an extent that all other disciplines, with the exception of 'science' and 'philosophy', cannot afford. Yet conventionally, if not logically, neither science nor philosophy, nor, indeed, history, are totally impervious to their subject-matters. Conventionally we do not write a history of the functioning of the human kidney – neither do we philosophise about it; but it provides rich material for the scientist. Conventionally we do not write a history of the nature of aesthetic consciousness, nor do we expect scientists to; but it is rich material for the philosopher. Just so, we do not expect scientists to write about the downfall of the Roman Republic, nor philosophers; but it is rich material for the historian.

So despite its enormous diversity of subject-matter, far beyond that of most other disciplines, it would seem that what the historian does *is* related to his subject-matter. What is this relationship? What determines what the historian does *not* study and write about? Is it that, in being an historian, certain subjects are closed to him? Or is it that certain subjects are simply unapproachable through history? Or do both questions come to the same thing? Whichever the case, what insight does it give us into the nature of history as a discipline?

THE HISTORIAN AND 'THE PAST'

The simplest and agreeably uncontroversial answer to the questions just posed regarding the relationship between the subject-matter of history and what it is the historian does with it revolves around the observation that the historian deals with the past.[1] In theory 'the past' encompasses any and every thing, and this accounts for the potentially overwhelming diversity of subject-matter for the historian. That political history may be more important, interesting, or instructive than, for instance, the history of wine-making, does not essentially affect the status of wine-making as a legitimate subject-matter since it 'has a past', and that is all which is required to render a subject-matter suitable for historians' attention. Ultimately the choice of subject-matter is a contingent matter, so long as it is located in the past. At any one point in time the practical concerns of a society, its current intellectual traditions, prevailing political ideologies, existing and developing stock of investigative techniques, and the particular, unpredictable interests of historians themselves – all are factors determining what subjects historians study and write about. The integrity of history as a discipline does not depend, then, on what the historian chooses from the past as an object of his attention; its integrity is assured, whatever his topic, so long as it belongs to the past.

Platitudinous as this answer might be, it does convey some truth. What seems implied by insisting history is essentially concerned with the past is that, in dealing with matters not present to us and which we therefore cannot know of 'immediately', we require some different approach, some method of knowing distinct from that by which we know things present to us – and the further implication is that the discipline of history is defined essentially in terms of this special problem regarding acquiring knowledge of the past. It is hardly necessary to engage in complex philosophical arguments regarding the nature of knowledge to identify what this special problem amounts to; an event or situation which is past is beyond our present experience and we can hence only be aware of it at second-hand, so to speak. What this means is that we regard some things which we can experience here and now as evidence of past things of which we cannot be immediately aware – and the essential technique here is that of *inference*. For example, we infer from these foundations uncovered by the archaeologist, along with objects found in the site, that there used to be a fortress, church, or market on this spot. The stones and other objects immediately present to us are seen as evidence from which we infer past circumstances no longer present to us. Similarly, we infer from this 1860s Irish Fenian newspaper present to us in the archives that, given the balance of its material, the movement's leaders regarded such-and-such as their principal enemies, and were relatively unconcerned with such-and-such a potential ally. We say this is an inference because the newspaper does not directly state these things. And even if it did, we would still be wise to ask whether we believe it – that is, we would again be involved in inferring something; in this case, the sincerity of the paper's statements.

Inferences do of course differ in strength. From seeing smoke pouring out of a revolver barrel I infer it has just been fired, and am unlikely to be wrong. But I could be, as must be the case with any inference. Or from finding a piece of pottery I infer there used to be trade between this and that town – a much more speculative inference but no different in

7

principle from the former. Inferences also vary in their credibility by virtue of the number of independent factors supporting them. For example, I search the room and find a warm corpse, a spent cartridge, and a blackmail note. By now, not only will my initial inference from seeing the smoking barrel have been strengthened, I will be inferring other matters such that I build up a 'theory' or hypothesis that a murder has recently been committed. This hypothesis is itself an inference derived from my present awareness of numerous objects and circumstances and from cross-checking separate inferences one with another both to test their individual strength and to test the validity of the overall inference that a murder has just been committed. Eventually I might reach the stage of feeling able to say that a murder was committed, that it was done in such-and-such a way, so-and-so were involved, with such-and-such motives, and that there is no other feasible inference from all the evidence. Short of having been privy to the events myself, or having a film of them, or of having and believing a detailed confession, I can go no further than inference, however full and compelling it may be.

What I did with respect to the smoking gun-barrel I can do with the piece of pottery, perhaps to achieve an (inferred) picture of some medieval trading pattern; or I can do the same with the copy of the Fenian newspaper, perhaps to achieve an (inferred) account of the movement's political strategy. In short, I can describe past situations, recount past events, explain past intentions, by regarding things present to me as evidence from which to infer the past. Whatever else might be said about inference – for example, that different individuals can infer different things from the same present evidence; that to make an inference is to apply some often unstated 'theory' about reality; that two or more inferences can go to make up another inference – it seems the method of inferring knowledge is essential to the historian insofar as his subject-matter is located in the past, out of his immediate experience. The philosopher does not essentially view Plato's *Republic* as evidence from which to infer things about the past. He deals with it as an amalgam of arguments whose cogency it is his business to estimate. The historian, however, views Plato's *Republic* as evidence from which to infer – what? It depends on the nature of the evidence, combined with the historian's background knowledge and interests. For example, had Plato changed his mind about certain matters? Why did he? Whom was he attacking? What events, if any, influenced his thinking? What interests, if any, was he trying to promote? To what present accounts of classical Athenian life and culture do these inferences add credibility?

As with the philosopher, we might say something similar of the scientist. Unlike the historian he is not essentially viewing present phenomena as evidence from which to infer knowledge of an otherwise unknown past. Rather, he examines present phenomena to discover how reality is structured and what 'laws' govern its manifold operations. It is true that, like the historian, the scientist is trying to discover things unknown, not immediately present to him, but they are not unknown in virtue of being in the past. They are unknown because they are general principles underlying the present. Hence we say the scientist induces and deduces his knowledge, whereas the historian infers his. For example, confronted by the Great Pyramid, the scientist would like to deduce the laws of mechanics its structure exemplifies; or deduce something about the rate of erosion of limestone. The historian, on the other hand, will wish to infer knowledge of, for instance, who built it and why.

It would seem, then, that because the historian's subject-matter is, for all its variety, located in the past, this is in itself sufficient to identify him as being essentially involved in a specific approach to his present material – namely, that he view it as *evidence*, from which he *infers* knowledge of past circumstances. It seems essential, for how else can he approach knowledge of the past which supersedes mere hearsay and allows him to judge how far to believe others' accounts? And it seems particular since neither the philosopher nor the scientist takes that approach to their present material. If valid, this claim gives insight into the interplay between the form and the content (between the approach and the subject-matter), of the discipline of history. Because his subject-matter is in the past, the historian approaches knowledge of it through inference. Alternatively, neither the philosopher nor the scientist are essentially involved in inferring knowledge, because their subject-matter's inaccessibility is nothing to do with its being in the past.

If at least this much can be derived from the convention that the historian deals specifically with 'the past', one further implication seems to proffer itself, albeit somewhat dimly. The historian seems limited, through his essentially inferential approach, to giving an account of his topic through the commonly accepted ways in which it is ordinarily understood. For example, if I notice egg on my colleague's beard, I infer he had an egg for breakfast; further, I may speculate as to whether he was in a hurry to get to work or whether his wife does not pay attention to his well-being. If sufficiently interested in either of these speculations prompted by my initial inference, I can seek other evidence with which to pursue their accuracy. The point is that, through inferring things about my colleague from his present appearance, I am not led to philosophise about the nature of man, nor his eating habits; neither am I led to investigate the glutinous qualities of eggs on beards. Rather, I am led into a world which is recognisably 'ordinary', requiring no special concepts of description or explanation other than those commonly appropriate to the subject-matter. If, then, I infer from certain stone foundations and objects that there used to be a fort on this site, the direction of my further investigations will be captive to the ordinarily understood matters pertaining to forts – for example, how many soldiers were stationed there, of which army, and what the fort's military purpose was. The same would apply to inferences from diplomatic notes and trade balance sheets; we would infer events and circumstances consistent with the 'language' of these different contexts (international politics, economic history), rather than conceptualise the knowledge of the past in some scientific, philosophical, or otherwise technical language brought from outside the manner in which the topic is immediately recognised.[2]

To put the matter more formally: if one's initial awareness is of egg on a colleague's beard, what one goes on to *infer* from this perception must relate to that initial conceptual context. I see egg on my colleague's beard, not a mess of chemicals adhering to an uneven surface; I see a note threatening war if the deadline is not met, not an exemplification of the moral problems posed by warfare.

It is along these lines, then, that we can bring to light this less obvious, albeit important implication of the historian's subject-matter's being in the past – important, because if his essential involvement in the technique of inference gives us insight into what is special regarding the historian's method of discovering knowledge (and the necessarily provisional nature of that knowledge), this further implication gives us insight into how he discusses this knowledge, how he presents it, what kinds of question he pursues, and, possibly, what kinds of explanation are available to him. To the extent he seems already entrapped into certain lines of thought by his initial understanding of a present phenomenon as evidence for a past which can be inferred, the historian lends a certain *kind* of awareness to his subject-matter. It is not a philosophical awareness, nor a scientific one, even where he is presenting a history of philosophy or of science. To investigate present evidence with a view to discovering, for example, what prompted Pasteur in his famous scientific researches, what existing scientific theory was available to him, in what areas he was innovative, and whom he had to argue against, is not to engage in scientific enquiry. On the other hand, to investigate whether the conclusions he arrived at regarding the nature of bacteria are valid is to engage in scientific enquiry. The question cannot be answered through inference. And it is along the same lines that we can draw the distinction between doing philosophy and offering a history of it. The philosopher cannot infer from evidence how adequate Hegel's concept of Mind is – on the other side of the coin the historian cannot deduce from Hegel's concept of Mind, as it stands, how Hegel came to have that concept, nor whose writing had influenced his thinking.

THE APPROACH OF THE HISTORIAN

To the extent the preceding arguments are correct, it does seem at least that some things helpful towards distinguishing history as a discipline can be derived from the conventional truth that the historian deals with subjects (however varied) in the past. He does not approach his topic either scientifically or philosophically, and we can assert this as both an empirical observation (in the main), and as a conceptual possibility, in the sense that it is possible to conceive of an approach to a topic which is neither philosophical nor scientific, and such a possibility has just been outlined, albeit not exhaustively. However it would be going too far to leave the matter at that, as if to have pointed to the implications of the historian's concern with 'the past' is to have said sufficient regarding the character of his activity to lend it an identifying distinctness. Firstly, the technique of inference is not associated exclusively with enquiry into the past; it is also used in enquiry into both the present and the future. I infer from seeing the curtain moving that the window *is* open. Again, as with any inference, I may be wrong – the cat may be playing behind the curtain. Or I infer from these foundations that the Department of the Environment is presently engaged in financing an archaeological dig; or I infer from seeing this product in the supermarket that Russia is presently trading with Britain. And any of these inferences may prompt further enquiry into the present, just as into the past, by searching for additional evidence of a fuller picture of the present state of affairs. For example, respectively, are my books on the window-sill getting wet? Is the Department of the Environment developing this region as a tourist centre? Is capitalism taking off in Russia? Also, it is not difficult to see how each of these examples could be cast into futuristic inferences, stimulating the endeavour, through inferring from present evidence, to gain a fuller picture of future circumstances and events.

To put the matter more formally: we can and do conceive of something present to us as evidence from which we infer something not immediately known to us; but its not being immediately known to us is not necessarily because it is in the past. It may be something in the present or in the future. All that is involved is inferring from evidence present to us knowledge of what was, is, or will be the case – and therefore if all knowledge of the past is necessarily acquired (initially) through inference, not all inferential knowledge is necessarily of the past. In short, the historian is not unique in approaching his knowledge through inference from evidence, and this is the first reason why those implications about his approach which can be drawn from his studying the *past* are insufficient to provide the unique hallmark, if there be one, of the historian's discipline.

The second reason this argument is insufficient is that the historian goes further than inferring knowledge of the past, for he also hopes where

11

possible to *prove* the truth of his statements about what was the case. Again, we need hardly go into complex epistemological analysis to see what kinds of things can constitute proof of the truth of statements as to what was (or is) the case. The important point is that there can in fact be numerous and diverse methods involved in demonstrating the truth of factual statements, and consequently the historian's discipline again becomes difficult, if not impossible, to define in terms of any one special methodology. For instance, I might infer from these foundations that a village used to be on this spot, and an investigation of local documents might 'prove' me right because I find a map drawn centuries ago which does indeed site a village on the spot in question. Proof itself, of course, varies from the tentative to the almost incontrovertible. How far should we believe the map-drawer? Was he completely accurate? Can the proof the map offers be strengthened by reference to other documents? Would a complete archaeological dig prove it was a village rather than a military encampment? What other ways are open to substantiate the inference that there used to be a village here? The resourceful historian will employ whatever methods are available and appropriate – for instance, carbon-dating, linguistic analysis, census returns, and geological science – to prove his inferences; and it is difficult to see any reason why he should not avail himself of all these, and any other techniques, in the attempt to validate inferences he makes. At this level of work it is clear the notion of some uniquely 'historical' methodology is absurd; if the subject-matter historians deal with is astonishingly diverse, so at one level are the techniques of approach to it. Chemical analysis might be crucial for an art historian; calligraphy crucial to a medieval historian; sociological science to an historian of popular movements; statistical science to an economic historian; and philosophical training to an historian of theology.

Another important implication is that there is a distinction to be drawn between evidence and proof, which depends more on the eye of the beholder than on what he is looking at. I can look at a centuries-old map from numerous points of view, of which three are directly relevant here. Firstly I can perceive (or understand) it at face-value as a map offering geographical information about an area of land – but if that is my interest I would do better to study the best up-to-date map available. Or, secondly, I can perceive the map as evidence, from which I infer various things about what was or is the case which the map itself does not display. Or, thirdly, I can perceive the map, not as *evidence* of this or that, but as *proof* of the validity of other inferences I made previously (from perceiving *other* phenomena as evidence). Often something such as an old map can be perceived both as evidence for certain inferences and as proof of others. What is certain, however, is that the map cannot constitute proof of inferences drawn from this same map. That would be tantamount to saying, 'I see a horse; I infer from this perception that I see a horse; that

I am seeing a horse proves my inference' – an unnecessarily tortuous account of what is a direct, immediate perception, the truth of which is not conventionally problematic given adequate eyesight and an understanding of language.

Put more formally: to construe something we see in the present as evidence from which to infer knowledge of something we do not 'see', is to do something different from construing something we see in the present as proof of some (inferred) knowledge already proposed – and both are different from construing something we see in the present for what it is. In the former case we might say the imagination is brought into play, whereas in the latter case it is the intellect that is at work. To infer something is to use the imagination, such that the logical validity of the inference is only a necessary, not a sufficient, condition of its adequacy, whereas to prove something is to use the intellect such that the logical validity of the proof is both a necessary and sufficient condition of its adequacy. For example, we can conceive the smoking gun-barrel as *evidence*, from which we can infer (that is, reasonably suppose or imagine), that the gun has just been fired. We need not have inferred that, however. We could have inferred that the barrel had just been cleaned, and an oil haze was issuing from it. But we would say we could not have (reasonably) inferred from the smoking gun-barrel that my trousers need pressing or some such other disconnected state of affairs.

If, on the other hand, we perceive the smoking gun-barrel as *proof* of something then we are precisely trying to rule out alternatives. For example, we might construe it as proof of a previous inference, from hearing a loud bang, that a shot had just been fired. We enter the room, see the smoking gun-barrel and regard it as proof of our inference that a shot had just been fired. This does of course involve inferring from the smoking gun-barrel that the gun has just been fired – but this stage in the thinking process is left unexamined. What is important is that the chain of reasoning is internal in its adequacy – namely, I hear a bang; I infer a gun has just been fired; I reason that if so, then nearby there is such a gun; here *is* such a gun; this proves the truth of my inference, from hearing a loud bang, that a gun has just been fired.

The above demonstrates two things. Firstly, to infer something is to do something different from proving something. Secondly, to prove one thing from another thing is, like it or not, to involve at least one inference (which necessarily need not be true – in the example just given, it is the unexamined inference, within the reasoning involved in the proof, that the gun-barrel was smoking because it had just been fired). It may be the case that the historian, as anyone else, mixes up the business of inferring and proving. There is ample scope for this since not only can, for example, the same document or stonework be construed as both evidence from which to infer something and as proof of an inference already made from something else; even in the latter case, fresh inferences are often also 'unconsciously' involved. Some historians even account for their activity as 'explaining the evidence', an odd formulation insofar as it ignores the fact that to construe something as 'evidence' in the first place is already to have 'explained' it.

Despite these potential confusions the point remains that in his approach to his primary material the historian is engaged in two different mental activities – inferring, and proving, knowledge of the past. Neither activity is unique to enquiry into the past, and of themselves neither invite any particular methodology. Inference requires imagination; proof requires logic. Both may involve a variety of specialist knowledge and techniques, depending on the subject-matter. Thus we are as yet no nearer identifying what distinguishes the historian's activity or 'discipline' (other than differentiating it from both philosophy and science), despite investigating not only his subject-matter but also his approach to knowledge of it, hidden as it is 'in the past'. In short, it would seem that in terms of both choice of subject-matter and appropriateness of method of enquiry for discovering and verifying the data involved, eclecticism rather than some specifically 'historical' approach has been, and should continue to be, the hallmark of the historian, paradoxical as this might seem.

OBJECTIVITY AND THE TREATMENT OF DATA

The historian, of course, must occupy a great deal of his time inferring and proving things from material in front of him – that is, from primary source material (unless he spends it on arguing about what others have written, a potentially parasitic activity, or on talking *about* history, a potentially uncreative activity). As we have seen, this work of 'data discovery and verification' does not of itself mark off the historian as being involved in any procedures unique to his discipline, despite his attention being located so specifically on 'the past'. However, the historian does of course go on to *do* something with the data he has established; indeed, were he not aware of what he proposes to do with the data he unravels, he would not know what data to collect in the first place. We have already argued that a map, for instance, can be looked at in at least three ways – as evidence from which to infer things, as proof of previous inferences, and at face-value as a map. But if we restrict ourselves to seeing the map as evidence there is no reason why numerous inferences cannot be drawn from it, and which of these the historian attends to depends upon what data he is pursuing – and in its turn this depends upon what he is trying to achieve. The only alternative to having such a guide to his approach to material is to have none at all. This would amount to presenting an historian with some object or document and asking him to view it as evidence of as many things as he can regarding the past (and presumably also as proof of as many things he can think of which have already been claimed about the past). No doubt this is theoretically a possible undertaking, but historians do not in fact proceed in this manner and there is no reason to suggest they ever should, unless for pure entertainment rather than serious intellectual endeavour.

What does the historian go on to do with the data he unravels? Perhaps the answer to this question will bring to light the special discipline of the historian, offering the answer to 'what is history?' But before proceeding with this investigation we should recognise that seeing things as 'evidence from which to make inferences', and as 'proof of previous inferences', already has implications for the important and controversial issue of objectivity in history; namely, insofar as we can perceive something as evidence of possibly a variety of states of affairs, it is reasonable to suppose we will draw that inference of most relevance to us. One source of such relevance is one's own present situation as a practical, social, emotional, busy individual with needs, hopes, principles, pressures, preferences, and responsibilities – such that one responds to what one is experiencing in terms of its practical implications for oneself as just such an individual living out what concerns him or her. In short, things can be relevant to us because they matter to us, and when it comes to seeing things as signs of other things (as when we make inferences), it can be that, because affairs already matter to us, we perceive things as signs or proofs relating to those affairs. Now it is fair to say that if our present involvement in the world around us gives a dominant direction to how we see things, and to what inferences regarding the past, present, and future we draw from things, then we may be accused of partiality and subjectivity – features of thinking in direct opposition to the standards of impartiality and objectivity to which most historians are committed.

Although we shall encounter further dimensions to this issue of objectivity later in this book, we can already point out that the nearer one approaches the present the more likely it is that one's present concerns give direction to which out of a variety of inferences one actually makes. What life was like in fifteenth-century Florence does not matter in practice to a twentieth-century Englishman, and therefore if he is confronted with some document or object from which a variety of things can be inferred regarding fifteenth-century Florence, but little else, we can anticipate his dealings with this 'evidence' will be objective and impartial. The direction his inferences take, however, with respect to a recent British Cabinet minute or to some expensive perfume in his wife's handbag, in terms of what these suggest to him about past events, are far more likely to stem from his practical interest in the world around him. Thus it is right to point out, even in advance of exploring what the historian goes on to do with the data he uncovers about the past, that already at this early stage in the process of his thinking his involvement with his present world *might*, through directing his inferential imagination, affect how he deals with 'the evidence' (primary source material), and is the more likely to do so (to the detriment of objectivity and impartiality), the more contemporary the material he is looking at.

If it is important not to overlook this difficulty it is equally important not to exaggerate it, for it does not follow that it leads to deliberately biased historical work, as where someone sets out to persuade others of his own values by distorting his account of a matter. In the case of blatantly 'ideological' history not only the selection of data, but also the whole direction of its ensuing presentation, is biased because the presenter deliberately uncovers only what suits the axe he has to grind. His work does not merely reflect his present concerns; it is intended as an engagement in them, and such an ambition is a different source of partiality and subjectivity from that threatened merely by the recentness of an historian's topic. The difference can be highlighted by conceiving of someone trying to infer something damaging regarding the Jewish people from a fifteenth-century Florentine document despite all the other inferences it invites, compared to someone who, aware of the danger of bias in working on recent Irish history, infers something about the status of women in Northern Ireland from the 1982 Assembly election returns, deliberately refraining from inferring more controversial matters. Of the first, anti-Semitic, individual we can easily say he is biased in his treatment of material, whereas of the second we may be tempted to point to his objectivity and impartiality despite the odds against this given the material he is dealing with. However, our second individual is not entirely objective and impartial, for his seeing the election returns as evidence from which to infer something about the status of women reflects his involvement in a time and culture which makes this topic relevant to him. In this sense any historian is a child of his time, irrespective of that *other* potent direction given to his thinking which derives from the traditions of the discipline of history itself (again, part of his present). Looked at in this light, the most important implication to be drawn is not so much that objectivity and impartiality are more difficult to attain the more recent the source material (possibly leading historians to some philosophical doubt as to whether objectivity is possible at all), but rather that in certain cases historians' writings can themselves constitute a form of primary source material for inferring what kind of world they experienced themselves as inhabiting.

DESCRIPTIVE HISTORY

We have claimed no historian approaches his material arbitrarily; that if he did not indeed already know what he wanted data for, he would not even know whether something was relevant source material in the first place. The historian *does* something with the data he uncovers, and if there appears to be no special 'historical' methodology involved in establishing data (that is, in inferring and demonstrating statements about the past by perceiving present phenomena as 'evidence' and 'proof'), then we may perhaps find the special hallmark of his discipline located in what he proceeds to do with his data.

One way of talking about the past is to *describe* past circumstances as accurately and fully as possible (on the basis of inferring from primary source material). For example, an historian may wish to describe what London was like at the time of the Civil War in the 1640s, or 'what life was like' for a Roman soldier stationed along Hadrian's Wall, or for a wage-labourer in the Lancashire cotton-mills of the early nineteenth century. As a descriptive account his project is primarily neither explanatory nor that of narrative, although he may find it helpful, for instance, to explain the shift-work routine of the Roman soldier or to narrate certain events in the London of the 1640s. Rather, his task is to present information of a descriptive (or 'ascriptive'), nature such that one 'gets a picture' of circumstances, rather than an explanation of them or a reference to them as part of a story.

Description, then, addresses itself to particular circumstances held *in stasis*, and offers contingent information about them, such that the reader who, for example, already knows what a medieval castle was, now knows what this particular castle looked like, how many towers and rooms it had, whether it had a moat, and what armaments it had. But if one limits oneself to describing it the reader will not know why it had that particular design, why it was put there, or who had it constructed.

Taken in isolation, then, descriptive history has its limitations, so much so that it is usually to be found in children's history books rather than presented as satisfying in itself to the mature intellect. Yet it should not be neglected for it can achieve at least three objects worthy of recognition. Firstly, it can satisfy one's curiosity regarding the particularity of the past; any description is potentially interesting, even fascinating, when dealing with things long past and gone. Moreover it satisfies one's curiosity in a concrete way, by offering direct information of a positive, generally non-controversial nature, such that what such knowledge lacks in analytic or explanatory sophistication is perhaps compensated for by the directness of its impact. One can only welcome the trend in museums towards presenting their objects in a more overall descriptive context by removing them from their glass cases and arranging them so as to contribute to a 'picture' of what things were like. Museum parks, where whole buildings are presented (schools, artisan dwellings, middle-class houses, and work-shops), and similar efforts such as HMS Belfast, HMS Victory, and the Mary Rose, are clear examples of how satisfying to the curiosity a descriptive knowledge of the particulars can be.

17

Secondly, in addition to satisfying one's curiosity descriptive history can excite further curiosity, prompting a host of questions ranging from the particular to the increasingly analytic and abstract. To the extent it can excite the imagination and stimulate the intellect, it can supersede what may be its only intended function – namely, to satisfy curiosity. To be taken back to a nine-feet wide, dirt street, with sewage running down a channel in its middle; and narrow, precarious, wooden buildings which overhang the street such that one could shake hands across it in places; to have beggars, cripples, and the weakminded, as well as the carts, children's toys, and women's dress, all described in particular detail (as in some of Brueghel's paintings), cannot but make a potent contribution to knowledge of the past as well as give a rich stimulus for further enquiry into it.

Thirdly, to the extent that a descriptive account of some aspect of the past – for instance, a city, a landed estate, a fleet of warships, domestic circumstances – is sufficiently generous to provide a cameo of particular modes of life rather than isolated aspects, then it 'brings to life' an awareness of 'what it was really like'. Such awareness may not be particularly perceptive or complex; for example, it may not explain important political trends or the social significance of class-structures. Yet in 'bringing the past to life' through its necessary concentration on particulars (as with any description), it serves the function of realistically locating one in that past. And insofar as it can achieve this, descriptive history can lend its subject-matter a kind of intelligibility, even though that is not its original rationale.

The famous Detective Superintendent Maigret insists on visiting and familiarising himself with the scene of the crime. Just so might we encourage a more determined and imaginative attempt by historians to first locate their readers and students within the mode of life they are going on to analyse, explain, or interpret, by 'bringing it to life' through descriptive history. Maigret familiarises himself with the locale, though he already has the immense advantage of being familiar with so many facets of the situation. Unlike the student approaching, for instance, an aspect of seventeenth-century England, he already knows what the modes of transport are in twentieth-century Paris, how far and fast a car, bus, train, metro, or bicycle can go; he knows there are telephones, radio, TV, local and national newspapers. In short, Maigret already knows an enormous amount about communications alone, and such information, along with a wealth of other details, serves a crucial function in his understanding of his environment. And yet he still feels the need to visit the actual scene of the crime.

The student of seventeenth-century England knows, of course, there was no radio, TV, or telephone. But to be given a cameo description of, for instance, 'life in the port of Bristol' at the outbreak of the Civil War might help him realise, merely with respect to communications, that there was no national press, no comprehensive road system, that one either walked or went places by horse (or barge or boat where possible), that few could read, that the pulpit was an important political communicator, that one usually reckoned to travel between ten and fifteen miles in a day, that inns were abundant and rather like our garages, being hotels, post offices, and pubs all rolled into one, there being numerous people employed in looking after horses and fetching and carrying with handcarts. This, simply with respect to 'communications'. In advance of undertaking more sophisticated and interpretive study, the student should already be aware, from such material, of how comparatively slowly things happened, how parochial most people's awareness necessarily was, and how uncertain was long-distance communication; and it is likely that such concrete, practical, particular information can be of considerable assistance to him as he moves forward to more complex understandings of the past.

Descriptive history, then, has its own virtues which spring directly from the very rationale of description – namely, its essential concern with particulars. There is probably a sense in which it could even be argued we should harbour special respect for it insofar as it is concerned with particulars, since when it comes down to it they are all we have – the rest is analysis, interpretation, explanation, and increasing abstraction, which may amount to no more than speculation or even fantasy if not rooted in the kind of realistic knowledge of particulars which descriptive history (increasingly a feature of films and television), provides.

However, this is to overstate the case. Firstly, if a chief attraction of descriptive history is its empirical character, holding out the promise of objectivity, we should be aware the historian inevitably selects those aspects he describes (and by definition omits others). Sometimes the lack of evidence can do the job of selection for him. But even where this is not a problem we may say as a general rule that the 'larger' the thing he has to describe – for instance, a city compared to a peasant's mode of dress – the more selective and 'interpretive' his description will be. The latter is sufficiently manageable to describe in complete detail ('complete' in the conventional sense – one would not expect each thread of the peasant's smock to be described), such that we do not feel we are given *this* historian's description, implicating his own ideas of what is important, interesting, or significant. In the former case, however, the scope for such subjectivity is much greater, to the extreme possibility of blatantly 'ideological' descriptions.

If, then, we should not overestimate one of descriptive history's chief attractions, neither, secondly, for all its virtues, should we underestimate its limitations, which stem from the inherent rationale of what it is to describe phenomena. Properly speaking, description deals with a static situation; it is limited to attributive statements of particular, contingent features; it is neither analytic, argumentative, deliberately interpretive, nor explanatory in form (although it may border on some of these where it is particularly selective). So even before proceeding to investigate what other things the historian can and does say about the past (on the basis of data he unravels), it seems clear that to the extent he limits himself to the task of description, he is that much less an historian proper. In short, if there is no special method or discipline which we can uniquely ascribe to the historian in his unravelling of data, such that we are led to seek his special hallmark in what he proceeds to do *with* his data, we are unlikely to feel we have encountered it with descriptive history, despite its being a coherent undertaking. Indeed, arguing more formally and *a priori*, we can say that to describe something is to do just that, and that others beside historians engage in the activity. It is true the descriptive historian is dealing with past phenomena, and therefore has to infer his data, yet for all that we may still deny what he does warrants his being singled out as an historian proper. He may be no more nor less than an expert on the seventeenth-century port of Bristol, and his only link with an expert on, for example, the Greek tragic theatre is that both are describing past phenomena. There is of course a sense in which it would be churlish to deny the term 'historian' to such an individual, insisting on merely semantic grounds that he be termed, for instance, an 'antiquarian'; and in any event historians do not restrict themselves to descriptive history as a pure type. The point here is that in its logic *as* a pure type there is simply nothing sufficiently distinctive, given what historians actually do with their data, nor adequately arguable, given the rationale of what is involved in describing phenomena, on which to rest an identification of the intellectual activity of history properly understood as having its own disciplinary identity.

ANALYTIC HISTORY

In addition to making descriptive statements about past phenomena and circumstances, the historian can proffer analytic statements about them, leading away from particulars towards more general statements derived from comparing and/or collating different phenomena, abstracting aspects they have in common. The reasons for doing this can be twofold, although they are usually combined. Firstly, to be able to abstract common features from otherwise different phenomena is, by producing a kind of shorthand, to assist in describing them. For example, one can abstract certain features common to most medieval towns, such that it can abridge the task of describing, for instance, medieval Florence by saying it was a typical medieval town. Just so it would help describe a play by saying it is a Shakespearean play. Secondly (and here we see why the two reasons for analytic statements usually combine in practice), to abstract common features of otherwise discrete phenomena appears to impart some explanatory power to statements. For example, to call thirteenth-century Florence a typical medieval town is not only to suggest many of its features but also to 'explain' their presence, just as to call a building a town hall is to 'explain' many of *its* features.

We should recognise that, in the sense of the term used above, the process of 'analysis' is complex, as is the status of its achievements, since understanding it principally involves one in an investigation into the nature of language and definitions, and their relation to 'reality'. For our purposes of characterising and assessing 'analytic history' it is, then, necessary to explore relevant aspects of this interesting problematic – all the more so since certain points emerge which are of recurring relevance throughout the remainder of this book.

To begin with we can say that to call an object 'a chair' is to distinguish it from other objects, not in virtue of its unique particularity (its *description* achieves that, insofar as it shows this chair is different from that chair in certain inessential, contingent, respects), but in virtue of features it shares with other, otherwise discrete, objects. We thereby distinguish a class of objects ('chairs'), different from other classes of objects (for example, 'tables', 'cities'). Thus, we isolate certain features – for instance, shape and function – and ignore others – for example, colour and weight. We add together those features we have isolated to make up an abstraction which we award a common name, 'chair'. The features selected thus constitute the meaning, that is, the definition, of the word 'chair', which any dictionary provides. Obviously we do not, in practice, undertake this process when we use words to identify things, but that is how they originate, and we find ourselves replicating their origination when teaching a child the meaning of words prior to simply being able to give him definitions in terms of other words – that is, we point to this and that chair, but not to this table or door, and say 'chair', drawing to his attention something which both chairs have in common but which neither the door nor the table share.

Many words, then (including all common nouns), are not merely denotive of particular phenomena but are to a certain extent explanatory of them. What, after all, is the function of any language (and here we might refer to *its* definition), if not to convey meaning – that is, render phenomena intelligible? Hence to call a thing a 'chair' is to appear to explain many of its features in the sense that if asked by a child why this object has legs we can reply, 'because it is a chair, and chairs have legs'. What we achieve by this, however, is not an explanation of why this object has legs, but why, in virtue of its having legs, it is called a 'chair' – that is, we have given part of the rationale (or meaning) of the word 'chair', and related this object's having legs to it. As a logical argument it is of course circular, but this is not to say nothing has been achieved by it. It is true it has not achieved what it pretended to – namely, explain why this object has legs

21

– and we should always be alert to this pretension in order to avoid the fallacy of, for instance, claiming to explain an individual's behaviour in terms of 'his belonging to the working class', or claiming to explain a fall in employment as 'belonging to a recession'. However, what this mode of argument does achieve, in addition to (partly) explaining the meaning of words, is to suggest with a force ranging from the insistent to the merely intimative that real individual things are predictable in terms of their characteristics and, sometimes, their behaviour. And to the extent we can rely on these suggestions, such that our anticipations of the real world are indeed realised, the elaboration of the meaning of words is incalculably valuable.

Before demonstrating the relevance of these points to 'analytic history' it is as well to add some of their implications. Firstly, if to 'explain' this object's having legs by saying it is a 'chair' is to (in part) explain what we mean by the word 'chair', this does not explain *why* we mean what we mean by the word 'chair'. But if we approach matters the other way round we can see how a word's meaning is itself suggestive of why it has that meaning. For instance, if we were to define the word 'chair' as an object designed to comfortably situate a seated person, this suggests the rationale behind making that abstraction and generalisation of features from otherwise different particular things. We identify things in terms of their relevance to us (a vast field of reference given the complex nature of human beings – for example, usefulness, danger, beauty, and curiosity), such that we can say there is a reason for the meaning of words (not proper names), derived from an expectation that the same relevant features are shared by some otherwise different phenomena. If, then, 'all knives are sharp', such that sharpness is (part of) the rationale of knives, this is not to say there is reason in or to the nature of things, but rather, there is reason in how we conceptualise them. And it is difficult to see in what sense the 'reasoning' involved in conceptualising things (via abstracting and generalising certain common features), does not amount to the same as 'the reason *for*' conceptualising them – that is, there is nothing inherently 'reasonable', 'logical', or 'rational' in things themselves, to which our conceptions of them have to accord. Our conceptions must be relevant and workable; that constitutes their 'rationality', their 'reason', or 'the reason' for them.

Secondly, it follows from the above that language (that is, meanings, or our conceptions), implies things about us, its creators and users, as well as about the reality we inhabit, for it demonstrates in what ways and for what reasons reality is relevant to us – for it is *we* who perform the business of abstracting relevant common features from an otherwise random, undifferentiated reality. Most languages, we might expect, will have included a word for 'tree' from their beginnings. However, not until people took to the air did the word 'air-pocket' emerge, and we could no doubt find cultures today in which the word 'teenager' or its equivalent does not feature as part of their language. Whether this point applies not only to the meaning of words, but also to tenses and general grammatical structures, is outside the scope of the present argument, as is any need to elaborate on the fact that we accept the meaning of most words but change the meaning of others, discard some altogether, and also invent new ones. The point is, it is *we* who are tree-perceiving, air-pocket-perceiving, and teenager-perceiving people, and it is in this sense that the words we use imply what we are like. And because we are human beings rather than gods or beasts, or 'pure intellects', then whatever meaning we give to the term 'objectivity' cannot itself exceed this limitation.

But thirdly, if the words we use imply things about us, they also imply things about the reality surrounding us since, in addition to the need for our conceptions to be relevant to us, they must also be workable. This requires that what the application of a word to a particular thing tells us of its necessary, or at least usually anticipated, features does indeed turn out to be the case. We single out things we call 'trees' on the basis of certain common features relevant to us in some way, and the extent to which the word's meaning remains unchanged as part of our language demonstrates real regularities, or reliably predictable connections, in our environment. We do not abstract from our environment a number of people in virtue of their sharing the features of being male, wearing ties, and painting their front doors, and award this generality a word. But we do have the words, 'a regiment at drill'. Although it might be argued the reason we do not have a special word for the former situation is because, even were it a regular occurrence, it would be irrelevant to us, in this case one could equally argue it is because it is not a regular occurrence that we do not have a word for it.

Just so with natural, 'given' phenomena – for instance, the situation where something grows out of the soil to a height taller than a man, is made of wood, and has branches and leaves, is sufficiently ubiquitous and persevering to make it worthwhile individualising it into the word (or meaning) 'tree', despite every particular 'tree' being unique in other respects. Were this a one-off phenomenon, or at least markedly unreliable in its major correlations, then we would not invent the word (that is, abstract the meaning), 'tree' – or if we did our conception would not work, and the word would never be used, or only as part of a fantasy. Thus the function of words: and if on the one hand they must therefore have relevance for us, on the other hand their meanings must be more or less accurate regarding the real world. Insofar as they are, they thus tell us things about that real world as well as about ourselves.

Fourthly, the previous passages have already intimated that words have meanings ranging from the exactly precise to the markedly vague, imply- ing that the generalisations words derive from point to differing degrees of predictability regarding the anticipated features of things we identify. Indeed, in the hurly-burly of everyday life our tendency is to manage rather than approach affairs with scrupulous scientific precision, and a great many words we use are in practice correspondingly vague or even ambiguous in their meanings (which doubtless helps them persist). Thus we are often content to abstract out only one or two essential features of things, and leave others as usual, but not strictly necessary. Science, however, aims at strict definitions whose fixity stems from a necessary correlation of certain features shared by otherwise discrete particulars, this necessity being construed in terms of the causal connections and processes discoverable in the natural world. For instance, a tree *must* grow leaves; its leaves *must* be of a certain substance.

Another source of strictly defined meanings is provided by things being deliberately fashioned *by us*, where the relationship between the rationale of the thing and the reason in conceiving of it coincide so directly, as in a 'crown and pinion', a 'swimming-pool', or a 'camera'. Here, it is not we who abstract relevant features from natural objects – it is we creating objects of relevance to us. Clearly, insofar as much of our environment is now man-made, numerous words have relatively strict definitions. Their rationale is that much more obvious since we are actually *making* a meaningful world rather than discovering, through trial and error, in what ways the given world is meaningful to us.

Finally there is the interesting special case provided by the science of statistics, where phenomena are abstracted out (through the process of generalising common features of otherwise discrete particular things) via the technique of randomly searching for 'significant correlations' within situations. Here, a feature is generalised not because, in being relevant and common, it is noticed; neither because, conceived of causally, it *must* be present. Rather, in advance of having noticed anything in common between things, many known features of a number of particular things are collated and subjected to quantitative analysis to discover if they 'correlate significantly' in respect of one or more feature. In this way phenomena are identified which would otherwise remain unknown and whose status is not explicable causally (although statistical correlations of course often point to causal connections). The rationale of these phenomena cannot but remain problematic, since there is no 'reason in them' (until or unless a causal explanation is found), and no 'reason for them' (insofar as they are not conceived of in virtue of their relevance and workability). An example of such a phenomenon is the individual (who might just as well be given a single meaningful word to denote him) who is a pet-owner who survives beyond sixty despite a lifestyle putting him at special risk of heart-failure.

Statistical phenomena are special, then, as the exception which proves the rule, the rule being that in inventing words we are abstracting certain features common to otherwise different things, thereby denoting classes of things meaningful to us because of their relevance and predictability. Some words have strict meanings, others remain vague. Some point to necessary causal connections in the world, some to deliberately intended connections (manufactured by human beings), and some point to more or less vaguely defined phenomena, abstracted in a fairly haphazard way but with sufficient rationale for managing in practical terms. We know with some precision what a 'crown and pinion' is; with less precision what a 'chair' is; with even less, what 'air' is. There would be no point in asking a scientist to tighten up the definition of a crown and pinion since it is a man-made object. But there is a point in asking him to define 'air' more closely, since it is both a possible and useful thing to do, affording greater insight both into our environment and ourselves insofar as what he discovers is of relevance (that is, is meaningful), to us. As with 'objects', so with 'actions'. We know with some precision what 'skiing' is; with less precision what 'having a holiday' is; with even less what 'thinking' is. Yet again it is the latter, rather than either of the former, which it is both possible and, in certain contexts, useful to define more closely than for everyday purposes.[3]

Words, then, have meanings for a reason. Some are precise, others vague. Some bear further enquiry into their rationale, others do not. Most intimate something more or less precise about reality, and all imply something about us. The word 'history', or the term, 'doing history', is of course no exception. It has a meaning, albeit a rather vague one with which we do no more than manage in a fairly rough and ready fashion – (like the examples of 'air' and 'thinking', it bears closer enquiry) – and insofar as it has meaning, there is a rationale to it; that is, there is a reason for it. Thus the term tells us something about the world. It suggests there is something 'out there', in this case, an activity, which is sufficiently prevalent, relevant, and predictable to make it worthwhile generalising into a word – 'history'. This constitutes its workability. (Why the word 'history' rather than some other word is, of course, a separate etymological matter.)[4] And the term also tells us something about ourselves in the sense that it is *we*, after all, who abstract the concept, *we* who find it useful.

The preceding paragraphs have tried to show, through the simpler means of examining the way words are meaningful and pointing to some of the implications of what is confessedly a complex and controversial topic for technical philosophy, what it is to conceive a generality as distinct from describing individual, particular things. It is true that from one point of view the distinction is evasive insofar as generalisations are abstracted from features of individual, particular things, which in their turn are denoted via prior generalisations, and so on *ad infinitum* – in other words, there is a sense in which any dictionary is one immense tautology.

But rather than be dismayed at the ambiguities such a dialectic offers, we should apply what instruction it contains and note what difficulties it uncovers for 'analytic history'.

With reference to doing history, then, by 'analytic' statements as distinct from 'descriptive' statements I mean statements (by historians) derived from deliberate attempts to generalise from particulars (by abstracting common features), in such a way as to indicate in what respects particular things, circumstances, or situations are predictable in terms of their composition, behaviour, origins, and outcomes. For example, insofar as the composition of a particular medieval prince's court, the activities of a particular Victorian craft-union, or the style of a particular Renaissance sculptor, can be predicted, hypothesised, or assumed in advance or in lieu of the particular facts being established, 'analytic' history is clearly a potent method of uncovering and conveying information about the past. Having studied numerous (particular) medieval courts, Victorian craft-unions, or Renaissance sculptors, and having discovered certain features common within each group, this process of analysis abstracts the notions, respectively, of 'the typical medieval court', 'the typical Victorian craft-union', and 'the typical Renaissance sculptor' – and to do this is to achieve three things.

Firstly, to be able to talk, for example, of 'a typical Renaissance sculptor' is to assist descriptive history by providing abridgements of detail in the same way we have argued single words such as 'chair' and 'holiday' do. To the extent Michelangelo was a typical Renaissance sculptor, we can say so, and be spared spelling-out those features of his work, and perhaps person, we would otherwise include in a description of him in particular. This was the point of the preceding examination of the rationale of words, for as concerns the process of abstracting out features from individual things to achieve a general notion, there is no difference in principle between 'a chair' and 'a typical Renaissance sculptor' (other than that in the latter case we do not have a single word, but a phrase). Both the single word, 'chair', and the phrase, 'the typical Renaissance sculptor', are a kind of shorthand which can be applied to individual phenomena to convey particular descriptive information.

This may appear inconsistent when we recognise the information they contain is conveyed by the definition of the respective words or phrases, whereas we have insisted that to describe a thing is to do something different from defining it. However, this inconsistency is merely apparent, since we are brought up against that slide into an infinite regression which the dialectic between the general and the particular provokes. To say of a particular thing, 'it is a chair', is to identify it – that is, to define it, not to describe it. But to say of 'a piece of furniture' that, 'it is a chair', is not to define the piece of furniture but to describe aspects of it in particular. To say of an individual, 'he was a typical Renaissance sculptor', is to identify him, not to describe him. But to say of a sculptor that 'he was a typical Renaissance sculptor', is to describe aspects of him as a *particular* sculptor.

The historian needs to take care, then, that he does not confuse the way he uses generalisations abstracted via analysis. For example, if he achieves the notion of 'a typical Roman fort' he can use that term descriptively of a particular fort, as a kind of shorthand. He may leave his description at that or add details not already implicit in his idea of a typical Roman fort. But insofar as he uses the term purely descriptively he is not attempting to explain anything about the fort. As for the term itself, the more explicitly it is the product of analysing phenomena the more open it is to potential objections that his analysis was inadequate, incorrect, or even biased, in terms of the features he isolated in order to generalise. Not surprisingly, the historian risks this more especially when describing political and social phenomena, as in describing a regime as 'a typical totalitarian government', or a society as 'a class society'. The potential objections here are not that such-and-such a regime was *not* totalitarian, or such-and-such a society was not a class society, although others *were* – but that the very terms are derived from generalisations open to question regarding their rationale and should hence not be used at all, or at least not in that ostensibly less controversial type of history, namely, descriptive history.

The second and more significant achievement of analytic history is its ability to explain rather than describe things, and here again there is a parallel between the explicit generalisations reached by historians and those implicit in single words, such that all we said about the explanatory suggestiveness of words applies to the more openly arrived at general notions historians abstract, except that this 'suggestiveness' is correspondingly more obvious. Just as single words such as 'tree' and 'chair' point to regularities in (natural and man-made) phenomena, so do the general notions of which we have given examples. The regularities discovered in phenomena – for instance, medieval princely courts, permitting a concept of 'the' medieval court – are usually suggestive of a rationale governing certain of their aspects. In short, the ability to generalise about some features of otherwise different phenomena suggests there is a reason for the way certain phenomena are structured, composed, or behave – and to say there is a reason for the way something is, is to claim to be able to explain why it is as it is. With 'analytic' history, then, we encounter one way in which historians engage in 'explaining' the past rather than merely recording and describing it. As a way of explaining things this generalising process shares the same varieties and ambiguities we noted respecting the explanatory role of single words, where characteristics of a particular thing range from being causally determined, or 'scientifically necessary', to being no more than usually predictable, based on vague intimations that such predictions make common sense. Between these extremes are varying degrees of clarity and precision.

27

Examples of generalisations abound in historians' writings, ranging from the almost absurdly broad (yet obviously manageable, because so persistent), such as 'eighteenth-century', 'medieval', and 'German', to somewhat more precise, conscious generalisations such as 'Renaissance', 'Edwardian', and 'republican', to far more careful efforts such as 'the typical Elizabethan planter in Ireland', 'the typical nineteenth-century Russian aristocratic liberal', or 'the typical commercial life of a fourteenth-century northern Italian city'. Rarely, however, do we find analytic concepts in historical writings whose constituents are awarded the determinateness of scientific causality. To the extent economics is properly a science such causally determined constituents may be presented within economic history, and alluring indeed would be an analogous status for the analytic work of some social historians, who would be only too pleased to lend their generalisations the strict conviction of scientific necessity – (for example, to be able to use the term, 'a mob', in such a sense as to enable certain features of any mob's behaviour and composition to be scientifically predictable, or 'explicable', with the full and inescapable force of necessary causality). Yet if 'economic science' is perhaps controversial regarding its status, 'social science' definitely is, along with 'political science'. To the extent the economic, sociological, and political sciences do, or could, succeed in establishing genuinely 'law-governed' aspects in their respective areas, backward indeed would be the historian who failed to use the fruits of such science where applicable to his topic. For instance, in the unlikely event that socio-political science could establish a universal law that all political revolutions are *necessarily* led by a charismatic populist leader who *must* have been a member of a suppressed generation of the intelligentsia, then the historian whose account of a particular revolution failed to take this necessary law into account, or even worse, whose account (wrongly) contradicted it, would justly be considered uneducated.

However, with the possible exception of economic science, the social and political sciences have yet to confront historians with propositions of an unequivocally scientific status, except for the occasional attempt (desperate in its deliberate generality), such as 'goal achievement reduces the drive-value of the stimulus', which even then remains not so much controversial regarding its scientific status as trivial regarding the instructive use to which such platitudes can be put. Indeed, we must expect that responsible social scientists themselves would be sufficiently hesitant about the status of the 'laws' they propose as to be alarmed rather than flattered at the prospect of historians adopting them wholesale and implicitly into their accounts in the same way they do the law of gravity and other established scientific laws regarding the structure and operation of the natural world. The response of most historians is equally hesitant in the other direction, ranging from downright rejection of the more assertive products of the social sciences, to the titillated sceptic, to the cautiously

28

hopeful. No doubt this broadly equivocal reception of the social sciences by historians is partly explicable in terms of the former's association with 'determinism' in general (professionally unpalatable to most historians, who, define them as we may, have always displayed a special respect for particulars), and to Marxism in particular as the most elegant, comprehensive, yet politically charged species of 'determinism' in the areas of social science and history. Some historians, we may expect, will continue the eternal search for necessity whilst their colleagues will remain satisfied with intelligibility, and the debate over history versus the social sciences will, correspondingly, continue as a potential source of stimulus to both camps.

The more prevalent generalisations historians produce via the process of analysis, however, are those whose explanatory status is not attributable to the causally law-governed model of pure science but derives more from intimations of regularities in otherwise discrete phenomena which common sense suggests. For instance, we might expect social historians to abstract a notion of 'the typical Victorian domestic servant', or political historians to abstract a notion of 'the typical French diplomat', and other such modest generalisations, readily acceptable insofar as they derive from actual data and do not involve intimations of either too broad a nature (as in 'the typical American', for example), or of too speculative a nature (as in 'the typical alienated proletarian', for example, where the generalisation involves specific and debatable sociological/psychological theories). So long as his generalisations remain within these modest boundaries, intuited as justifiable in common-sense terms, they fulfil a useful and non-controversial explanatory function.

For example, an historian may abstract a notion of the typical French diplomat which defines him (*sic*) in terms of class, education, status, and political attitudes, such that the historian might feel well able to use this generalisation not simply to describe a particular individual, but to explain certain of his attributes and actions without having to spell out a detailed explanation as one would with a unique phenomenon. His actions, then, can be 'explained' as those predictable, in common-sense terms, of 'the typical French diplomat', in just the same way that 'a typical chair' has a predictable and understandable relationship between its legs, back, seat, and size (in this case, the product of a deliberately imposed rationale, through human design). Likewise with 'the typical French diplomat' – there is not only a predictable but also an understandable relationship between his class, education, status, political attitudes, and working-style. The intelligibility of these relationships is not derived from, nor dependent upon, any causal law-governed model, nor derived from any particular sociological or psychological theory. Neither are these relationships simply randomly discovered (in which case they would be correlations, not intelligible relationships). Rather, we would be content to say they are understandable (that is, accountable for, or explicable), in terms of intelligent and experienced common sense,[5] (akin to Aristotle's notion of *phronesis* or 'practical wisdom'). Thus, these attributes might have been other than those discovered – there is no necessary law governing them. And yet whatever they are, they will display an appropriateness understandable to the observer who is not naive about 'how the world works'.

It is true this source of intelligibility is philosophically untidy, verging on the intuitive rather than the rational, and yet many would argue the attributes of human beings are themselves inherently 'untidy', as are their affairs. A diplomat, after all, is not a manufactured object like a chair. On the other hand there is an element of imposed rationale insofar as diplomats are, after all, selected and trained. Yet all are individuals who have responded rather than mechanistically reacted to their upbringing, education, and class. In short, the diplomat is neither like a crown and pinion, nor a programmed robot, though he does have to be 'suitable' for the job – he is, then, an 'untidy' phenomenon for the purposes of either scientific or philosophical explanation. Yet he is an intelligible phenomenon for the heterogeneous approach of worldly common sense, as are other phenomena historians reveal via a process of analysis, such as 'the typical nineteenth-century Russian aristocratic liberal'.

By analogy with the meaning of single words, we may say of such common-sense historical abstractions that they need to meet the same two criteria, namely, workability and relevance. So long as the research has been thorough and not superseded by newly discovered data contradicting its findings, the workability of such concepts should be assured (that is, the reliability of their knowledge when matched against the objective world). Their relevance, on the other hand, is both more complicated and interesting an issue, partly because it tells us something of how historians think both about the world and the subject of history itself. If, as claimed, the word 'chair' needs to be meaningful *to us*, and is only so if relevant *for us*, just so with abstractions produced by analytic history. For example, there were clearly at any one time in the Victorian era a number of individuals between the ages of thirteen and twenty – yet not only did the Victorians not have the concept of 'teenagers', we who find the concept relevant today do not use it when discussing Victorian times, even though there is a sense in which there *were* 'teenagers' in that era. But there is equally a sense in which there were not, because the 'teenage' generations did not impose any felt special relevance on circumstances and events. Thus, whether 'the typical Victorian teenager' existed or not is not so much a question of fact as of relevance – and of relevance to us now, it is important to add, rather than to the Victorians themselves. This is so because there are other concepts which, although not conceived of at the time (because not felt to be relevant), we are now aware of *and* regard as relevant to earlier periods. A clear example of this is where an historian

30

regards the concept of 'class' and its accompanying refinements as relevant to many (if not all) past societies, even though those societies lacked the concept.

More generally, however, we can say that succeeding generations, and differing schools, of historians will tend to shift the emphasis of what they find relevant in their understanding of 'how the world works', such that the concept of, for instance, 'a typical Bourbon prince', intimating an intelligibility to some episode of French history in terms of heredity and individual agency, although important to an eighteenth-century historian, might now be regarded by some historians as irrelevant to understanding the episode compared to the concept of 'a typical peasant area', with all its attendant sociological ingredients. What this points to, in short, is that the way we perceive and think about 'the past' is part of our present. That we now find some things noticeable which previous generations did not, locates our own understanding as 'historical' (that is, relative to our time and circumstances), such that while we may now view earlier historians' approaches as themselves part of the history of how sophisticated, but nevertheless common, sense has altered, so future historians will be able to view today's historians as interesting and instructive in the same terms. To the extent, then, that one explores preceding historians' ideas in this light, especially their analytic concepts, one is engaged in nothing less than reconstructing the history of refined common-sense awareness of 'how the world works'. How instructive such a project might be is open to speculation – all the more reason, then, for its being attempted, such that we might eventually be able to add to the history of political, scientific, religious, economic, and philosophical thought, a kind of history of 'practical' thought. My suggestion is that an available and philosophically sound insertion point, so to speak, for such work is to view previous analytic history, in the sense of the term used here, as primary evidence.

The third achievement of analytic history in addition to its descriptive and explanatory uses, and closely allied to the latter, is it potential for prediction. To revert again to our analysis of the meaning and rationale of single words, we have noted that once the workability and relevance of a generalisation has been established, then insofar as a particular object is known to be, for instance, a chair, we can safely predict certain of its features in advance of witnessing them. The same applies to general concepts arrived at through analytic history, not so much in terms of predicting the future (although there seems no reason why historians should not attempt this where possible), but more in the way of making sense of past circumstances and events in terms of their predictability or 'reasonableness' given what preceded them. Thus, for example, we might say of a hypothetical historian who had a good analytic grasp of modern Russian history up to 1916, that he might *expect* to discover something like the political events of 1917. We hypothesize he has a notion of the typical Russian bureaucrat, Russian peasant, and war-time economy – maybe even of 'the typical revolutionary situation'. Armed with such general notions and a knowledge of particulars up to 1916, he might well be surprised if at least the principal events of 1917 (for example, the downfall of Tsarism), had *not* occurred. Should one regard this as an exaggeration, observe how many examination questions are couched in terms of why such-and-such a course of events did *not* occur. Indeed, the business of rendering events and circumstances intelligible is so close to rendering them predictable that historians are likely to be particularly interested in situations which contradict expectation. This highlights just how important a foundation is provided by the notion of 'the typical' for many historians. Its converse cries out for explanation, often providing the very stimulus for steering away from generalisations and moving more into the area of particular narrative. In respect of individual figures in history, 'greatness' always supersedes 'the typical', of course, and has correspondingly attracted special interest from historians and laymen alike, as have fame and infamy.

In talking of the predictive value of generalisations arrived at via analysis, their workability (that is, their reliability when matched to the real world), is the obvious concern – (for instance, how *true* is this or that historian's concept of 'the typical Leveller'?). Just as the predictive value of single words varies significantly in respect of both the number and certainty of the features they predict, so with historical generalisations. For instance, from such a concept as 'a typical town of the Industrial Revolution' we might anticipate only such broad predictions as still to leave scope for important differences between those phenomena the concept embraces. On the other hand, such a notion as 'a typical Lancashire cotton town' offers more, and more certain, predictive information, in the same way the term 'a motel' is more precise than 'a building'. And if our intellectual instinct is wont to complain about such disparities, perhaps especially regretting concepts which are 'too' general, let us bear in mind that markedly general concepts such as 'a building', or 'medieval', are in fact extremely useful and eminently workable. What this amounts to is that there are no good or bad generalisations other than those which are useful or otherwise – and vague ones can be as useful as precise ones.

COMPARATIVE HISTORY AND QUANTITATIVE HISTORY

Before relating what I have called 'analytic history' to the question, 'what is history?', we should note two explicit and ambitious species of analytic history, one of ancient lineage and the other of recent times. The former is comparative history, previously more a preoccupation of political theorists and speculative philosophers of history such as Aristotle, Machiavelli,

Bodin, Hegel, and Marx, but also now a recognised feature of some contemporary historians' work. The latter is quantitative history, a recent undertaking made plausible by an increasing awareness of the uses of statistical techniques.

Of comparative history, where, for instance, different revolutions such as the English, American, French, and Russian examples – or different nationalist movements such as the German, Italian, Indian, and Chinese – are put under comparative scrutiny, the hope is that certain common features (in addition to those already implied by the concepts, 'revolution' and 'nationalism') might be discerned. Where this is fulfilled, generalis-ations of what is 'typical' emerge (ranging from the broad to the precise), which at the least add a dimension to the understanding of particular historical episodes, and more significantly may point to explanations other-wise hidden in particular cases. For instance, to discover by comparative analysis that all revolutions undergo identifiably similar phases and that their leaderships face similar problems *vis-à-vis* counter-revolution, foreign interference, and the aspirations of their own supporters, is to tentatively build up a picture of 'the typical revolution', potentially replete with that explanatory and predictive suggestiveness afforded by the gradual elaboration of a common-sense, empirically based notion of 'how revolu-tions generally work'. Here again the untypical is thus allowed to emerge, suggestive of lines of enquiry and explanation which might have gone unnoticed had one only studied a single revolution, however exhaustively.

Even more interesting and potentially valuable is the case where a comparative approach to history suggests regularities in situations hitherto regarded as entirely separate; for example, economic historians' discovery of 'the trade cycle', or early-modern historians' concept of 'pre-industrial capitalist societies'. Here, comparative history is not merely analysing phenomena already known about, such as revolutions and nationalist movements, but actually discovering phenomena – that is, revealing 'things going on' within history which were previously unknown. This possibility must make comparative history the most stimulating to bolder, and some would say, speculative minds. Yet for all that, the chief virtue of such work carried out by historians, rather than by political theorists and speculative philosophers of history, must remain its empirical basis, raising it above the realms of 'mere' theory or speculation.

Apart from this danger to comparative history's integrity – namely, to skip or even deliberately neglect the facts because under the influence of some elegant and plausible hypothesis from political or social theory – another danger is the temptation to *explain* particular circumstances or events in terms of their being 'typical' of a (necessarily abstract) generality, as in our example of the fallacious argument of an object's having legs 'because it is a chair'. We have to remember 'the typical chair' is but an ideal type, conceived of by human beings because of its relevance and workability. In short, a concept cannot explain the existence of particular empirical phenomena, even in the deceptive case where they are produced by human beings. Actual trees do not exist because of our concept of a tree; neither do things we make, such as chairs. The proper explanation of why this object has legs is that it was manufactured to seat someone comfortably; it thus requires to be of a certain height and dimensions; legs are an economical use of material to help achieve this. Incidentally, we call such objects 'chairs'; (that is, it does not have legs 'because it is a chair'). If it is important to insist on these points respecting the simplest things it is even more important to do so as we move to more complex situations where the questions may be, not 'why does this object have legs?', but, 'how inevitable was multinational war by 1914?', or, 'why did republicanism fail in seventeenth-century England?'

At such levels of abstraction the danger is that concepts rather than facts are appealed to in explanations. Because, for instance, 'the typical pre-industrial capitalist society' could never have caused or even influenced anything, then to *explain* any feature of an *actual* society in terms of its being a typical pre-industrial capitalist society is at the least misleading, and at worst silly. To be sure, to elaborate upon the *meaning* of the concept may be of great value in explaining certain features of a particular society; but to the extent historians are especially valued for their insistence upon the hard-won facts and for their common sense rather than speculative approach to them, one might almost prefer them to offer their concrete explanation and then add that, incidentally, it was inspired by a useful concept, namely, the notion of 'a pre-industrial capitalist society'. In short, 'capitalism', 'the Enlightenment', 'the trade cycle', or 'imperialism', never caused, influenced, or contributed to any actual circumstance, situation, or event. The latter remain unassailable, whilst many of the former concepts may be superseded by new ones regarded as more relevant and workable. And this is to say that whilst our understanding of the past may change, since what is relevant and workable for the human intellect is subject to alteration, the historical world is fixed; Voltaire wrote what he wrote, irrespective of whether we find the concept of 'the Enlightenment' useful or not either in giving an account of, or in accounting for, what he wrote.

Comparative history, then, in being the most explicit and deliberately developed example of analytic history, is adventurous in its ambition, promising valuable new insights and even discoveries; and in its pursuit historians need only be mindful that in so clearly highlighting the possibilities of the analytic approach, the caveats are equally highlighted.

The other explicit species of analytic history is quantitative history, where statistical techniques are applied to acquired data in order to discover regularities, exceptions, significant correlations, suggestive connections, and trends, and to prove or disprove long-held beliefs and new hypotheses.

Although the predictive value of statistical science has been established beyond doubt, it has much less of a direct explanatory value, being adumbrative rather than demonstrative of explanations. The scatter-graph abstracts 'the typical' in the solely quantitative terms of a normal distribution curve. Given large enough numbers its predictive value is remarkable in cases of highly significant correlations – 'significant', that is, in the specialist statistical sense – yet it is no part of the rationale of the exercise to produce any explanation, even in worldly common-sense terms, of why various factors correlate. In this sense statistical 'facts' and phenomena are unintelligible in themselves, and whether one is prompted to find an explanation for what lies *behind* them depends on whether one wants to do more than predict things, or (dis)prove assertions of a quantitative nature, such as, 'the vast majority of Belfast Protestant workers earned higher wages and suffered less unemployment than their Catholic counterparts throughout the period of Stormont rule'.

Today's historian faces two problems here. Firstly, even in the absence of any clear definition of what an historian is, he will surely recognise historians are and should be involved in giving an account of, and explaining, past circumstances and events – that is, rendering the past knowable and intelligible – and for this reason he will wish to go beyond quantitative analysis *per se*. At most, then, it is an extra tool in his bag, not the occupation itself. Secondly, moreover, one must query how useful this tool is for the historian in particular as distinct from, for example, the physicist, medic, or traffic-planner, because as a tool its success is so dependent upon collations of data sufficiently numerous to permit the emergence of the statistically significant. A coin tossed ten times may roughly divide fifty-fifty between heads and tails. Tossed a hundred times, the picture becomes clearer. But the statistician would rather toss the coin a hundred times, plot the result, and then repeat the exercise a hundred times, and this he can do. The medic can deal with millions of individuals; the physicist can repeat his experiment over and over again. But the historian does not deal with thousands let alone millions of wars, revolutions, famines, churches, or political parties. Were he able to, as in Asimov's science-fiction idea of 'psycho-history',[6] where the rise, duration, and fall of regimes is statistically predictable in terms of numerous factors discovered to be statistically significant, he would need to be projected into that futuristic universe whose recorded history spanned millions of years and millions of cultures. For these reasons, then, there is a world of difference between the concept of 'the typical' produced by comparative history and the same produced by quantitative analysis. The former is intelligible, that is, 'meaningful', and is not denied access to the larger movements of history, whilst the latter seems both an inherently limited tool and to have a markedly restricted use for today's historian.

THE LIMITATIONS OF ANALYTIC HISTORY

Having identified and elaborated upon what I have called analytic history as one answer to the question of what essentially demarcates the historian (since it is not his data-unravelling activity), the question arises as to whether the proffering of analytic statements derived from comparing different situations with a view to abstracting instructive generalisations is a sufficient answer to 'what is history?'

The answer to this must be no. Empirically, historians have rarely limited themselves to descriptive and/or analytic history, but have also engaged in the writing of narrative. The subject of history tells us not only 'what it was like', with accompanying explanations of why, but also 'what happened' – that is, historians have always concerned themselves with *events*, and as will presently be examined as central to the nature of history, it is the piecing together of data into the structure of narrative which is the essential technique of apprehending them. To say this is also to offer the *conceptual* grounds for denying that history can be demarcated in terms of descriptive and/or analytic history. History, whatever else it might deal with, deals with events. Events cannot be described in the same (ascriptive) way objects are; they have to be narrated. They may require explanation; they may offer themselves to a comparative treatment, where the analytic mind abstracts illuminating common features; but first and foremost they have to be presented, and it is difficult to see how else the intellect can apprehend events other than through the logic of narrative, essentially construed as *a* happening, then *b*, then *c*, and so on. Furthermore, in dealing with events history necessarily feeds on a changing world – in the conventionally accepted version of what history is, a changeless world would literally 'have no history'. The very way the word 'history' is commonly employed is strongly suggestive of this and should not be eclipsed by more esoteric reflections. To describe a medieval village is not to give its history; to analyse a medieval village and compare it with others, possibly permitting the emergence of a concept of 'the typical medieval village', is not to give its history. The history of a medieval village is its story – the story of how it began, how it developed, how it changed in various ways, and how it finally disappeared, or at least became something no longer recognisable as a medieval village. To offer the history of something, then, is to centre attention upon a changing identity, to recount change in an intelligible way. This cannot but imply apprehending the past in terms of 'things happening' – that is, in terms of 'events' – and the intellectual activity involved in understanding situations as sequential and continuous, albeit changing, is that of narrating. One narrates events – there is no other way of conveying 'what happened'.

Analytic history is not essentially involved in narrating events; indeed, it is not essentially concerned with a changing world. An expert on 'the medieval village' or on 'the pre-industrial capitalist society' may have enough to occupy him without studying the (changing) history of any actual medieval village or pre-industrial capitalist society. In short, just as the descriptive historian deals with phenomena held *in stasis*, so to an extent does the analytic historian inasmuch as he is not so concerned to trace a changing sequence of events as to abstract factors common to otherwise different situations, thereby producing a useful generalisation or concept. It is true the comparative historian in particular may compare different sequences of events (for example, revolutions), in order to discover common factors, but once discovered he can stop the film rolling, so to speak, as he will already have many times, in order to analyse the different factors involved from a comparative viewpoint. Also implicit here is movement away from concrete particulars to abstract concepts (for instance, movement away from this and that revolution to, for example, 'the typical nationalist revolution') and these, like any concepts, are not intrinsically to do with change. On the contrary the hope is that a general concept such as 'the typical nationalist revolution' remains applicable for a useful period despite changing particulars, such that we might almost evaluate an analytic concept's success in terms of how far it manages to supersede the world of changing particulars with which narrative is concerned. After all, is not that one sign of the relevance and workability of *single* words, such as 'chair' – namely, that in successfully persisting they denote *unchanging* things? And, to return to the starting-point of our argument, what is the status of a concept such as 'the typical nationalist revolution' if not that of an (elaborate) single word; and vice-versa?

SUMMARY – THE QUESTION OF NARRATIVE

In approaching the question, 'what is history?', we noted its bewilderingly wide subject-matter and, finding little there to guide us, turned attention to those special features involved in acquiring knowledge of the subject-matter which particularly arise from its being in the past – most notably, the business of inferring from evidence. But again it seemed difficult to claim such intellectual activities as specifically the province of the historian, however clearly they distinguish him from the philosopher and the scientist. Thus we suggested that, if it is neither the subject-matter nor the methods of acquiring knowledge of it which demarcate the discipline of history, attention must be turned upon what historians *do with* the data they unravel. In the broadest terms three modes of treatment have been distinguished on both empirical and conceptual grounds; namely, descriptive, analytic, and narrative history – and examination of the former two suggests that although both are eminently instructive, demanding, and coherent undertakings, neither involve a sufficiently unique intellectual structuring to allow us to claim we have singled out something only historians do.

Commensurately, both descriptive and analytic history fail to relate fully to the ordinary intimations of the word 'history', since however much we may regret its vagueness the common wisdom of language does at least centre attention upon the notion of a story of changing events. The kind of 'intellectual structuring' or 'mode of treatment' this necessitates is the narrative approach, and we should straight away note that we look in vain for sustained (factual) narrative as the form in which any other discipline's knowledge is or can be structured and conveyed. And yet it must be conceded that if we survey the writings of many recent and contemporary historians we look equally in vain for narrative as the core of their endeavour.[7] Indeed, that recent historians have turned away from narrative has been noted both by historians themselves and by analytic philosophers of history, and what the former have continued to justify by their practice the latter have attempted to justify in argument.

The accusation – for such it is – against narrative history is that it is naive. Historians insist explanation rather than story-telling is their principal business, whilst philosophers argue out the same point by attempting to show the very form of narrative is non-explanatory of its subject-matter. The latter then embark on the quest for what has become a veritable philosopher's stone, namely, 'historical explanation', trying to isolate some mode of explanation peculiar to the historian, premised on the rejection of what stands before their eyes in both convention and logic – namely, narrative explanation.[8]

That historians themselves have tended to turn away from the narrative form is probably explicable, and partly understandable, in terms of the rise of the 'social sciences', widely conceived to include sociology, political science, economics, and even aspects of psychology. Arguably 'a product of the Enlightenment', these disciplines became increasingly established through the course of the nineteenth century, such that they are now accepted as crucially important in understanding societies and human conduct. Facing this challenge, many historians have clearly felt that the potential for sophisticated explanation of events and circumstances revealed by the social sciences has rendered the telling of stories an unsatisfactory vehicle for conveying knowledge of the past in terms of what happened and why. Economic systems, organisation, and development; social structures, class consciousness, and sociological laws; the comparative study of political systems, power structures, and the nature and function of ideology; the growing awareness and organised study of the media's influence; all have provided a massive panorama of factors potentially involved in giving a full and adequate account of the past. In short, the social sciences have transformed not only the specialist intellectual but increasingly the ordinary common-sense understanding of 'how the world works'. There is now so much more, and different, to be said about 'the rise and fall of the Roman Empire' that it seems hardly possible to expect the story-form to be anywhere near adequate to the task – the very form of narrative seems to invite a naive treatment, and to this extent we may be heartened rather than dismayed at many of today's historians' rejection of narrative, for their motivation is in good faith.

However, when all is said and done, the introduction of new and added insights into past circumstances and events means the old story should be rewritten rather than not written at all. People in the seventeenth century did not stop telling stories of past times because of their growing disbelief in divine miracles and growing confidence in the natural sciences; they merely incorporated their new beliefs into the fabric of their accounts, just as the early Christians expunged belief in the intervention of the Graeco-Roman gods from their stories of the past. Just so in this, the late twentieth, century; after a phase of confusion we might expect historians to return to the narrative form having mastered the ability to incorporate those most general features of that revolution in knowledge of 'how the world works' constituted by the social sciences. The alternative is nothing less than the disappearance of history – that is, stories of the past – and its replacement by an intricate and confusing criss-cross of specialist analyses, explanations, and interpretations under the misguided assumption that narrative is intellectually obsolete.

Although it is doubtful whether historians take any guidance from those philosophers who turn their attention to the logic of the discipline of history, it is probable that what philosophers say is influential when it happens to confirm in its more rigorous way the general atmosphere of what historians have been doing anyway. Such has been narrative history's misfortune, where even its most sympathetic analysts have felt obliged to reiterate the essential claim of fellow philosophers that narrative *per se* is at the very least a simplistic vehicle of explanation, and at the worst is not such a vehicle in any sense at all.[9] In the latter case it is consequently recommended that historians abandon narrative altogether, whilst in the former case the function of explanation is denied to the narrative form itself, and is instead to be supplied by the inclusion, or intrusion, of explanatory glosses interrupting its flow.

Yet even prior to close examination this negative stance towards the narrative form in terms of its ability to explain circumstances and events must surely be challenged on the straightforward grounds that, whether in the profusion of mundane conversation or in the drama of the court-room, the narrative form is the commonest vehicle of explanation it is possible to identify. 'Why are you in debt?', 'why didn't he apply for the job?', 'how come she got home so late last night?', 'why did they emigrate?', are all queries exemplifying the stuff of which everyday conversation is made, and for which no more satisfactory answer is sought than 'the story of what happened', or what might be regarded, significantly, as the same thing, 'the story of why it happened'. Likewise, the courtroom is all too familiar with individuals giving markedly different 'stories' of the same events, in effect giving differing explanations of them. If we follow the story (necessarily structured as a narrative), we will know why he is in debt, or why they emigrated, so long as the story makes sense. But even to know what happened at all (leaving *why* it happened as separate for the sake of argument), we need to follow a story, and insofar as we can classify events along with objects as 'phenomena' in the world – for instance, wars, elections, mergers, divorces, and holidays, as distinct from chairs, trains, cities, and mice – this class of phenomena is constituted through the narrative form. It is not possible to particularise them in any other way. In short, if we are dealing with events, narrative is essential in the most compulsory sense of the term.

Narrative, then, has the property of both establishing events in the first place and of explaining their occurrence. Furthermore, if we stop at a certain point in the narrative of a sequence of events, and call this *status quo* a situation or circumstance, narrative is also explanatory of circumstances as well as of events. As in ordinary conversation, the question, 'why is (or was) this so?', can be treated as synonymous with 'how did this come about?'

Provisionally these arguments point to the importance of the narrative form to the historian, contrary to much current practice and to analyses produced by philosophers. But these arguments *are* only provisional as yet, for two matters require proper demonstration – firstly, that the very form of narrative is indeed a mode of explanation *per se*. Secondly, it is necessary to demonstrate what *kind* of explanation is intrinsic to it in order to assess the claim of those who accept narrative's explanatory function but nevertheless regard it as inherently naive or simplistic. If the narrative form is non-explanatory in the first place then we must in all common sense accede to the views of those historians who do not see the telling of stories as that which essentially makes them historians as distinct from, for instance, political sociologists, conflict-study scientists, or Byzantine-art experts. Likewise, if the narrative form *is* shown to be explanatory, but inadequately so (that is, in terms of naivety or any other sense worthy of complaint), then we must in all fairness reject it as the historian's special hallmark rather than condemn him to a technique intrinsically incapable of an adequate treatment of his often complex and hard-won material.

On the other hand, to the extent we can demonstrate the narrative form to be above these criticisms (as I intend), we should examine its peculiar properties and their implications, encouraged in the belief that in so doing we are indeed probing into the special characteristics and possibilities of history as a distinct, identifiable discipline requiring its own approach, despite the enormous variety of subject-matter, and techniques of discovery, discussed in this chapter.

2

THE STRUCTURE OF
NARRATIVE

WHAT IS A NARRATIVE?

We will not go far wrong in equating a 'narrative' with a 'story', so long as we are not immediately insistent that a 'story' is something with a beginning, middle, and end, in such a strong sense as to sustain its overall coherence. Perhaps the archetypal story is of this character, but not all stories begin on a new dawn and end with a satisfying completeness. Many, as we finish the last page or watch the last scene or film-roll, are simply adjourned; they are nonetheless stories. Alternatively (to concede to the strong sense of the term), they are incomplete, unfinished stories – but they remain *stories* for all that, rather than something else. And what makes them stories is that they are purposeful accounts of continuous events. It is true there are many types of story, one of the major distinctions being between factual and fictional ones. But what enables us to subsume them all under the term 'story' is that at the minimum, and necessarily, they assume the narrative form. They narrate events.

Put another way, we can say that because *any* kind of story is necessarily structured on events ('happenings', 'actions', 'changing situations'), then its form of discourse must be capable of communicating events, of saying 'what happened'. That form of discourse (for there is only one), is *narrative*. The term denotes that kind of discourse which has the form or structure, 'this happened, *then* that', or 'this was the situation, *then* that occurred'. Despite the obvious ubiquity and apparent simplicity of this form of discourse, reflection reveals it has epistemological implications of such complexity that they threaten to be intractable. Rather than approach the matter *a priori*, let us first raise some questions about the construction of stories as we conventionally know them.

STORIES AND CHRONICLES

Stories are of course constructed by human beings, and obviously for a wide variety of reasons, ranging from the simple (for instance, the moral fable, the excitation of a few basic emotions, the joke), to the increasingly complex (as in most good literature, drama, and film-making). Further, some stories are purely fictional, others purely factual, whilst many combine both fact and fiction. Some are told in order to answer questions, others in order to raise them. In short, we should remark upon the flexibility of the story-form to suit an impressive variety of purposes. Yet in all cases the form remains the same at root – 'this happened, *then* that' – whereby events, situations, or actions are presented as succeeding each other in such a manner as to appear to 'follow on'. The story 'develops', 'progresses', 'evolves' – whatever term we use, we mean to indicate an essential continuity in a sequence of events.

The case is different with a mere chronicle of events, for a chronicle is a kind of calendar. It lists events (or other data) in the order of their dates. For example, one could produce a list of every Act of Parliament ordered (sequentially) according to their dates; or one could chronicle the offspring of a family over the generations. Insofar as their succession in time is the sole principle underlying their manner of presentation, it would appear continuity is the essence of the matter in the construction of a chronicle – and if so, then the chronicle is the narrative in its starkest, hence purest, form. But of course this is not the case.[1] A chronicle's 'continuity' is merely abstract, superimposed by the purely formal rationale of the numerical ordering of dates; it is a meaningless continuity. Put more formally, the chronicle is structured in terms of 'this (then) that', whereas the narrative is structured in terms of 'this *then* that'. In the narrative form, the 'then' has a peculiar, distinctive significance which transforms a succession of events into a meaningful sequence. Insofar as this transformation is somewhat mysterious and yet is the heart of the matter, it cries out for explication.

When we offer someone a story, a narrative account of 'what happened' – it might be the story of the Falklands War or of my friend's arrival at the cinema late, soaking wet, and penniless – we cannot but structure this discourse in terms of a sequence of events. But unlike in a chronicle, this structuring is done intentionally by us, for our purposes, rather than being formally imposed by the anonymous requirements of dates succeeding each other. Our structuring is meaningful; it manifests the reasons we have in doing it; it constitutes a rationale. A computer can produce a chronicle, and do so more quickly, accurately, and hence efficiently, than can a human being. But only human beings can produce stories, because only they have reasons for doing something, whereby they endow what they do with meaning – and in proportion as that meaning is communicated by means of the story form, the story is more or less intelligible. At the minimum, intelligibility is the criterion of success for the construction of a story. It has to 'make sense', whatever else it might also achieve.

How is it, then, that to put events into a sequence can *of itself* be

43

to construct meaning, to communicate intelligibility? And *what* is made intelligible by the very form of narrative? The chronicle is a 'sequence' but is not intelligible. It might imply a story; one might infer an intelligibility from or in it; but its form is not in itself meaningful. What is happening in a narrative which makes it so different?

FICTIONAL NARRATIVE

Common sense and experience tell us no one ever *invents* a (thereby fictional) story simply for the sake of it. One must have a purpose over and above that of simply rendering a sequence of events intelligible, for one is, after all, inventing them. Moreover, one is inventing them in such a manner as to construct a continuity. This may even require inventing some which in themselves are of no significance apart from serving the function of 'joining together' those which, given one's purposes (for instance, amusement, or moral instruction), one *does* have a reason to invent. We note such mere 'joining together' events are often dealt with perfunctorily by novelists, such that our hero's move from London to Jamaica is treated of in a sentence or two whereas his departure from his flat and mistress warranted several pages. Alternatively, some novelists exploit these otherwise merely 'necessary' events in such a manner as to reflect style, humour, or some personal 'gripe' – (for example, the alleged dishonesty of taxi-drivers). Some omit them altogether, leaving them to our imagination. But even in the latter case our imagination must be within the bounds of reasonable inference. We cannot be left astounded the hero has suddenly gone to Jamaica. It can never be the novelist's intention to perplex his readers regarding the sequence of events he narrates. (Temporarily, as in the thriller, yes: but such constructions only prove the point. By the end of the story earlier events which were unintelligible precisely because of their 'intrusion' into the narrative sequence are made understandable in retrospect – finally, one understands what 'actually' happened.)

The novelist, then, can be said to exploit the narrative form always in order to achieve something *by* recounting a sequence of events over and above merely inventing it for its own sake. (And the same can be said of that other sense of the term 'fiction' – namely, that kind of lie where, although the events are factual, their sequence is deliberately distorted.) He chooses the events (via a process of selection *and* omission), but his choice is restrained by the narrative form. He must needs include some which have no relevance to his purposes other than that of sustaining the story's 'flow' – that is, of rendering it intelligible. We all recognise cases where an author clearly feels this restraint a merely formal burden; his overwhelming interest is to present dramatic, amusing, or titillating scenarios. In such cases his exploitation of the narrative form is easy and instinctive, and however skilfully he presents these scenarios we are wont to say he is a poor story-teller because his overall 'story' barely escapes being no more than a chronicle, artificially 'strung together' by the inclusion of tediously bland episodes. An alternative is for the novelist to invent such merely formally demanded events in such a manner as to contribute to what he is trying to achieve. For instance, he may exploit such 'joining together' passages to add to the description of a character, or to present relevant background information about a town or work-place.

But we should not hesitate to identify the serious novelist as he whose purpose is principally achieved not by using the narrative form as merely a peg upon which to hang his descriptions, explanations, exhortations, or perceptions about the meaning of life, but as he who achieves his purpose(s) essentially *through* the narrative form. For example, descriptive, philosophical, and scientific writings are not novels; they do not need the narrative form. For the serious novelist, however, the narrative form is taken seriously; it is the form of discourse by which he hopes to realise his purposes in writing at all. Unlike our virtual chronicler of a succession of interesting, amusing, or morally instructive scenarios where the narrative form is merely formal, the serious novelist constructs his sequence of events with deliberation, such that their sequentiality of itself conveys the meaning, or 'message', he intends his story to convey. It may be he could have conveyed it by other means – for example, the message of a moral fable can be presented in exhortative form or in the form of explanatory moral philosophy. On the other hand it may be certain 'messages' can only be conveyed by the narrative form, and that some novelists intuit such a necessary correlation between the form and the content of what they want to 'say'. Indeed, there may be a mystery here – namely, what kind of 'message' could intrinsically necessitate a *fictional* narrative to convey its content? – such that exploration of its potential rationale may suggest a distinctive approach to literary criticism.

Such a pursuit is not to our purposes here, however. All we are concerned to establish by regarding fictional narrative is that it must meet the minimum requirement of constructing a sequence of events in such a manner as to achieve an intelligible continuity; and that it is difficult to see how this can ever be more than a minimum requirement since the novelist must be attempting to achieve something more than simply inventing a series of fictional events in such a manner as to construct their intelligible continuity. That this 'something more' may necessitate the narrative form we leave for speculation. And in any event, perhaps Plato was right – namely, there *is* no message so mysterious that it can only be communicated through fictional narrative; rather, the teller of fictional stories merely exploits the narrative form, the essence of the matter being fiction, not narrative. And why is *fiction* the essence of the matter? –

because in permitting free play to the imagination it enables the story-teller to intensify the emotions he wishes to excite in a manner and to a degree a factual story could not achieve. We know of Plato's consequent disapproval of the freedom of the arts, his no less logical recognition of their power, and hence his recommendation of censorship.[2]

In short, could Cervantes have communicated such a rueful critique of the obsolete medieval concepts of honour and chivalry by means of a rationally argued moral essay rather than by a fictional narrative which included Don Quixote's famous tilt at the windmills? Could Evelyn Waugh have communicated such a persuasive view of the contingencies of individuals' fates and the ironies of the politics of the Second World War if he had written an explanatory discourse on them rather than the *Sword of Honour* trilogy? The case is different, however, with factual narrative – or rather, it *can* be.

FACTUAL NARRATIVE

In deference to what has just been said, let us immediately concede that *factual* narrative can be constructed for purposes similar to the above – that is, for its persuasive, 'message-laden' effect. Valuably, Tudor has pointed this out, arguing that a narrative account of the past may be constructed from 'the facts' (rather than from imagination or wishful thinking), but in such a manner as to have either the explicit or implicit purpose of persuading an audience to adopt certain moral or political stances.[3] Whether this is a species of that other kind of 'fiction' already noted, namely, the deliberate lie, is an interesting issue. But Tudor argues that the question of whether the narrative is fictional or factual is of secondary importance: of primary significance is whether the story-teller's purpose is so to select his facts (or invent his falsehoods) that he can construct a story which is persuasive of the moral or political message dear to his heart. And if this is really what is going on, how do we account for significant changes, revisions, and amendments in such narratives, perhaps particularly those of long-standing public credence? To a large extent the right approach to answering such questions is already implicit in Tudor's analysis of the character of such stories, narratives, 'histories', or 'myths' – namely, to attend to their function rather than their veracity.

A contemporary example of such a problematic is afforded by those Anglican bishops and savants who attempt to get public acceptance of certain revisions in the life-story, or 'history', of Jesus of Nazareth (particularly regarding the claim that he was neither 'actually' born of a virgin, nor 'actually' resurrected). What is the point of such attempted revisions? Surely not historical truth for the sake of it, for if that were the case one wonders why the State appointed individuals so afflicted by the intoxicant of factual truth – so much so, indeed, that they ignore so many of their predecessors' recognition that the practical business of persuasively communicating moral truths demands a technique which fetishises neither logical consistency nor factual truth.

In short, it is possible to construct a narrative, from fact rather than fiction, in such a manner as to deliver a 'message' in the mind of the narrator, determining what he chooses to include, omit, and amend in his story. Such a process *must* characterise fictional narratives: it *may* characterise factual narratives.

The recognition, then, that neither fictional nor factual stories tell themselves, but have to be more or less painstakingly constructed by human beings, is important despite its mundaneness. It highlights that constructing a narrative involves selection, and thus omission, of events, and thereby inescapably implies a governing purpose to the narrator's activity. The narrative will thus manifest a rationale (unlike a chronicle where, although there must be a motive in producing it, the logic of its actual construction, or its 'reason', is purely abstract and formal). Attention to its structuring may in each case reveal what this rationale is. Is this woman in the dock so structuring her story (the facts of which may or may not be true), in order to incriminate the defendant? Is my friend so structuring his story of the match (the facts of which may or may not be true), in order to impress upon me his skill? Is this historian so structuring his story of the English Civil War (the facts of which he would be foolish to falsify), in order to present himself as a radical? – or, for example, in order to denigrate monarchism?

In all these cases where the facts in a narrative may be true, the story is being 'angled' in order to achieve a practical purpose – namely, the persuasive communication of a 'message'. The question thus arises: insofar as historians especially are supposed to have no extrinsic practical purposes of their own in constructing their narrative accounts of past events but are supposed to adhere to 'the truth' for its own sake, what determines *their* selection and ordering of events? The centrality of this question to our enquiry warrants its elaboration.

Insofar as the constructing of a narrative necessitates deliberate selection and omission of events, some purpose or 'reason' must determine this process. Such a determinant is usually not difficult to perceive where it derives from a practical purpose and we are right to regard such narratives as 'merely' subjective accounts, 'angled' or distorted away from the 'true', 'objective' account by the domination of the story-teller's practical purposes governing what he selects and omits. But what if he has no practical purposes, no 'axe to grind', or 'message' to deliver? (Some, of course, rashly deny this is possible.) What determines, not his narrative's fundamental structure – for that must always be the same, namely, 'this happened, *then* that' – but his handling of the actual content? Can the narrative *form* of itself determine the *content* of the narrative? 'Caesar crossed the Rubicon, and then . . .'? Got his servant to dry him off? Called his generals together to plan his next move? Marched on Rome? There are numerous alternatives to choose from even in factual narrative, all of which necessitate the omission of intervening events, and also correspondingly varying time-scales.[4] Where the narrator has a practical purpose – for instance, to criticise Caesar's ambitious nature – this should sooner or later become clear from his choice of alternatives. But in the absence of any such extrinsic purposes, how does one proceed with the narrative? Can 'sticking to the truth for its own sake' perform the same function as does an extrinsic purpose – namely, that of being the determinant of what to select and omit? At first glance this seems unlikely, if only because 'the truth' is not itself a 'message' in the sense we have found that term revealing.

NARRATIVE FOR ITS OWN SAKE

Is it possible, then, to construct a narrative 'for its own sake' – that is, not in order to amuse the reader, thrill him, preach a moral message to him, raise or answer questions the narrator believes he should pay attention to, or to achieve whatever other extrinsic practical purpose can be imagined? In other words, is it possible simply to inform the reader of 'what happened'? (For the sake of argument, we leave why the reader wants to know as a vicarious issue.) The answer to this must surely be yes; it is precisely what some historians, some investigative journalists, and hopefully all jury members, understand themselves to be doing. And it is important to show it is not an impossible task. However, its logic requires explication.

Suppose someone was asked to give an account of what he did on a certain day. His reply might be: 'I got up rather late and in my hurry over breakfast didn't really pay attention to what my wife was saying. Anyway, I got to work on time. I went to lunch at a rather nice restaurant because I was entertaining a client. When I got back to the office my boss wanted to see me, and when I did get to see him it turned out he wanted me to move district, home and all, to take charge of a new branch. Thinking about it on the train home, I reckoned I hadn't got much option, but I was worried how my wife would take the news. When I got home we had a first-class row, actually, because I'd forgotten to pick up her prescription (which she'd asked me to do at breakfast) – and in trying to excuse myself I divulged we were going to have to move, and that this had been so much on my mind that I'd walked straight past the chemist's. Rather than mollify her, this made her even more angry, so I went out, and came back late, hoping she was already asleep. But she wasn't – she'd packed her bags and gone. Yes, that was quite a day; I remember it well!'

Now, as in any such story where the narrator is not answering a *specific* question, making a particular point, or trying to persuade people to a particular view of the world, we should notice two things about the above narrative. Firstly, irrespective of its articulation, its fundamental structure is cast in terms of 'this happened then that'. Secondly, despite there being no extrinsic practical purpose behind the story's construction, it is still selective regarding which occurrences, actions, or situations are recounted. The story could conceivably have been much longer or much shorter. Its being a story simply demands the form, 'this happened then that happened'. What, then, determines which events are included and excluded?

The first point is that the story 'makes sense', and what is this to say other than the events recounted are intelligible in and because of their temporal ordering? Had the story gone, 'I got up rather late, and when I got home last thing at night my wife had packed her bags and gone', her disappearance would not be intelligible. Less dramatically, had it gone, 'In my hurry over breakfast I didn't pay attention to what my wife was saying, and then my boss wanted to see me', again the story would be unintelligible. This shows that 'prior' and 'subsequent' events are interdependent, as any logician would affirm. Any particular event is only a prior event in the light of one which is subsequent, and vice versa. They are both sides of the same coin. What cements them together is their conventionally acceptable contiguity, such that the nature and occurrence of the 'subsequent' event is rendered intelligible precisely inasmuch as it is acceptably 'subsequent'. And the technique of narrative is to treat this 'subsequent' event as one which is also 'prior' to yet another 'subsequent' event. And so on the story goes.

In our example the narrator could have recounted numerous occurrences and/or actions as 'subsequent' to getting up, even *before* recounting his having breakfast – for instance, washing, shaving, dressing, and going downstairs. Alternatively, he could have omitted not only those, but also having breakfast, and instead moved from getting up late to nevertheless arriving at work on time. But there comes a point where to move forward from one event to a later one fails to achieve intelligibility despite linking them by the word, 'then'. 'He got up and then went to work', succeeds. 'He got up and then got home late', does not succeed. 'Hitler was elected Chancellor and then conspired to have no more to do with elections', succeeds; but, 'Hitler was elected Chancellor and then committed suicide in his bunker', clearly does not.

What this points to is that to put two events as contiguous to each other is, *ipso facto*, to achieve a kind of intelligibility. But it also shows that, even in the absence of any 'exterior' motivation governing which events are selected, there are parameters to one's selection which are determined by the form of narrative *per se*, in combination with the generality of assumptions about 'how the world works' which the narrator believes his audience shares. The more alien to his audience the narrator's culture, the less intelligible his story may be to them. We cannot see why, after having delivered bad news, the messenger's throat was 'then' cut, since in our time and culture these two events cannot be understood as conventionally contiguous, as 'prior' and 'subsequent'.

But to understand the form of narrative *per se*, let us assume we share the narrator's culture such that we can discuss the narrative form in the absence of any 'external' influences whatsoever. This leads to the second point, for in this case the narrative form presents itself purely as 'this *then* that', being thereby immediately intelligible. Thus, 'he woke up, stretched, yawned, looked out of the window, got out of bed, and put his slippers on', makes for an intelligible sequence of 'prior' and 'sub-sequent' events – but a clearly *unnecessary* sequence. And we should note that even this tedious sequence could be considerably lengthened by detail-ing each otherwise discrete action, as in 'he moved his left leg to the side of the bed, then raised himself up on one elbow, put his right leg on the floor, and then swung his body out of bed' – and all this merely with respect to 'getting out of bed'. On the other hand, as already noted, 'he got up and then arrived home late', is unintelligible. In the first case too many events are narrated; in the second, not enough. What, then, deter-mines which events should be recorded to meet the necessary requirements of the narrative form?

Bearing in mind a narrative must always be more than a chronicle – (it must manifest *meaning*) – and that it cannot be exhaustive of *every* occur-rence, the *a priori* answer is that the narrative must strive towards an economy of intelligibility. This implies the narrator beginning with a certain event – for instance, 'he woke up' (event 'a') – and moving forward in his mind through a continuous sequence of 'subsequent' and 'prior' events until he reaches one (call it event 'y'), which is not intelligibly 'subsequent' to the original event – or put the other way around, until he reaches one to which the original event cannot be understood as (meaning-fully) 'prior'. In other words, although it would make sense to say 'a then b', or 'a then c', or 'a then t', it would not make sense to say 'a then y'.

It would, however, make sense to say 'a then x', and also to say 'x then y'. Thus the principle of economic intelligibility dictates the narrative should proceed, 'a then x then y'. Abstractly, then, 'pure' narrative should be structured 'a to y minus 1', given that by 'y' we mean that point in a sequence which cannot be understood as conventionally contiguous to the original event, 'a', and given also that 'y' becomes a new starting-point (that is, a new 'a', namely, '$a1$'). Hence the 'pure' or 'unadorned' narrative would be structured, 'a then x then y' (which becomes '$a1$') – 'then $x1$ then $y1$' (which becomes '$a2$') – 'then $x2$', and so on. For example, 'he got up and then slammed the door on his way out to work', does not make much sense; it is like 'a then y'. 'He got up, and then argued with his wife over who should make breakfast, and then slammed the door on his way to work', does make sense – that is, it is like '*a* then *x* then *y*'.

What does this 'model' of narrative imply? Firstly, it shows how it is both possible to construct a narrative without its being virtually infinite in detail, and hence impossible – and also how to do so without any extrinsic practical purpose governing the selection and spacing of content. The narrative form of itself, construed as the achievement of a maximum of economy in the relating of conventionally contiguous events, affords an intelligible, meaningful discourse. It thereby surpasses mere chronicle whilst simultaneously remaining independent of any *necessary* subjectivity of purpose on behalf of the narrator (unlike fictional narrative). In short, in this sense it *is* possible to offer an 'objective' account of 'what happened'.

Secondly, this 'model' demonstrates that to establish a continuity to successive events is to achieve an intelligibility for them. The narrative form conveys an understanding of events, thereby achieving intelligibility. But, more closely, *what* is it that is explained, and what *kind* of an understanding is achieved?

NARRATIVE EXPLANATION

Firstly, then, *what* is explained by means of the narrative form? Mundanely enough it is already clear that, at the minimum, it is the nature and occurrence of events presented as 'subsequent' to 'prior' events (or situations or circumstances). To present an event as 'subsequent' to a 'prior' event is to do more than narrate the event – it is to say why it happened. And the way we do this is to preface the statement that '*x* happened' with the term, '*then*'. But this term must be meaningful rather than merely formal. 'He began to feel the cold and then closed the window', is an example. Not only do we know he closed the window; we know why. He did it 'because' he felt the cold. Alternatively one could say, 'he closed the window because he felt the cold' – that is, narrate an event and then add its explanation, rather than use the narrative form to provide it. Thus on the face of it both statements mean the same thing despite the former taking the form of narrative, and the latter the form of analytic discourse. If they amount to the same thing, we can say the kind of explanation is identical despite the different forms of discourse. And insofar as to say, 'this happened because of that', is to suggest a simple causal model of explanation, we could conclude that the kind of explanation inherent in narrative is causal. Were this so, there would be no special virtue, nor singularity, in writing factual narrative rather than straightforwardly causal explanations.

However, it is wrong to equate the kind of explanation achieved in narrative with causal explanation, even in the above example of 'feeling the cold and then closing the window'. Yet the difference is more a matter of intimation than of logic. To state, 'he closed the window because he felt the cold', is to intimate the exclusion of alternative explanations; in intimating that his feeling the cold 'caused' him to close the window, it is dogmatic. In other words, the mode of discourse structured in terms of 'this happened *because* of that' is strongly suggestive of that mode of (causal) explanation employed by the natural sciences, whereby the necessary interdeterminations between natural phenomena are displayed, construed as the product of 'laws'. In short, to employ this mode of discourse is to intimate the human 'behaviour' under scrutiny is a 'reaction' to 'stimuli'.

Those who take this view of human conduct may or may not be correct – at present the only point is that the narrative form of discourse does not bear the same dogmatic intimations. When we say, 'he felt the cold and then closed the window' ('this happened and *then* he did that') we are leaving him some elbow-room to have behaved differently; nevertheless, elbow-room only, since we wish to account for his subsequent action as indeed his 'next' action by using the term, *'then'*; that is, we wish to render his conduct intelligible, and this places parameters to what he can (intelligibly) do *'next'* (that is, subsequent to feeling the cold). He may have turned up the heater, or put on a cardigan, or left the room, or chosen to suffer the cold. But it would not make sense to present his 'next' action as playing the piano, or standing on his head, or coming home from work.

In short, the narrative form presents his conduct as a response to situations rather than as the effect of causes, because it is intelligible to us in terms of our more or less hazy, or systematically reflective, view of 'how the world works', especially of the factors which influence (but do not *determine*) human conduct. Now it is true the very form of narrative thus begs the question, 'is human behaviour a caused reaction or an intelligible response?' The form of narrative reflects the latter position (and in so doing is replete with tautology), but does not argue it. It is simply the most universal and therefore appropriate form of explanation adopted by those who, reflectively or not, draw a line (usually at the point where human beings are involved) between causally deterministic explanations of events and those which leave room for 'human freedom', 'human motivation', or 'human reason'. As a mode of explanation it is inherently 'messy' for philosophical or scientific purposes. It lacks the coherence of a philosophy because it does not examine its premises – indeed, when exposed, the assumptions regarding 'the way the world works' may vary so much that they are found to be contradictory. And it lacks the coherence of science for similar reasons – namely, it does not subsume events under tried and tested 'laws' of causality, determinateness, and inevitability. Further, it lacks the *objectivity* of science insofar as its explanations depend perhaps just as much upon the way the narrator understands 'the way things work' as upon the objective events available for verification. But at the moment none of this matters; the overriding point is that the narrative form *is* explanatory. It is necessary to identify it as such, and analyse how it works. Evaluation is a separate project best undertaken only after the topic to be evaluated is thoroughly understood.

What, then, can be said so far regarding narrative as a mode of explanatory discourse? It does not seem to offer an understanding of events as determinately caused. Rather, it seems to achieve an understanding in the sense that the reader can see an action as an appropriate response by an agent. He can say, 'given that such-and-such was the situation at point *a* in time, I can see why the agent did *x* at point *b* in time'. Certainly he could have done things other than *x* – for instance, *f*, *g*, or *h*; but he could not have done *m*, *n*, or *p*. Or at least, if he *had*, the action would be unintelligible to the reader. He would be unable to imagine why he did it, given the narrative so far. What this demonstrates, as already indicated, is that the narrator assumes a certain credulity in his readers. If the event in question is, 'he closed the window', it is sufficient to say he did this subsequent upon feeling the cold. Thus the narrator is assuming, either himself and/or on behalf of his readers, certain notions about the way individuals behave. Whether he admits it or is even aware of it, he is implying a 'theory' about individuals and about the world in general insofar as he selects (and omits) data on the basis of assumptions about what is reasonable, predictable, or appropriate for their conduct in different contexts.[5]

Narrative, then, assumes a general theory about human conduct, meaning by this not an explicit, specific theory but a set of assumptions about how people behave and how the world works, which may even be contradictory. And the writing of narrative is itself a potent bulwark to these 'ordinary', conventional assumptions since, if it does not establish them, it certainly reinforces them. They are not, then, derived from any particular theory – for instance, Marxian, or Freudian – but are taken to be common to all people of a similar culture, received through tradition, experience, and indeed the writing of history and fictional stories. To the extent these assumptions are thus unexamined rather than the product of reflection, some would argue they are the worst kind upon which to base any explanation or understanding. Hence we arrive at a claim encountered earlier – namely, that if there is such a thing as 'narrative explanation', it is a weak, naive, and unreflective kind of explanation for the purposes of precise historical work.

But although a fuller refutation of this critique must emerge from deeper examination of the logic of narrative, we can even now retort that a mode of explanation which focuses upon human beings as responding agents rather than reacting animals, nor again as god-like masters of their conduct, can hardly be called weak. Moreover, that this mode of explanation does not need articulating on each occasion through explanatory and analytic discourse but is actually embedded in a *form* of discourse exclusive to itself (viz., narrative), suggests that narrative explanation is sophisticated rather than naive. Finally, as to its being unreflective let us for the moment at least concede that, whilst reflective theories come and go in profusion, it has stood the test of time all over the world.

I have argued up to now that the basic form of narrative is, 'this happened *then* that'; that to put two occurrences as contiguous to each other is to achieve a kind of intelligibility; that in the absence of any extrinsic purpose governing the narrator's inevitable selection (and hence omission) of events, intelligibility is achieved through the economic establishment of continuity (viz., '*a* to *y* minus 1'). And what this amounts to is that the establishing of continuity is not only a necessary condition for the intelligibility of any kind of narrative, but can also be a sufficient condition. The latter is the case in 'narrative for its own sake'. Not only is this crucial relationship between continuity and intelligibility somewhat mysterious, but such is the pertinence of this case to our overall enquiry that it cries out for elaboration. This leads into an area of philosophy replete with paradoxes – namely, the concept of *change*.

CONTINUITY, DIFFERENCE, AND CHANGE

Of two things we treat as distinct from each other, we say they are '*different*' things. Mr Anon is a different individual from Mr Brown. They are different phenomena. 'This differs from that', is the basic formulation of the logic of 'difference', and we note that in no sense is temporal sequence relevant. Now suppose we perceive a thing at two points in time; at point 1 it is yellow, and at point 2, blue. Are we perceiving two *different* things, time again being irrelevant? For instance, in June we saw our neighbour's car, and it was yellow; in July we saw our neighbour's car, and it was blue. Is the June car a different car from the July one, or are we dealing with just one car which has changed (that is, has been resprayed)? Has our neighbour got two different cars or has he changed the colour of his car, such that we can say the car is the same one at points 1 and 2 in time, but that it has changed? In the absence of any further information we cannot say whether the two things in question are different things or whether it is the same thing which has changed. Are we dealing with a different thing, or with a changing (or changed) thing?

It is not hard to imagine circumstances where the answer to this general problematic is of practical as well as intellectual importance. Is that my girlfriend of years ago or someone different? Is this document a different will, to be invoked in alternative circumstances, or are you changing your will? Do these statistics indicate a different economic situation or has the recession simply changed its direction? Is marriage a dead, or a changing, institution?

One thing, then, differs from another thing; but a thing is said to 'change' when it *now* differs from what it *was*. It is not a different thing – it is the *same* thing which is different now from how it was then; that is, it 'has changed'. As for the paradox, 'how can it be the same thing if it is now different?', the reply is simply that in some respects it *is* different, but that in others the observer regards as dominant it is not different, such that the thing in question has not assumed a new identity. And as for the paradox, 'can a thing change so much that it becomes a different thing?', the reply must be that it indeed can, inasmuch as a thing may be judged in the mind of the observer to have changed in respects which are dominant or 'essential', such that it is now a different thing rather than one which has changed. But even here we can still say of the new, different thing, that it *was* the previous thing, whereas this cannot be said of two things which differ from each other at the same point in time. For instance, as we heat some water we say it is still the same water, although now different in some 'inessential' respects (that is, its volume and temperature). But when it boils we say we are now confronted by a different thing, namely, steam. The point is, however, that unlike saying this water here differs from that oil there, we can say this steam here differs from that (previous) water, but it used to be that water.

This highlights that if the temporal sequence into which a thing or state of affairs falls is irrelevant to it, then it is difficult to see where the concept of 'change' figures in anything we say about it. In short, if to say a thing differs is to say it changes, and to say it changes is to say it differs, then this is tantamount to saying change and difference are identical, which is nonsense. A thing differs *from* something else, whereas a thing changes *over* time. When a thing differs from something else, time is irrelevant. When a thing changes, however, time and the continuance of the single identity are essentially relevant. By 'continuity', then, we do not mean the static persistence of a state of affairs, but something persisting through changing states of affairs. Thus it is as well to reserve the term, 'persist', for changeless states of affairs and employ the term, 'continue', for situations involving a sequence of occurrences where a thing changes (over time).

This brief exploration of the threateningly paradoxical concepts of difference, change, identity, and continuity, has prepared the way for an important general proposition regarding narrative; namely, what is common to all narrative is that continuity is a necessary condition of its intelligibility, and this demand for continuity itself generates a demand for an identity or 'subject', which in its turn must undergo change.

In addition, the clarification of these principles affords further insight into what narrative explains, and how. Narrative is structured on what happened *next* – ('this happened *then* that'). We know there could be any number of 'nexts' – today's scientists can measure time in millionths of a second – but where there is no extrinsic purpose or message to the narrative governing what to choose as 'next' in terms of *relevance*, what is selected is that event or state of affairs penultimate to that which does *not* 'follow on from', or can 'reasonably' be construed as subsequent to, the initial situation. This – '*a* to *y* minus 1' – preserves continuity, and hence intelligibility. It supersedes mere chronicle (which is meaningless), because it endows the term, 'then', in the formula, 'this then that', with a power it lacks in the mere ordering of events according to dates. By saying a thing happened *next*, we know why it happens. However, the formula does *not* explain why it happens *next*. Neither does it explain why *it* happens rather than something else which might equally 'reasonably' have happened next.

It is, then, confirmed as an 'indeterministic' mode of explanation, and as noted is perhaps peculiarly defensible when dealing with human affairs – and therefore of special appropriateness for the historian, as will emerge. What we can say straight away, however, is that where the historian employs the narrative form, that form of itself imposes the above limitations on his scope for explanation – or, put in a positive light, allows him the freedom or 'open-endedness' of explanation appropriate to human affairs. From the opposite side of the fence we can note the narrative form does not commonly appear in discourse regarding the (solely) physical world, nor in those sciences which seek to explain aspects of reality construed as consisting solely of material objects and states of affairs. Hence we again encounter the recurring intimation of some special link between narrative and the world of human beings. Pursuit of this intimation not only proves its validity but also reveals further principles underlying the narrative form which add to its significance.

NARRATIVE AGENTS

The considerations which throw light on this adumbrated connection between the narrative form and the specifically *human* world derive from what has already been uncovered regarding the need for 'continuity' in a narrative, the manner in which that need generates the demand for something which 'persists' through 'change', and the way in which 'explanation' is implicit in the logic of narrative structure. Given these principles, the question arises as to whether *anything* can constitute this 'something which changes' in a narrative, or whether there are inherent constraints. For example, apart from a person, can a town, make of car, or even '*the* car', provide the focus of a narrative? Can an activity, such as wine-making, or governing? Can a religion, or a country?

On the face of it the answer to all these cases is yes, since not only can, for example, 'the story of Birmingham' be told in common-or-garden terms, but there are numerous professional factual stories – called, indeed, 'histories' – of cities, paintings, activities, universals such as 'the motor car', and of such complex phenomena as 'the British Empire' and 'Christianity'. However, we should note the story of Birmingham only becomes a *story* when the script ceases being simply a description of that city at successive points in time – that is, a chronicle – and achieves some continuity by Birmingham at one point in time being linked to Birmingham at 'the next' point in time, such that one gets a sense of *change* (for instance, expansion, recession, or modernisation). Now, at all such points we note the involvement of people who make things happen. The same is the case with, for example, 'the story of the motor car' – it stops being an unintelligible succession of model names and designs only when individuals such as entrepreneurs, financiers, engineers, and designers play a role as agents.

Putting the matter *a priori*, if all we do is describe Birmingham at one point in time and describe a Birmingham different in some respects at a later point, then so far as we know we are presenting two different states of affairs unrelated to each other in time – and this is to give none of that special force or significance to the term, '*then*' (or '*next*'), which lies at the heart of narrative structure. Rather, for these two otherwise merely *different* states of affairs to be intelligibly connected into one *changing* state of affairs, there must be a *reason* why Birmingham is now different from how it was.

Now Birmingham, this piano, or that car, cannot change themselves – that is, make themselves different from how they are. As (merely) physical objects they cannot effect or do anything. They can only suffer being acted upon. They cannot change themselves; they can only be changed. And if the most we can offer as, for instance, 'the story of Birmingham' is, 'this happened to it, and then that happened to it', and so on, then we are confronted by a (necessarily unintelligible) chronicle of discrete happenings where what occurs *next* (or '*then*') is an arbitrary choice of the chronicler rather than the painstaking discovery of intelligible continuity by the narrator.

What narrative requires, then, is agents which are active, which, in responding to states of affairs, are *responsible* for their temporal sequentiality, thereby binding them together as, in fact, the *same* state of affairs changed (for a reason). Only thus are narrative's interrelated conditions of change, continuity, and intelligibility secured – and in *factual* narrative this points to the necessity for the agents to be *human* because, for it to be possible to employ the narrative form, there must be a reason why 'this happened *then* that'. So far as we know, only human beings (with the possible exception of animals), 'have reasons' for what they do – or put another way, a necessary condition of *action* (as distinct from mechanistic

57

'reaction') is 'having a reason' to do something. Narrative, then, requires agents which have reasons for behaving as they do. In each case, this 'reason' can only be the agent's reason, not someone else's. In other words, the agent must be self-moving, must generate its own behaviour; and one of the perennial themes of philosophy is that it is precisely this capacity which distinguishes human beings from all other known phenomena.

Now, whether one agrees with this last proposition regarding the uniqueness of human beings or not, what is clear is that, in requiring subjects capable of reasoned agency, inanimate objects or abstract universals cannot play this role in (factual) narrative. In short, it is as impossible for 'Birmingham', 'the motor car', or 'wine-making' to be the subjects in a narrative as it is for 'blueness', 'silence', or 'intelligence'. We are confronted by categorial distinctions on *a priori* grounds. Another way of demonstrating this is to develop these arguments where they imply a distinction between 'scientific' and narrative explanation. This is all the more necessary since it may be objected that things do properly 'change' *without* the agency of human beings. For example, 'Mount Vesuvius erupted, and then (or 'next') Pompeii was engulfed in ashes', or, 'the red billiard ball was near the pocket, then the white ball struck it, and the next thing was that the red ball rolled into the pocket'. In other words, does not 'science' frequently use the narrative form to convey an intelligibility to natural sequences rather than present them as meaningless chronicles of differing states of affairs which 'happen to occur' at different points in time?

In reply it must be conceded that events where human agency is absent can of course be linked together in terms of 'prior' and 'subsequent' – namely, when we talk of *causal* sequences; a causes b, b causes c, and so on. This can be expressed as 'a happens, then b, then c'. Thus these different events or circumstances are genuinely related in time, such that the term, 'then', in 'a happened then b', is not merely formal as in a chronicle. Indeed, the concept of temporal succession is crucial, for b would not have occurred at all if a had not happened first.

But this is also where a difference is apparent between the narrative form and the relating of a causal sequence. In the latter, what happens 'next' (or 'then') happens necessarily, and happens necessarily 'next'; 'a caused b', or, 'a happened, then b'. The occurrence of b rather than of something else is (construed as) necessary, and its 'nextness' is (construed as) literal rather than some events intervening between a and b having been omitted.[6] In the narrative structure we have already noted that in saying, 'he did this then that', *why* he did 'that' rather than something else is not explained, nor why he did 'that' *next*. All that is explained is 'why he did that' (namely, 'because' he had 'just' done this). In a causal sequence, however, why b rather than x happened (next) *is* explained, and also why *b* happened *next*. Further, that what happens next in a causal sequence must occur *literally* next is crucial, for where *a* causes *b*, which causes *c*, which causes *d*, and so on, every moment of that sequence must be recounted to preserve intelligibility. In short, *a* does not cause *d*; to say, '*a* happened then *d*', would not make sense. In a narrative, however, we have already observed a different principle at work, where what is presented as happening 'next' is not presented because it *is* literally next, but because it precedes a situation which could not (conventionally) be construed as 'next'. The narrative is structured in terms of '*a* to *y* minus 1', whereas causal sequences are structured in terms of *a*, *b*, *c*, *d*, and so on.

The clarification of this fundamental difference in structure and logic between the narrative form and causal sequences (albeit one more intimated in, than articulated by, the ordinary use of language) thus helps substantiate (factual) narrative's need for agents which, in turn, must be *human*. All a causal sequence requires is a starting point; for instance, a thunderstorm, which (then) causes a flooding river, which causes the collapse of a section of river-bank, which causes the local otters to move habitat. Nowhere does a subject figure in this sequence, such that it is difficult to see how the concept of continuity is relevant. Rather than being taken through a changing situation, we are presented with a number of different, discrete situations, and are told what caused each. But there is nothing which persists throughout the causal sequence to allow the notion of one ongoing, changing state of affairs. The case is entirely different where we are taken through the various situations engendered by Mr Anon's agency in the world as he, for example, mends his fence. Urged by his wife to get on with it, he looks at the sky to check the weather, fetches his tool bag, studies the fence, digs away its crumbling supports, discovers he has misjudged the kind of brackets needed, changes his clothes, and goes down to the shop to buy the right kind. In this sequence of events or different situations, each is related to a *selected* 'prior' event in terms of being an intelligible response by an agent who 'has a reason' for what he does 'next'. To present this as a causal sequence in the strict sense would be absurdly difficult, involving exhaustive detail regarding each action the man took and relying on any number of laws of, for instance, physiology and psychology under which to subsume the causes at work.

The easy way out of these difficulties, of course, would be to treat the man's reason for doing something as a cause. But even were one to countenance this, it is to add something crucial to the notion of causality which it properly lacks in scientific discourse. Where a sequence of events can be explained causally – that is, be subsumed under general laws – human reason or response plays no part, and there is no 'story' to be told.

Finally, we may be reminded of the manner in which in ancient times certain especially important or relevant sequences of natural events were made intelligible, not through particular causal explanations (of which they were ignorant), but by being made into stories. What this essentially required was a subject, or agent, who responded to situations, who had reasons for doing things; namely, one or other of 'the gods'. In this way what we now understand as causal sequences of events – for instance, terrible natural disasters, the origin and spread of plague, the geographical dispersion of species, and the revolution of the seasons – were converted from discrete states of affairs merely happening to succeed each other in time into an intelligible continuity where what occurred happened as a response by an 'agent'. In such a way did ancient myths make certain events meaningful, which is another way of saying they made events intelligible by presenting them as 'meant' by a reasoning subject. However much we may scorn such explanations today, we must concede that their form, given the presence of familiar gods, had integrity. Where the form fails lamentably in its explanatory potential is, as Spinoza noted, where events are explained by referring them to 'the will of God', God being inscrutable. What he castigated as 'truly, a ridiculous way of expressing ignorance',[7] we might gloss as 'an abortive approach to narrative explanation'.

Thus although the ordinary use of language can indeed disguise the differences in both logic and structure between causal and narrative explanations, analysis reveals their distinctness from each other, and perhaps no more pointedly than where the narrative form is demonstrated to necessitate, not merely agents, but (at least in factual narrative) *human* agents at that.

NARRATIVE EXPLICATION

Thus far, enquiry into narrative as an explanatory form of discourse has revealed the need for continuity, change, and agency. Further analysis of these interrelated conditions of the intelligibility of narrative has revealed that, for them to be met, the agents or subjects must be human beings, and this helped substantiate the recurring surmise that (factual) narrative explanation is somehow peculiarly appropriate when dealing with human affairs.

There is, however, a further and different sense in which the narrative form 'explains' things, which we must now examine to do full justice to its explanatory potential. The foregoing has treated of the manner in which the narrative form explains *why* (what I have indifferently called) the separate 'events', 'states of affairs', or 'happenings' *within* a narrative sequence take place. Now, to say why a thing happened is to *account for* its happening, and this is precisely one of the meanings of the term, 'explain'. But to 'explain' a thing can also mean to make a thing intelligible

– that is, to show its meaning – and where it is important to distinguish these different senses then the latter can be more closely denoted by the term, 'explicate', meaning to 'develop the notion of something', or to 'unfold' or 'make explicit the nature of something'. Now it is in just these terms of being *explicatory* that there is an additional sense in which the narrative form is explanatory over and above its ability to account for things happening. What, then, is this additional 'explicatory' sense in which the narrative form, of itself, achieves 'explanations'?

In first distinguishing narrative from both descriptive and analytic discourse, we noted that what is immediately clear is that narrative is the form used to articulate 'things happening'. As put initially, the only way to articulate 'something happening' is to narrate it, and this involves relating states of affairs into prior and subsequent, suggesting a genuine sequential interdependence. But this analysis has nevertheless kept silent so far about precisely that crucial ingredient, 'things *happening*'. What exactly is this link between narrative and 'things happening'? Narrative feeds on 'things happening'. We can put states of affairs into a sequence of prior and subsequent but our analysis has already intimated that no *narrative* is involved unless something *happens* to make this link intelligible. Further, narrative feeds on explaining *why* things happen, through its formula, 'this happened, *then* (or *next*) that happened'. So necessarily is this an achievement of the narrative form that it is more correct to say narrative feeds, not on things happening, but on things happening 'next'. Nevertheless nothing can happen next if nothing happens in the first place, so there remains an obvious sense in which 'things happening' is as important as things 'happening next' for narrative to be possible at all.

This same problematic can be revealed in less abstract terms. To use an earlier example, we can talk of a 'happening' such as someone getting out of bed, and intelligibly link this with a subsequent happening – for example, 'he got out of bed and then put on his slippers'. Insofar as there are now two happenings linked sequentially, we are engaged in the narrative form. However, as we follow subsequent happenings such as getting washed and then going downstairs, we recognise that all these sequentially linked happenings can, precisely insofar as they *are* linkable, be conceived and expressed as one happening – namely, 'he got up' (after which, the 'next' happening might be, 'he had breakfast'). Are we, then, confronted with one happening, 'he got up', or a sequence of happenings, 'he got out of bed, then put on his slippers, then went to the bathroom and washed', and so on? In the latter case the narrative form comes into play, but not in the former case where we simply state the single happening, 'he got up'. In this former case his 'getting out of bed' is simply an (implied, or conventionally understood) part of 'getting up'.

The same problem also extends backwards in time, for if 'getting out of bed' can be seen as merely part of a 'larger' happening – namely, 'getting up' – then 'getting out of bed' can itself be seen as constituting a 'larger' happening made up of a sequence of happenings such as, 'he moved his left leg to the side of the bed, then raised himself up on one elbow, and then put his left leg on the floor'. Thus from both directions it becomes increasingly obscure as to whether, in talking of someone 'getting out of bed', we are treating of one happening or of several in sequence – and if the latter, then *which* sequence?

Thus the distinction between 'things happening' and 'things happening *next*' seems elusive, even paradoxical; and so long as this remains the case the apparently obvious link between the narrative form and 'things happening' must remain something of a mystery. Is the narrative form structured around things happening, or around *sequences* of things happening? Or do both amount to the same thing? How is it that a happening can be made up of other happenings, somehow connected, possibly *ad infinitum*? Or can we safely talk of happenings as if they have beginnings and endings? And if they do have such parameters, how do we proceed to nevertheless link up happenings which have 'ended' with subsequent happenings, such that despite 'endings' some kind of continuity is preserved?

In short, we will not attain a full understanding of narrative logic whilst such basic questions remain, and it is all the more important to pursue them since only such an investigation can set out what I have referred to as the 'explicatory' potential of narrative. We need, then, a further grasp of the logic, grammar, and semantics of 'happenings', and for purposes of exposition it is now necessary to find terms which will enable the pursuit of that elusive distinction within 'happenings' to which I have just alluded. In order to make relevant distinctions which avoid unnecessary jargon, I will use two terms which are otherwise indifferently equated with 'happenings' – namely, 'occurrences' and 'events' – but give them a narrower compass than has been necessary so far in this exposition.

OCCURRENCES

There are occasions when the only way to say 'what happened' is to give a 'blow-by-blow' account – for instance, 'the boy ran into the barn'. There are other cases, however, where we can summarise 'what happened' by using a single term, such as in 'a theft took place' or 'an avalanche occurred'. What happened blow-by-blow is not spelt out, but a general term replaces an account, and the only verb required is (indifferently) one denoting the *general* condition of *anything* happening – that is, the theft 'occurred', 'happened', or 'took place'. In the former (blow-by-blow) case, however, a particularising verb is used, as in 'the boy ran'. This draws attention to *verbs* in relation to the logic and grammar of what we have repeatedly pointed to as the business of narrative structure; namely, 'things *happening*'.

In dealing with 'objects' or 'things' we use nouns. A noun denotes a thing – 'thinghood' is articulated through nouns. This noun rather than that one denotes this rather than that thing – for example, 'a cat', meaning 'any cat'. Individual nouns, then, denote individual universals; and in the course of Chapter One we went on to draw a number of implications regarding the nature of 'things' and the manner in which we 'perceive' them or find them meaningful. In analysing 'occurrences' a parallel treatment is salutary for the sake of clarity.

Thus: in dealing with 'occurrences' we use verbs. 'Occurrings' are articulated through verbs. An individual verb denotes this rather than that kind of occurrence – for instance, 'to fall', meaning any falling. Thus, individual verbs denote individual universal occurrences; for example, the verb 'to fall' denotes a class of occurrences, otherwise discrete, for what they have in common.

It is clear from this that 'occurrence in general' is, so to speak, an irreducible datum. One may define as many individual verbs as one likes – (that is, specify what kind of occurrence is denoted in each case) – without getting any closer to breaking down into analytic form what 'occurrence in general' is. That we experience the world in terms of occurrences is a given, as also is our experiencing it in terms of objects, qualities, and properties. Or at least, these matters are 'given' in relation to the grammar of the respective modes in which we articulate them. Thus, although occurrences are articulated through verbs, that there are 'occurrings' perhaps remains impenetrable.

The case is different, however, when we deal with individual occurrences. Here, the verb used tells us what *kind* of occurrence we are dealing with – for instance, to fall, estimate, love, dissolve; and we have only to consult a dictionary to find the meaning of these verbs. It tells us what *kind* of occurrence a verb denotes, as in, for example, the various meanings of 'to swim'; '1. Float on or at surface of liquid; 2. Progress at or below surface of water by working legs, arms, tail, webbed feet, fins, flippers, wings, body, etc.; 3. Appear to undulate or reel or whirl, have dizzy effect or sensation; 4. Be flooded and overflow with'.[8] What the dictionary does not, need not, and cannot tell us is in what sense 'to swim' (in any of its meanings) is an occurrence rather than, for example, an object or a quality. Rather, in drawing attention to those particular features which assist in distinguishing an individual kind of occurrence from others, the definition of a verb invariably involves other verbs, as is clear from the example just given. And the only relevant considerations here are the same we suggested regarding 'things' or 'objects' – not, then, 'do trees really exist?', or, 'do objects in general really exist?', nor, 'do things really swim?', nor, indeed, 'do occurrences actually occur?', but, 'how far is this individual kind of occurrence a relevant abstraction from the world of occurrences in general, and how reliable and workable is it?' And just as nouns denoting things can come and go and change meaning, so can verbs, as with the emergence, for instance, of 'to commute' (re travel). Again, just as with nouns denoting objects, verbs denote occurrences ranging from the precise, as in specialised contexts such as law – 'conveyancing', 'arraigning' – to the vague – 'to go', 'to move'. Finally, different cultures can find different 'occurrings' worth individuating; for example, German has the verb, '*spazieren*' and French, '*se promener*', whilst English has no equivalent individuation but makes do with phrases such as 'to go for a walk', or 'to take a stroll'.

A further parallel between the world of objects and occurrences is worth pursuing, for it concerns the intelligibility of 'occurrences'. In relation to objects, it was argued earlier that the meaning of a noun (for instance, 'chair'), manifests the reason we have for abstracting and individuating the object denoted; in that sense, objects are 'meaningful', 'reasonable', or 'intelligible'. Just so with occurrences. The intelligibility of an individual kind of occurrence (for instance, 'falling'), is conveyed by nothing other than the definition of the verb denoting it, which exposes in what ways it is meaningful to us – or put another way, exposes the reason we have for abstracting and identifying it. Hence, just as 'the reason this object has legs is that it is a chair, and all chairs have legs', so 'the reason this is going down is that it is falling, and all things which fall go downwards'. In this way we revert to the point that an individual occurrence (articulated by a verb) is made intelligible through other verbs – that is, through refining and differentiating it from other kinds of occurrences – but that 'occurrencehood' itself is not thereby made intelligible. It remains a given – the ground, so to speak, of individual kinds of occurrences. *Their* intelligibility is specific to their definitions rather than being derived from some prior principle underlying the intelligibility of 'occurrence in general'.

Sufficient has been clarified, I hope, to sustain an observation which is both important and paradoxical; namely, although narrative is the form we use to tell of 'things happening' or of 'what occurred', and is essentially structured in terms of 'this happened *then* (next) that' – involving concepts of time, continuity, change, *et al.* – nevertheless the fundamental nature of occurrences is nothing to do with time, continuity, or temporal succession. An individual occurrence is articulated through an individual verb, and we have seen its intelligibility derives from the meaning or definition of that verb. But the meaning of an individual verb – that is, the intelligibility of the particular kind of occurrence – is *not* spelt out in terms of 'this happened *then* that'. This is the form narrative demands, but it is not the form of occurrences.

Thus, contrary to what we might expect when analysing the world of events, or of 'things happening', where we know we are dealing with one thing happening after another, what nevertheless lies at the core of this world (namely, the individual occurrence), is not intelligible in terms of temporal succession, or 'this *then* that'. Although it seems difficult to conceive of 'time' when nothing happens, or conversely of something 'happening' where time does not enter into the matter, this is nevertheless the case in this area of analysis. In dealing with occurrences we are not, unlike in a narrative, dealing in a 'this *then* that' context. For instance, 'to swim' is, after all, in one of its meanings, to 'float on or at surface of liquid' – no 'then and now' is either stated or implied. If, then, one 'is swimming', the explanation of what this means in no way rests upon the notion that one is doing this and then (or next) that. It is true 'swimming' may *involve* doing one thing and then another in a purposeful sequence, as it does in another of its meanings, 'to progress at or below surface of water by working legs, arms, tail, webbed feet, fins, flippers, wings, body, etc.' – but this is to explain *how* to swim rather than what it *means* to swim (just as in our earlier example of 'getting up', where it *involves*, but does not *mean*, 'getting out of bed, washing', and so on). Time, change, continuity, and temporal succession are not relevant to the intelligibility of this occurrence. But they are the heart of the matter when it comes to the intelligibility of a narrative. Hence, and in short, we do not narrate occurrences; occurrences are not made intelligible through the narrative form; they are not structured narratively; they are not 'narrative identities'.

Finally, in discussing 'occurrences' there remains the particular, 'actual' occurrence; for instance, 'the boy ran into the barn'. Here our task is that of articulating *this* particular occurrence, akin to identifying *this* particular cat. This particular cat is identified by describing it – that is, stating what is particular rather than essential about it as a cat. Similarly with occurrences. In stating 'the boy ran into the barn' we articulate not only the general kind of occurrence in question (by using the verb, 'run'), but also what is particular about this instance of it. As such, we are *describing* this or that occurrence when we say, 'the boy ran into the barn'. Again, neither time, continuity, change, nor temporal succession enter the matter. It is not essentially a 'this *then* that' context, despite appearances. Thus with a particular occurrence, we state it; we do not narrate it. To say, 'the boy ran into the barn', is not to tell a story. The intelligibility of that particular occurrence is derived from principles entirely different from those we have set out as underlying the constructing of narrative.

Thus the question arises, what *does* narrative achieve if it is not the form in which we either define or describe 'occurrences'? If narrative does not make occurrences intelligible, what *does* it make intelligible? The answer to this emerges from what can now be understood more clearly – namely, that although narrative neither defines nor describes occurrences,

65

it does link them together. Indeed, occurrences are its essential ingredient. It is occurrences, in the stricter sense in which I have used the term, which narrative links up in its basic structure, 'this *happened* and then that *happened*', or 'this *occurred* and then that *occurred*'. If nothing occurred, narrative would be impossible. Equally, if only one thing ever occurred, again narrative would be impossible. Narrative does not articulate particular occurrences, then; rather, it articulates something else *by means of* ordering occurrences sequentially in an intelligible manner. Thus we can state, 'the boy ran into the barn', but this is to describe a single occurrence. We only begin a narrative, begin 'telling a story', when we add a ('the') subsequent occurrence – for example, 'the boy ran into the barn and then climbed into the hayloft'.

Thus the formula, 'this *then* that', can be given proper precision by extending it to, 'this *occurred* and then that *occurred*', thereby making it clear that narrative is the form whereby we articulate, not occurrences, but the *ordering* of occurrences. Hence the connection between narrative and occurrences, between narrative and 'things happening', is evident. To state, 'the boy ran into the barn and *then* the boy was blue-eyed', does not make sense; nor, 'the boy ran into the barn and *then* the barn belonged to Farmer Brown'. Necessarily in every case, what is 'next' or 'then' in the narrative form must be an occurrence rather than a circumstance, state of affairs, or situation. Similarly regarding that which is 'prior' to the 'subsequent' occurrence – it must also be an occurrence. 'The boy was blue-eyed and *then* ran into the barn', does not make sense, nor, 'the barn belonged to Farmer Brown and *then* the boy ran into it'.

NARRATIVE IDENTITIES

Narrative, then, links occurrences to one another in terms of 'prior' and 'subsequent'. But, as already observed, this formula does not simply put occurrences into the temporal order in which they occur – indeed, in the teeming world of occurrences such a task seems beyond human ability and also peculiarly pointless. Rather, narrative links them up so that (or insofar as), they follow on from the 'prior' to the 'next'. And we have already gone some way in exploring how this is worked and what is achieved – namely, the explanation of why the 'next' occurrence took place. But this does not exhaust the function of the narrative form, for it would imply that the *sequencing* of occurrences (which it essentially constitutes), is no more than an abstract by-product, of no relevance to actuality – or put another way, to view narrative orderings of occurrences as merely (one) way in which we explain discrete occurrences is to lose that ordinary sense in which a narrative or 'story' can have a completeness which, if cut short, leaves one curious to know, not what happened next, but what happened 'in the end'. And both observations amount to suggesting narrative can achieve something unitary in itself, over and above being the vehicle for explaining discrete occurrences.

Let us recall the salutary fact that narrative has to be narrated. It is not so much, then, a question of 'what narrative can achieve', as of 'what do narrators achieve by narrating a sequence of occurrences?' Insofar as they are narrating we know they are not chronicling occurrences but linking them up into an order which makes sense. And this is not a difficult thing to do; indeed, both the perceiving and the constructing of intelligible sequences of occurrences is a universal, instinctive human characteristic. By comparison, the production of some kind of chronicle is a painstaking, deliberate, artificial contrivance with far less immediate and obvious a point to it.

People can tell or make stories, then, with an easy facility. We have already remarked in general terms upon the variety of purposes served by telling stories. In the case of fiction it was urged the story-teller must have some purpose beyond simply that of putting invented occurrences into an invented (albeit intelligible) order. And it was pointed out that the factual story-teller *may* share the same purposes. In the case of the discipline of history, however, our attention is focused on the exploitation of factual narrative solely for its informative and explanatory possibilities – that is, for the sole purpose of achieving and conveying knowledge. And the question we are approaching is, knowledge of *what*? When stripped of the numerous extrinsic purposes to which it can be put, what is it in general terms that narrative informs us of, and what is it that it explains in addition to why 'things happened'?

There is an agreeable sense in which no special mystery looms here, inasmuch as ordinary language suggests that what narrative achieves is a story – narrative conveys knowledge of 'a story', and closer analysis does not refute this. As we have seen, narrative links occurrences into an intelligible sequence, into an *order*; narrative orders occurrences intelligibly or meaningfully. Now this would remain an empty tautology – 'it is an order because it is intelligible, and it is intelligible because it is an order' – were it not that 'an order' of occurrences is, so to speak, an actual phenomenon. It has a unity, a particular identity; or at least this is what is proposed through the narrative form. Now, what is 'a story' other than 'an order' or sequence of occurrences? And what is this to say other than that 'stories' articulate a distinct class of phenomena in the world; that is, that just as we perceive objects and occurrences as 'real' things in the world, so we perceive 'story-objects' as real things in the world? From a virtually infinite number of occurrences happening at a virtually infinite range of temporal points we extract or abstract lines of continuity. We posit some *real* sequential relationships within an otherwise undifferentiated, meaningless flux of occurrences happening at different times. This ordering of occurrences is proposed as constituting an identity in itself, over and above the discrete occurrences contained in it. This implies the ordering of occurrences achieved by the narrative *form* is itself the *content* of that form – that is, this specific form is the form of a specific content which has its own identity or unity. Hence, the contents within a narrative (that is, occurrences), are not the content the narrative itself constitutes. As Spinoza argued, dealing in the same general problematic when differentiating between *natura naturans* and *natura naturata*, a system can be more than a mere 'thing of reason'. It can, if it is a real system, be a unity – that is, constitute what we might refer to as an 'organic unity' over and above, but inextricably determined by, its parts.

A story or narrative, then, is more than the sum of its parts. Its parts are occurrences, and intelligibility *within* a narrative relates to 'the reason' for its occurrences, intimated through the 'this occurred and *then* (or 'next') that occurred' formula. But insofar as something unitary is achieved through this formula we have yet to see in what sense a 'story-as-a-whole' is intelligible. That is, there are two kinds of intelligibility with respect to narrative – that contained *within* it (which I have termed its explanatory potential), and that constituted *by* it as a whole, which I term its *explicatory* potential. In examining this latter, we are thus not concerned with how 'this *then* that' is meaningful, but with how a '*this*' (this story-as-a-whole), is meaningful or intelligible. In short, narratives do more than show occurrences following on from each other – they articulate meaningful overall entities.

Hence the full understanding of the narrative form, especially in terms of its overall explanatory characteristics (often so glibly denied or under-estimated), must involve grasping in what sense this class of phenomenon – namely, the story as an entity in itself – is meaningful or intelligible. Now, if seeing a narrative as an entity in itself involves seeing it as more than the sum of its parts, the other side of the coin is that this involves seeing the entity it articulates as something distinct both from *other* kinds of entity, and from other 'story-objects'. To constitute a distinct identity it must have parameters, and to ask what these are is to ask in what sense a 'story-object' or 'narrative identity' is a meaningful or intelligible phenomenon. By analogy, we not only know what kinds of things make up a 'city', we also know where the city stops and something else (even a different city), begins. Moreover we know a city is not a quality, nor an occurrence. Likewise we need to understand what principles underlie the distinction between one 'narrative identity' and another, and the categorial distinction between 'narrative identities' and objects, qualities, and other such classes of phenomena.

What, then, is the nature of the unitary identity the story-form articulates? Or put the other way around, in what sense is a story a unity? Clearly, the 'identity' involved is that of an order or sequence of occurrences, and it as well to point out straight away that the integrity of the entities articulated through narrative varies in different cases. Some stories articulate more strongly parametered phenomena than others. By analogy, we have seen the world of objects, and of occurrences, exhibit this same characteristic – respectively, 'a building' articulates a vaguer object than 'an abattoir'; 'to move' articulates a vaguer occurrence than 'to arraign'. Reference to this analogy points to those same cardinal principles of the intelligibility or meaningfulness of any class of phenomenon – namely, relevance and workability. The case is no different respecting narrative entities. The narrator is the articulator of real lines of continuity between occurrences; he perceives them as 'there' rather than inventing them. But this does not mean his own principles of perception, understanding or 'reasoning' are not involved. He is not Marx's 'contemplative materialist' whose perceptions simply mirror a given, meaningful reality; neither does he construct lines of continuity from logical categories indifferent to the external world.[9] Rather, he abstracts a particular line of continuity between different occurrences for its relevance to him. From within the same general *mélange* of occurrences over a period, different individuals can extract or abstract different stories, different lines of continuity. But a line of continuity abstracted for its relevance to *us* must also be credible in relation to the world of narrative entities – that is, it must be a workable way of experiencing orderings of occurrences in the real world. There is, after all, a distinction between fanciful and absurd stories. Given our normal way of perceiving lines of continuity, or 'stories', in the world, the fanciful story at least *could* be true. But the absurd story could not – or at least, the world has not yet taught us it could. We are not referring here, of course, to an absurd story proposing, for instance, that 'the house swam across the river', since that is an absurd *occurrence*, and absurd stories do not essentially derive from absurd occurrences. Rather, its absurdity stems from an absurd line of continuity which it proposes; for example, 'he made a cup of tea and then the house collapsed', or, 'the House of Lords adjourned and then swam to the surface'.

Additionally, that we understand there to be 'stories' or 'sequences of occurrences' in general, let alone this or that particular story, is explained along the same lines of relevance and workability. From the one side it seems such a way of experiencing the world has always been of relevance to human beings. From the other side, the world has not let human beings down, so to speak, in respect of the notion that there are 'real' continuities of occurrences rather than merely potential or absurd ones. Thus the same can be said of the status of particular 'narrative identities' as has been argued respecting particular 'objects' and 'occurrences' – namely, it is not a question of whether this or that connecting-up of occurrences into an intelligible line of continuity is 'real' or 'objective', but whether it is relevant and workable. Where such continuities are not found, perceived, or noticed, the temporal relationships between occurrences remain an abstract kaleidoscope of possible sequences of occurrences – a meaningless turmoil. Hence, that part of our understanding of the world is in terms of this and that story, tells as much about ourselves as it does about the world. One of our characteristics is that we are 'story-perceiving' beings; one of the characteristics of the world is that it generates stories, that is, 'story-objects'.

Stories or narratives are, then, more than the sum of their parts. They articulate a valid class of things in the world I have variously called 'story-objects', 'story-entities', or 'narrative identities', and the issue of the 'external reality' of these phenomena has been shown to be no different from that in relation to other kinds of phenomena such as physical objects and occurrences. As entities which we perceive and/or abstract, particular 'story-objects' are therefore intelligible; they are meaningful things. Although they are formed in terms of 'this occurred and then that occurred and then that', *what* occurred 'then' or 'next' is not randomly selected from out of a hat containing all later occurrences. Rather, the 'story-object' has parameters and it is up to the story-teller to ensure he gets them right, that he makes the story he tells correspond to the story to be told – that is, that he uses the narrative form to delineate correctly the narrative identity or 'story-object'. What, then, are these 'story-objects' or 'narrative identities' when translated into familiar phenomena?

EVENTS

If presented with a completely unfamiliar object, what do we make of it? How do we understand it? It is not a cat, house, or bottle – in fact, we cannot give it a name. We can attempt to describe it, but because we cannot classify it as a particular type of object (for instance, 'a house'), it remains a meaningless object – it is unintelligible. Or rather, its only intelligibility is that it is indeed 'an object' rather than, for instance, an occurrence or a quality. And that is precisely what we call it – 'an object'. As such we have said something meaningful, but not very much. The class of things we have put it in to give it a minimum of meaning is that class of things we call 'objects'. It is 'an object', and that is as far as it is an intelligible phenomenon.

But even in saying this, we may be wrong. The 'it' we are dealing with may not be a single object; it may be two or more objects adjoining each other. In the real world, indeed, it is only because we have, for instance, already identified other objects on a table-top as individual things (the table-cloth, bottle, and ashtray), that *this* strange conglomeration of matter stands out as a (supposed) single object. But this *is* a supposition. As for an object we *do* recognise – for instance, the bottle – we know it *can* be viewed as a collection of many separate individual things, including the cork, the label, and the glass structure. And we know in turn that the cork, for instance, can be seen as a collection of particles; and so on until we arrive at the collection of otherwise discrete 'objects' which make up what we call 'atoms'. Yet we collect all these things together, call the object, 'a bottle', and thereby indicate a unity, a single object somehow parametered off from other objects such as the table-cloth and the ashtray. Theoretically every atom adjoins the next; but we do not experience, nor articulate, the world as a soup of atoms. We extract individual, separate objects; and as so frequently argued up to now, we do this in terms of relevance and workability. 'Air-pockets' were recurrable and predictable, but were not recognised and individuated phenomena until they were relevant to us. Conversely, the phenomenon known as an 'air-pocket' was not established by the first encounter. 'It' had to be a recurring, reliable phenomenon. And the same applies to occurrences, denoted by such verbs as 'to swim', 'to hiccup', 'to commute' – that is, we 'individuate' particular occurrences through the same general principles of relevance and work-ability which apply in individuating particular objects.

These same principles of individuation also apply to 'story-objects' or 'narrative identities', and the most appropriate term for this type of entity or 'individual thing' is 'an *event*'. If the world of objects is differentiated by the use of (different) nouns and the world of occurrences by (different) verbs, so there is a world of events differentiated by the use (where available) of different 'event-nouns' (such as 'a wedding') – otherwise, by the narration of their particulars.

By 'an event', then, I mean a sequence of occurrences singled out for notice. As an individual ordering of occurrences it must, like an individual object, have parameters. In this case, however, the parameters are not to do with physical properties – 'the bottle stops here and the table-top begins' – but with the succession of occurrences; that is, an event must have a beginning, an end, and thus some kind of 'middle'. And what is sandwiched, so to speak, between the beginning and the end must consti-tute a sequence of occurrences which not only make sense in terms of 'following on', but also specifically contribute to the intelligibility of the event construed as a whole, over and above its constituent parts. Thus in the more precise sense of the terms necessary for proper analysis, an 'event' is different from an 'occurrence' despite what might appear as an impenetrably dialectical interdependence between them, and despite dictionaries usually equating the terms. An event is an individuated order-ing of occurrences; it is not a single occurrence, nor a sequence of occur-rences which follow on from each other as in the basic narrative form but have no beginning and ending – that is, constitute no overall individual phenomenon. In referring to 'events', then, the kind of phenomena under consideration are those such as wars, arguments, holidays, divorces, births, deaths, examinations, parties, elections, revolutions, evenings-out, and journeys. In other words, the stricter meaning it has been necessary

71

to give the term, 'event', does not remove it from everyday associations, where it does generally refer to more than a single occurrence and is understood to have parameters.

We do, then, individuate, or classify, many events; others, it is true, are so individual as not to attract classification. They simply have to be narrated, which equates with describing them. But particular instances of the former, classifiable events, can of course also be described, and this is done by stating what is particular rather than essential about them as, for instance, wars or weddings. This involves narrating the event in individual detail – that is, 'telling its story', or 'saying what happened' *within* the context of that *kind* of event.

Thus we arrive at the formula that to tell a story is to describe an event. Put more formally, the narrative structure is that by which we apprehend events – or again, the 'content' of an event has the 'form' of a narrative. Events are no more nor less 'real' or 'objective' phenomena in the world than occurrences and physical objects; like them, they are classifiable through that same logic which individuates an otherwise teeming and meaningless world into separable, intelligible phenomena.[10] Or we can put the matter the other way; namely, the fact that events are classifiable and describable on the same general principles which apply to, for example, physical objects and occurrences, indicates we are confronted by phenomena just as 'real', 'objective', and 'individual' as any object or occurrence.

Thus we see what it is that narrative achieves through its *explicatory* potential, and hence what a substantive and significant role it plays in our perception or construction of a world made intelligible to us through the process of discrimination and classification. Part of our understanding of 'the real world out there' is constituted by our awareness of events. For example, wars, revolutions, dinner parties, road accidents, and domestic arguments, actually take place; they are objective phenomena, not mere abstractions, imaginings, or inventions. Or at least, as individual, intelligible phenomena, events have as much or as little integrity as do physical objects and occurrences, for their logical status as concrete phenomena (with corresponding functional modes of articulation) is the same. Thus if we were incapable of narrative that entire aspect of reality constituted by events would be beyond our awareness.

Correspondingly, then, we owe an enormous debt to those who involve themselves in the activity of discovering, establishing, and communicating (almost necessarily past) 'events'. They are exploring an aspect of reality no more nor less valid, and certainly no less important, than that of physical objects. Their work is factual, their standards rigorous, and their conclusions provisional. One always hopes they get events right; but in the first place and above all one hopes the nature and significance of what they strive to achieve – namely, the revelation of an entire dimension of reality otherwise only dimly perceived and so often held to be 'merely a matter of interpretation' – is understood and appreciated. 'They', of course, are the historians; and especially, then, the narrative historians, for although we have yet to relate these general principles of narrative to historical knowledge in particular, it follows from what has already been said regarding 'story-objects', 'narrative identities', or 'events', that they are narrative phenomena which correspondingly require the narrative form in order to be perceived and communicated.

Since I have claimed the above use of the term, 'event', is not so different from its ordinary usage, we can advance our understanding of these phenomena by discussing them *a posteriori* rather than from first principles. Firstly, regarding the reality and integrity of events, we have already claimed no one disputes the reality of, for instance, wars, revolutions, football matches, and weddings. These are not regarded as mere inventions or 'matters of interpretation'. On the contrary they are regarded as real, objective phenomena which can be described in their particularity, about which errors of perception and judgement can be made, and which can be classified into different types. In practice it does indeed matter whether the event one has been invited to is a dinner party, seance, interview, or auction. In short, certain orderings of occurrences are intelligible to us in their distinctness; they are meaningful phenomena, capable of being described and classified.

Secondly – and nevertheless – if asked exactly when, for example, the dinner party we attended yesterday began, which occurrences were part of it and which not, and when it finished, we would be hard-pressed to come up with precise answers. That is, the event may be a little ragged at the edges and imprecise in the middle; yet in cases such as dinner parties, boxing matches, and even wars and revolutions, we feel the event in question is sufficiently recognisable in the major character and ordering of its occurrences as to be capable of being parametered off both from other events and from other occurrences which happened either before, after, and indeed during it.

In the boxing match, for instance, we can narrate that 'the bell rang, and then the boxers stopped fighting. Next, a woman stepped into the ring, carrying a card. Then she proceeded to walk around the ring, showing the card with the number of the next round on it'. We would be right to view these occurrences as part of the overall event. But if whilst the boxing match was in progress a brawl broke out amongst some spectators, we would regard this as a separate event, begun when one spectator attacked another and finished when the staff had dragged off the offenders and peace was restored. (Indeed, we might well call the brawl 'an incident', which the dictionary defines appropriately as a 'subordinate or accessory event; a detached event attracting general attention'.[11] Both the boxing match and the brawl are, of course, 'events' in the strict sense of the term; but they are separate events.) Yet during the boxing match there will obviously be numerous other occurrences and sequences of occurrences, such as people entering and leaving the stadium, others lighting cigars, and moving around to talk to different people, such that the singularity or integrity of the event does remain somewhat imprecise. In giving an account of the boxing match, which occurrences should be selected and which omitted, and in what sequence should they be narrated? In other words, what happened 'next'? How does the narrator proceed?

It is clear that, although 'telling the story' of the boxing match poses somewhat of a problem, the narrator is greatly assisted by knowing there will be one distinct event, and what it will be. He already has a model or paradigm of that kind of event; indeed, it is so familiar that it has its own 'event-noun' – namely, 'a boxing match'. Moreover, events such as boxing matches, weddings, and board meetings are to a large extent deliberately planned 'orderings of occurrences'; their intelligibility is given them by human design, enabling their outlines and characteristics to be pinpointed with a confident accuracy, just as we previously noted regarding such manufactured *objects* as a 'crown and pinion' or a 'tea dispenser'. Rituals and art-objects are similar phenomena, except that in being symbolic their intelligibility is not so directly approachable, and may in certain details be recondite to the point of obscurity, despite their precision.

But where deliberately designed events do not contain large elements of obscure ritual the narrator can proceed to say 'what happened' without having to puzzle overmuch. His paradigm instructs him which are the principal occurrences to look for and what order he can expect them to follow. And as for how he decides, within this paradigmatic order, what *in particular* to include in his 'this happened then that happened' account, the previously displayed skeletal model, 'a to y minus 1', will guide his art. He moves from one occurrence to 'the next' by determining which is the first subsequent occurrence not conventionally contiguous to the former, and then 'retracks' a little in order to maintain the internal intelligibility of the sequence.

Indeed, we can see from this why it happens that in certain cases – for example, 'yesterday's examination' – 'there is no story to tell', since nothing untoward occurred during it, and its overall nature is so familiar as to require no further articulation than, 'it was an exam, that's all, just like any other exam – there's nothing to tell'. In other words there are cases where, from the observer's and/or participant's viewpoint there were, so to speak, no ys at all in the 'a to y minus 1' formula. But more usually in human affairs something out of the ordinary occurs such that there is usually a story to be told – that is, reality is always individual rather than paradigmatic, thereby providing the narrator with those y points so crucial in determining his process of selection and omission. In fact, many human-designed events, such as sporting occasions, board-meetings, and auctions, are of course designed precisely to promote or give play to uncertainty, and to provide mechanisms for its solution. In such cases there is always a story to be told.

A further point more easily revealed *a posteriori* is the manner in which our understanding of individual occurrences and sequences can be modified when it is recognised they are not discrete happenings but part of a 'larger' event. For example, if we know a football match is taking place we sometimes abandon the language of discrete occurrences, such as 'kicking the ball', and transform it into, for instance, 'passing the ball', or transform an otherwise discrete *sequence* of occurrences into, 'making an attack down the wing'. Aided by an awareness of the nature of the event as a whole we refine our discrimination and understanding of the occurrences and sequences of occurrences within it. Some are rightly discarded altogether as distractions from the reality we are trying to apprehend, just as one would ignore a flea on a dog's back in trying to sort out what this object, 'the dog', is.

Other occurrences and sequences would, however, be more properly understood. Indeed, it can be seen there is a strong sense in which to identify an occurrence as, for instance, 'he kicked the ball', is to misunderstand what happened if he in fact *passed* the ball. The 'neutrality' of the former terminology is akin to identifying an object as 'a creature' rather than 'a dog'. Similarly with sequences of occurrences. To say, 'this player moved there and then that player moved there', is to misunderstand what is going on *if* what happened is 'the defence broke out' – or if 'misunderstand' is too strong a term, let us say the former terminology at least manifests such a *lack* of understanding as to invite the erroneous notion that the players were warming up or performing some dance.

In short, if someone is 'passing the ball' then failure to recognise this is a failure to understand reality, and this *a posteriori* viewpoint vindicates the *a priori* notion of the 'organic' or 'dialectical' nature of events and the sequences of occurrences which constitute them. If one fails to discover those real lines of continuity present within the myriad world of occurrences, one tells the wrong story; one has either not understood the actual 'story-object' or 'event' in front of one, or even, perhaps, that there is any 'story-object' or 'event' there at all.[12]

In discussing contrived events such as boxing matches we have thus been considering strongly paradigmed events which correlate well with the ordinary use of the term. But not all orderings of occurrences exhibit such strongly parametered identities. Domestic arguments, journeys, and conversations are examples of less structured ones whose beginnings, endings, and intrinsic contents are far less specific. Nevertheless that we can manage to identify them for what they are, and tell the story of particular instances, means they are still 'events' in our analytic sense of the term. By analogy, to single out something and denote it as 'a building' is to carry out a valid (that is, relevant and workable), individuation of an 'object', even though it is vaguer than 'a factory' or 'a cathedral'. Where the 'building', or the 'domestic argument', starts and stops, and what we include as part of them, is more a matter of relevance and workability than of logic.

Indeed, to pursue the analogy to the extreme, some 'events' may be as vaguely parametered as are such physical 'objects' as 'a country scene' or 'a view' (where, nevertheless, one can say 'look at the view', just as one can say 'look at that cathedral'). For instance, 'a day in the life of' an individual is such a case, whose only recognised parameters are 'getting up' and 'going to bed', the remainder of the 'relevant' occurrences being so random that one is thrown back on no more specific guidelines than the pure formalism of our 'a to y minus 1' framework. Finally, there are those sequences of occurrences so trite, brief, or inconsequential – for instance, someone leaving his house, going down the street, buying some chocolate, and then returning home – that, although constituting 'events' in the analytic sense, their brevity and/or banality sits ill with the ordinary, and in this case, grander use of the term, 'an event'.

But in every case, from the boxing match to going out to buy some chocolate, the logic is the same – a continuum of otherwise separate occurrences which has a beginning, middle, and end, is pointed to and thus individuated from other continuums or 'events'. And as already observed, to fail to perceive, or to misconstrue, these discrete sequences of occurrences is respectively to be blind to, or misunderstand, part of the nature of reality. And it is worth repeating that insofar as to perceive a continuum is to make sense out of a myriad of occurrences taking place at different times and in diverse time-scales, then we transform our understanding from the mere chronicling of, 'he did this, then that, then that', into the notion that what *in fact* was going on was, for instance, that he was playing football, staging a coup, or going out to the shops.

Conversely, of course, we must not claim a continuity between occurrences where it does not pertain. Events, after all, have endings; the story, however long, must come to an end. Narratives which we feel might as well go on forever are almost dismissable as 'real' stories. 'What happens' is virtually a matter of the narrator's whim, so tenuous is the real narrative force of the term, 'next', or 'then'. Thus, for example, media soap-operas, although replete with strong events, go on and on, such that although the narrative appears to flow endlessly, it is not *one* story. It does not describe one, single (infinite?) 'story-object'; rather, in being more nearly a chronicle of different 'story-objects' or 'events' tenuously linked together, it is a pseudo-narrative. In short, the content of a chronicle does not articulate a real phenomenon. Biographies can provide another example of this syndrome; were it not that the subject finally died, the 'narrative' would have continued. But sooner or later real 'events' such as wars, parties, journeys, or philosophical expositions constitutive of chapters in a book, come to an end, and new ones begin.

SUMMARY

The previous chapter concluded that in the search for what, if anything, peculiarly distinguishes the discipline of history, there are good reasons for focusing upon narrative history despite its current unfashionability amongst some historians and philosophers. Four issues in particular stood out as needing examination – to what extent narrative is a specific mode of discourse in its own right; what it achieves; in what sense, if any, it is explanatory; and how satisfactory it is as a formal framework for historians to work within.

The first three of these issues largely converge into the general question with which this chapter began – namely, what *is* a narrative? – and hence their treatment has been subsumed under this more general enquiry. Thus: the essential nature and distinctness of narrative as a structure or form has been analysed; it has been identified as that mode of discourse which puts otherwise discrete occurrences into an intelligible order. Throughout, the distinction between (mere) chronicles and (meaningful) narratives or 'stories' has been of recurring relevance, drawing attention to the special function of the (often implied) terms, 'then', or, 'next', in the logic of a narrative. Regarding its explanatory power, narrative was shown to convey intelligibility (and in that sense constitute the form of an explanation), at two different levels. On the first, a treatment of the concepts of continuity and change clarified the manner in which the narrative form renders occurrences intelligible as regards their happening – that is, explains why they take place. At the second level, narrative was shown to achieve something additional, for in our disentangling of the paradoxical dialectics of 'happenings' (by positing a distinction between 'occurrences' and 'events'), it was argued the narrative form is *explicative* of a distinct and familiar dimension of reality – namely, the world of 'story-objects', or 'events'. This explicatory power of narrative was shown to consist in rendering its own class of phenomena intelligible through those same principles of meaning and identification (and the attendant logic of individuation) outlined in Chapter One.

The fourth issue – that of how adequate narrative is as a framework for historians in particular to work within – now remains. Although much of relevance has already been adumbrated, the issue has not been fully subsumed under the course of this general exposition of the principles of narrative. Given the centrality of the issue to our overall topic, such questions which do remain regarding *historical* narrative now need to be brought into direct focus. In short, given the logic of narrative generally, there is still the need to see where the narrative historian stands in all this.

For instance, that the historian who engages primarily in narrative is doing something which has its own distinct identity, has already been shown to the extent that narrative itself has been uniquely individuated from other modes of discourse. But within the realm of narrative it is necessary to restrict the historian to *factual* narrative; further, within these confines it is necessary to examine more closely how historical narrative differs from other narratives which, although equally factual, can serve a variety of purposes. In other words, we cannot blandly fit the historian into his narrative jacket without further investigation; indeed, this evidences that, although we have set out how narrative in general proceeds, questions remain in any event regarding the actual practice of constructing them, and perhaps no more so than in the case of the historian.

Similarly, although much of relevance to the historian has already been said regarding narrative's explanatory and explicatory potential, again the need remains to focus more directly on that issue as it relates specifically to *historical* narrative. For example, given the twofold nature of narrative explanation in general, is the *narrative* historian thereby restricted to explaining only certain things because of the narrative form? In other words, to what extent is his *narrative* jacket a strait-jacket? Or conversely, in what ways are the explanatory and explicatory possibilities of narrative perhaps limited or modified in *historical* narrative? What, for instance, are the 'story-objects' or 'events' which constitute the material of *historical* narrative?

In these ways and for these reasons, then, we need to clarify where the narrative historian stands in relation to narrative generally before we can properly determine the overriding issue of how adequate narrative is as a framework for history. As for this issue itself, our general enquiry into narrative has already uncovered some relevant intimations. In particular, we have had occasion to approach the notion that the dimension of the world articulated through narrative in some sense specifically involves human beings. It was argued, for example, that any narrative must have subjects who are agents – and that in factual narrative these must be (responding) human beings. In addition, the first level of explanation achieved through narrative was characterised as peculiarly appropriate to human affairs, in contrast to the causal mode of explanation employed when treating of 'natural' (non-human), phenomena. And concerning that second level of explanation – narrative's power of *explication* – it would seem to follow that so-called 'natural events', such as avalanches and earthquakes, are not 'events' in the stricter sense of the term I have used.[13] In this connection it is interesting to note the old-fashioned curricular distinction between 'natural' and 'civil' history, a discrimination even the materialist Thomas Hobbes was anxious to insist upon.[14] These intimations of a necessarily 'humanist' character to the discipline of history are interesting enough in themselves, but are worth pursuing all the more, as the occasion arises, as we now turn to explore where the historian in particular stands in relation to narrative, so we can properly assess its adequacy as a formal framework for his discipline.

3

THE PRACTISING HISTORIAN

Chapter One surveyed the various types of historical enquiry and presentation, and singled out narrative history as that form whose intellectual structuring promises both a uniquely coherent identity and an equation with what history is traditionally regarded as being about. Chapter Two therefore studied the structure of narrative in general in order to become as intimate as possible with its rationale, subject-matter, parameters, and potential. At certain points that analysis generated issues of special relevance to the historian because of their direct implications for his/her practice. The purpose now of Chapter Three is to explore and elaborate upon these issues; not so much, however, with a view to instructing historians how to prepare valid narrative, but more to encourage that practice by defending its integrity where it might be subject to untutored criticism, and to suggest ways of overcoming certain inherent difficulties in its construction. Primarily concerned here, then, with the practising historian, I leave to the next chapter the explicit derivation of *theoretical* principles intimated by this practice – and to the final chapter an exemplification of narrative history, where I will treat of the history of (political) thought. This chapter therefore restricts attention to those especially pertinent and potentially problematic issues appertaining to *any* kind of historical narrative.

INDIVIDUALS IN HISTORY

The complex abstract model which emerged from the formal analysis of narrative is nevertheless clear in its implications and easy to follow if one is writing fiction. Gaps, obscurities, abortive beginnings, sudden endings – all can be resolved or avoided merely by the exercise of inventive imagination. And in the case of factual narrative (where such freedom is denied), we have noted the ease with which we nevertheless engage in narrative accounts, demonstrating a natural facility in conforming to its requirements without need of theoretical insight into its methodological subtleties – this, so long as we are involved in ordinary conversation. But put us in the witness-box in a trial, subject our story to meticulous examination, and soon enough our account will exhibit weaknesses, if not be exposed as nonsensical. Ordinary conversation is not obliged, after all, to make the right sense of what actually happened. However, this *is* the challenge the narrative historian faces – namely, to escape the vague, misleading impressions in Plato's cave. The practice of constructing valid (that is, historical) narrative is, then, far removed from the unconscious ease with which both the fictional writer and the busy conversationalist conform to its logical requirements.

Our prior analysis revealed that one of those logical requirements is that since narrative must be centred on a changing identity (because its form is not structured in terms of mechanistic cause and effect, but through its continuity being construed in terms of an agent's conventional responses to his context), then one cannot but be dealing with some human being's intentional conduct. However, although writers such as Hobbes and Marx delivered severe blows to philosophical idealism, confused remnants remain to clutter and obscure the task of valid history, and from a variety of sources. Some continue to reflect a pseudo-Hegelianism by attempting to present the history of, for example, socialism as 'socialism determining itself'.[1] Others, whilst eschewing any philosophical extravagances, nevertheless people their narratives with agents no less abstract than the phantasms of idealism, whereby seductively 'empiricist' concepts such as classes, governments, electorates, economies, and public opinion, are intruded as agents into historical narrative, filling gaps in its flow in a way no serious historian should contemplate. Such, I believe, is the prevalence of this kind of confusion, manifest in the slap-happy treatment of this aspect of the formal requirements of factual narrative, that it is worth spelling out the issue of agency clearly. (In addition it is only proper that where analysis impinges upon traditional themes within the philosophy of history, as here *vis-à-vis* the role of individuals in history, its implications should be made clear.)

Given, then, that the narrative historian must deal with some human being's intentional conduct, what are the implications of this requirement? Firstly, the historian cannot construct (narrative) histories of natural events – in fact, of course, he does not. But in restricting himself to human affairs (leaving natural events to the physical scientists), he is not merely following a fashion or maintaining a tradition; rather, he is conforming to one of the prime categorial imperatives of the narrative form. In short, he is bowing to necessity whether he knows it or not. Secondly, the historian should not people his narrative with pseudo-human agents such as animals, angels, ghosts, or gods. Neither, thirdly, should he exploit abstract agents, such as 'the spirit of liberty', 'imperialism', 'racialism', or 'the Enlightenment'. It is only in a manner of speaking that, for example, 'nationalism' can do anything, respond to circumstances, or initiate different situations. To present 'nationalism' in all seriousness as an agent in the logic of narrative is to fall into the kind of categorial muddle with which pub-talk is replete, but which has no place in the serious business of trying to extract real events from a world of occurrences sufficiently kaleidoscopic without such hopeless extra confusion.

Fourthly, and similarly, it is only 'in a manner of speaking' that a corporate body (for example, Germany, the Labour Party, a crowd) can be said to be affected by or to effect things. Strictly speaking, the Labour Party does not 'do' anything – it is a constituted body whose members do things such as write pamphlets, consider tactics, and vote for delegates. Its members do these things as individuals, not as collective entities. In short, the fact that the Labour Party is an authoritatively constituted body renders it no more capable of doing anything than is any other collective, such as a mob, the Ford Motor Company, the public, the working class, or 'society'.

Now it might be objected that to deny agency to constituted bodies in particular is to be over-scrupulous – that (although correct), it would be trivial to insist that the statement, for example, 'the Labour Party changed its defence policy in 1989', is only a figure of speech, because for all practical purposes it makes no difference and is a recognised form of shorthand for expressing what happened. As stated, this objection might be upheld so long as it is indeed continually recognised that a kind of figurative shorthand is in use. But if forgotten it can so easily seduce its user into peopling his narrative with governments which respond to pressure, mobs which become incensed, and electorates which change their minds! Dangerously, even the historian can be so seduced, such that his conceptual framework begins to *generate* such questions as 'what prompted the government to call an election then?', or, 'why didn't the mob lose interest earlier?'; and to propose absurd conclusions such as a hung parliament being 'the will of the electorate' despite most individual voters probably willing no such thing, voting uncompromisingly for the party of their choice. If the historian compounds such errors by trying to sustain a continuous narrative peopled with such pseudo-agents, it will disperse into loose ends. Sooner or later the shorthand must be dropped and the reality of single individuals deciding this, being affected by that, voting this way, recommending that policy, or enforcing this command, will take over as the historian brings a closer and more realistic scrutiny to events.

An alternative objection to denying agency to constituted bodies is the assertion that they really *are* agents rather than merely figuratively so. This would hardly warrant considered refutation were it not that corporate bodies and institutions are so much part of human affairs, and so often written about as if they *literally* are agents, that it is worth clarifying why they are not. Perhaps the most convincing example of a collection of individuals appearing to be a genuine agent is that of an authoritatively constituted body carrying out actions in accordance with, and in pursuance of, its regulations and responsibilities – as where a committee proposes a policy or where an electoral college decides a party's leadership.

But a moment's reflection will determine these are not special cases of genuinely corporate agency. An electoral college does not choose x or y; rather, x or y is the *outcome* of a vote – that is, the result of individuals' choices collated into an abstraction. Similarly, a committee does not, for instance, determine this measure or exhibit that prejudice; these are the *outcomes* of individual agents' views, feelings, and votes. The only thing which can be said is that where outcomes are predictable or unexceptional then the shorthand conversion of corporate bodies into agents does no harm, despite being metaphorical. Where outcomes arouse interest, however, most historians instinctively focus upon individuals in order to get at the reality behind affairs, and rightly so.

Thus it is that analysis confirms and encourages what is still for many historians a preference for concentrating upon the actions of individuals in constructing their narratives. The fact is, they *must* do so in order to locate and sustain intelligible continuity in the real world. To raise this intuition to the level of conscious methodology can only alleviate, at its outset, the formidable task of establishing continuity as, and at, the heart of narrative. In this context it is appropriate to note the attraction history has for those many students whose fascination is drawn to individuals' conduct. Any tendency to dismiss this as naive is as dangerous as it is misguided. It may be the same fascination which attracts enjoyers of TV 'soaps' (as well as a telling impulse to discover what 'eventually' happens), but woe betide the author of 'soaps' who neglects to interweave, for example, current popular sociological ideas and reality into his narrative. Just so regarding narrative and 'analytic' history. The allegedly naive enthusiast for historical narrative is as likely as the keen 'analyst' to be interested in current sociological, economic, political, and psychological theories, and therefore be as impatient as any 'soap' addict with narrative which ignores that contextual background. The complaint in both cases would be that the (hi)story is simply unrealistic and outdated – that is, not in accordance with current conventional expectations of how people get into and respond to situations.

In short, a fascination in the conduct of individuals need not and usually does not go hand–in–hand with a disinterest in or ignorance of those more abstract factors which analytic historians suggest play a role in historical events. In this light one may ask whose approach to history is the more naive – the analyst who on methodological grounds is not only *not* interested in individuals but who even therefore either neglects narrative altogether or invents a fantastic one based on the interplay of abstract forces as if they were agents; or the student whose interest in history was first aroused by an historian's account of how some remarkable individual behaved and of what ensued?

Thus as the basis and at the heart of narrative history, as a necessary condition of its coherence, is the individual human being as 'an embodied, living, real, sentient, objective being'.[2] Real, individual living people are the prerequisite of historical narrative, since it is the activity of these real individuals of flesh and blood which cannot but constitute its material. And this is to say that, if in its structure and logic, historical narrative truly apprehends the structure and logic of the actual world, then it is people's activity, and solely that, which is responsible for the world's 'having a history' in the proper sense of the term, rather than its generating no more than discrete states of affairs which happen to succeed each other, or which are construed as causally (rather than temporally) linked.

It is worth reminding ourselves that if the temporal sequence into which a state of affairs falls is irrelevant to that state of affairs, then it is difficult to see where the concept of *change* figures in anything we say about it – and if nothing can be said to change, there is neither story nor history to be told. Conversely, narratives (and therefore stories and histories) are simply impossible in the absence of change. Thus we must deal with human activity, as made equally clear by the writer just cited, who, in addition to castigating idealist historians for peopling the world with abstract identities as agents of historical change, also warned materialist historians against conceiving of their subject-matter 'only in the form of the *object*' rather than as human activity.[3] Simple objects and states of affairs pertaining to them have no history of their own; it is only when they are enlivened by human beings deliberately involving them in their activity that the possibility arises for them to play a part in history's melody – as second fiddle to people themselves. Equally, however, in the absence of real objects and states of affairs people themselves would not have a history. Thus, to stay with Marx a little longer, it is just in his work upon the objective world that man really proves himself as an *historical* being, and thereby a *human* being at all (if we are to distinguish between a responding being and a reacting thing).[4] That it is solely people who are responsible for 'making' history, assures us they are human beings, an assurance which no natural science can give. Medicine, physiology, and the like, however useful, suffer the drawback that they cannot but dehumanise people. After all, one resigns oneself to a visit to the doctor whereas one enjoys oneself by reading (and maybe even making) history; the former reminds us of our animal origins, the latter of our human nature.

HUMAN ACTIVITY

I have presented the preceding arguments about the role of individuals in history as a fundamental step in alleviating the problems the practising historian encounters in conforming to the theoretical implications of narrative structure as they come home to roost. Factual narrative must focus on the activities of (ultimately, individual) human beings. Now it might be objected this places an unpalatable restriction on the subject-matter the (narrative) historian should deal with – indeed, that it sets unpalatable limits to the discipline of history itself. But it is more instructive to adopt a Hobbesian stance and see the matter in a positive light. Since water must of necessity run *down* a channel, he asks, is this to be seen as a limitation upon its 'freedom'? His reply is that necessity and liberty are consistent, such that it is more helpful to remark it is the very nature, 'virtue', or 'power', of water to run down a channel rather than (confusedly) bewail its lack of freedom.[5]

Just so should we view this limit to the discipline of (narrative) history; that is, recognise as the peculiar *virtue* of factual narrative that it focuses necessarily on the activity of human beings. And the same may be said of other properties innate to the structure of narrative, many already exposed in Chapter Two (such as its potential for explanation), and others yet to emerge. To identify the nature of a thing is as much to express its virtues as to restrict its scope, for to say what a thing is is to imply what it is not. Thus, in attempting to identify 'history' as a coherent discipline in the first place, and then undertaking to expose its nature, it depends more on the reader than on the intentions of the author whether he take a jaundiced view of its 'restrictions' or a positive view of its potential.

To restrain the focus of the historian to the activities of human beings is, then, to assist him in the task of achieving continuity in his narrative. But it by no means solves the problem since it is rash to assume all the 'successive' actions of an individual constitute an unbroken continuity. Even if they did, it would still be rash to assume there would be no problem in how to construe and present this. In short, that an agent does *x* and 'then' does *y* does not mean we are therefore witnessing a single changing identity; rather, this may or may not be the case. It is for these reasons that we need to enquire into those aspects of the nature of human activity which have implications for the concepts of continuity and change.

We begin this enquiry by remarking that the term 'activity' can denote something concrete, specific, and individual (for example, to engage in the activity of cooking a meal or arguing a case), or denote a mere abstraction, where we simply refer in general to all the different things a person does over a period of time as his 'activity'. In this latter case the temporal order of the different things the agent does may be irrelevant to understanding them – in other words, he may do one thing and then

85

another without any meaningful relationship of 'prior' and 'subsequent' in his actions. Some may be so related, but it seems reasonable to assert people are capable of simply stopping doing one thing and choosing to do something different – that is, doing 'this' and (then) 'that'. In such cases it would be spurious to insist the person is thereby 'continuing his activity'. It would be equally spurious to claim he is 'changing his activity', as if we were dealing with a single identity which is changing. In both cases the term 'activity' is only an abstraction.

Thus to say 'he did this, then this, and then that', *if* it is to do something different from producing a mere chronicle of discrete actions, is to find (or suppose) a real relationship between his now doing this and *then* (next) doing that. If there is no such relationship and yet we present his actions as if there were, then we have misunderstood them. Equally, if there *is* such a relationship and yet we interpret his actions as if there were not, we have again misunderstood them. In neither case have we understood what is really happening. It is in this manner, then, that valid narrative, the question of continuity in human conduct, and historical understanding – that is, the discovery and presentation of 'historical' or 'narrative' identities – are interdependent; and in practice what the historian needs are some pointers as to how to disentangle human actions with regard to their temporality, if only to be better able to defend his interpretations of 'what really happened'. How far is it possible to uncover such guidelines without imposing some specific theory of human conduct upon those (the historians) who perhaps more than any others need the most generously accommodating view of it?

ACTIONS

An appropriate beginning can be made by accepting and clarifying the conventional distinction between a specific activity and a specific action. For example, we talk of the *activity* of cooking a meal, and of the different *actions* involved (for example, adjusting the oven-heat and seasoning the sauce). Conventionally, that is, we distinguish between an action as a single, discrete piece of behaviour and an activity as a recognisable sequence of otherwise discrete actions. Quite where an activity begins, what it involves, and where it ends, may in many cases be difficult to discern with analytic accuracy. The same, however, is the case with a single action. Rather, we have conventional, workable ideas of its parameters, just as we have of the parameters between actions and activities. Some actions (construed as single, discrete pieces of behaviour), involve many otherwise different pieces of behaviour, yet we do not call them activities. Vice versa, some activities are expressed no differently from actions, as where they are denoted by a single verb (for instance, 'he cooked a meal', or 'composed a song').

Thus it is we draw these distinctions conventionally, even though in analytic terms the threat of infinite regression is ever present, whereby actions can be expanded into activities and activities be compressed into actions. In fact, of course, the logical paradoxes of this dialectic are analogous to those already encountered in the previous chapter relating to the analysis of 'happenings', 'occurrences', and 'events'. The problematic is similar, as is the manner and extent to which it can be resolved, because what we have here called 'a piece of behaviour' is simply a 'happening' conducted by an agent. Likewise, an action is simply an occurrence conducted by an agent, and an activity simply an event conducted by an agent. Thus it is along those same lines of argument used to extract 'occurrences' and 'events' from an otherwise undifferentiated realm of 'happenings', that we extract actions and activities from the general realm of 'pieces of behaviour', and distinguish between them.

PRACTICAL AND 'FINAL' ACTIONS

Having established the sense in which we can talk of individual actions, we can now clarify the logic of continuity in human conduct by resurrecting a distinction *within* actions (sporadically impressed upon us from philosophy) – namely, that between doing something 'for its own sake', and doing something for a practical purpose. We may recall, for example, Bodin's reliance on 'ancient wisdom' in declaring that 'those things which are least in order of dignity come first in order of necessity',[6] and Spinoza's reasoning in his central dictum that 'virtue is its own reward'.[7] Likewise we may be reminded of the young Marx's concept of 'self-activity' and his corresponding revulsion at the division of labour,[8] and of Oakeshott's presentation of what it is to be 'conservative', and his subsequent identification of 'civil conduct'.[9] We are, then, in good (if disparate) company in claiming an important distinction between actions undertaken to achieve an 'end' (I call these 'practical'), and actions undertaken as ends in themselves (that is, undertaken for the sake of experiencing them, which I call 'final').

Thus, for example, the football player must needs go through the business of putting on his boots and tying the laces, in order to play football. For our purposes it is peculiarly well put that he engages in such actions *in order* to play football. Although their precise ordering is relatively arbitrary, they are directed towards other actions undertaken for the experience of engaging in them – namely, those constitutive of playing football. (Let us immediately reject the crude reductionist hedonism which would insist this amounts to a desire to achieve an 'end', namely, pleasure. Eventually the footballer's lungs are screaming for air, his bruises aching, and his morale may be at rock-bottom. Similarly, for example, a writer can dread that blank sheet of paper before him, yet persist in his effort to write.)

It is true, of course, that the footballer may play football *not* because he enjoys it but *in order* to earn money, fame, or the admiration of his girl-friend, just as the writer may be similarly motivated. This, indeed, was the somewhat paranoiac fear behind the young Marx's representation of capitalism as distorting actions which should not be so, into the category of merely practical actions. Things which might otherwise be done for the sake of doing them become commodities to be sold, whilst things which might otherwise be done for a merely practical purpose (for instance, eating, defecating), are transformed by a sick and false consciousness into ritual actions of self-indulgence.[10] However, it is clear such arguments do not undermine the distinction between practical and final actions, but precisely originate from a heightened awareness of their relevance. For example, this particular footballer might actually play football *in order* to engage in tying his laces; this particular writer might write *in order* to experience blank sheets of paper. In both cases the common-sense judgement that there is something 'perverse' in their conduct evidences the faithfulness of this fundamental distinction between doing something in order to achieve an end and doing something as an end in itself.

Again, one may try to undermine this distinction by observing it is often the case that actions undertaken to achieve a practical end (for example, to earn money), are performed better than those same actions undertaken for the sake of undertaking them – in other words, that the professional's performance usually surpasses the amateur's, particularly, for example, in sports. Doubtless there is an unsavoury truth to this observation, but one solely related to the criterion of winning (which some claim is symptomatic of societies where, via a culture of 'efficiency', competition rather than social or human priorities determines the allocation of resources). The assumption is that individuals play football 'better' if practically motivated. However, such a claim in no way invalidates the distinction at issue; rather, it merely challenges the moral drawn from it. And if by 'doing a thing well' is meant facility in achieving the practical end motivating the performance, the challenge is surely well made. The time, training, and special equipment devoted to the professional's performance should pay off in those terms.

However there is another meaning, preferred by moralists, to the phrase 'doing a thing well', popularly intimated in the saying, 'If a thing's worth doing, it's worth doing well', and Biblically enjoined in the saying, 'Whatsoever thy hand findeth to do, do it with all thy might'. Indeed, what we encounter here might be put even more suggestively in the Platonic terms of 'doing a thing justice', whereby one strives to make one's performance of an action (or activity) conform to the intrinsic character of that action, rather than neglect or exaggerate certain of its features in order to achieve some extrinsic purpose. Here, our distinction could be expressed in terms of 'doing justice to the activity of playing football' rather than distorting its performance in pursuit of some unrelated end.

Here, however, mention of Plato should forewarn us of Socratic paradigms whereby, to demonstrate the distinction at issue, we imply an ideal way of, for example, playing football, cooking a meal, governing, arguing a case, or writing history. It seems to me to be unnecessary to appeal to such fantasies. To do something for the sake of doing it need mean nothing more than that; that is, one does it for the sake of doing it and for no further (extrinsic) purpose. Also, therefore, *how* one does it is entirely up to the agent's individuality rather than the action or activity exercising paradigmatic demands upon an agent's conduct via mystical means which cannot be conceived of. Hence, to make clear this is not a moral argument, let us concede there is nothing inherently perverse in a footballer engaging in that activity in order that he can tie his laces. It may be unusual – but our response must surely be, 'so what?' Repeatedly we are brought back to individual human beings' responses to their experience of being in the world. That is, we are confronted by what both the scientist and the philosopher most fear in their encounter with human conduct; namely, the subjective factor.

We may understand their distaste if we substitute 'inexplicable' for the term 'subjective', but it may now be readily appreciated that it can be precisely the narrative historian's achievement to identify and employ this irreducible factor in his account of events. An individual may like eating chocolate, or interfering with young boys. Whether he or she actually engages in these actions is another matter; respectively, fear of fatness or of a law may intervene. But to be able to say of someone that he did this, and did it in this way, because he enjoyed doing it, and doing it in that way, seems to me to put a stop to further enquiry. This is an avenue historians should not be reluctant to go down; on the contrary, it constitutes a route opened up by the logic of narrative which precisely generates successful perceptions rather than failures in explanation.

It is true, of course, that individuality ('arbitrariness', 'creativity') in the choice and performance of actions undertaken for their own sake is not as frequent as the foregoing arguments invite one to expect. This may be in appearance only, or possibly because many people do, in Sartre's terms, 'take themselves seriously', subordinating the way they perform activities to their belief in ideal forms. However, where this occurs one can only suppose it is the gratification of these fetishes which is the experience sought – a special case of undertaking an action for its own sake (possibly affiliated to 'ritual'). This is also an ironic case, however, because if idealists were correct regarding the reality of paradigmatic actions, one might have expected arbitrary individualism to be far more prevalent in the realm of practical rather than final actions. The fact is that it is not, of course. Practical actions are far more paradigmatic in their requirements, as anyone in employment knows. When efficiency is the criterion of performance, then technology, training, discipline, incentive, and time-and-motion study, are all brought into play to constrain the performance of actions into proved (rather than idealised) paradigms. In short, the one individual not welcome on a production line is he who actually enjoys screwing spark plugs into cylinder blocks in his own 'peculiar' way.

PRACTICAL ACTIONS

Following the above, and in pursuit of a salutary framework for the construction of narrative continuity, I turn now to a closer scrutiny of practical actions – (that is, those subordinated towards an end rather than performed for the experience of doing them). Extending the preceding argument, it is not difficult to determine guidelines or parameters for how practical actions 'should' be done. At any given time the state of technology, knowledge, and experience is the only, albeit severe, constraint. Thus, for example, if my objective is to produce light in a dark room, I switch on the lamp. The action of switching it on does not in this context invite subjective variations. Where subjectivity might come into play is if I have a choice of means (for example, opening a curtain), in which case, accounting for which I choose is a separate issue. The point at this juncture is that, given the means adopted, efficiency in achieving the objective determines how the action is undertaken.

If, then, I choose to switch on the lamp as the means of lighting the room, I will regard this action as necessitating determinate movements. I do not choose these movements. Rather, they appear as intrinsic to the action of switching on the lamp – I am constrained in which movements I make. As such it is justifiable to refer to actions undertaken for a practical purpose as mere labour, if by 'labour' we follow an ancient tradition of meaning activity forced upon one rather than issuing spontaneously, freely, or 'for its own sake'. Hence the desire, particularly in creative persons, children, and self-indulgent classes, to employ others to carry out practical activity (not, then, to make a profit; rather, I refer here to service).

Practically motivated actions are, then, actions constrained by the criterion of efficiency and therefore appear to have intrinsic parameters to their character. Yet analysis has shown that if by 'intrinsic' is meant some kind of innate, 'self-determining' nature, or equally obscurely, some fixed character determined by an ideal paradigm, such arguments accounting for the admittedly determinate nature of practical actions are as mystical as they are unnecessary. The sources of their determination are actual and intelligible, and of such a character that they are of course amenable to change over time. All that needs to be grasped regarding actions undertaken for a practical purpose is that they are identifiable as such through reference to their (extrinsic) purpose. Once so recognised, both the character of an action and the manner of its performance become intelligible in terms of the continuity of the otherwise discrete acts involved. In other words, *if* in all reasonableness the context and character of actions point to their practical nature, then the continuity of otherwise discrete actions can be spelt out in the terms, 'he did this, *then* that', and so on. That is, a narrative account in terms of an intelligible sequence of actions is demanded rather than a disjointed chronicle whereby one does this (then) that, (then) that, and so on.

The historian, of course, is different from the prosecuting advocate who may well find it necessary to focus on such trivia as what to make of the fact, and manner, of someone switching on a lamp. Conventionally the historian will be focusing upon 'grander' actions such as declaring war, resigning the whip, publishing *The Origin of the Species*, or denying the physical reality of Christ's resurrection. But the same principles apply. *If* the context and character of the actions suggest they are practical actions, then they can be singled, and sorted, out from amongst a myriad of intervening actions into an intelligible continuity of behaviour. What the agent does next is rendered immediately explicable in terms of what he did 'previously', given the observer's (or historian's) knowledge of the parameters surrounding practically motivated activity.

Thus, in short, we should be able to account in narrative terms for both the fact and manner of switching on the lamp and likewise for the former Bishop of Durham's public denial of the physical reality of Christ's resurrection. That the latter chose to do so at Easter, and himself declared he did so *in order* to make people reflect upon Easter's meaning, would encourage the observer to interpret this action as a practical one. This would then prompt him to extract and present the details of the action as part of the sequence of a genuine narrative continuity, involving a relevant discrimination of both 'prior' and 'subsequent' actions from within the mêlée of the Bishop's overall conduct.

Now it may be, of course, that 'getting people to reflect on Easter's meaning' is a situation the Bishop sought for its own sake, and that therefore this particular narrative identity stops there (of which general case I will treat shortly). On the other hand, 'getting people to reflect on Easter's meaning' might be practically motivated, in which case we can proceed in those terms to what the Bishop did 'next', and so on. Often, in fact, we encounter the instructive case (so frequent for the historian as to make it unexceptional), where the observer might identify actions as practical in advance of knowing what their distant objective is. In this case the very supposition of their practical character generates hypotheses, with genuinely argumentative evidence, of 'what actually took place'. Thus, aided by a clear grasp of the distinction between practical and final actions and of the issues surrounding the former, the historian is provided with at least one valid and instructive heuristic principle underlying the transformation of otherwise discrete pieces of behaviour into an intelligible narrative. We must now explore the heuristic value of that other species of action, namely, 'final' actions.

FINAL ACTIONS

I have already indicated examples, from moral philosophy, of the recurring recognition of a distinction between practical and 'final' actions. Whether upon closer scrutiny those philosophers all mean the same is a matter for doubt. But since our purposes are purely analytic then the relevant issues for us are different – namely, how can the identification of a 'final' action be substantiated, and what are the implications of its 'finality' for the construction of intelligible continuity within the narrative form?

Firstly, how do we know a certain action is 'final' – that is, undertaken for the experience of undertaking it rather than to achieve some (exterior) objective? If they are present we can ask the agent – but this is not an avenue often open to the historian. Rather, he must needs look to context, evidence of motivation, alternative hypotheses, and at the nature of the action and the manner in which it was performed. In addition he should also employ his common sense, if only to distinguish the likely from the unlikely. This latter observation is especially pertinent because of the initial importance of recognising the unlikelihood of actions being final actions 'by their nature'. That is, one looks in vain for any valid *theoretical* principle which would demand a particular sequence of movements must of its own nature be a final action.

The nearest vindication of such a principle would be afforded by the claim that there exist objective criteria for determining what constitutes, for example, art, literature, music, entertainment, and sports. Broad as these categories are, they conventionally exclude government, economic production, management, and housework. But the very mention of these excluded activities raises the suspicion that there is something wrong with the line of argument, for we know people can engage in literature for practical purposes, and in housework for its own sake.

What we are in fact confronted with is that same issue of the allegedly intrinsic character of actions encountered in the analysis of *practical* actions, and the same objection applies. For example, to say of a certain painting, 'that is art', and to mean that because of its objective characteristics it must have been undertaken for the sake of undertaking it, is to relapse into the fallacy of philosophical idealism. The supposition is that some paradigm determines that such-and-such actions constitute, for example, art, and also determines their precise manner of execution, therefore replacing the actual individual with its own mystic agency. The actual agent is thereby relinquished to servitude, albeit lightened by a necessarily 'false consciousness' of what he is doing and why. Here we may only observe that if by an individual's consciousness we mean his understanding, then although his understanding might involve incorrect conclusions this is different from claiming its very mode of operation is fallacious, as seems implied by idealists.

More to the point is to recognise the common knowledge that some of the most glorious works of art, exquisite pieces of literature, and most skilful achievements in sport, have self-confessedly on the part of the agents been undertaken for practical purposes – usually money, but sometimes prestige, power, or some other ambition. Likewise we should recognise that some of the worst works of art, most risible efforts in sport, most effective examples of management, and least irresponsible performances of housework, are undertaken for the sake of (experiencing) undertaking them. I say 'recognise' because we can reflect on our activities, and ask others about theirs.

Does this mean, then, there simply is no such thing as 'art', 'sport', or, indeed, 'housework'? The answer to this is surely no; rather, these are terms which distinguish different areas of activity along those cardinal principles of relevance and workability proposed earlier. Their parameters are correspondingly conventional rather than paradigmatic, and are neither derived from, nor dependent on, the distinction between doing a thing for a practical purpose and doing it for its own sake. If they *were* so determined then an extensive vocabulary would have emerged along those foundations, such that we would have different terms, for example, for what we now call 'art', 'sport', or 'housework', depending upon whether they are undertaken for practical purposes or as ends in themselves.

The fact is we have no such extensive vocabulary differentiating conduct in this way – rather, there is only a small number of terms expressive of this distinction, and they appear to be much more specific in reference than those broad areas mentioned above. For instance, one example of terminology denoting conduct performed for its own sake is the term, 'to make love'. A wealth of more sanguine but less savoury terms are also employed to denote the same actions, but of these popular and slang terms one cannot tell what they intimate about the practicality or finality of the activity (nor with the bland media term, 'having sex'). On the other hand it is interesting its scientific terminology ('copulation', 'mating', 'the reproductive act') is indicative of the activity when, or as if, undertaken to achieve a practical objective.

Another example is the term, 'going for a walk', where we are clearly invited to understand not only what approximate actions are involved but also that they are specifically undertaken for the sake of the experience. The term 'commute', however, which could equally apply to someone walking down the street, specifies that the actions are undertaken for a practical purpose. Thus, as in the case of walking or sexual intercourse, we can find examples where ordinary language is meant to convey the distinction under discussion. Nevertheless, as already suggested, their number is small, particularly where they denote the finality of an action or activity.

However, rather than take this to imply that final actions are rare or the distinction is seldom recognised, I suggest the common wisdom of language faithfully reflects further signs of that untidy ambivalence of human conduct often referred to earlier. To identify someone's activity as, for example, gardening, reading, or playing the piano, is not so much to overlook or deny the distinction between practical and final actions as to suspend judgement, leaving room for either interpretation; and to the extent language is our tutor on such issues, it seems eminently sensible. Sometimes closer observation of actions and their performance *is* sufficient to determine whether they are practically motivated or done for their own sake. Often, however, we encounter that inherent untidiness of human affairs – in this case, the situation where both species of motivation are present simultaneously. Thus, one may be gardening in order to keep fit but be fortunate to discover many of the actions involved are enjoyable in themselves. (Hence the frequent parental advice to children, to get work which they will enjoy – and the equally frequent admonition from employers, to 'get on with the job'. Both are partial. The parent should add that the child should also be good at the work he or she chooses, and the employer should note that people are more prone to 'get on with' a job they like doing.)

Sufficient has been said to vindicate the claim that neither the finality nor practicality of actions can easily, if at all, be established solely by reference to their objective nature. An individual, after all, may be tying his shoe-laces because he enjoys tying his shoe-laces, and there may be nothing in the way he does it to demonstrate this. However, common-sense dictates that if tying his shoe-laces is an experience desired for its own sake, he will be likely to engage in this action even when he does not need to. In addition there may be signs in the manner he executes the action to demonstrate, or suggest, his non-practical motivation. Careful attention to the nuances of a conversation, for instance, may generate the suspicion that, appearances notwithstanding, it is an exercise in persuasion rather than the enjoyment of good talk.

One further clarification is necessary to help discriminate between final and practical actions – and to help introduce an additional species of action whose explication is necessary for us to gain a sufficiently overall view of human activity based on the preceding interpretive techniques.

In human conduct we have noted that practical actions generate the formula, 'doing something in order to' do that, achieve this, or reach that situation – and that this is a notably strong case of the 'prior' and 'subsequent' ('this *then* that') logic axiomatic to narrative structure. The problem is, however, that final actions also have a purpose, and therefore might appear resolvable into practical actions. For example, one might argue that where an individual happens to enjoy tying his shoe-laces, or gardening, 'for its own sake', then nevertheless his purpose must be to engage in the actions *in order* to achieve their objective (namely, the tightly fitting shoe or the fertile garden). This difficulty is particularly met with in the performance of sports and games, where there seems a recognised tension between playing the game for the sake of it and playing to win. Scoring more goals than the opposition is, after all, the objective in playing football.

Firstly, however, we must remember all games are (artificially) rule-bound. But more importantly we must recognise that when an action is undertaken for practical purposes, the actual purpose which determines its undertaking, and the manner of its undertaking, can be one amongst many. I have called it 'exterior' in the sense that it has nothing to do with the activity itself. The 'intrinsic' purpose in playing football, however, is to score goals, and more than the opposition; there is no other. Likewise regarding the 'intrinsic' purpose of tying shoe-laces; namely, to secure the shoe to the foot. *All* actions are in this sense 'intrinsically' purposeful, but this is not to say they are necessarily undertaken for the sake of achieving their purpose. Rather, if it is a final action it is undertaken for the sake of experiencing doing those things demanded by the action.

We must repeat, however, that this does not mean some paradigm determines an action's parameters. Rather, whatever 'logic' a recognised action has (evidenced by language adopting a special term for it), is attributable to its recognised relevance and reliability in people's discriminatory experience of the world. People have not always 'smoked'; people in tropical zones do not 'ski'; 'manufacturing' is an historically recent activity, as is 'jiving'. And all of these actions and activities may disappear as circumstances and human proclivities alter. Whilst they prevail, however, they are perfectly 'real' activities with their 'own' logic. Sports and games are simply special cases where the 'logic' of the actions involved is primarily invented by people rather than being the outcome of the encounter between man and nature.

ACTIVITIES AND 'MEDIATE' ACTIONS

The preliminary distinction I drew between actions and activities has lain dormant, if not obscure, amongst the subsequent discussion of practical and final actions, and it is now necessary to return to that initial distinction. I argued the discrimination between a single action and an activity (involving several otherwise discrete actions) is as 'real' as it is conventional, so long as we avoid the term 'activity' denoting all someone does over a random period. Rather, it must denote an intentional connection between the actions involved. Thus we conventionally refer to playing football, or writing a book, as an activity rather than as a single action, because we wish to recognise a unity connecting different actions, worth individualising in terms of relevance and workability.

So far, then, it would seem an activity can be carried out for practical purposes (for example, servicing a car), or for its own sake (for example, playing a game). However, where engaged in an activity in order to achieve an 'exterior' purpose (as is probable in servicing a car or writing up the minutes of a meeting), we are just as likely to refer to such an activity as a task, job, or chore. By this we mean to indicate several different actions are involved in achieving an overall objective. As such, a 'task' would appear to be no more than a familiar sequence of practical actions to achieve a familiar purpose. Indeed, the very terms, 'task', 'chore', and 'job', precisely denote their practical motivation. Because of this, it seems to me there is little to interest us in the difference between a 'task' and a single practical action, since the formula 'he did this in order to achieve that' applies equally to both. It is simply extended in the former case, where, by means of different actions which constantly change the situation, one moves continually towards achieving the exterior objective.

The situation is different, however, where one performs an activity for its own sake. Here, the individual actions are not practical actions moving ever forward to an overall exterior objective. Neither, however, are they final actions, for nothing follows from a final action. Rather, they are performed as actually *constituting* the activity. Consider, for example, the actions of passing the ball, then regaining position, and then heading the ball, in the activity of playing football. They are not practical actions because they are not performed in order to change the state of affairs. Rather, they precisely *are* the continuation of the state of affairs – namely, to be playing football. Should one doubt this, it is only necessary to compare the action of passing the ball with the action of re-tying one's boot-laces during the game. The latter is a practical action, undertaken *in order to* play the game, whilst the former is not undertaken *in order to* play the game but as part *of* the game. The practical action of re-tying the laces interrupts the game; passing the ball is the continuing of the game.

Neither, however, are they final actions, because they are not undertaken for their own sake individually. We noted earlier what unpleasantries can be involved in doing things for their own sake – they are sometimes necessary as part of the overall activity. But if that activity *as a whole* were experienced as unpleasant, it would simply not be indulged in by the agent (at least, not for its own sake).

For these reasons, then, I say actions involved in an activity undertaken for its own sake are neither practical nor final actions, but partake of the flavour of both. Being in this kind of middle, and being best understood as *constitutive* of an activity, I call them 'mediate' actions.

Contrary to final actions, there are numerous examples where language indicates an action is a 'mediate' action, although it would be wrong to trust entirely to that avenue. This is because of that ambivalence in human conduct already remarked upon. We cannot automatically tell whether an 'activity' is 'final' or 'practical' from a perfunctory observation, nor always definitively from the language used, however suggestive. Although I have preferred to call the latter by such terms as 'a task' or 'chore', wherein each action involved is simply practical rather than 'mediate', others might claim 'tasks' have constitutive (hence 'mediate') actions. Content to leave this a marginal case, let us at least note where language denotes an action as part of an activity, and leave as merely indicative the question of how far it also denotes the activity's finality or practicality.

Thus, for example, if a person is playing football we do not speak of his kicking the ball to his team-mate – we speak of his passing the ball or making a pass. Again, we do not speak of his kicking the ball at goal – rather, he 'takes a shot at goal'. Here, the very words used 'explain' or 'account for' the agent's conduct; to say, 'he took a shot at goal' is to account for his kicking the ball in a particular manner.

Of course, sporting activities being so well defined, we find numerous examples of special terminology for mediate actions in this area; for example, 'he returned the service' (in the activity of playing tennis), a mediate action. 'He hit the ball back to his opponent' (so that they could resume the game, the ball having gone astray), is on the contrary an example of a practical action.

Outside sport, consider the example, 'he trimmed the hedge', indicating an engagement in the activity of gardening. Alternatively, he may not have been gardening, but wanted to get a better view, or provide himself with some decorative foliage. In these contexts of *practical* action we could describe him as 'cutting branch-ends off the hedge' rather than use the mediate term which would denote his actions as constitutive of an overall, on going activity. Again, we would consider 'he ordered another round' (in the activity of 'having a drink') a mediate action, whereas 'he asked for drinks to be served to the company' (in order to relax his juniors, or to impress with his generosity) would express the action as a practical one.

Thus in these examples of mediate actions, when trimming the hedge he is not cutting the hedge for the sake of doing it, nor in order to achieve some specific, different state of affairs. He is undertaking the action as both contributive to, and as a continuation of, the activity of gardening. When returning service he is not hitting the ball back to his opponent for the sake of it, nor to achieve some specific exterior objective; he is continuing to play tennis. When he orders another round he is not ordering

97

drinks for the company for the sake of it, nor to achieve some particular purpose. He is continuing the activity of 'having a drink with friends', or whatever other terms are appropriate to capture the fact he is engaged in a recognisable activity with its own 'rules' or 'structure' – that is, an activity which requires actions intrinsic to it, and which therefore *is* such (rather than a series of discrete actions), precisely because it requires 'mediate' actions.

CHANGE AND CONTINUITY IN HUMAN CONDUCT

Chapter Two presented the structure of narrative as articulating one thing following on from another in the manner of an agent's conventional responses to his situation. Necessarily, at points, we were drawn to a close analysis of the concepts of agency, change, difference, continuity, occurrences, events, and identity, in order to penetrate how narrative works, upon what suppositions it rests, what it can and cannot achieve, and how far and in what sense it is an explanatory form of discourse. In talking now of the practising historian, it has been our aim to show how those general theoretical principles relate specifically to the construction of narrative history, and thus in a sense to bring them down to earth. Towards this end the first section discussed the question of agency as it relates to factual (that is, historical) narrative. The succeeding discussion of activities, and of practical, final, and mediate actions, has not been offered as an exhaustive theory of human conduct (which would impose speculative and ideological restrictions on historians), but rather as a common-sense perspective by which it can be understood in terms of continuity and change. Although indications have emerged regarding how this perspective facilitates that aim, it now behoves us to give a systematic exposition of the matter.

To remind ourselves of the general problematic: I have argued the narrative historian must be able to establish and present continuity in human conduct. He cannot achieve this by simply chronicling all the successive actions of an individual, as if their mere succession were equivalent to a genuine continuity. Rather, he must establish continuity through demonstrating real relationships of 'prior' and 'subsequent' ('this *then* that') in the agent's conduct – and we recall that, insofar as we are dealing with conduct, we are inevitably confronting change and its problematic relation to continuity and identity. Without resurrecting the complexities of Chapter Two's detailed analysis of those concepts, let us now see how the distinctions within human conduct suggested in this chapter accommodate those theoretical principles of the narrative form. I leave actual examples of the application of this overall approach to Chapter Five's focus on the history of political thought.

PRACTICAL CONDUCT

In making the kind of sense of human conduct suited to the construction of narrative, I first outlined the notion of a 'practical' action. We may imagine, for example, a man sitting in a chair, who then gets out of the chair in order to switch on the light. He switches on the light in order to read his newspaper, and he reads his newspaper in order to find out what local entertainments are available – and so on. We have already remarked that language itself indicates the *ordering* of these actions into an intelligible continuity, such that in dealing with practical actions the historian has no problem in constructing continuity in an agent's conduct so long as he perceives their practical nature, and so long as his perception is correct.

The only caution advisable here lies, not so much in accepting the possibility of alternative actions being available to the agent to achieve his purpose, but in whether this should influence our understanding and presentation of his conduct. That is, where technical or other constraints do not make the performance of a practical action paradigmatic, an agent has a choice of how to achieve his purpose. In our example the seated man may have stayed in his chair and asked his nearby child to switch on the light; or he may have got out of his chair to open the curtain rather than to switch on the light. Other means of achieving the purpose of being able to see better to read his newspaper can also be imagined, such that following his conduct may generate the question as to why he chose to achieve his purpose in this rather than another way.

Indeed, it might be thought that a legitimate and largish part of an historian's task is to explain why individuals chose the particular means they did in order to achieve their objectives; in short, to explain not only why an individual did x, but also why he did it in the way he did. After all, there must be a reason, we may say, why (if it were the case) the seated man asked his child to switch on the light rather than do it himself. He may, for instance, have felt tired, in which case it is not only legitimate but also informative for the observer to say so in his account of the man's conduct. Given Hitler's objective of invading England, surely part of the historian's business is to explain why Hitler set about the project in the way he chose?[11]

Unexceptional as this appeal may be, I do not, however, believe it to be a realistic expectation of the scope of historians' work. Firstly, we must recognise it is only in virtue of those actions which Hitler actually did that we establish his objective of invading England. It would be nonsense to argue we know Hitler intended to invade England, not because of what he did, but because he did it in this rather than some other way. Such an upside-down logic leads into an Alice's Wonderland of absurdity where I propose, for example, that I can tell you intended to go to town because you were walking there rather than taking the bus, cycling, or driving there!

Secondly, we should recall and respect the fact that the logic of the narrative form, in putting occurrences into a sequence of 'prior' and 'subsequent', explains why a thing occurred, but not why *it* rather than something else occurred. The narrative form gives us 'the reason' a thing happened, but not 'the reason' why this rather than that happened. To return to our seated man, we can follow his subsequent actions and find in them a continuity (in this case, via the notion of practical actions). Thus, through the implicit explanatory nature of the narrative form, we can explain his action of getting out of the chair. He did so in order to switch on the light. But why he got out of the chair to switch it on when he could, for instance, have asked his child to do so, is neither a question implicitly posed nor implicitly answered by the narrative form. Nor, I suggest, can it be answered by any other means.

To make this important point clearer, let us pose the common-sense objection that there are numerous occasions when we *do* explain why someone chose this rather than another way to achieve an objective. In the above example let us suppose he got out of the chair, rather than ask his child, because he did not want to disturb the child's homework. Our reply to this is, simply, 'how do you know?' *If* all that is available to one is the seated man then getting out of the chair and switching on the light, we have no warrant to suggest why he chose to get the light switched on by that rather than by some other method. If we nevertheless pose the question, all we can do is *assume* some likely explanation, and to assume something means precisely to guess. It may be an intelligent, informed guess, but it remains a guess for all that; and in painfully reconstructing their factual accounts guesswork is not the business of historians.

The case is different, however, with inference. If we *assume* a thing precisely because we have no information, we *infer* a thing on the basis of *evidence*, and it is of course *this* process which lies at the heart of the historian's business. Now, in the above example, what would be needed in between the man sitting in his chair, and eventually getting up, is evidence of the interposition of some additional occurrence if we are to be in a position to claim he got up to switch the light on rather than ask his child to do so. And what this means is the narrative is extended. Instead of the man now sitting in his chair, and then getting up, and then switching on the light, we must extend the narrative along such lines as the man sitting in the chair, then wanting the light put on, then considering asking his child to do it for him, then noticing the child's absorption in his homework, and then choosing to get up and switch it on himself. What this narrative seems to achieve is the explanation, via the narrative form, of why the man chose to get up to switch on the light rather than ask his child to do it – in short, why he chose this rather than that way to achieve his aim (that is, why this rather than that happened, precisely the ability we have denied the narrative form).

But looking more closely, I believe our original claim stands. Although the narrative does tell us why the man did not ask the child to switch the light on, it does not tell us why he switched it on rather than achieve his objective in some other way. It merely tells us why he did *not* do it in one *particular* way; it does not tell us why he did it in this rather than in some other way. Further, although each occurrence in our extended narrative is explicable as 'subsequent' to the 'prior' point, what is still not explained is why, at each point, this rather than that occurred. We know, for example, he paid attention to the child's absorption; we do not know, however, why he paid that attention rather than do something else. As argued, the narrative form does not implicate that kind of explanation. If one nevertheless seeks it, all one can do (if the evidence is there to be inferred from) is produce an extended narrative which explains, not why he attended to the child's absorption rather than do something else, but merely why he did *not*, for example, do some other *particular* thing.

Thus to conclude this point; I may for instance get on the bus in order to go to town. There are many other ways I can get to town. In myself I know I considered walking, but it was raining. Also, in myself I know I considered therefore driving to town, but could not face the parking problems. I then chose to go on the bus, not having considered any further ways of getting to town. Now, even with my intimate knowledge of what I did, I am likely to say I went to town on the bus because it was raining, glossing over the fact that I got on the bus, not because it was raining, but in order to get to town – and also glossing over the fact that although I know why I took the bus rather than drove, I do not know why I got on the bus to go to town rather than get there in some way other than either walking or driving. Thus, even given my own intimate awareness of what I did and why, there remains a strong sense in which I do not know why I went about it in the way I did. What remains clear, however, is that I got on the bus in order to go to town.

Now if these lacunae characterise the self-knowing individual's ability to explain what is happening, how much more limited is the observer's ability! He sees me come out of the house, then get on the bus, and get off when I arrive in town. We may be generous in accepting his conclusion that I got on the bus in order to go to town (since I may, for example, have changed my destination during the journey), but let us be so. Further, as we have argued, he may *assume* 'reasons' why I got on the bus to go to town rather than used some other means of getting there. In the absence of evidence they remain mere guesses. There may, however, be certain things he notices me doing, or he may have knowledge of my habits and preferences, such that they constitute evidence from which he infers 'reasons' why I got on the bus rather than use some other means of travel.

101

But he is unlikely to be able to infer as full an account as I, the agent, can offer (which is itself incomplete). And if this is the case respecting a present observer of occurrences, how much more limited will usually be the *historian's* ability to explain what happened. He is not present, and must function solely through inference, ever-cautious of that fine line historians tread between assumptions, which are bound only by the imagination, and inferences, which are bound by evidence.

Thus to return to the notion that it behoves the historian, particularly in tracing an intelligible sequence of *practical* actions, to explain not only why an individual did *x* but also why he did it in the way he did, we have seen that in addition to the practical limitations often imposed by his position, there are also theoretical restrictions at work. We can ask why that person got on the bus; the answer is, in order to get to town – that was his reason. But we cannot sensibly then ask, 'but why did he get on the bus in order to go to town?' – (for example, that it was raining does *not* explain it). It is like asking, 'why do you brush your teeth in order to keep them healthy?'

The fundamental error revealed here is that, in asking why someone pursued his objective in the way he did – in effect, why this rather than that happened – what is being sought is the reason for a reason, and historians should beware of going in search of this chimera.[12] The logic of narrative does not accommodate it, and it is difficult to conceive of any other logic doing so either.[13] The flight from narrative towards 'analytic' history (although welcome insofar as it has been associated with the emergence of new *branches* of history), might have been prompted partly by the prospect of some sort of 'total' explanation of events, revolving around the illusion that, in addition to explaining what happened, one can also explain why this rather than that happened. Thus the multiplication of, for instance, social, economic, psephological, cultural, and psychological 'factors' interwoven into analytic history. But can we be sure there are not occasions when a faulty logic is at work here – namely, a supposition that explanations for occurrences have themselves somehow to be 'explained'?

Be this as it may, in noting the 'limitations' of the narrative form *vis-à-vis* what it does and does not explain, we should yet again remark upon that happy correlation between the logic of the narrative form and that of human affairs. In being brought to focus ultimately upon human conduct, historians should, then, restrict themselves to explaining why individuals did what they did, and rest content that in revealing the way individuals acted (for example, in realising practical objectives), they are *characterising* individuals' responses rather than explaining them. 'The action is the man', it is said. Police forces can recognise the '*modus operandi*' of some criminals as if it were an identification badge; they do not need, however, to explain why a criminal has this rather than that 'MO'.

The above discussion was prompted by the recognition that in the sphere of practical actions there are often different ways of achieving the same objective. However, there are occasions when only one means is available, and here we should note the possibility of deliberate inaction because the agent regards the price of undertaking the necessary action as too high. Where such is the case it is often worth the historian recording this. Not only does it tell us much about the intricacies of the real situation and the responses of those agents involved; it also adds to the explanation of what *was* actually done. For example, it is surely worth lending a hand to those burdened with power and responsibility by pointing out Machiavellian means which, although available, they rejected as involving actions they were not prepared to take. To reduce history to the ruthless achievement of practical objectives would be as unreasonable as it would be unpalatable. Room should be left for principles, morals, and ideology to play a part in even the powerfuls' conduct. Certainly, the reductionism of certain historical approaches which would resolve all actions of the powerful to the merely practical (for example, the quest for profit, security, domination, or power), is an object of belief rather than of rational enquiry. The cry, 'megalomania!', is simply a way of expressing ignorance.

To conclude this consideration of practical actions we can note how those formal concepts of change, difference, continuity, and identity implicit in the logic of the narrative form apply. In performing a practical action an individual is *now* in situation x, desires to be in a *different* situation, y, and thus *then* performs action a in order to achieve situation y, thereby *changing* the situation. Thus, in presenting a practical action we are establishing a *continuity* through change. To say that someone did this in order to achieve that is to point to a single *identity*, namely, the agent's changing the state of affairs so that it is *now different* from how it was *then* – and this applies equally to whether we are dealing with a single practical action which leads no further than the desired objective (that is, a situation sought for its own sake), or with a sequence of practical actions leading to a distant objective (sometimes conventionally individualised into a single 'task', 'chore', or 'job').

CHANGE AND CONTINUITY IN FINAL ACTIONS

The second notion I advanced in analysing human conduct in a manner designed to facilitate the construction of narrative continuity was that of a 'final' action. Here, however, the logic of that notion might seem to rest less easily with the spirit of our endeavour, since an action (or, indeed, activity), which is 'final' seems to lead nowhere 'next' – and where we cannot go on to identify some succeeding action as 'next' or 'subsequent', the structure of narrative breaks down. In short, a 'final' action is precisely not 'prior' to any further action or state of affairs. Now although I do not think this is a conclusion which can be resisted, let us nevertheless examine the logic of final actions more closely before assessing them as therefore incongruent with the rationale of narrative.

Returning to our seated man, let us suppose he gets out of the chair not in order to switch on the light but because he feels stiff. Getting up from the chair relieves his stiffness. He does not perform the action with a view to facilitating some further action or state of affairs (as in a practical action). Rather, his getting up *is* his relief from feeling stiff. In this example of a *final* action we therefore see it is undertaken not *in order to* create a different state of affairs, but immediately *as* the different state of affairs desired by the agent. The action *is* the desired change in circumstances rather than being undertaken in order to change circumstances.

Yet language often blurs this distinction, for we would normally find nothing incongruous in saying, 'he got up in order to relieve his stiffness'. To say this, however, is to imply that getting up and relieving his stiffness are two separate actions put into temporal succession by the agent, as in a sequence of cause and effect. But in fact, not only are the two circumstances contemporaneous (getting up and relief from stiffness), one might just as well go further by claiming there is only one circumstance involved, call it 'getting out of the chair', or 'relieving stiffness'.

It is this (Spinozist) point which is often distorted in ordinary speech, with the effect that human experience is presented as consequential upon circumstances, or caused by them, rather than being the mental counterpart in the individual *of* those very circumstances. In short, if the same logic is involved in saying, 'he got out of the chair in order to relieve his stiffness', as in saying, 'he got out of the chair in order to switch on the light', then this is tantamount to saying his getting out of the chair *was* his switching on the light, which is absurd. But there is nothing absurd in saying that his getting out of the chair *was* his relieving of stiffness; on the contrary, this is precisely the case. That is why I have defined final actions (and activities) as those undertaken for the sake of the experience accompanying them.

If, on the other hand, our seated man got out of the chair as a way of relieving stiffness, in order better to prepare himself for an imminent tennis match, then his action is a practical one, not performed for its own sake, but ordained to a future situation – and we have already seen how practical actions are accommodated by the narrative form.

Clearly, final actions cannot be accommodated in the same way since their rationale does not refer to any future, or 'subsequent', situation. However, on two counts this does not mean they therefore fall outside the scope of narrative treatment, rendering its logic unable in this instance to correlate with the way people behave. On the contrary, we should note that just as occurrences and events have endings, so do human actions and activities, such that people are capable of now doing something different without intending any relationship with what they were doing. Secondly we should note that, just as occurrences and events have *beginnings*, so also do human actions and activities. Narrative structure accommodates both these counts.

As to the first, I say that when an individual has performed a final action (or activity), this is a complete action which does not lead to any further related action or situation. Certainly it will be *succeeded* by some new action – indeed, its completeness precisely invites that – but whatever an individual goes on to do 'next' is not explicable in terms of what he has just done. That was done for its own sake, not in order to do something further. We must, in other words, leave room for stories to end and for new ones to begin. Not to do so would be to reduce human conduct to the monotone of a single, ceaseless undertaking, be it a never-achieved practical project or a permanently performed final activity. Neither alternative is remotely realistic; and thus we must recognise *discontinuity* in human conduct, know where it is likely to be found, and be prepared to present it as such.

For example, suppose someone plays a game of football for its own sake. At quite what point the game ends as an activity enjoyed by him is not as clear-cut as the final whistle. He may go on to enjoy the crowd's applause, and exchanging shirts with the other team. But at some point the game ends for him, and he does something which is no longer conventionally contiguous to the final whistle. (That is, as in Chapter Two's analytic model of narrative, we omit numerous actions when giving an account of an individual's conduct). Supposing he takes a shower, we are likely to say he now takes a shower because he has just been playing football, thereby imposing continuity in his conduct. This, however, is a fallacy. He takes a shower because he feels hot and dirty, not because he has just played football. Between feeling hot and dirty and taking a shower there is a genuine continuity intentionally established by the agent, but not between his finishing the game and taking a shower. He might equally have gone for a drink or attended a press interview.

People must, then, be understood as capable of now doing one thing and 'then' a different thing, without a real temporal relationship of 'this *then* that' between the two. Individuals can simply stop doing a thing, and 'then' do something else. To present this succession nevertheless as a genuine continuity is an error, for it suggests a changing identity where no such thing exists. In short, it is to invent a pseudo-action and is thus to impart a falsely grounded intelligibility to conduct, through supposed intentionality. Put formally, where there is no temporal relationship of 'prior' and 'subsequent', then all we are presented with is a *difference*, not a change. To suggest, for example, that our footballer has 'changed his activity' from playing football to taking a shower would be to relapse into that useless abstraction whereby 'activity' simply means everything someone does. Where someone *can* properly be said to 'change his activity' is where he deliberately alters the way he performs a concrete activity; for instance, where he *now* plays football *differently* from how he *was* playing it, because of an injury, the onset of rain, or whatever other reason *he* has. Here, we are confronted by a genuine change *in* his activity, only expressible through the narrative form. The case is different, however, where someone simply turns from doing one thing to doing something different.

This leads to the other side of the coin, for if actions and activities have endings, so they have beginnings. In our example the individual has finished playing football. It was an activity engaged in for its own sake, not directed towards any subsequent action or state of affairs. Whatever he did next was something new, or *different*. In this example the 'next' thing he did was take a shower, and I have argued it would be wrong to present this as an action intentionally subsequent to playing football. Rather, we presented his taking a shower as his response to feeling hot and dirty. But he could have made other equally intelligible responses. Further, his feeling hot and dirty is likely to be merely one amongst numerous features of his situation after the game, any of which he may have responded to. He has fans clamouring to see him, a manager ready to pay him.

What this points to is that, given the completion of a final action or activity, we cannot link what the individual did 'next' to what he just did. We have to accept discontinuity. However, this does not mean his 'next' actions are therefore unintelligible. Rather, we are obliged to deal with what he actually did (in this case, take a shower), and explore what it was in his situation to which his taking a shower was the most likely response.

It is in this way that we explain any 'new' action – not, then, with reference to a prior action with which we establish its continuity (as in practical actions, and tasks), but by accepting it as a *different* action which happened to occur in succession, but not in genuine continuity. We must therefore construe it as the agent's response to some aspect of his present context, and this involves familiarity with the diverse claims upon his attention, and with the complex of his personality, preferences, ambitions, principles, and habits. The more intimate such knowledge the more likely it is one can infer what has prompted this (new, different) course of action – in other words, present it as the individual's response to something in his situation, thereby making his action intelligible.

Now this may appear to ask a lot of the historian were it not that, in addressing himself to the individual's context 'here and now', what that individual has 'just' finished doing will nevertheless often be a relevant feature of it. In our example, the individual took a shower in response to feeling hot and dirty. He was hot and dirty because he had 'just' finished playing football. Thus, although we have already argued he did not take a shower because he had finished playing football, there is nevertheless a link between the two, such that it makes sense to employ the narrative grammar, 'he played football and then took a shower'. Here, we are brought back to Chapter Two's formula of elementary narrative structure whereby we present actions as conventionally contiguous. To an extent, then, we appear to have rescued continuity, and therefore the intelligibility afforded through the formula, 'he did this, *then* that'. However, there are two considerations which should prevent us from rashly concluding that therefore the fact of endings and beginnings in human conduct does *not* interfere with presenting a continuous narrative.

The first is to remind ourselves that, although the effect of an individual's 'previous' action is always part of his context here and now, it may be some entirely unrelated part of that context to which his 'next' action is a response, such that no continuity or contiguity pertains in his move from one action to another. A clear example is where, 'out of the blue', one suddenly remembers something one promised to do, and proceeds to do it. More commonplace is the unexpected phone call inviting one out, to which one responds positively. Respectively, that is, our footballer may not take a shower after the game, but ring his car-insurance firm, or accept a drink from an unexpected invitation. These examples are salutary because they impress upon us that individuals do indeed exhibit stops and starts in their actions, and that where we encounter such 'beginnings' and 'endings' we must understand the individual's 'new' action as a response to something in his present context rather than insist upon linking it to his previous action in order to preserve continuity.

The second consideration to dissuade us from the belief that continuity is always *in principle* to be found in human behaviour (implying a disbelief in 'beginnings' and 'endings'), is that, even where we appear to rescue continuity by presenting a 'next' action as an agent's response to something in his context which was caused by his 'previous' action, the continuity thereby restored is not a continuity in *conduct*. Rather, it is a continuity construed as an agent's response to something in his *present*, occasioned by his preceding (final) action or activity, such that his next action appears to follow on. But unlike a sequence of practical actions, where an agent does this in order to do that (this *then* that), thereby himself imposing a continuity in his conduct, in this case he intended no such continuity. In short, our footballer did not play football in order to take a shower, whereas he did put on his boots in order to play football. In the former case there is no continuity in his conduct whereas there is in the latter case.

DISCONTINUITY

If, then, discontinuity is a feature of human conduct, what are the implications for the construction of narrative? On the face of it they may appear daunting, since narrative could be seen as feeding on a constant search for continuity. However, the apparent contradiction disappears if we recognise the rationale of narrative is not to perceive and present 'continuity in general' (an abstraction), but rather to seek out real continuit*ies* – that is, occurrences, events, actions, and activities. The form of narrative is not obliged, after all, to make a further, overall continuity out of the discrete continuities it unravels (and neither does it in reality, either in fictional or factual narrative). To demand this would be to say that, having managed to extract, for example, a real occurrence, or an agent's engagement in an activity, from the kaleidoscopic world of happenings (through employing the concepts of change and continuity), one is then obliged on formal grounds to make it part of some 'larger' occurrence or of some more comprehensive activity, thereby depriving it of the very status one has just awarded it!

On the contrary, rather than approach the phenomenon of discontinuity as threatening frequent failures on the part of narrative form to accommodate reality, we should recognise the perception of endings and beginnings as precisely one of the achievements of narrative. The lesson this contains for the historian is straightforward enough – namely, that he recognise and deal with the fact that 'the history' of something is most unlikely to constitute a single line of continuity whereby a real story (that is, a single 'story-event'), can be told. This applies even in the case of an individual's conduct. Rather, wherever final actions and activities are identified, discontinuities necessarily punctuate that particular flow which is extracted from the general flood of affairs.

EVENTS

In addressing the problems faced by the practising narrative historian vis-à-vis the construction and presentation of continuity, I have so far in this chapter concentrated upon the conduct of individual agents. As I argued at its beginning, the demand that narrative be centred on a changing identity generates the further demand that one therefore deal ultimately with a human being's intentional conduct. Since individual conduct lies at the heart of history, I have suggested a way of looking at it which might assist in making sense of it in narrative terms.

But the historian, of course, is not exclusively a biographer. His topic is not the conduct of a single individual, but *events* such as wars, revolutions, migrations, discoveries, reforms, and debates, which involve the conduct of *numerous* individuals.

In Chapter Two I called events 'story-objects', or 'historical identities', and offered a formal analysis of their nature and logical status. Further, I argued that the apprehension and presentation of this class of phenomena was the peculiar and praiseworthy province of the historian, whereby in addition to explaining human conduct in narrative terms he also explicates the nature of events through construing them as real continuities in an otherwise undifferentiated complex of successive occurrences. What is required here, in addressing the actual practice of the historian, is that we explore the implications of those general analytic principles of 'events' with a view to identifying potential problems and suggesting ways of dealing with them.

SELECTION

The first implication of this overall analytic derives precisely from the fact that the historian does indeed examine more than the conduct of single individuals. Instead, his narrative involves the genuine interplay (rather than meaningless juxtapositions) of individuals with each other and with a multiplicity of phenomena such as groups, parties, institutions, and ideas. The question arises as to how, confronted by such a multi-faceted world, the historian achieves coherent narrative?

The obvious first point is that historians do not jump feet-first into the general mêlée of 'all occurrences' in the hope of making some sense of them. Rather, their attention is drawn to a recognised area of interest (for example, politics, art, warfare, science, religion), and within that area, to important developments – and further, regarding those developments, to their genesis, progress, and results. And this is to say that the subject-matter historians approach is already significantly selected out from the kaleidoscopic world of occurrences even before they locate their precise topics.

However, it is not mere tradition, or preference, that lie behind this 'selecting-out', facilitating the discrimination of complex, multi-faceted stories, but the (perhaps insufficiently understood) fact that there is a rationale or logic underlying historians' practice which necessitates that occurrences are indeed manageable in narrative terms. In theory, one could *chronicle* every occurrence over a period of time; but one could surely not treat of them in the narrative form, and what this points to is that only certain aspects of 'what happened' can be treated through narrative. Now, some may argue this is to impose restrictions from a merely literary form (narrative) upon what historians can deal with. However, it is truer to argue that aspects of occurrences do congeal into narrative structures whether one likes it or not, and can thus only be explicated via the narrative form. In fact both outlooks are different sides of the same coin; if there is something in people which makes them approach affairs narratively, there is equally something in 'affairs' which prompts people to connect them up into 'stories' and 'events'.

The lessons of this might appear clear for the historian, for as a *narrative* historian he must deal with phenomena which properly constitute *events*, and as a narrative *historian* he must of course avoid fiction. However, it is in guarding both these requirements that he must ensure he is dealing with sequences which really do constitute events rather than pseudo-events, and this merits clarification.

Firstly, we have earlier argued that events construed as involving agents other than individual human beings (for instance, spirits, corporate bodies, and abstractions), are not real events since the connectives which otherwise only real human beings insert into affairs, through their responsive and purposive conduct, cannot be real. These cases, then, do not represent merely a species of fiction – they represent a species of fantasy.

A second kind of pseudo-event is that where occurrences are wrongly juxtaposed into continuums, thereby trying to extract a continuity in affairs which is simply not there. This indeed would be a case of the narrative historian *imposing* an unwarranted form on his subject-matter, and because I believe it is in this territory that historians do encounter challenges, it is helpful to elaborate the point.

Mindful of Chapter Two's formal analysis, let us take an analogy from the spatial world. For example, a lily may simply appear in a garden; no one intended it should be there. As such, its position has no meaning or significance. The case is different with this rose-tree because the gardener has deliberately positioned it near the window, so that it can be seen from the lounge. There is, then, a real relationship between the location of the rose-tree and the lounge, but not between the rose-tree and the lily. And we may go on to suppose the gardener relates where he directs a crazy-paving path to where he has positioned the rose-tree – and likewise with other items, such that we can say the location of numerous features in the garden is related to the location of not just one but of many other things, in a more or less complex web of spatial interrelationships. But this does not apply to *every* plant or blade of grass in the garden – that is, the position of many things are devoid of 'meaning', 'significance', or 'relevance'. In short, they are not real spatial relationships but merely abstract spatial juxtapositionings.

Now, if it makes sense to talk of spatial relationships in these terms, so it does to talk of *temporal* relationships. Here, we are dealing not with the location of objects in the spatial world, and the relationships between their locations, but with the temporality of occurrences in the temporal world, and the relationships between their temporality. By analogy, in any period of time (akin to any area of space), a myriad of occurrences happen, only some of which bear a temporal relationship of 'this *then* that' to each other. The remainder comprise the abstract formalism ('meaninglessness', or 'irrelevance'), of mere chronicle.

What can usefully be observed from this analogy is that the general area of affairs is already known. In our spatial analogy we already know we are dealing with a garden. Therefore we expect certain determinate, intended spatial relationships between at least some of the numerous objects in that conventional space. Its being a garden already selects out an intelligible and manageable area of space.

The same discrimination is generally operating in the historian, albeit probably instinctively, when he works within a conventionally recognised area of interest. It may be political or maritime history, or the history of science. Whichever, it is akin to a garden in our spatial analogy, for rather than being confronted by a random torrent of all occurrences within a given time period in the blind hope of stumbling upon meaningful temporal relationships between them, the historian has selected out an aspect of occurrences where he can expect to find genuinely related temporalities – that is, what might normally be called a 'subject-area', or 'branch of history'. Further, within that area, which nonetheless houses a vast edifice, his attention focuses upon those parts which can be regarded as the principal pillars of its architecture – for example, on the make-up of governments, legislation, revolutions, wars, and organs of public opinion, in the subject-area of political history.

This can be seen as evidencing the intuition that amidst the kaleidoscopic confusion of all that happens even within a chosen subject-area, some occurrences are more important than others. Why? Because where occurrences take place amongst the principal pillars of an edifice, the more likely it is we will locate the sources of the dynamic of intelligible, explicable change. And we must remind ourselves of the truism that if nothing changes, there is no history to tell. So, finally, we find the historians narrowing their attention down to those occurrences which relate to charting the origins, development, and results of important changes in the overall landscape.

Now, although this 'selecting out', or 'narrowing down', process is likely to be construed in terms of historians' instinct for the significant rather than trivial in history, we can equally construe that the *effect* of this discriminatory process is to make it very likely they will locate contexts of occurrences where meaningful sequences (that is, genuinely related temporalities), are to be found. Let us again recall that where they are not to be found, no narrative is possible. It might, then, be regarded as a piece of good fortune, akin to 'the cunning of Reason', that most historians' instincts motivate them, through a concern for 'historical significance', towards the very contexts of occurrences which enable them to carry out their craft in the first place.

However, a more down-to-earth assessment is that historians have

111

found the above way of delineating their focus of interest to work reliably in practice, such that recognisable branches of the discipline have emerged within the general study of history. In short, people have successfully studied, for example, political history (that is, it has endured as a viable branch of historical studies), because it *is* possible to establish genuine historical continuities and identities within that context. People know there are stories there, and where they are likely to be found.

'BRANCHES' OF HISTORY

Reassuring as the above observations may be, there is nevertheless still room for some disquiet over the topic of subject-areas, or 'branches', within history, for although we have noted the often happy correlation between historians' instincts and the suitability of discriminated contexts for historical treatment, this is not automatically the case. Real challenges and substantial problems do confront the practising historian from this direction, particularly those associated with attempts to introduce *new* branches of the discipline, for example, social history or women's history. What underlies the unease amongst some 'conventional' historians about the emergence of these new branches of the study of history does not reflect upon their importance, relevance, or significance, but rather upon a concern for how amenable they are to a specifically *historical* treatment. That these concerns have been variously felt and expressed is, then, intimative of deeper intuitions regarding the logic of historical work, such that it is as well to bring the matter to deliberate analysis.

Let us take the example of 'social history'. Does it mean, 'the history of society', or 'the history of societies'? Whichever, it does appear to select out occurrences in '*society*' for special scrutiny, and therefore, within that area, the crucial pillars of its architecture at any given time; and further, the charting of the origins, development, and results of important changes amongst those determining pillars. The problem here lies in the *initial* selecting out of such a thing as 'society' from the general pandemonium of affairs, presumably inviting an awareness of *social* conduct and occurrences rather than, for example, political, scientific, or artistic ones.

But is there a clear, sufficiently workable idea of what a 'society' is to accommodate an identification of what constitute its principal pillars?[14] Social historians have variously treated of such topics as the family, leisure, domestic contexts, sexuality, class structures, religious affiliations, income levels, and sport.[15] If I have an interest in the changing pattern of drug addiction, for example, I may present my studies as contributing to 'social history', thereby lending them an added significance lacking if left as 'an historical study of drug addiction'. Whether such studies are accepted as an integral part of 'social history', and thus contribute to a larger forum of related stories which all interweave so as to add to our understanding of either this society or societies in general, remains problematic, however.

This is because despite, or perhaps owing to, the reflections of sociologists,[16] 'society' is not at present a sufficiently parametered subject-area to safely invite those further processes of discrimination necessary to provide the historian with reliable grist for his mill. How successfully, for example, will he be able to link up into real continuities what is going on in the world of drug addiction with sexual practices? What, if any, are the real continuities between leisure activities and church attendance? Indeed, how can we be sure it is to this, or even a, *social* aspect of his existence which an individual is responding in his religious or leisure-oriented conduct? And thus how, in short, can we be sure we are not inventing 'pseudo-events', whereby what are mere unintended juxtapositions of discrete occurrences are converted into allegedly meaningful (that is, genuinely related), occurrences?

The answer to these questions is not, however, to be found *a priori*. Thought, after all, does not determine reality, either to convince us that social history is possible or impossible. Instead, we have to wait and see where the practitioners of a new branch of a discipline such as social history take us before we assess its validity, rather than pontificate in advance as methodologists. In other words, the projects of, for example, social history and womens' history will be more or less convincing as their practitioners are more or less successful in establishing genuine and recurrent continuities of occurrences across the (sometimes alarming) breadth of otherwise discrete topics they deal with. However, there is at least one lesson to be taken from the realm of methodology; namely, that historians hoping to establish new branches of their discipline (or alternatively, subjects such as Black studies which might wish to *become* historical), give thought to whether their initial discrimination of a subject-area holds out the hope of finding genuine narrative continuities and identities. Will the subject-area permit of a treatment which supersedes merely 'descriptive' and 'analytic' history, such that in studying it one can enter the rarefied atmosphere of narrative history? Or is the subject-area such that it invites the presentation of slap-happy juxtapositionings of occurrences as if they constitute real phenomena, that is, real continuities and events? (Established subject-areas, of course, are not free from this vice).

Clearly, social historians are one group who believe their practice viable, and one might suggest that if they can succeed in discovering and presenting genuinely coherent stories which are evidently emanating from, of significance to, and *specific* to, something we now loosely call 'society', then whatever the parameters and content of that concept of 'society' implied by *their* work, it will be in a class of its own compared to the various concepts of 'society' and 'the social' produced by theoreticians.[17]

THE 'RELEVANT'

A further aspect of Chapter Two's analytic regarding 'events' which has implications for the historian follows from the preceding argument. We examined how historians find their initial bearings amongst (otherwise) undifferentiated complexes of successive occurrences, both in terms of their own motivations and of the covert rationale which colludes to promise success. Given he *is* on safe bearings, however, how does the historian know what to include in his narrative? This is to ask, how does he choose what is *relevant*? This issue so frequently bedevils students' essays and examination answers that one suspects they are more often in doubt as to what they are supposed to do rather than dull, or ignorant of the requisite facts. Professional historians, on the other hand, do not as a rule find the issue a problem in their work. In addition to the experience they bring to it, they are more likely in their own research and writings to be addressing specific questions of limited scope rather than constructing large overall historical accounts of block-buster proportions. In this latter task, such are the problems of selectivity that even the professional historian finds the issue of relevance daunting.

But this aside, if professional historians do not ordinarily find the issue a problem in their own work, this does not mean it is not a problem for them as teachers. How easy it is to identify where a student's essay goes off the point! The blue pencil is applied with confident instinct to the offending passages. But how difficult it is to instruct a student in what it is he is supposed to do when, surrounded by copious notes, he is unsure what he is expected to produce from them! Often, that is, students know the answer to a question, but do not know *how* to answer it, particularly regarding what to include and omit – and it is difficult to offer instruction on this without a more explicit grasp of the issue of 'relevance'.

In Chapter Two we claimed it is possible to tell a factual story 'for its own sake' as distinct from angling its content towards, for instance, raising or answering a particular question, persuading the reader of a moral view, or amusing him. This involves moving through a sequence of occurrences until we reach one which is not conventionally contiguous to point '*a*' (our starting-point), for example, point '*k*'. Thus, although it would not make sense to say '*a*' occurred and then '*k*', it would make sense to begin at '*a*', omit intervening occurrences up to '*j*', and thus present the sequence, '*a*' then '*j*' then '*k*', treating '*k*' as another starting-point.

In the abstract this basic model thus demonstrates what to exclude from an account, and what to include. Before seeing how this helps us understand 'relevance' in concrete terms, let us also recall the claim later in Chapter Two; namely, that in addition to explaining 'why *x* occurred', one of narrative's achievements is to articulate or explicate 'story-objects' – that is, *events* such as journeys, wars, divorces, evenings out, and boxing matches. By putting these two arguments together we can derive some concrete implications for the issue of 'relevance' in historical (that is, factual, message-free narrative) accounts.

Journeys, wars, divorces, boxing matches, and other 'events' have beginnings, endings, and a content of (genuinely) temporally related occurrences sandwiched in between (otherwise they would remain as single occurrences). By 'giving an account of' such events it is difficult to see what this means other than a narrative account, and therefore one necessarily in terms of 'this happened, *then* that', and so on. However, we cannot and do not chronicle every single occurrence which is conventionally contiguous within the parameters provided by the beginning and ending of an event. Rather, if we are objective, message-free reporters, we exploit the basic model referred to above ('*a*' to '*j*' to '*k*').

Thus, for example, if it is a journey we are giving an account of, some things can be taken for granted and thus omitted, whilst others are unique to that journey or at least require explanation. Now there are no journeys which can simply be denoted as such. At a minimum one wants to know who made the journey, from where, to where, by what means, and for what reason. Beyond this, if everything went smoothly according to conventional expectations, there is no more to be said about the event. In theory the same may be said of a war; having established who the contenders were, and assuming its outcome to be predictable, there is little more to be said in giving an account of it. Like Chapter Two's example of an examination, 'it was a typical war, that's all'.

In reality, however, many events cannot be dismissed as 'obvious'. Particular things occur as part of them which, if not surprising, at least require explanation since their occurrence is not obvious. In short, given we are offering, for example, an account of Mr Brown's journey by car from Detroit to Chicago, it is unlikely we can find nothing more to say about it because it turned out to be so 'paradigmatic'. Even those events which are conventionally, and strongly, parametered, are nevertheless not paradigmatic in their content. Indeed, if they *were* there would be no need for narrative. Thus, for example, even if the details of Mr Brown's journey are obvious to him, not all of them will be to the observer. Why, for example, did he take that route? Or regarding our student's assessment that 'it was an examination just like any other', we still want to know which questions he chose and why.

These observations should lead us to recognise that what we are in fact involved with here is the logic of *description*. In Chapter One we distinguished between defining and describing a thing by arguing that the definition of a thing involves saying what the word denoting it essentially means, whereas its description involves saying what is particular about it. Also, for the purposes of subsequent argument I claimed one describes an object, but narrates an event. Now, however, we see that to narrate an event within the above guidelines is analogous to describing an object for the sake of describing it. For example, in describing this post-box we omit that it is cylindrical, red, and has a slot for posting letters into. Instead our description will focus on those inessential features which, without being exhaustive, render it particular. In describing it we are pointing to what is not to be taken for granted; in short, we select those features relevant to identifying *this* particular post-box.

Similarly, then, in narrating an event (such as a journey or war) within the guidelines, '*a*' then '*j*' then '*k*', the logic of such narrative is, in effect, descriptive. We do not include every single occurrence, nor the obviously essential. Rather, we omit trivial and obvious occurrences by moving forward in our selection of 'what happened next' to that occurrence which is not conventionally contiguous to where we are at the moment. We thereby rescue intelligibility by tracing back a step in the sequence, thus restoring continuity. This directs attention to what is particular about *this* event, which is to *describe* it; and what I am proposing is that to narrate an event in this manner is, in fact, to nullify the problem of 'relevance', because all one includes will be relevant, and all that is relevant will be included.

In short, the concept of 'relevance' in telling a story is not some mysterious extra category which has to be applied in the business of selection – rather, it is swallowed up in the rationale of what it is to 'describe' an event. Thus, for example, in giving a (narrative) account of last night's boxing match, we present it as having a beginning, middle, and end. Unless we have some exterior purpose in constructing our account, those occurrences we choose to include as constituting the 'middle' will be solely those which gave that boxing match its particularity. Those are the 'relevant' occurrences.

THE 'SIGNIFICANT'

These same arguments also assist in clarifying the notion of the 'significant' as it relates to the construction of historical accounts. Here, we appear to be confronted by another category involved in discriminating what to include and exclude in accounts of complex events – and on the face of it, the selection of what is 'significant' not only commands greater importance than applying the criterion of 'relevance' but also invites greater subjectivity on behalf of the observer. What is it which makes this or that occurrence a *significant* part of an event?

We proposed 'last night's boxing match' as an example of a complex event involving many individuals and implicating a variety of objects, institutions, practices, and ideas. We have already seen how to narrate such an event in terms of what to select and omit from amongst this complex mixture. Now, little imagination is needed to recognise that such an account will differ from a running commentary on the event, for the running commentator will point out many things which simply happen to capture his attention, some because they are unusual, some because awaited, some to fill in a gap in the proceedings, and some because he believes they will influence the result of the contest. In other words, although he is dealing with a parametered event, his approach to selecting what to recount will be a mixture of arbitrary description and momentary prediction. Because the event is ongoing he cannot discriminate between all that is happening with a view to offering a controlled narrative account, setting out the event as a coherent continuity of occurrences (neither, of course, is he attempting to).

Rather, he can only guess at what will, after the event, turn out to be relevant for an account of it. The historian, on the other hand, *has* to have the wisdom of hindsight to permit of such a discriminatory process. (This is why, if meant literally, 'contemporary history' is impossible – if, that is, for the discipline of *history*, the Owl of Minerva does indeed only take flight at dusk, this is for rather more precise, albeit prosaic, reasons than underly Hegel's famous dictum.)

After the event, then, the historian can apply those elementary principles outlined earlier to select what to include and exclude – and this, as I have argued, is to discriminate what is relevant to (that is, descriptive of), the event. But suppose we were asked to decide which occurrences should be included in our account of the boxing match because they were *significant*?

If by 'significant' we mean that which is important, or especially note-worthy, it is difficult to see how they may differ from, or be additional to, those already selected for their relevance. That is, so long as we are not referring to events subsequent to the boxing match, the notion of 'significance' appears to coincide with that of 'relevance'. Only those occurrences which *made* this boxing match into this boxing match bore any importance or 'significance'.

If this is correct, there appears to be no difference between the relevant and the significant when we come to select what to include in our construc-tion of an intelligible continuity of occurrences. Left at that, the logic or rationale of the 'significant' appears to coincide with that of the 'relevant'.

Now this is clearly an unsatisfactory conclusion, for although difficult to evade in the above terms, it would render the notion of 'significance' redundant, and thereby remove a way of talking about events which historians are familiar with.

The key to unlocking such a paradoxical outcome lies in the terms in which the above problematic are set out. As given, we cannot distinguish between the relevant and the significant in the account of the boxing match; but this is only because the terms are too restrictive. Indeed, asked to construct a narrative account of last night's contest 'for the sake of it', it would be truer to say it is not possible to select *anything* for its significance. If the only event in question is the boxing match then there is no basis for singling out certain of its occurrences for their significance to it. What this points to is that something which occurs in an event is only *significant* in the light of some *other* event or story.

For example, suppose one of the numerous occurrences at last night's contest was the arrival of a promoter, and he was impressed by one of the boxers' performances. Let us further suppose that at some later date he therefore offers the boxer a prestigious match which subsequently proves his successful debut on the big scene. Now, if we were to construct an account of that boxer's career we would include the promoter's attendance at last night's contest on the (already explained) grounds of relevance; but further, we would also say that of the numerous occurrences at last night's fight, that which was of *significance* for our account of the boxer's career was the promoter's attendance.

Viewed in this light it follows that none of the occurrences constituting the boxing match are significant in themselves, whereas any one of them may be significant depending upon a number of *other* events or stories in which they play a *relevant* part. Mrs Brown, for example, shouted so much at the fight that she was hoarse the following day, too embarrassed to attend an important job interview. The stadium's manager made a large enough profit from the boxing match to permit him to expand his business. In short, there were many occurrences at last night's contest which might constitute *relevant* episodes in *other* events or stories. Just, then, as a complex argument is multi-directional in its implications, so is an event multi-faceted in its significance, depending respectively on which further line of argument one is interested in or which other events have one's attention.

Thus we arrive at the formula that 'the significant' is that within one event which is 'relevant' in another – and three observations are worth making from this. Firstly, a grasp of the notion of 'significance' depends on a prior understanding of the notion of 'relevance'. For example, our boxer's fight last night was of course part of the sequence of occurrences which make up his career; but the only aspects of that event *relevant* to his career, and therefore needful of inclusion in a narrative account of it along our model lines, were his performance and the promoter's attendance. Thus, what renders the promoter's attendance 'significant' is that it is 'relevant' to the story of our boxer's career. Were it not relevant to this latter story it would not be singled out as a significant occurrence in that other story, namely, the account of last night's boxing match.

A second observation follows – namely, that an account of an event in terms of what is relevant in it by no means automatically includes occurrences which may be relevant in *other* events and stories, and which may therefore be significant. For instance, our model account of last night's contest might well have ignored the promoter's attendance, Mrs Brown's enthusiastic shouting, and the profitable takings of the stadium's manager. Thus, to unlock and defeat our earlier paradox, the 'relevant' and the 'significant', far from being indistinguishable, become markedly different criteria. And yet, as we have seen, they are not entirely separate, since nothing is significant in one context which is not relevant in another – and this is not a reversible proposition, since 'the significant' depends upon 'the relevant', but not vice versa.

The third observation is this; the identification of what is significant within an event is not a subjective matter, if by 'subjective' we mean to refer to historians' prejudices or opinions. It is, however, an arbitrary matter, because it depends (in our example) upon whether our historian happens to be interested in giving an account of the boxer's, Mrs Brown's, or the stadium manager's career. That is a question unamenable to logical determination. But the more important point is that, given an interest in the boxer's career, then the inclusion of the promoter's attendance in his account is not whimsical, subjective, or opinionated; rather, it is objectively required via the criterion of relevance. Thus, to pinpoint the promoter's attendance as a *significant* occurrence within last night's contest (and thus to include it in his narrative account of the boxer's career), is to select 'the significant' along objective lines. It is the logic underlying what the historian is doing, rather than any personal bias, which determines his designation of this or that occurrence as significant. His 'personal bias' is only involved in the sense that what he designates as significant within one event depends upon what other event or story he 'happens' to be interested in.

Of course, there are some events conventionally regarded as universally worthy of interest. So great was their impact (for example, the Holocaust), that they command a significance of rock-like, unarguable permanence. Compared to these the significance awarded to other occurrences seems a more subjective matter – that is, a matter of judgement, if not of mere opinion. But we can see this is an illusion. An occurrence is either significant or not, in quite objective terms, depending upon what other story or event one is considering. In short, if I am interested in the history of modern British architecture, or of Welsh nationalism, Hitler's assumption of power has no significance, whereas other parts of the story of German political development in the 1930s might possibly be significant in the light of one or other of these interests.

HISTORICAL REAPPRAISALS AND RE-INTERPRETATIONS

In summary of the relationship between 'relevance' and 'significance', we have seen that every story has its relevant components, only discriminated after the story has ended (supposing it to be a familiarly parametered event such as a boxing match). If we have to wait until the end of an event to discriminate what is relevant in it – that is, put simply, it is not possible to 'describe' an event until it is over – we likewise have to wait until *other* events or stories are over before we can discriminate what is *significant* in the former event. This is because until we know what is *relevant* in other stories we cannot say whether occurrences in the former event play a relevant part in them, thereby lending these occurrences a *significance*.

Thus, if one has to await the ending of an event to be able to discern what would be relevant in an account of it, one will generally have to wait even longer to discriminate what is significant in it, because one has to await the conclusion of other, generally subsequent, events in order to see what is relevant in an account of *them*. This is why certain aspects of past events, already known, can nevertheless acquire a significance never recognised before. This does not of itself imply the need for any re-interpretation of events, but it does involve their reappraisal – namely, a fresh look at the significance of past events afforded by necessarily changing perspectives as succeeding events unfold. But also, of course, this possibility of new insights into old events invites enquiry into previously untouched aspects of them because, as already noted, an account of an event may have excluded from its selection of relevant occurrences something which turns out to be significant. It is in this way that hitherto unknown or ignored features of the past are opened up to scrutiny, offering the prospects, not merely of a reappraisal of events, but of actual re-interpretations (reconstructions), of them.

Such an impetus to enquire where no one has before can originate from either end of the spectrum. For instance, it might be it was only because our boxer became world champion that earlier episodes in his career are now looked at in greater detail, uncovering the previously unmentioned (or possibly unknown) fact of the promoter's attendance at 'last night's boxing match'. Alternatively, someone might just happen on this hitherto unrecorded occurrence whilst researching the boxing match because dissatisfied with existing accounts, and, aware of the boxer's subsequent career, recognise its significance. Either way, it is this dialectic between 'the significant' and 'the relevant' which, in relating otherwise separate events or stories to each other, generates both reappraisals and reconstructions. As such, we may describe it as the motor of fresh historical interpretations and knowledge, although it is of course the historian who is the driver – and it can be seen he will be all the better at exploiting this motor the more adequately he fuels it with two ingredients implied by the foregoing analysis.

Firstly, he needs to be well-read over his subject-area, and hopefully within closely related ones, such that in being knowledgeable over a wide compass (that is, knowing a great many stories within his branch of

history), he is in the right position to discern hitherto unnoticed signifi-
cances, offering him the possibility of reappraisals and even re-interpretations. Secondly, he needs to be disposed to enquire 'for its own sake'
into the details of events, such that he goes beyond existing accounts; we
may call this the capacity to browse at length, or simply insatiable curiosity. Whichever, it is a trait which, if combined with the former qualification, greatly enhances the prospect of coming across and recognising
the relevance of data previously ignored. These arguments, then, suggest
that what the good historian is favoured with is, amongst other things,
an impressively 'general' knowledge within his area plus a disposition to
collect and cherish particular detailed information which might appear,
and remain, both irrelevant and insignificant.

NON-PARAMETERED 'EVENTS'

In this exploration of the implications of Chapter Two's analysis for the
practising historian, our discussion has so far not moved beyond 'events'
which have conventionally parametered beginnings, middles, and endings.
In this connection we have discussed the extraction of such events from
the teeming chaos of occurrences, the concept of 'relevance' in selecting
which occurrences to include and exclude in constructing a (narrative)
account of an event, and how the notion of 'the significant' relates one
event to another. But as noted in Chapter Two, not all 'events' or narrative
identities are so clearly parametered that they can be subsumed within the
class of this or that 'event-noun' (such as 'wars', 'discoveries', or 'boxing
matches'). This is particularly the case where, as often, the historian is
endeavouring to answer a specific question rather than write the story of
a given event. In this latter case, where he may for instance be preparing
the story of the 1917 Russian Revolution, it is true he will be re-writing
the story in order (in his view) to present it more adequately than it has
been before. But we can assume that unless he adopts a most radical
approach the parameters of the event remain as before, whilst it is what
is sandwiched within them that he is revising.

Where, on the other hand, he is answering a specific question, more
often than not regarding either the origins or consequences of an event,
then the boundaries to the story he has to tell are not so obviously
parametered. For example, if he is addressing a question regarding the
origins of the 1917 Revolution (for instance, 'what were its causes?'), then
only the *ending* of his story is fixed – namely, the outbreak of revolution.
His task is to render this occurrence intelligible through constructing a
narrative account of a preceding (genuine) continuity of occurrences which
culminates, or 'eventuates', in the 1917 Revolution.

The familiar difficulty here is, where does one begin? – that is, how
far back does one go in retracing the sequence of occurrences which

culminated in 1917? And if we do not have a recognised beginning to our story, it is difficult to see what would constitute its middle as we attempt to construct a controlled narrative, selecting content via our criterion of relevance. In short, we seem not to have 'a story', but rather a threatening chronicle stretching back arbitrarily in time. To the extent this *is* the case, and mindful that historians do indeed devote much and frequent attention to the origins of affairs, then it would appear the proper logic and integrity of the narrative treatment is denied them. This would be a startling misfortune for it would imply, in effect, that it is not possible (in our terms) to deal 'historically' with the origins of things!

BEGINNINGS

We will best find the solution to this apparent dilemma by reminding ourselves what ordinary stories are actually like. The archetypal fairy-story begins, 'Once upon a time there was a little girl called Red Riding Hood who had a grandmother who lived alone in the woods . . .'. Arbitrary as 'once upon a time' appears to be, it is nothing of the kind. The story does not begin with the birth of Little Red Riding Hood, nor her mother's, nor her grandmother's. Neither does it begin where the wolf has consumed the grandmother. Rather, its point of departure is precise – it is that point 'immediately' preceding the first in that sequence of occurrences which lead up to the final denouement. It is not necessary to go back further in time because any prior occurrences are by definition irrelevant to *this* story. If, on the other hand, one began half-way through the story, the occurrences would not follow on from each other in conventional terms and would therefore lack intelligibility.

Thus it is that the story begins by setting that scene of 'normality' which one assumes would either have persisted, or changed in some way other than it does in *this* story, but for the first occurrence we encounter in it. This 'first' occurrence does not have to be especially unusual or unexpected so long as it represents that particular departure from the previous normality which leads into the 'next' occurrence in that line of continuity leading to the denouement. The principal point to notice is that, unlike in a 'running commentary', it is the prior knowledge of the denouement which determines, for the author, *where* he begins his story and *what* he selects as its 'middle' content. Unlike, then, our elementary '*a* to *y* minus 1' narrative model which applies when determining what to say happened 'next' when looking forward in time, a different principle seems to be involved here, for we are tracing a line of continuity *back* in time.

However, there is no need to abandon altogether our elementary model; rather, those same principles which select and 'glue together' occurrences into economically intelligible sequences still apply, but in reverse. The apparent difference is that both the starting and ending-points of our *elementary* model (going forward), seem arbitrary, whereas when answering a specific question about origins not only the ending but also the beginning of the sequence is prescribed, the latter didactically, the former by implication. This is to say that our task in answering a specific question about the origins of a situation or event is to isolate that (genuine) continuity of occurrences which led to it. The ending of the story is given. But its starting-point is also, in principle, determinate (albeit a matter of judgement) – and once *given* this starting-point, our elementary model applies.

What this teaches is that if, when looking backwards, it is the specificity of the *ending* of the story which determines both its beginning point and middle, there is likewise, despite appearances, a specificity to the *starting-point* of any story which looks 'blindly' forward via the '*a* to *y* minus 1' formula. To be succinct, what lay hidden in this formula was that it very much matters what the '*a*' point is, from which we go forward to derive the 'next' occurrence.

To clarify these arguments, and move from archetypal fictional to mundane factual stories, suppose my son arrives home late at night, soaking wet and penniless. I ask him how this has come about. I am impatient with any sociological, psychological, meteorological, or economic 'causes'; I want to know what happened to bring him home late, wet, and penniless. His story (that is, his explanation), does not begin with his getting up that morning, nor with he and a friend being accosted by a gang outside a night-club he had never been to before. Rather, aware he is explaining the eventuality to me, and thus assuming what I would regard as normal circumstances and behaviour, his narrative begins with his lounging around at home after dinner. 'Then' (or 'next'), his friend rang to say his elder brother had unexpectedly turned up, and had invited them out to the aforementioned night-club. Having agreed to this, the painful story unfolds, and can be left to readers' imaginations. But supposing my son, as most people, to have an instinctive grasp of what is relevant in a flow of occurrences, I understand why he came home late, wet, and penniless.

His mother, however, has a different question to ask – namely, 'why isn't your sister with you, since she accompanied you this evening?' To answer this he has to tell a different story, which can again be left to the imagination. It may or may not begin at the same point, and parts of its middle may coincide with his other story – but it will be a different story culminating, for instance, in her remaining on at the night-club because she was promised a lift home later.

'INTERPRETATION' AND ALTERNATIVE ACCOUNTS

Such realistic examples of the rationale of narratives which answer specific questions reveal, then, that where they concern *why* a particular state of affairs pertained (that is, where they relate to the origins of a situation), there are recognisable, rational parameters which render practicable the proper telling of 'a story'. Its coherence and accuracy depend upon the perception, judgement, impartiality, and veracity of the teller (and in the historian's, unlike the participant's, case, its details have to be inferred from evidence) – but it *is* there, to be told. As is clear from the preceding arguments, 'it' is far from being merely a matter of 'interpretation', if this implies that (within some ill-defined, yet 'sensible' limits) all accounts of the same eventuality are necessarily subjective, albeit equally valid! What confusion! Presumably one then proceeds to accept this rather than that account on equally subjective grounds – and then it is up to others, again on equally subjective grounds, whether they approve of one's selection, and so on *ad infinitum*. What happens to 'truth' amidst all of this?

The retort to such confusion should surely be that one's answers to a question (for example, '1+1=?'), are one's own, rather than borrowed from someone else out of laziness or cowed respect. In this sense they are one's own 'opinion' or 'interpretation' (rather than someone else's). But this says nothing about their veracity – certainly, it does not imply they are therefore invalid. In short, the truth has to be 'interpreted', and by someone. Were one a concerned parent, a policeman investigating a crime, a general deliberating upon military action, or an historian offering an account, one would check respectively relevant stories related to one both in terms of their factual accuracy and of whether they not only make sense of what had transpired, but the best sense. The supposition governing such caution is not only that some accounts are better than others, but, because such judgements *can* be made, they inevitably (or logically) point to the viability of that ultimate standard – namely, the correct or true account.

The only qualification necessary to this embarrassingly forthright concept is that already pointed out in both Chapters One and Two – namely, that whether *x* did or did not occur is not (theoretically) open to dispute; (for example, the emperor Nero either did or did not fiddle while Rome burned). But whether this needs to be included in the 'true' account of an ordained (that is, question-determined), story is a matter which is culture bound. It depends on the reader's understanding of what is, and is not, conventionally contiguous in sequences of occurrences. In the absence of a correlation between teller and listener regarding 'how the world works', or how people behave, the likelihood of the story told being accepted as correct is in jeopardy (even assuming the facts therein as indisputable). And to the extent that 'correct' equals 'true', there is a sense in which the truth of *any* account is culture-bound, as competent foreign ambassadors know.[18]

A further point clarified by the foregoing examples is that, where one constructs a narrative answer to a question regarding the origins or 'causes' of a situation, there are many different stories to be told depending upon the exact question asked. The more precise the question the easier to locate the implicit beginning of the required story. This is why general questions such as, 'what caused the 1917 Russian Revolution?' or 'why have you come home like this?' are more difficult to answer through narrative. 'How far was the 1917 Russian Revolution a consequence of the failings of tsarism?' or 'why have you come home in such a dishevelled state?' immediately narrow down the range of occurrences under consideration and point more clearly at the implicit beginning of the requisite story.

Likewise this is why singular questions are easier to answer. In our example the father asks the son why he has arrived home late, wet, and penniless, whereas the mother asks why his sister is not with him. There may be two distinct stories to be told here, and yet he may have been asked why he arrived home late, wet, penniless, *and* without his sister. At most he can intertwine the two stories (if they *do* intertwine) by pointing out what is significant in the one story because relevant in the other, and vice versa – a technique employed at structural points in fiction in order to obviate too frequent a resort to 'coincidence'.

Taken together, then, these considerations show that where the historian is answering a question regarding the origins of a situation, he is not threatened with a chronicle stretching back arbitrarily in time; rather, there is a genuine narrative to be told which, as such, has a beginning, middle, and end. Neither, we have claimed, is the selection and content of the story merely 'a matter of interpretation', although the more general and multi-faceted the actual terms of the question the more likely his treatment will appear subjective, or even akin to an arbitrary collection of different stories which he occasionally relates to each other by suggesting what is significant in one for its relevance in another. But it is not unlikely that some ill-defined muddle might ensue, whose lack of overall rationale invites the false notion that such accounts are necessarily 'subjective'; rather, they are confused.

ENDINGS

Now, if there appeared to be a problem in constructing integral narratives regarding the origins of situations (because of the apparent arbitrariness of where to begin), the parallel problem also seems to arise where asked about the consequences or 'effects' of something. Here, the starting-point of a story is given but not the ending. A never-ending story threatens, which, in therefore lacking rationale for its 'middle', again approaches a random chronicle. Wars, journeys, and boxing matches have endings, whereas once we look at the consequences or 'effects' of an occurrence in the narrative terms of what happened 'next', then although our elementary '*a* to *y* minus 1' formula does control our selection, it does not appear to offer any integral ending-point.

The first response to this, however, is akin to that regarding the degree of specificity in questions about the *origins* or 'causes' of occurrences. Questions may be general, as in 'what were the consequences of the Treaty of Versailles?' or 'what were the consequences of my son's receiving that phone-call from his friend?' – or they may specify *which* consequences, as in 'what were the consequences of the Treaty of Versailles for Franco-German relations?' or 'what were the consequences of that phone-call for my son's social life?' Although there may appear to be a difference between the former (unspecified) and latter (specified) questions, common sense dictates they are not essentially distinct. In the latter case the specification is spelt out; but in the former case there is still an implicit specification regarding the consequences *for what?*, even though it remains more general.

For example, where the question concerns the unspecified consequences of the Treaty of Versailles, the very context of that treaty suggests what is sought are its consequences for subsequent international relations rather than, for instance, for architecture or economic theory. Hence, appearances notwithstanding, we can treat both non-specific and specific questions regarding consequences as the same in kind, albeit differing in degrees of specificity. In short, just as in our analysis of origins, there are different stories to be told depending upon how specific is the actual question asked.

The second response about 'endings' is that, conventionally, a distinction is made between 'immediate' and 'long-term' consequences (the same is made regarding immediate and more remote *origins*). But the logic of our present argument demands we bypass the concepts of immediate and intermediate consequences and concentrate upon 'long-term' consequences, for these seem most to threaten either the never-ending chronicle or the arbitrarily (that is, 'subjectively'), ended story. Indeed, questions about *intermediate* consequences are artificial (for instance, 'what were the consequences of the Versailles Treaty for Franco-German relations up to 1924?'). They are posed for merely pedagogic reasons and cannot be answered without an implicit knowledge of the 'entire' story (that is, without a knowledge of the long-term consequences). In short, they are like asking what the consequences were, up to a point three-quarters along in the story of Little Red Riding Hood, of the wolf eating her grandmother. We would be given either an inconsequential (*sic*) answer, or one that assumes knowledge of the whole story.

What this all points to, in fact, is the supposition that even 'long-term' consequences are finite. The very language historians use regarding sequences of occurences intimates they eventually come to an end (after which there are new beginnings, as in our analysis of 'final' actions within individual human conduct). It would be a peculiar irony were historians themselves to doubt that consequences (or origins) are finite, for they would be cutting the ground from under their own feet. It may be that in some philosophical sense both origins and consequences respectively stretch backwards or forwards to infinity, but that is not the supposition governing either the conventional, or the historians', frequent reference to them. Thus, either the way people treat these terms is wrong (which would be an oddity), or there is a workable way of conceiving both origins *and* consequences as finite. I have suggested the logic behind the former – we now need to pinpoint that behind the latter.

Once again it will do no harm to be reminded of archetypal fairy-stories. We noted and commented upon the usual starting-point, 'once upon a time . . .', which is followed by, 'one day . . .', introducing the 'first' occurrence in the ensuing story. The usual ending consists of some 'culminating' eventuality (often a dramatic denouement), succeeded by the familiar words, 'and they all lived happily ever after'. The rationale behind this phrase is not that nothing occurred after that point, but that nothing unusual or remarkable happened as remaining consequences of the preceding occurrences. In other words a point is reached where, in our elementary '*a* to *y* minus 1' formula, that implicit dynamic which drives a narrative forward becomes exhausted, such that there is nothing which can *obviously* be said to happen 'next'. Let us be reminded that when asked of an occurrence in a narrative, 'why did that happen?', it should always be possible to reply that it happened because such-and-such had just happened 'previously'. Many fairy-stories conclude with the princess marrying the hero, after which they proceed to 'live happily ever after'. Now it could be that at a later date the princess has a son, but even in the case where a new story begins with the birth of the prince, it is unlikely to be relevant to ask why she had a child, and to answer by saying she had 'just' got married.

Now although fairy-stories, in addition to being fictional, are dramatically structured such that their endings are strongly parametered, that same general rationale underlying their endings applies to those less deliberately crafted 'stories' which constitute accounts of the 'consequences' of actions, occurrences, or circumstances. For example, suppose the consequences of my son's phone-call were that he went out to a night-club, got involved in a fight, arrived home late, wet, and penniless, and was 'grounded' for the following fortnight. Only if something noteworthy occurred because of his being grounded would the consequences of that phone-call stretch further than that point. Otherwise, the story stops there in response to the unspecific question, 'what were the consequences of your son's phone-call?' If, on the other hand, the question specified its consequences upon his school-work, and his grounding enabled him to produce exceptionally good and punctual work remarked upon by his school, then these occurrences subsequent to his being grounded *would* continue the story beyond that former point.

Thus we see a parallel between the treatment of 'origins' and 'consequences', whereby different stories are required depending on how far, and in what way, the question is specific. Another is that, just as we found determinate 'beginnings' to origins, so there are determinate 'endings' to consequences. Equally, *where* one ends a sequence of consequences is of course a matter of judgement, just as where one begins a sequence of origins, but again this does not relegate such parameters to the arbitrary or subjective; rather, the point is, are they correct?

'CAUSES' AND 'EFFECTS'

We should note one further parallel from the above arguments, particularly since the investigation into origins and consequences is such an expected feature in the study of history. Often the terminology used is that of 'causes' and 'effects', and it would appear churlish to quibble over the semantics involved; indeed, where one approaches affairs *analytically* (involving, as we saw in Chapter One, the isolation of apparently identical determining factors in otherwise different scenarios), then the mechanistic and abstract overtones of the terms 'cause' and 'effect' could be viewed as more appropriate. The same overtones are also suggested by those questions, not about stories' beginnings and endings, but regarding their 'middles', where what is sought is an estimation of how important or significant a particular action, occurrence, or circumstance was – as in, for example, 'how far did the weakness of Kerensky's provisional government contribute to the Bolshevik coup?' or 'assess the role of Britain in the Versailles Conference'. In fact, these kinds of questions come from the direction of analytic history since, although they do not necessarily involve comparisons between different events, they do invite consideration of an event in terms of 'factors', thereby inviting the terminology of 'causes' and 'effects'.

In narrative history, however, I have already argued a distaste for the non-humanist, deterministic language of cause and effect, and hence a preference for the terms, 'origins' and 'consequences', is clear enough. The logic of narrative, as we have seen, is to treat 'effects' as understandable outcomes, consequences, or results, and 'causes' as intelligible responses by originating (human) agents. Where, however, the 'origins' of a situation are seen analytically in terms of the operation of various *factors* (for example, a rise in the price of oil, a falling birth-rate, or a revival of evangelism), then the language of 'causes' seems more appropriate than that of 'origins', the preserve of narrative history. The logic of causes and effects replaces that of intelligible sequences of occurrences.

What our analysis of 'events' implies, on the other hand, is that where the origins of a state of affairs are abstracted as 'factors', inviting the language and logic of causality, it must nevertheless be possible in principle to spell out what happened as a genuine narrative, intimately dependent upon human agency and response (in terms of practical, final, or mediate conduct). Where such an underlying reality cannot in principle be spelt out, we are presented with a phony or pseudo 'history'; that is, one which cannot ultimately be elevated into a story. This may be because its agents are, as previously discussed, mere abstractions rather than individual human beings, or because it simply cannot be made to hold together as a credible narrative, such are the gaps in its construction (sometimes filled in by the random appearance of 'factors' neither previously introduced nor subsequently appealed to).

For example, if it is proposed that a fall in the rate of interest caused people to have more disposable income, this is correctly put. But if I, therefore now having more income, move to a more expensive house, it is more appropriate to explain the move as *originating* in a fall in the rate of interest rather than being caused by it. In short, having more money does not cause one to move house; that conduct is a response to having more money, such that moving house is a *consequence* rather than an 'effect' of a fall in the rate of interest. I might have moved in any event, of course. Alternatively, although a fall in the rate of interest did *cause* me to have more money, I might have saved it or spent it in some other way.

What this demonstrates is that even where it is true that I move house because I have more money, and I have more money because of a fall in the rate of interest, it is only insofar as this sequence of occurrences can be spelt out as (crucially) including moving house as my *response* to *that* aspect of my circumstances that the fall in the rate of interest can be said, in justifiable metaphor, to be the 'cause' of my moving house. Once we move from the causal interaction of abstract mechanisms and structures such as the relation between rates of interest and liquidity, or between class, occupation, and education, into the area of actual human conduct, then the logic and language of 'causes' must in principle be genuinely transformable into that of 'origins' – for, as we have seen, in appealing to (economic, sociological) factors as causes of human conduct, there is potentially 'many a slip 'twixt cup and lip'.

If, then, in talking of the 'causes' of things it behoves the historian to be ready in principle to show he can transform his discourse into that of a narrative intimately involving human conduct as a *response* to situations, the same applies to the notions of 'effects' and 'consequences'. Where what ensued from an occurrence is construed as an 'effect', such terminology intimates the logic of causality, and it must again be possible in principle to spell out this sequence in narrative terms, for otherwise the 'explanation' is, in one or other of the senses noted earlier, false. For example, if it is proposed that the effect of a minister of state's resignation was a fall in the pound or a difficult cabinet reshuffle, then if one wants to stay within the discipline of history it is necessary to be able, in principle, to present either eventuality as a consequence within a genuine narrative, thereby involving the responsive agency of human conduct rather than the knee-jerk reactions of abstract factors in a determinate context. As such, the tighter language of 'effects' must be genuinely resolvable into the looser language of 'consequences' appropriate to narrative.

This parallel between 'causes' and 'effects' has been all the more worth drawing because there is a sense in which *any* historical account revolves around origins and consequences ('causes' and 'effects'), since all history is located around *change* – again we insist that where nothing changes there is no (hi)story to be told. So far, I have focused on problems involved in locating both where to begin an account of *the* origins, and end an account of *the* consequences, of things. Ultimately, however, we must recognise that, although these are junctures of special interest, there is a sense in which *every* part of a story is both a consequence and an origin (both an 'effect' and a 'cause'). Thus, all I have just argued about the principles underlying their semantics (apart from the specific case of beginnings and endings), continually applies throughout a narrative presentation.

In short, in the middle of an intelligible narrative (necessarily set out in terms of individuals' responses to their perceived circumstances), it is no good suddenly to interject a 'factor' such as someone's class origins, a deficit in the balance of payments, a psephological statistic, or some sociological trend, as 'the' explanation for the ensuing conduct. Equally it is no good to present 'what happens next' (that is, subsequent to some human conduct), as a fall in the birth-rate, an electoral defeat, or a relaxation of East/West tension, unless the individuals had both the means and intention to produce such a consequence.

'Mr Brown, as was his wont after dinner, took his dog for a walk. Then, as he entered the park, he saw two muggers assailing a young man, and turned back home to ring the police' – this despite, or because of, his being right-wing, middle-class, homosexual, self-employed, heavily mortgaged in a context of rising interest-rates, and an immigrant. Now it may well be true that it was in response to being middle-class, or homosexual, or an immigrant, that Mr Brown acted in such a way. But do we mean to apply such suppositions to his taking the dog for a walk, or his choosing the park, or his turning back home, or his ringing the police? Some of these? Only one of them? All of them? One, some, or all of these may be true; but unless it can be spelt out in terms of Mr Brown's response to his own perceptions of the succeeding situations it remains surmise. The narrative, however, remains true.

'Subsequent to phoning the police, Mr Brown discovered that no action had been taken. Angry, he complained to the Chief Inspector, who in turn was glad to pursue the complaint since he wanted rid of certain staff. Eventually, however, local police procedures were changed, rather than heads rolling'. Now, this was not 'the' effect of Mr Brown's conduct consequent upon his experience – rather, as it turned out, it was 'an' intelligible consequence of it given the responses of the various people involved (including the intervention of such alleged 'agents' as committees and boards of enquiry). Again, unless it can be spelt out as such, it remains mere surmise. Worse, it may be phony, concocted story-telling which resorts to abstract 'factors' as explanatory devices, arbitrarily intruded (or perhaps ideologically selected), to fill in what would otherwise be gaps in the flow of conventional narrative. We should not be fooled by them. 'Factors' such as a fall in the pound, a rise in violent crime figures, or a drop in the birth-rate, never *did* anything, and never will. Categorially, they cannot be agents in a narrative. Only responsive individuals can fulfil that categorial role, so that if we wish to get at the truth behind 'what happened' (almost indistinguishable from 'what happened next'), such factors have to be shown as constituting not only a, but *the*, consideration at work in forming the relevant individuals' responses to their perceived circumstances, pressures, responsibilities, or ambitions.

Inevitably this often brings us back to those in power, and it is no coincidence that it is exactly in this scenario that historians so often instinctively locate themselves. In fact, the very logic of their discipline (revolving as it does around the rationale of narrative structure), drives them to sharpen, even restrict, their focus on to the effective agents of change rather than on to 'agents' (more hopeful than effective) such as public opinion, elites, and the revolutionary classes. In having to focus upon change, factual narrative (that is, history), has to focus upon agency, which means power – not the power we all have to make things happen, but the power to bring *important* things about. Excursions into stories of failed movements, abortive organisations, and ineffective individuals, however interesting, are only relevant in history insofar as they may illuminate what *did* importantly happen. In themselves they warrant no further attention than clarifying the impact they had, if any, upon the experience and responses of those in power, be they in British government or General Motors. Interest exceeding these limitations belongs to the 'expert', or 'antiquarian'; it is not that of the historian.

SUMMARY

In returning so forcibly to the singularity of the notion of the practising *historian*, I reserve a fuller elaboration of its implicit 'theoretical' foundations to the next chapter. However, since I will claim its arguments derive significantly from this present chapter, I now turn to summarise it.

Following from Chapter Two's analysis of the narrative form I began by drawing attention to the uniqueness of individual human agency as that which is the very condition of history – namely, change. This topic re-emerged latterly in discussing 'causes' and 'effects' as distinct from 'origins' and 'consequences', where it was claimed that when abstract 'factors' are appealed to in an historical account, they should in principle be resolvable into the responses and actions of individuals if one is to sustain the logic of credible and coherent narrative. Thus, regarding agency, we know, for example, that Charles I was careful about which *individuals* composed the Star Chamber. Regarding 'factors', if, in addition to particular individuals' actions, Puritanism was an important factor (not agent), in the Civil War period, we must be prepared in principle to resolve this into a demonstrable part of the context to which relevant *individuals* actually responded.

But if change is the very condition of history, continuity is its paradoxical and symbiotic bedfellow. Marrying these two stipulations, we were thus led to attend to the topic of *continuity* in *individual* conduct, and I proposed a workable, non-ideological framework for such a scrutiny; namely, the concepts of practical, final, and mediate actions, and activities. One of the outcomes of that analysis was that 'the reason' for any occurrence (ultimately contributive to the 'explanation' of events), could not but be the outcome of individuals' responses to, and aspirations within, their own experiential context. Where evidence is lacking or inconclusive for such insight (as is the case, for instance – and despite meticulous documentation – in Cromwell's refusal of the Crown), it is reassuring to find historians reserving judgement, recognising the difference between mere supposition and valid inference.

Yet if individuals' actions are the bedrock of coherent factual narrative, the recognition that the study of history supersedes individual biography by treating of complex events (involving numerous individuals, occurrences, circumstances, and relationships), prompted enquiry into the rationale of their construction and presentation. In particular, we explored the process of discriminating genuine lines of continuity from amidst a kaleidoscopic mêlée of occurrences, whereby different 'branches' of the study of history are generated. But we found that an understanding of this process does not of itself provide immediate instruction regarding the intimate construction of historical narrative. In pursuit of this, and for ease of treatment, we first considered strongly parametered sequences ('story-objects', 'narrative identities') – namely, conventionally recognised events such as wars or journeys. We there encountered the practising historian's familiar problems of selection, relevance, significance, and objectivity, and noted that the logic underlying and connecting these criteria is, if only by analogy, that of the rationale of how to '*describe* an event'.

We then turned to non-paradigmatic sequences – that is, apparently open-ended 'stories' where either the beginning or ending, or both, seem indeterminate. Here, the problem of selection seemed to be accompanied by the problem of direction, for in the absence of a governing paradigm there can be numerous occurrences genuinely and simultaneously 'subsequent' to the same, single circumstance. This generated discussion not only of where to start and stop a (hi)story, but also of the factors making both for different interpretations and alternative accounts. As with strongly parametered events the key to these discussions, albeit more concealed, lay yet again in an appreciation of that dialectic between explanation and 'description' in the narrative form, whereby the *explaining* of occurrences via narrative logic achieves the 'description', or, as I prefer, *explication*, of an overall narrative identity. In recalling that the rationale of description is that of identifying what is *particular* about a phenomenon (for instance, about *this* war, or *that* journey), we traced the logic of selection, relevance, and direction in non-conventionally parametered events.

This led to the implication that what is going on in constructing a narrative account of something non-individuated (that is, not of this as distinct from that war or journey), is nonetheless the describing of a distinct phenomenon. It was argued that although such non-individuated 'events' (for example, Cromwell's rise to power), fit into no generalised paradigm, this does not detract from their validity, reality, and objectivity. Rather, by analogy with the world of fiction, we are confronted by such particular stories or narratives as that of Little Red Riding Hood – or to transfer to the factual world, that of my son's evening out.

The lesson to emerge was that there are, 'out there' amidst a virtual infinity of occurrences, *real* stories to be *truly* told, and that their telling must conform to those criteria uncovered in this chapter. In short, and by way of analogy, it is up to the art-critic to demonstrate that an 'abstract' painting is as intelligible as any immediately recognisable representational painting, rather than a random, and thus meaningless, juxtaposition of discrete images.

4

HISTORY AND THEORY

In treating of the implications for the historian of Chapter Two's general analysis of narrative, Chapter Three focused on those which relate particularly to the actual practice of construing, constructing, and presenting history. Its *theoretical* content emerged from examining the needs of that practice when conceived of as unequivocally narrative in structure, and therefore more from the nature of the practice of history than from some *a priori* general principles. Nevertheless, this is not to say that Chapter Three's theoretical content does not point to some general 'principles', as should be clear from its concluding summary.

Now there is nothing wrong in proposing that certain 'principles' (or a 'body of theory'), underly the discipline of history, so long as they are the correct ones. Where wrong, we should not be surprised if the historian regards the intermixing of 'theory' with history as a threat, or nuisance, or irrelevance. But to the extent that a body of theory, in elucidating his practice, might confirm it as resting on sound principles, the working historian should welcome rather than eschew what the theorist has to say. If soundly based, he may even find such theoretical insight helpful, if only as an antidote to whatever self-doubts may assail him when confronted by the more strident and castigatory theorists of history.

Now it is my contention that those general principles intimated by Chapter Three's theoretical content are more likely to be sound because they are derived from the actual practice of history rather than from some imagined practice or from some prior general 'philosophy'. Thus the aim of this chapter is to extend and elaborate upon these intimations such that the 'set of principles' or 'body of theory' they point to as underlying the discipline of history emerges clearly to view. I say 'emerge', because rather than set out these principles didactically it is more instructive (and, from above, potentially 'antidotal'), to argue them within, and where necessary against, traditional themes in theoretical writings on the discipline of history – for example, 'reason in history', 'historical explanation', 'determinism', and the speculative and analytic 'philosophy of history' generally. Thus although in a separate chapter, I nonetheless offer the following sections as in a sense a continuation of considerations relevant to the actual practice of history.

REASON IN HISTORY

What is generally meant by this phrase is the notion of an underlying rationality to the course of past (and sometimes future) events. What might otherwise be regarded as random, directionless, arbitrarily and sporadically connected events are instead seen to exhibit (or at least imply), some overall unfolding pattern or design. Now such a notion can be advanced *a priori* (for example, in the teleology of Christian eschatology), or *a posteriori* (for example, in loose talk of 'progress' by those who compare recent to distant times); or even as an apparent mixture of both (as in Hegel's concept of the 'cunning of Reason').

Advanced *a priori*, the supposition is that history must exhibit a design because there simply *is* an underlying reason for the way things turn out. If, *a priori*, one already 'knows' what this 'reason' dictates then all one can hope is that, when or *if* studied, the occurrence and arrangement of actual past events do not disillusion one. If, however, all one 'knows' is that, *a priori*, there is an underlying reason for the way things turn out but does not know what that reason is, one surveys events with a view to discovering it – in short, one looks for 'signs', as in the doctrine of Providence. Here, as in our analysis of 'significance', an occurrence which is part of one story is deemed significant if *relevant to* (that is, part of), some *other* story. All that can be said about this providential doctrine is that if one does not know what this other story is then anything can be seen as a 'sign' of some imagined design – any event can be deemed 'significant'.

More interesting than *a priori* approaches to 'reason in history' are *a posteriori* cases. Here we encounter the possibility of someone, previously regarding history as random, now noticing some kind of pattern or direction whereby he infers an underlying rationale ('reason') governing events. By analogy, we may scatter a handful of iron-filings on a sheet of paper and be unable to detect any pattern. Secrete a magnet underneath the paper, however, and we would hardly fail to notice a pattern into which the fragments gathered. We would thence be led to infer some underlying cause of, or reason for, the design; in other words, propose hypotheses explaining it (as do conspiracy theorists regarding various events in history).

Now, it is quite common to do what I have just exemplified – namely, equate 'the cause' of something with 'the reason' for something. Yet we already encountered this problematic in Chapter Two, where a difference was proffered between them, and here again the opportunity to do so presents itself, but from another angle. Regarding the iron-filings we may safely say the *cause* of their forming a pattern was magnetic force upon

135

them – this is a necessary effect according to scientific laws. Put *any* handful of iron-filings near *any* magnet at *any* time and it will be distributed into this predictable pattern. That they behave in this way is neither reasonable nor unreasonable, as is the case with any naturally necessary occurrence. It is the way things are.

The case is different, however, if we seek an explanation for why these *particular* iron-filings formed into a pattern on this *particular* piece of paper on this *particular* occasion.[1] There are potentially two different answers to this, depending on the case. The first is that there is no explanation as such, it being pure chance or accident. For instance, the wind blew the paper on top of a magnet and we had no knowledge of this before throwing the iron-filings. (In saying the wind blew the paper there we are not explaining the overall event we have been asked to explain since equally important in this chance configuration of circumstances is that we chose to throw the iron-filings on this rather than some other piece of paper.)

The second potential answer is that there is a *reason* why these particular iron-filings formed a pattern, and it is that I knowingly placed a magnet under the paper. If I did it unknowingly then we are back to pure chance or accident, whereby we say there was no reason (and, by definition, no cause) for what happened with the iron-filings *on this occasion*. The matter is transformed, however, if I knowingly put the magnet there. There is now a reason for the pattern's appearance on the paper – and this, I suggest, is where the terms, 'reason', 'cause', and 'chance' correspond to categorially different situations in the real world. The cause of the iron-filings forming a pattern was the proximity of a magnet. There may have been a reason why these particular iron-filings formed a pattern on this occasion; namely, someone knowingly put a magnet under the paper. Or there may have been no reason for that configuration of circumstances, in which case, that these particular iron-filings formed a pattern on this particular occasion was chance. It was a chance occurrence.[2]

Having thus distinguished realistically (rather than merely abstractly or semantically) between causes, reasons, and chance in occurrences, we now need to focus more closely on the notion of 'reason' in order to complete this discussion of the notion of 'reason in history'. In the iron-filings example I have posited the case where we arrive at the formula that there was a reason for what occurred inasmuch as I knowingly placed a magnet under the paper (that is, intentionally to produce a pattern). But what does the term, 'a reason', mean in this context? We have already ruled out the case of my unknowingly having placed the magnet there – this would relegate the pattern's appearance on this (as on any *particular*) occasion, to chance. What we are left with, therefore, is that the notion that 'there is a reason' for the pattern's appearance translates into 'I had a reason' for bringing this about (by deliberately placing a magnet under the paper). Now, what do we mean by the notion of someone 'having a reason' for what he does?

The term, 'reason', seems suggestive of some kind of 'logic', and this sits uneasily with much human conduct, especially that which manifests emotion rather than the cold calculation of means and ends; 'the reason he committed suicide was that he loved her', for example, as distinct from, 'the reason he married her was for her money'. Yet the same formula, 'the reason he . . .', is used with equal facility in both situations. Either, then, both are alike despite appearances, and language faithfully reflects this – or they are different and language overlooks this. In my view the former situation prevails, for when asked, for example, why that madman killed his family, we can faithfully report that the reason he did so was because he believed they were trying to kill him. That he was under a paranoic illusion in no way undermines the validity of his 'reason'.

This example shows that when we say an individual 'has a reason' for doing something, be it marrying for money or 'familicide' for self-defence, what we mean is that, whatever 'reason' prevailed, it was *his* reason – and I suggest we call this a 'reason' rather than a 'motive' or 'intention' because we mean to intimate there is something of the 'logical' (so akin to 'reasonable'), in his conduct. If, for instance, I believe my family is trying to kill me and I wish to avoid this, *it follows* that one way to avoid it is to kill them. Another would be to flee them. Playing the piano, however, would *not* 'follow', as we argued previously respecting the analysis of an individual's response to feeling cold, where some actions would be 'rational' (for example, closing the window or stoking the fire), whilst others (such as dousing the fire or whistling), would not be 'rational', or would not 'follow'.

It is in this way we arrive at the formula that by 'the reason' people do what they do we mean the *calculating* they happen upon in response to their present experience. So long as such calculation takes place, as in Hobbes' account of 'reasoning',[3] we say they 'have a reason' (their reason), for what they do. Their calculations may be faulty or superficial, such that we may say their reasoning was faulty or inadequate – in other words, that their reasoning was unreasonable. But all this means is that in imagining ourselves in the same situation we would have acted differently, a proposition obviously fraught with paradoxes. Rather, what is increasingly apparent is that to ask whether 'the reason' someone had for an action is itself 'reasonable' is to commit an error. Once we have ascertained what an individual's reason was for doing what he did (that is, presented it as a response to, or as 'following on' from, his experienced circumstances), we have shown 'the reason' for, or in, what he did. To go on to ask whether this reason for what he did was itself 'reasonable' is the same as asking what the reason was for his reason, an error already exposed at some length in Chapter Three.

One thing that follows from this, as more than one philosopher has insisted, is that there is no reason in things themselves; rather, it is a term denoting that property the human mind has to make one proposition 'follow from' another. Perhaps the notion that 'reason' is something more than this, providing some extra, ultimate, underlying criterion with which to judge matters independently of human idiosyncrasies, is prompted by the purity of mathematical reasoning. This seems the prime example of there being 'reason' in things. However, we should first note that the serene autonomy 'reason' appears to have in mathematics derives, rather, from the exact definitions within that discipline, whereby what 'follows' to a properly functioning mind is almost determinate, as if it were captive to some power other than its own *modus operandi*.

But we must note it is only in virtue of how we define our terms that, for example, $1+1=2$. Given this, however, it may still be argued that, *once* defined, mathematical propositions are fixed as by some external standard. For instance, we say that if $1+1=2$ then it follows that $2-1=1$, and this 'following on' appears exclusive and determinate. To say, however, 'if Mr Brown feels cold in the room it follows that he turns up the heat', appears far less exclusive and determinate because there is so much more, and imprecise, in that situation. There were many other things which would equally 'follow' from his feeling cold, including leaving the room; but equally, as in earlier such analyses, there are many things which would *not* follow. What confronts us here, then, is simply a difference of degree (in precision), rather than a difference in kind, between the 'reason' which inheres in mathematics as distinct from that inherent in more mundane examples of human conduct (mathematics, of course, being a species of human conduct).

To conclude this point I will only add that even in the exact and apparently autonomous world of mathematics the operation of 'reason' still exhibits a degree of indeterminacy, thereby confirming that the 'reason' inherent in mathematics is no different in *kind* from that inherent in other things people do, such as Mr Brown's leaving the room. This is because, if $1+1=2$, it follows not only that $2-1=1$ but equally, for example, that $2+1$ must be greater than 2 and that $1-1$ will be less than 2. Neither consequence is more nor less 'reasonable' than the original. 'Reason' does not, then, dictate what follows from, 'if $1+1=2$ . . .'. Rather, if I say that what follows is that $2+1$ must therefore be greater than 2, *that is my reasoning*. So long, then, as it does 'follow on' it is pointless to ask whether my reasoning is itself 'reasonable'. Having established Mr Brown's reason for leaving the room was that it was cold, it is like asking what the reason was for his reason, an absurdity which should now be amply manifest.

What emerges from this is that where we say there is 'reason' in a course of events this translates into there being a reason *for* the course of events – and this in turn translates into its being the expression of an agent's 'reasoning', which, as noted even in the case of mathematics, is multi-directional albeit not arbitrary. We will recall that in our example of the iron-filings it was not the pattern they formed which was 'reasonable' but the fact they formed *any* pattern, as distinct from being an arbitrary scattering, which prompted the notion of 'reason' being involved in the state of affairs (or course of events), because of the inference that there must be a reason *for* the pattern's occurrence. In our example we showed in what sense such an inference may be wrong by considering the notion of chance. We also showed that where the inference was right the presence of a pattern was brought about through an agent's knowing exploitation of the laws of magnetism in order to produce it, and it was the agent's *reason for* doing this which located where 'reason' was involved.

Thus to return to the *a posteriori* notion of 'reason in history', we can see more clearly what this would involve. Firstly, the course of past events would need to exhibit some kind of pattern, regularity, or direction, contradictory of the expectation that it is no more overall than an arbitrary kaleidoscope stretched through time (that is, that 'the course of history' is simply that). Secondly, whatever this characteristic is (for example, a pattern or direction), it does not of itself have to be 'reasonable' or 'logical'. Rather (thirdly), the perceiving of this characteristic prompts the inference (fourthly), that there must be 'a reason' for it. This implies (fifthly), that some agent had a reason for producing this characteristic (and continues to unless 'reason in history' stopped at, for instance, 1066 AD). Sixthly, whatever reason it is, it is his (the agent's), reason. Seventhly, to discover what his reason is we would need to find out about his circumstances in order to see what he was responding to, and to what end, in his fashioning of the course of history. Is the agent involved in an ongoing activity undertaken for its own sake, as in, perhaps, the Graeco-Roman gods playing a game? Or is he engaged in a practical project, a constant labour designed to achieve some end result desired for its own sake?

Now, most historians would have abandoned interest in the (*a posteriori*) notion of 'reason in history' from point five onwards; and so would others who, as I, see agency only in terms of individual human beings. It is surely only theologians and certain philosophers who might pursue the above analysis to the end, although many of the former would stop at point six (albeit in what appears a most confused reasoning sequence), declaring the ways of God mysterious. It must be to the credit of Hegel that he pursued the above logic to its end, thereby producing his astonishingly comprehensive philosophy. Such an effort cannot fail to inspire admiration and interest.

Equally interesting to some is where Marx might be seen as standing with regard to 'reason in history', given his so-called 'historical materialist' approach. Following our above analysis it is clear Marx believed he perceived something which denied the course of history as an arbitrary kaleidoscope of events over time. By analogy, he saw a pattern in the iron-filings – this, we might add, after he had expressly denied the presence of any superhuman agency governing history.[4] This pattern was in the nature of a (recurring) regularity which, doubtless for the purposes of argument, he exaggerated and simplified into the proposition, 'The history of all hitherto existing society is the history of class-struggles'.[5] Observing this regularity, he enquired, not into its reason, but into the causes producing it, and emerged with the socio-economic causal formula of the mode of production 'determining' the relations of production (class relations based on property rights), which in their turn 'determine' the 'superstructure' of a society. But he did not go on to draw any inference regarding the existence of any 'reason for' (and thus of an agent behind), this. By our iron-filing analogy, he noted a 'pattern' and claimed to identify the causal mechanisms producing it (plus associated necessary effects such as the nature and role of ideology in the superstructural arena). But on 'philosophical' grounds he did not infer any 'reason for' this. His deliberate, albeit somewhat equivocal, use of the term 'materialism' is expressive of this.[6] Rather, he specifically presented the operation of these socio-economic causal mechanisms as a 'fact of life', analogous (in that sense only) to gravity in the physical world.[7]

In presenting these causal mechanisms as a crucial part of the context in which individuals respond to affairs and generate projects and ends, Marx never explicitly, nor by implication, denied individual agency in history (unlike subsequent 'dialectical materialists'), nor suggested any 'superhuman' agency responsible for exploiting these mechanisms. Whatever their illusions regarding their conduct individuals are as captive to the causal factors underlying their situations as is anyone, despite his illusions, to the laws of gravity, such that he will sink or swim irrespective of what he happens to believe.[8]

So far this must be unexceptional to the historian. He merely needs to decide whether, or how far, he accepts Marx's causal economic and social laws as a fact of life, whose operation is continually dispersed in events, as are the laws of gravity. But how far, and in what ways, accepting these 'laws' would affect the (narrative) historian's account of particular actions and events is another matter. What *is* clear is that although, for example, the cause of this golf-ball's trajectory through the air is to be found in the laws of motion and mechanics, the *reason for* it on any particular occasion is to be found in the reasoning of the golfer. He exploits these causal laws whether he understands, or is even aware of, them or not. Just so, up to this point, with Marx's 'laws' of 'historical materialism'; they will not provide 'the reason' for particular occurrences and there is nothing in

Marx's logic so far, and neither in the practice of his specifically historical works, to suggest he thought they could.

Thus in perceiving a regularity and enquiring into the causal laws underlying it, it does not so far seem Marx was claiming any overall 'reason in history'. However, this is true only of his notion of history up to a certain point in (historical) time. He calls this period 'pre-history' and looks forward to a future he calls 'human history'[9] when there will indeed be, in our terms, an approximation to 'reason in history'. This is because he believed in the emerging possibility of human beings' ability to impose their own pattern or direction on the course of events through their knowledge of the causal laws of society.

Our analogy with the iron-filings example breaks down to an extent at this point, however, because whereas the laws of magnetism operate independently of human assistance or connivance (such that in understanding them one chooses to exploit them or not but cannot alter how they operate), 'social' laws, for Marx, only operate insofar as human beings execute them. Through knowledge and alternative action these 'social' laws can actually be transformed, and it would seem the 'historical materialist' Marx had this in mind rather than subsequent 'dialectical' materialists' more simplistic notion of exploiting 'laws' of society which they regarded as operating in an unassailable way, independent of human control (thereby treating them as if they are the same as 'natural' laws – for example, the laws of magnetism).[10]

Although an important distinction for social science, this involves only a minor amendment to our iron-filings analogy. More substantial, potentially, is the issue of individual human agency, because in his pre–1845 writings Marx refers to 'the species' human-being as if it were an agent capable of governing 'history'.[11] Although the term is dropped by 1846, it remains obscure whether Marx subsequently thought in terms of *individuals'* agency effecting a (transformed) pattern to future history or whether he continued to think in terms of a genuinely collective agency, namely, 'the species' – or indeed, as he appeared to become increasingly empiricist in approach, whether he abandoned the whole idea of 'human history' as a youthful philosophical indulgence.

Whichever, sufficient of our analogy with the iron-filings example remains to sustain the notion that for the young Marx the period of 'prehistory' is that in which some kind of pattern (including a direction), can be discerned, evidential of the persistent operation of certain 'laws' or causes, although there cannot be said to be any 'reason for' the fact of their operation. But there remains the prospect of 'human history' where humankind will understand, exploit, and where necessary transform, the 'social' causes underlying and dispersed throughout the future history of societies, such that there will then be a reason for (or 'reason in'), that history. It will be humankind's (*sic*) reason, whereby the pattern or direc-

141

tion subsequent history takes will reflect the collective (*sic*) responses and aims of humankind. What that pattern or direction, and what the reasons *for* it, might be is not answered through the above logic. Moreover, as we have seen, 'reason', although not arbitrary, *is* multi-directional. For Marx, however, given his well-known predispositions and perhaps more particularly certain philosophical pointers residual from his Hegelian heritage, we know enough to say he himself thought in optimistic terms of the fashioning of a context for the self-fulfilment of individuals within a harmonious, abundantly enabling society.

What we see in Marx, then, regarding this issue of 'reason in history', is an interesting and complex case where there is no 'reason' in 'pre-history' (either *a priori* or *a posteriori*), although there is a pattern and direction discernible *a posteriori*, the causes of which Marx, in his headlong flight from Hegelianism, is reluctant to call 'premises' in the philosophical sense of the term.[12] But the very direction these causes are conspiring to produce, according to Marx, is towards generating the arrival of 'reason in history'. That these causes so conspire appears to be a notion he arrived at *a posteriori*, in the sense that it was his observation of his contemporary world which led him to the notion that, in its course, history had exposed its mechanisms to adequate human understanding, this being a necessary (albeit not sole), condition for the beginning of 'human history'. As already noted there is of course no *reason* for (or 'reason in') the underlying causes of history producing this transformation, and in his rejection of Hegel's 'cunning of Reason' Marx would be the last to suggest there was.

Thus on Marx's reasoning we are left to conclude it is simply mankind's astonishingly good luck that the course of history conspires to supersede its own lack of reason, and with such beneficial results for mankind. It is not surprising this latter strains the credulity of many critics, prompting at least one to hint this is merely the esoteric Marx making political myth.[13] An alternative would be to suggest this is yet one more piece of evidence in favour of those who claim, of Marx's relation to Hegel, that 'he protesteth too much' – in other words, that he failed to extricate himself from the allure of Hegel's ontology. It is not to our purposes here to adjudicate on these criticisms since the only way to do so is to enquire into Marx's 'reason for' writing what he did, and I reserve treatment of the rationale of the history of thought (with its implied techniques of explanation), to my final chapter. What *is* to our present purposes, however, is to comment on the logic of what he *wrote*, and here I return to the issue of individual as opposed to collective agency.

Regarding 'pre-history' Marx's logic provokes no problems in the terms we have set out for 'reason in history'. It does not arise and there is no logical demand it should if our reconstruction of what Marx wrote is correct. The case is different, however, when he writes of 'human history' because the 'reason' clearly implied in that future history is the reasoning of 'humankind' (an abstraction in our terms), rather than that of individual human beings. Leaving aside whether this was an error corrected by Lenin's insistence on the role of the Party (itself subject to his veto), this issue of agency in history is not one Marx wrote about in relation to 'human history'. Nowhere as yet has he been found to explicate the notion of 'the species' as a collective agent.

This is a point similar to that made by Tucker, who argues (dubiously) that in 1844 Marx himself was uneasy about transferring *individuals'* potential for existential alienation into a clash between *collectives* (in this case, 'classes' rather than 'the species'). Tucker also calls this crucial jump from individual to collective personality or agency, 'myth-making'.[14]

From related angles, then, both Tudor's and Tucker's analyses accord with the implication that the validity of Marx's logic regarding 'reason in history' is prima facie wrong unless he can be understood at some later date, whilst retaining his notion of 'human history', to construe agency in ultimately individual terms. Meanwhile, Sartre's dictum, 'Hell is other people', must threaten a particular poignancy in relation to the young Marx's revelatory, hence intensely individual, intellectual constructions.

Enough has been said, particularly with the concrete example of Marx's writings, to clarify what the notion of 'reason in history' means and implies. It is up to others to suggest how to make some other sense of the notion. In our unashamedly *a priori* terms (defended at the beginning of Chapter Three), the notion of 'reason' permeating 'history as a whole' is ruled out because of the issue of individual human agency. Individuals reason differently, not in unison. However, the converse to our propositions regarding this topic is that if there is no 'reason' to, for, or in, history as a whole, there would be no history *at all* were it not for the ceaseless appearance of 'reason' *within* history. In other words, what transforms a teeming scenario of occurrences succeeding each other randomly, or through mechanistic cause and effect, into *history* is the intelligibility lent to multitudinous discrete sequences by the presence of humans' reasoning.

If there is not *a* reason in history, nevertheless a multiplicity of *reasons* abound in history – indeed, they constitute its precondition. The phenomenon of human reasoning informs, not 'history as a whole', but numerous discrete episodes in diverse aspects of what happened in the past. This 'human reasoning' is instanced whenever we can say of something which happened, that someone 'had a reason' for effecting it, or wherever we can identify sequences involving interplay between individuals whose continuity depends upon their responding to each other – that is, where an individual's reasons for his conduct relate to another individual's reasons for *his* conduct and vice versa. Such sequences superseding a single individual's conduct range from simple short sequences involving two individuals – for example, a chess game or a conversation – to complex, longer sequences involving numerous individuals, such as those constituted by wars or other complicated stories.

HISTORICAL EXPLANATION

This examination of the concept of 'reason in history' has, then, both a negative and positive outcome, for if we dismissed the grand idea of 'reason in history', no different arguments were needed to propose the idea that history abounds with 'reasons' as, indeed, its very condition. Now I have argued that the 'reasons' with which history abounds consist of 'the reasons for', or 'the reasoning in', individuals' conduct, and it is clear that in constructing coherent narrative a goodly proportion of the historian's activity is devoted to unravelling this species of 'reason'.

In *accounting for* occurrences in terms of the reasons individuals have for their conduct, he is *explaining* these occurrences (as clarified in Chapter Two) – and to the extent this process lies at the heart of the logic of narrative we may be prompted to ask whether this explaining process is what is called 'historical explanation'.

This is a term used by theorists whereby they propose there is an historical way of explaining things as distinct from other ways of explaining them (for instance, 'scientific' and 'practical' ways). Accordingly they go in search of what constitutes 'historical explanation' as if it were, if not the philosophers', then at least the historians', stone. It must be noted this search often proceeds from abstract propositions of logic rather than from the obvious starting-point of what practising historians actually do, and it is therefore not surprising it ends up in correspondingly unreal locations. (Indeed, in his shrewd monograph, *Historical Explanation Reconsidered*, Graham argues that 'most modern [philosophical] discussions of historical explanation are wide of the mark';[15] further, that it is 'not a topic which presents any aspects of great philosophical interest'[16] because, properly understood, 'questions about the nature of historical explanation can be settled very simply').[17]

Let us instead ground our discussion on what people actually do and ask what they do when they 'explain' something. The verb, 'to explain', denotes a particular kind of occurrence which has been abstracted from the world of occurrences in general – and (following Chapter Two's analysis), to discover *what* kind of occurrence we have only to consult a dictionary to find the verb's definition. In this case the 1989 *Oxford English Dictionary* gives a list which includes; (1) 'to make clear the cause, origins, or reason of; to account for': and (2) of the phrase, 'to explain oneself', 'to make one's meaning clear and intelligible . . . also, to give an account of one's intentions or motives'.

This, then, is what people do when they 'explain' things, and to the extent it is possible not only to define but also to explain what it *is* to explain something, we can use definition (1) in conjunction with Chapter Two's analysis of 'occurrences' to say this particular kind of occurrence has been abstracted and articulated because it is relevant to us and has proved a reliable, workable abstraction in relation to our experience in the world. We can also note that the kind of occurrence the verb 'to explain' denotes is neither highly specific nor overly vague. It rests somewhere in the middle, and the only consideration is – not, is 'explaining' a *real* occurrence and if so does the dictionary definition *truly* correlate with this 'objective reality'? – but how far is this particular kind of occurrence a relevant abstraction from the world of occurrences in general (in this case, intellectual ones), and how reliable and workable is it?

Thus, that we 'explain' things is a feature noticed *by* human beings, *of* human beings, and I suggest reflection on the above definitions reveals that 'to explain' something is to show how what is to be explained *'follows on'*. For example, 'to explain one's conduct' is to show how it 'follows' from one's motives or intentions – or, 'to make one's meaning clear' is to show (often via a rewording) how what one has said does actually 'follow on' from one word to the next (definition (2), both parts). Again (now looking at definition (1)), we can note that although the distinction drawn earlier between generalised scientific causality and 'the reasons for' particular occurrences is glossed over in that definition (possibly rightly, since usage rather than theoretical nicety is the arbiter of non-technical language), the notion of one thing 'following on' from another remains. For example, if one adopts Newton's law of gravity, 'it follows' that an object not restrained will fall to the earth's surface, and at a predictable rate of acceleration, just as it 'follows' that if $1+1=2$, then $2-1=1$. Although there *are* differences in these propositions (revealed in the previous section regarding 'reason'), they are differences *in* the way things 'follow on', not differences which suggest that 'explaining' a thing sometimes involves the notion of 'following on' and at other times does *not* involve this notion but some other operative principle instead.

So much, then, for what it is to 'explain' something. In meaning 'to account for', 'to make sense of', or 'to make intelligible', it revolves around making what one states 'follow on' (through scientific causality, logic, or conventional wisdom regarding human conduct and discourse). Another term for this process, no worse for its antiquity, is 'to bring a thing into the understanding', whereby we do not simply say, 'the cat was on the mat', or '$2-1=1$', but make these statements intelligible (that is, *explain* them), by making them 'follow on' from earlier statements pregnant with 'effects' or 'consequences'. Whether this 'following on' in the logic of discourse correlates with what actually occurs is for our purposes a different question – and thus I restrict myself here to saying that where discourse is shown not to be relevant, useful, or workable, it is the terms of that discourse which should be altered. Only if there were

145

aspects of 'the way things are' which are capable of alteration through human agency would we encounter the converse; that is, rather than accommodate our discourse to 'the way the world works', bring 'the way the world works' into accord with our discourse, a god-like potential already explored in our examination of Marx's notion of 'human history'.

Not surprisingly, terms such as 'reason', 'understanding', 'explanation', and 'account for', are mutually intermixed in dictionary definitions, and I have suggested the phenomenon of 'following on' underlies them all. Further, we have only to adopt the view of many philosophers to propose that this propensity of the human mind (one amongst many – for example, memory), to think in terms of one thing 'following on from' another is a given feature or 'law' of the mind; that is, this is the way it works, from the paranoiac who kills his family to the mathematician investigating the circle. Were it not a 'law' as severe as that of gravity, no one, for example, would dare get into a car for fear he may encounter a driver to whom it does not follow that keeping to the left side of the road avoids head-on collisions – or worse, but even more strictly to our point, a driver whose mind does not function in terms of things 'following on' at all, but in some other way. Philosophers have variously referred to this *modus operandi* of the mind as 'reason' or 'understanding', and those who have suggested the mind can work in no other way (as do we), have consequently been at pains to explain error. (For Spinoza, for example, error cannot arise from an individual's mind operating 'wrongly', but only from his ignorance or from confusion over the meaning of words – that is, from a 'privation of knowledge').[18]

However, this is not an aspect of the topic to be pursued here (despite the particular error we wish to expose). Rather, having argued that the essence of 'explaining' things lies in showing how they 'follow on', what we are concerned with is the claim that things 'follow on' in different ways, one of them being the historical way, such that we can sensibly talk of 'historical explanation' as distinct from other kinds of explanation. To this I retort that just as things do not *fall* biologically, psychologically, or historically, neither do things *'follow'* biologically, psychologically, or historically. It is true things may fall either quickly or slowly, noisily or silently, by design or accidentally; again, one may sleep soundly or fitfully. In each case the adverbial qualifier serves only a descriptive function and thus draws attention to a merely contingent feature of what is essentially occurring. As indicated, qualitative features of occurrences have to be appropriate or applicable to what they qualify, just as adjectives have to be applicable to, for example, material objects. We can talk of yellow dresses but not of silent or quick dresses.[19]

Now, of things which 'follow on' we can say they follow on more nearly or distantly, or more obviously than other things which also follow on. Just so of the process of *demonstrating* that one thing follows on another

146

– that is, of explaining things. One may explain something clearly or confusedly, lengthily or succinctly, conventionally or originally. In all these cases the qualifying adverbs draw attention to merely contingent features of what is the same essential phenomenon in each case, namely, that of 'following on'.

What is clear from this is that nothing 'follows on' mathematically, artistically, scientifically, or historically, particularly if what is suggested is that 'following on' somehow works according to different principles in each case. Were that so then we would indeed need to become acquainted, for example as mathematicians, with the special way things follow mathematically, or as historians with the special way things follow historically. We are being invited, thereby, into categorially distinct modes of explanation, a self-defeating world inasmuch as if it makes any sense it can do so by no other means than demonstrating its arguments 'follow on' in precisely that singular way whose sovereignty we assert, but they deny.

In thus rejecting this kind of notion of 'historical explanation' – and we note practising historians manage perfectly well without being versed in its mysteries – the most that can be said is that distinct areas, activities, and topics often generate their own terminology and consequent terms of reference for explaining matters pertaining to them. For example, to explain why an internal combustion engine needs a flywheel one is to an extent captive to the topic of mechanics, such that one's explanation will consist of demonstrating how the need for a flywheel 'follows on' from those laws of mechanics exploited in engine design. Being thus couched in terms of mechanics there seems nothing wrong in thereby referring to a 'mechanical' explanation so long as one does not mean there is a 'mechanical' way of explaining things.[20] As already noted, there is a lucid, or long-winded, or succinct, way of explaining things, but not a mechanical, psychological, ethical, or historical way.

Finally, even where we might wish to draw categorial distinctions between areas of study, such as that between the world of scientific causality as distinct from that of reasons for particular occurrences, those distinctions nevertheless remain *contingent* features of explanations. Thus although we might for good reasons distinguish between explanations of things which 'follow on' via subsumption under general causal laws ('science'), from things which 'follow on' as individuals' contingent responses to their circumstances ('human conduct'), the manner of their 'following on' remains true to the same sovereign principle whereby anything is said to 'follow on'.

All this, however, is not to deny that the historian explains things. On the contrary, particularly if he is a narrative historian who thereby centres his activity on giving an account of past events, we have demonstrated at length and in detail how the narrative form depends on presenting one thing 'following on' another (that is, the concepts of 'nextness', 'this *then* that', 'prior and subsequent', referred to in Chapter Two). In other words, in giving an account of a sequence of occurrences the historian is constantly explaining each occurrence by presenting it as 'following on' from the previous. And there can be no objection to referring to an historian's account of something as an *historical* account rather than, for example, a biological or psychological account. For instance, to give a biological account of something is to give an account of it within the terms of reference of biological matters – and clearly the thing in question must be amenable to such referents. One cannot give a biological account of the internal combustion engine nor of the Peloponnesian Wars. One can, however, give a military account of the latter since any warfare is clearly amenable to military terms of reference. One can also, of course, give an historical account of the Peloponnesian Wars; but this is simply because they constitute a sequence of occurrences rather than in virtue of any specialised 'discipline' to whose terms of reference these wars also happen to be amenable.

What I am suggesting, then, is that amongst the different kinds of accounts of things which can be given we can include *historical* accounts – and that the term, 'historical', is an unusually broad term denoting that a thing will be treated within the reference of sequences of occurrences. In short, an account is 'historical' simply and solely insofar as it deals with *any* sequence of particular occurrences by making it identifiable as such, whether it involves the outbreak of a war, the invention of a medicine, or the outcome of last night's boxing match. (Just so, in talking of a *scientific* account of something we again encounter an unusually broad term denoting a thing's treatment within the terms of reference of causal law-determined phenomena. Wherever something, be it the composition of a star, the strength of a bridge, or the course of an illness, is amenable to demonstration as causally determined, then to do so is to engage in a 'scientific' account of it.)

Thus it is, then, that historians know how to give an historical account of something; but they do not know how to give an historical *explanation* of something (that is, account historically *for* something). And neither, I suggest, does anyone else. Certainly, historians know how to *explain* something, as aware as anyone else of what is involved in demonstrating that one thing follows from another. But they are as wary of the notion that they are explaining things 'historically' as certain philosophers should be of the notion that *they* hold the key to explaining things 'philosophically'. Rather, historians get on with their activity instead of making it revolve around defining its own nature, a criticism from which philosophy, in particular, can claim no special exemption.[21] If some find it problematic to identify the rationale of 'philosophy' (and as with 'history' they are the more likely to the less they attend to what those called philosophers, or historians, actually do), one thing is nevertheless clear;

148

the object of philosophy cannot be the 'discipline' itself (even if philosophy might be the 'discipline' through which that object can be discovered).

In arriving at the formulation that the historian gives an historical account *of* something (by accounting *for*, or *explaining*, occurrences), but that this is not to be confused with accounting historically *for* something (that is, the chimera of explaining something 'historically'), we are in fact paralleling an earlier point regarding 'reason' in history, itself derived from our analysis of human conduct. It reverts to the example of someone entering a room, feeling cold, and closing the window, whereof we say we can account for, or explain, his closing the window as his response to feeling cold. He closed it 'because' he felt cold. But, as argued, it makes no sense to seek an explanation of why he closed the window because he felt cold.

This, then, is an elementary example of giving an account *of* a sequence of occurrences by accounting *for* them (through the selective abridgement intrinsic to narrative structure). The sequence itself, however, is not accounted for. Rather, in constructing it we have given an ('historical') account *of* a genuine continuity of occurrences (extracted from an otherwise kaleidoscopic jumble of earlier, simultaneous, and later occurrences). But we have not *explained* this sequence and thus it is not in this region that the alleged phenomenon of 'historical explanation' can be found.

To be sure, the individual's action of closing the window has been explained, but simply in the same way anything is explained – by presenting it as 'following on'. So again, we are not confronted by the alleged phenomenon of specifically 'historical' explanation. I conclude, then, that if by 'historical explanation' is meant 'accounting for a thing historically', or 'explaining a thing in an historical way', then the very concept of 'historical explanation' is confused at the core and correspondingly not worth further enquiry.

Now, conceptual confusion is always serious and often the product of the lesser mischief of mere linguistic ambiguity. Such may be the case with the term, 'historical explanation', for there is a way of restoring value to the notion by introducing a linguistic refinement whereby, without straining language, the term takes on a different meaning. In Chapter Two's section entitled 'Narrative explication', having previously shown how narrative is structured on explaining why occurrences happen (via 'following on'), I examined that other property of narrative which 'makes explicit' the nature of *sequences* of occurrences (that is, 'events', 'story-objects', or 'narrative identities'). I referred to this latter property as 'explicatory', meaning 'to develop the notion of something' or 'to unfold or make explicit the nature of something'. This exactly expressed our claim that, over and above explaining why individual occurrences happen, narrative thereby also unfolds before us, or makes intelligible to us, phenomena just as 'real' or 'objective' as material objects – namely, those

149

'narrative identities' variously signified above. It does not *explain* these phenomena in the sense of accounting for them; rather, it reveals them to our view. As such, we might say with respect to narrative identities that to 'explicate' them is more akin to 'describing' than to 'explaining' them.

However, if the dictionary defines 'explicate' as 'to make explicit the nature of something', we also find that one of its definitions of '*explain*' is, 'to make [something] clear or intelligible with detailed information'.[22] We can, then, use the term 'explain' to mean 'explicate', and in *that* sense the notion of 'historical explanation' does indeed have a peculiar applicability. This is because 'story-objects' are of such a nature as to require their own distinct technique or 'kind' of explication, by which they are uniquely brought to view or made intelligible – namely, the narrative form. Through this linguistic adjustment, then (well-supported by the dictionary), the concept of 'historical explanation' *can* be afforded a specific meaning which is relevant, workable, and useful. That in this form it does not hold out the promise of 'accounting for' something, or 'making clear the cause, origins, or reason of' something – that is, answering the question, 'why'? – is clear from the argument; and so long as that remains clear we have a worthwhile sense in which we can talk of, and about, 'historical explanation' as distinct from some other kind of 'explanation' – otherwise, not.

PHILOSOPHY OF HISTORY

In popular intimation 'philosophy' is an even more indefinite term than 'history', which at the very least is understood by everyone to concern the past. Through the ages, indeed, such has been the uncertainty over what 'philosophy' is (evinced by philosophers themselves), that it is justifiable to engage in contentious propositions regarding it, albeit in a work devoted to the discipline of history. What seems clear is that whereas other disciplines have their own object and/or method of study (however dimly or generally perceived, as, respectively, with 'history' and 'science'), this is not the case with philosophy. In some cases the study of something is called by the same name as that which it studies; for example, 'music', 'French', or 'electronics'. In others the study of something is given a different name from that which it studies because it seems more appropriate to designate it, not in terms of its object (for example, French), but in terms of its method, as in science or mathematics, whereby numerous different phenomena are amenable to, respectively, a scientific or mathematical treatment.

Now where does 'philosophy' stand in relation to this? Since we should think only in terms of what actual philosophers have done (rather than pluck some *a priori* notion out of the air), we note the *objects* of philosophers' studies have included the universe, justice, the State, happiness, language, dreams, love, lenses, art, God, motion, understanding – and nowadays, sport, nursing, science, and, indeed, history. Thus it would seem impossible to define philosophy in terms of some object which is peculiarly its own.

The alternative is to see whether it can be designated as having its own method or approach. Ostensibly, however, this seems a difficult proposition to uphold. Certainly, writings known as 'philosophical' are constituted by closely reasoned argumentation (as distinct, for instance, from the looser, more imaginative, writings of rhetoricians), but they share this feature with many other disciplines including the natural and social sciences. As already argued, there is only one way in which things 'follow on', such that it makes no sense to talk of explaining things 'historically', 'scientifically', 'mathematically', or 'philosophically', as if reasoning operated differently in each case. We will recall that the most which can be said is that an explanation, argument, or 'piece of reasoning', may be described as, for example, mathematical, biological, or socio-logical, when the subject-matter in question generates its own terms of reference. Being descriptive, such terms as 'biological', or, indeed, 'rhe-torical', refer to merely contingent features of explanations, arguments, or 'reasonings'.

If, then, we are to talk of 'philosophical' explanations we cannot talk of some special kind or way of reasoning; rather, we must regard the term as merely descriptive, drawing attention to the fact that in this particular case the argumentation is captive to the terms of reference generated by philosophy's *object* of study. But since philosophy does not have its own object it can have no special terms of reference, generated by that object, within which it discusses things.

Thus we appear to arrive at an unreasonable impasse inasmuch as 'philo-sophy' evaporates into something indefinable. This is unreasonable because there must be a reasoning in (that is, a 'reason for'), the term's use, particularly since it has proved so enduring. Thus, despite the foregoing arguments undermining its rationale, the reason for its persistence should be sought even if the logic which underpins the identification of other disciplines is lacking in its case.

The supposition is, then, that amidst the wide array of topics which have been discussed by philosophers (and discounting their use of reasoned argumentation), there has been something sufficiently common to warrant calling them all by that name. As for what this is, one would not be alone in suggesting that although it is true there is no one kind of object, however broadly conceived, which philosophers have studied, this is pre-cisely because it is the very existence, or nature, of *any* phenomenon which is (potentially) the object of the philosopher's study. I say 'poten-tially' because it appears that where a question regarding the nature of something has been answered to the satisfaction of intellectual circles, by reference to accepted disciplines, then philosophy is mute.

For example, prior to what we now regard as satisfactory (scientific) explanations for why the sky is blue, for what a star is, for why things fall, or for what a dream is, philosophers pondered these topics, using reasoned argumentation rather than reiterating myths, folklore, or Revelation. But once questions regarding a thing's nature were demonstrably answered, philosophers would retreat from that topic and concentrate on things whose nature remained unanswered, as well as finding new such things. The principally seventeenth-century discoveries in what we now call astronomy, biology, physics, and medicine, prompted one of the most massive retreats by philosophy from topics previously in its domain. This continued in the following century of 'Enlightenment' when, amongst others, geography, botany, and geology were added to the growing list of disciplines. Again, another largish retreat was occasioned by the establishment of the social and psychological sciences in the late nineteenth century, whilst for those who comprehensively accept Marx's 'historical materialism' even venerable topics such as 'human nature', morality, and the nature of justice, were removed from philosophy's orbit through being rendered demonstrably explicable.

I cite these as some examples supporting the proposition that philosophy is the investigation into things whose natures remain either unexplored or inexplicable through (other) accepted disciplines. For instance, although we do not yet have all the answers regarding cancer, or the galaxies, we regard them as potentially reachable via medicine and astronomy respectively – we no longer 'philosophise'. In short, then, philosophy is the exploration of the nature of something insofar as we do not already know the answer, or how to get it.

This may seem a hostile statement, corresponding to Marx's judgement that, 'when reality is depicted, philosophy as an independent branch of knowledge loses its medium of existence'.[23] However, neither formulation need be derogatory since there remain numerous phenomena whose exploration falls under no accepted discipline, or where the capacity of a relevant discipline to 'deliver the goods' is subject to dispute. Regarding the former, a pertinent example is 'the nature of history' and/or 'the nature of the discipline of history'. These topics remain, then, the preserve of 'philosophy'; that is, of reasoned argumentation in the absence of their falling under the terms of reference of any established discipline. Regarding the latter, our meaning might better be conveyed by hypothesising an example whereby our present foundations of the science of physics were entirely overthrown, reversing that seventeenth (and subsequent twentieth) century philosophical retreat. What an outpouring of philosophy we would witness![24] But even without such dramatic hypotheses there remain numerous areas of enquiry into the nature of things which are as yet not subject to demonstrable explanation or explication. As the nature of the physical universe is increasingly laid bare the scope of philosophy may be correspondingly restricted – but questions always remain, not least, for example, regarding the rationale (and hence validity) of 'scientific' explanations themselves (itself merely one topic within the 'world of mind').

From this perspective the value of philosophy is perhaps more to raise rather than answer questions, such that it encourages individuals to advance knowledge and understanding beyond the boundaries encompassed by existing disciplines. In the Socratic sense good philosophy points out what one does *not* know or understand, and it may well be that individuals are more prompted to respond to such probings because dissatisfied with the *answers* philosophers give, than by simply being told that they, the non-philosophers, do not know the answers. In this connection we should be reminded that questions such as, 'why is the sky blue?' or 'what is illness?' were just as difficult to answer in the fifth century BC via any demonstrably sure argumentation as the questions, 'are there different kinds of understanding?' or 'what is the nature of mind?' remain today.

There. is a sense, then, in which the literal translation of the term 'philosophy' – namely, 'love of knowledge' or 'love of wisdom' – is ironically misleading since its rationale may be better designated as 'love of the unknown'. This accords well with that *amazement* at the nature of things which is properly characteristic of the philosophical temperament, whereby the mind leaves aside things already understood in search of things still to be wondered at, or carves out the genuine opportunity to challenge even the former. In short, philosophy 'reaches parts other disciplines don't reach', and would only disappear through a final fulfilment of its own progress, whereby its probings prompted the emergence of disciplines to answer *all* questions via demonstrable argumentation – an eventuality so distant, if not impossible, as to cause no alarm to those who define human beings as (essentially), philosophers.

This said about the nature of philosophy in general, we can proceed to examine the notion of that branch known as 'the philosophy of history' with a view to assessing its relevance, if any, to the practising historian. Philosophers now usually distinguish between 'speculative' philosophies of history, which attempt some overall interpretation of the course of past events, and 'analytic' philosophy of history,[25] which, in being primarily concerned to examine the nature of the *discipline* of history, is thereby also interested in the suppositions informing 'speculative' philosophies of history. Rightly, some see these two projects as interconnected[26] – others do not. The latters' thinking, however, is based more on *a priori*, or imaginative, notions of the discipline of history than on what stares them in the face – namely, what those recognised as historians actually do. Consequently a 'white elephant' literature has arisen, busily debating topics such as 'determinism', 'causality', 'responsibility', 'truth criteria', 'objectivity', and 'historical explanation', and from which a variety of criticisms, prescriptions, and encouragements is showered upon our poor practitioners.

Now although some argue the very precondition of philosophy is that its proponents be 'disinterested' in their conclusions (as if, peculiarly, 'truth' were the sole preserve of philosophy rather than applying with at least equal poignancy to anyone wiring an electric plug), a better alternative is to appeal to those who have a considerable 'interest' in their conclusions regarding the matters at hand because directly involved in trying to manage them. In other words, we should not be particularly interested in what individuals who have no direct experience of a thing have to say about it.

However, neither should we lack caution when listening to what those whose interests are intimately involved in the understanding of a thing have to say about it, since their account is likely to be, not false, but partial because limited to that aspect of the matter which affects them.

The upshot of this is that analytic philosophers of history should pay attention to what historians actually do, ideally by engaging in that discipline themselves, before attempting to examine the nature of the discipline of history. Vice versa, of course, historians who wish to dispute the conclusions advanced by analytic philosophers of history should pay respect to the function of philosophy, ideally by engaging in that activity themselves – and, in addition, examine their objections for partiality.

The point has been sufficiently made, I hope, to pursue the topic of the philosophy of history in the light of what historians actually do. Within that broad orbit I have singled out factual narrative as that which has a rationale sufficiently distinct to sustain the notion of history as a discrete, identifiable discipline rather than a slap-happy juxtapositioning of various discourses loosely associated in virtue of being concerned with 'the past'. Proceeding from here we should first observe that the current disassociation of analytic from 'speculative' (or 'substantive') philosophy of history is a mixed blessing. If by the latter is meant, 'the central aspiration to afford a total explanatory account of the past'[27] – that is, in our terms, to see history as a pattern or design evidencing 'reason' – then we have already dismissed this possibility and will have yet more to say on this.

If, on the other hand, 'speculative' or 'substantive' philosophy of history is primarily meant to refer to the actual *content* of history as distinct from the form in which that content is apprehended (that is, the *discipline* of history), then the attempt to understand the nature of that content is, far from misguided, essential. Where form and content are divorced intellectual misfortune can only follow. What appears to have happened in many cases is that analytic philosophers of history, rightly deciding not to waste time on analysing attempts to render the 'course of history' as the manifestation of some 'mind', or even of some mind*less* pattern, have turned their backs on the content of history *per se*. Instead they concentrate solely on the form in which that content (which will not go away), is presented – namely, on the *discipline* of history. They thereby 'throw out the baby with the bathwater'.

Let us reiterate that there is 'out there' a reality of 'events', 'story-objects', 'narrative' or 'historical' identities or phenomena, which is apprehended and explicated via an already existing discipline, namely, history. It is *their* presence which invites that discipline as the 'form' appropriate to apprehending the nature of that 'content'. To ignore that content and concentrate on the form alone (that is, to look solely at what formulations and presuppositions the discipline displays, irrespective of the substantive content it deals with), is akin to arriving half-way through an unfamiliar symphony and picking at aspects of its composition in the light of some abstract concept of 'what music is' – or akin to listening to an art-critic who exercises his intellect in criticising the brush-strokes in a painting without seeing the whole of it, or imagining it is some *other* painting than, for instance, this Van Gogh. It is not difficult to gain the impression that much of the work of analytic philosophers of history, however refined (and indeed recondite), suffers this drawback; that they 'nit-pick' at what historians do. A kind of randomised critique emerges, interspersed with alternative idealised petty paradigms, whereby they are not so much concerned to understand the nature of the discipline of history (which necessitates attention to the 'content' of history), as to find 'logical' contradictions, paradoxes, and inadequacies in that discourse without reference to its overall rationale.[28] It can only be instructive to note the indifference historians afford such analytic philosophy of history.

Rather, then, than dissociate form from content, one needs an overall vision of the sense in which the actual rationale of the discipline of history corresponds to its object or content before one can locate what is relevant to understanding the nature of the discipline. Conversely it can equally be said one needs an understanding of the discipline of history before one can properly locate what is relevant in understanding the nature of the 'content' of history, or 'history' as the 'object'. In fact the two (the discipline of history and its object), are of course so intermingled that in understanding the one, one understands the other.

It happens that in the case of history the proper understanding of it as 'object' or 'content' is peculiarly difficult compared to, for example, astronomy or psychology. Their 'objects' seem given and easily recognisable – the problem has been to establish viable disciplines with which to apprehend their nature. If anything the case has been the reverse with history, where, despite the long-established discipline of factual narrative, it has variously been discarded or subjected to random criticisms because many have either taken for granted a notion of 'history as content' so vague as to offer no coherent guide to its form (that is, to the *discipline*), or have no such notion at all.

In this dialectic between form and content, or a discipline (*any* discipline) and its object, primacy must be given to content, for if reality did not include phenomena which were intelligible there would be no forms (disciplines) by which the nature of phenomena are understood. Put simply, if reality were undifferentiated then the process of differentiating would not exist – or if one tried it it would not work. Thus if there were no difference between *a* and *b* then that elementary condition for the discipline of logic would be absent, such that logic would not be a form, or discipline, by which individuals apprehended the nature of (discrete aspects of) reality. Alternatively they could propose whatever 'logic' took their fancy, with correspondingly fanciful results.

It is of course true there needs to *be* an individual thinking mind to make whatever differentiations (or 'understandings'), are possible, but even more important is that there be something offering itself *to* differentiation. Were there not discrete 'objects' in reality then disciplines (that is, forms of apprehending the nature of these objects), would not arise.

On the other hand, in giving logical primacy to the 'contents' of reality it would be wrong to regard them as given, self-sufficient, or 'objective'. Just as in that dialectic between master and slave where neither would be what they are without the other (albeit the initiative for their respective existences lies with the master), so the form in which discrete parts of reality are apprehended depends upon the dialectic between the apprehender and the rest of reality. Obviously we can say that without the apprehender no form would be recognised – but we can also say the nature of the form recognised depends upon how that reality impinges in relevant, hence notable, ways upon the apprehender. This draws attention as much to the nature of the apprehender as to the nature of the reality he apprehends, whereby the dialectical circle is closed.

As Feuerbach laboured to clarify, the nature of man is discovered by paying attention to what is an 'object' for him,[29] and although it may be true he made subsequent mistakes which allowed Marx (eventually) to accuse him of 'contemplative materialism',[30] (regarding 'the object' as given – as if, so to speak, there could be masters without slaves), he may be forgiven for overstating his case regarding the irreducability of the 'content' of reality given the dominant (Hegelian) position he saw himself as opposing – namely, that the differentiations we make within reality are solely the product of self-determining Mind driven to resolve what, to it, is the logical paradox of 'Being'. His central insistence on 'content' was, in that context, entirely salutary.

Thus, with respect to 'history' we arrive at the formulation that as a discipline (or 'form') its nature cannot be divorced from its content (that is, from 'substantive', or 'actual' history), *pace* much analytic philosophy of history. Rather, this 'content' is only established as such not only because there *are* 'happenings', 'occurrences', and 'events' – that is, intelligible sequences, themselves worth differentiating – but also because the perception or 'abstracting' of them has proved a relevant, useful, and workable feature of human experience. I say, then, that there are events and such, not in the sense of their being 'objective' or given, but in the sense and to the extent that any phenomenon, be it a rock or a downpour of rain, can be said to be 'real' (as explored in Chapter Two).

There is, however, this difference; whereas the intelligibility of material objects is that much more explicit when they are man-made (because the 'reason' for abstracting them from the world of objects is the same as the 'reason' for *making* them), so to a degree in the world of 'events', 'story-objects', or 'narrative identities', the intelligibility of sequences is, by those necessities of the narrative form we have set out, more generally equatable with the 'reason for' (or 'reason in') human conduct. We cannot give a narrative account of an ant's behaviour; we can only chronicle one movement to the next (an empty description rather than a narrative account), and propose understandings or explanations with reference to causal laws.

Human conduct, on the contrary, creates intelligible sequences (or is the factor upon which their intelligibility is grounded), such that perceiving/abstracting narrative identities is akin to perceiving/abstracting man-made artefacts. The reason 'for' or 'in' them does not so much equate with what we happen to find relevant in an otherwise undifferentiated world, but more immediately with the fact that individuals 'have reasons' for their conduct. Thus of an action such as closing the window its sequentiality coincides with the 'reason for' closing it – that is, its intelligibility as a sequence is secured via the intelligibility afforded by the general sense of human conduct.

However, I have qualified the parallel with man-made artefacts by adding the term, 'to a degree'. This is because, although the source of the intelligibility of a sequence coincides with the reasons for someone's conduct in the case of *individual* actions, the matter is not so straightforward when dealing with interpersonal sequences such as wars, revolutions, or constitutional reforms. Here, individuals respond to each other, in different ways to a variety of factors, such that although we may find the *outcome* intelligible in terms of numerous individuals' reasons for what they do, none of these 'events', 'stories', or 'narrative identities' are the product of a single individual's conduct (despite the illusions of certain politicians, generals, or economic advisers).

Thus it is that ultimately the material most frequently dealt with by historians – that is, portentous changes in the 'human-dominated' world – is in a kind of middle. Although the intelligibility of such sequences does not equate with the 'reason for' a single individual's conduct, its source nevertheless derives from that intelligibility whereby the 'reasons for' things are equatable with the manner in which human 'reasoning' is involved in human conduct.

By analogy, I am intimate with the intelligibility of an object I made because I conferred the 'reason' in it (that is, its 'nature'). I did not abstract it from the world of objects because it imposed its relevance on me – rather, I created it. The case is different regarding an object made by someone else. I am not immediately intimate with its intelligibility. However, I *am* intimate with the *source* of its intelligibility – it equates with that someone else's reasoning. I might not know what that 'reasoning' is but I do recognise 'reasoning' as the principle underlying the object's intelligibility. The same applies to an object contributed to by *many* people, its nature being the outcome of different individuals' reasonings.

When it comes to 'natural' objects, however, we say that in themselves they have no intelligibility. (Indeed, their very status as discrete objects is not self-sufficient). Rather, it is the process of their abstracting which is intelligible, not they themselves directly. In short, it is not this rock or that tree which is intelligible in itself, but the *word* 'tree', or 'rock'. Of such words denoting natural objects we ask, what is the source of the meaning or intelligibility of these words? And the answer cannot lie in the reason for *creating* the objects (they were not created), but in the reason for inventing the words denoting them – that is, the 'reason for' attending to, or abstracting, or individuating, them as denoted objects. In the cases of both created and natural objects 'reason' is involved in what we call their 'nature', but in the former case their 'reason', 'nature', or 'intelligibility' is imposed upon them by us, whereas 'reason' is only associated with *natural* objects inasmuch as they provoke reasons *for* noticing them. They themselves (for instance, their shape, size, colour, weight, or chemical composition), are neither reasonable nor unreasonable. What we call their 'nature' is simply whatever it is about them which provokes us to individuate them and is encapsulated in the meaning of the word we use to denote them (at hand in the dictionary). In short, man is a tree-perceiving but kettle-creating being, such that the source of intelligibility for natural objects is different from that of man-made objects despite both involving what we have called 'reasoning'.

Now the same can be said of the world of happenings, occurrences, and events as of the world of material objects. Some of the sequences making up this world are attended to and individuated by us insofar as they press their relevance upon us – that is, *natural* sequences such as earthquakes and volcanic eruptions. Other natural sequences which claim our attention are not individuated but are spelt out in particular 'pseudo-stories' or narrations, such as 'the cat came into the room and then chased a mouse under the sideboard'. Individuated or not, such sequences are not intelligible in themselves; they have no 'reason' *in* them. Their intelligibility is that afforded by the language in which they are denoted. As a *content*, or 'object', the *form* or discipline appropriate to exploring their 'nature' is the area of linguistics, grammar, and logic.

The case is different, however, with sequences *created* by human beings, for here, as with other things made (for instance, chairs, clocks), their nature is produced by 'reasoning' human beings and is therefore 'reasonable'. Thus in understanding their nature we are involved in recapturing the reasoning process which led to their formation. In other words, the form in which these sequences, as *content*, are apprehended equates with the manner in which reasoning inheres directly in that content itself. Just, then, as we can understand the *nature* of a chair, not simply what the *word* 'chair' means, so we can understand the nature of sequences formed through human conduct, in terms of one thing 'following on from' another.

This form demanded by the nature of the content (that is, the discipline appropriate to the object), is factual narrative; that is, history. The content of history is intelligible because the components of sequences are made to 'follow on' by individuals who have reasons for what they do. In reconstructing this 'following on' input by individuals we lay bare a sequence as an intelligible phenomenon. It is the (only) way in which we *understand* the *nature* of the *content*, just as it is the (only) way in which the content *is* intelligible 'in itself'.

What emerges from this analysis of the dialectic between form and content (or between a discipline and its object), is, then, that the intelligibility of the content of history coincides with the manner (that is, form, or discipline), in which the nature of that content is apprehended; and there must be a strong sense in which anything not subsumed under this analysis is merely contingent both to history as 'substantive content' and to history as a discipline. Thus, if by 'the philosophy of history' we are referring to an understanding of the nature of the content of history, or of the discipline of history, or of both, then the foregoing arguments are perhaps sufficient to satisfy those criteria. Of course one can talk *about* both the content and discipline of history from as many angles and for as long as one wishes, but the exploration of such contingencies is not our concern here. Our understanding of 'the philosophy of history' is restricted to enquiring into the nature of the 'form' and 'content' of history (that is, the discipline and its object), both of which I have laboured to make clear. Philosophy, I have argued, is the investigation into the nature of things, inspired by astonishment rather than mere curiosity. The latter may be satisfied by pursuing the heuristic techniques of a given discipline whereas one's astonishment at something is prompted partly by the inaccessibility of its nature via existing disciplines – whereby, to put the matter in a more negative light than previously (where philosophy reaches the parts other disciplines cannot), we have as a last resort to depend on consulting our wits.

CONCLUSION: THE DISCIPLINE OF HISTORY

Having made clear, within those sections analysing the topics of 'reason in history' and 'historical explanation', what relevance they have for the practising historian, I hope also to have shown in what respects 'the philosophy of history' (under which some would subsume those two prior topics) should and should not impinge on the historian's practice. More precisely, since this is not a prescriptive work, I have laboured to expose the rationale underlying narrative historians' work, offering this as a bench-mark by which to assess the worth of those various discussions which constitute the now substantial body of literature known as 'philosophy of history'.

It has thus been important to derive this rationale not from some *a priori* nor imaginative notion of the discipline of history; nor from some *a priori* nor fuzzy notion of what the 'content' of 'actual' history is. Rather, it has been important to establish from what historians actually do, the rationale underlying their discipline; the nature of the object (or general 'subject-matter') of that discipline; the extent to which an implicit dialectic pertains between discipline and object ('form' and 'content'); and the degree to which the historian's practice is thereby self-composed, or intelligible.

What ensues is that the bulk of historians are engaged in an activity which is remarkably coherent. This is to say that although in both the popular *and* philosophical mind confusions and illusions respectively abound regarding 'what is history?' (both as substantive content and as a discipline), the bulk of those practising the discipline exhibit a sureness of touch often absent in some philosophers of history, whose business it is to reveal either the fullness or paucity of its nature through informed argument. As for those who are called historians but do not centre their activity on the construction of narrative, or do so whilst betraying those categorial imperatives I have argued as integral to its construction (thereby inventing 'pseudo-narrative'), I say that to the extent they publicly succeed in warranting this denotion the scarcer the authentic practice of the historian will become. Such an eventuality would not merely be intellectually messy; it would run the graver risk of relegating to the sidelines an intellectual activity responsible for revealing the nature of (or 'explicating'), an entire class of phenomena which form (or are extricated as) a fundamental component of the reality we experience. Whether this concern is expressive of a crisis not, then, solely within historiography but within the wider orbit of our ability to understand reality, is paradoxically a question only answerable by future historians.

Historians, then, are not those who talk interestingly albeit randomly about the past; rather, they are those who painstakingly extract intelligible phenomena from a kaleidoscopic scenario of happenings which would otherwise remain a teeming chaos. Some of the causal mechanisms operative within this chaos can be disclosed by the scientists, and in *that* sense aspects of it are rendered intelligible. Historians, on the other hand, explicate the contents of this real world of occurrences and events through the only form or discipline appropriate to this categorial object. However, we do not say this is every historian's conscious intention. He is not a philosopher, amazed at the nature of things and thus consciously pursuing that kind of enquiry. Rather he is the historian, already immersed in his contextual world, whereby his curiosity (rather than amazement) is aroused when he does not know why something happened or is dissatisfied with existing accounts. This latter is more prevalent, particularly where new evidence interferes with existing accounts. But in addition, new methodologies or original thinking may equally raise queries over the adequacy of existing explanations of 'what happened'. Whichever, the upshot is that the historian is led to amend, reconstruct, or 're-explicate' the nature of that overall sequence which involves the particular occurrences or actions he finds puzzling.

To develop this point regarding what historians achieve in their work we may take as an example the origins of the First World War. In one form or another the question of why that war occurred appears on students' question papers with (justifiable) regularity; and what is sought is an explanation of why it occurred via giving an account *of* something. In other words, we hope to receive a narrative which eventuates in war breaking out, and in which that eventuality is explained in terms of its following from previous events. Also we hope the choice of relevant preceding events will comprise as comprehensive and likely an account as can be expected. If carried out well, at least respecting its rationale as a piece of writing, what we will receive will amount to a description or exploration of something, in the course of which the war's outbreak will be explained. Whatever that 'something' *is* which is being described, explored, or explicated as to its nature, it must be some singular, real identity in the world (that is, a 'narrative' or 'historical' identity). In this case, of course, it is a notoriously complex identity for which there is no adequate individuating term, although to call it 'a particular multilateral international argument' comes somewhere near the mark.

The point here is that in a practice which appears to revolve around explaining why this or that event occurred, or how this or that state of affairs came about, the historian is led into proffering explications of the nature of sequences or 'narrative identities'. The former endeavour is always deliberate or intentional. The latter *may* be equally so, especially where numerous junctures of an existing explanation seem dubious to him such that he becomes aware of the need to reconstruct an entire account, within whose compass the intelligibility of that merely *particular* event or situation originally appeared questionable. (Such circumstances generate

161

re-writings, rather than mere amendments, of previously accepted narrative identities.)

More usually, however, we can suppose the work of most historians originates in their impulse to better explain why something occurred or turned into this or that situation, rather than to achieve what is *implied* by such activity; namely, the more 'philosophical' prize of explicating the nature of a phenomenon in the world of happenings.

By way of analogy we may cite the skilful tennis-player, adept at all the shots. But the *complete* tennis-player recognises his activity is not devoted to, nor exemplified by, demonstrating his stroke ability. Rather, what makes the exercise of his skills worthwhile (thereby rendering them subservient to a higher rationale), is winning the match. However, just as one does not initially coach tennis-players in how to win, but in how to play the shots, so there is little point in training aspiring historians in the ultimate rationale of explicating the nature of real narrative identities before they are familiar with the prerequisite – namely, the accurate use of narrative logic to explain why this or that occurred.

On the other hand, no top tennis coach will waste his time on those who are not already in command of all the shots. Rather, he begins by telling his pupils that, now they *are* adept at all the shots, he is going to instruct them in what the game is *actually* about, and that if they thought they already knew, they had better forget their previous illusions.

Just so, ideally, with the complete historian. Although he will have 'cut his teeth' on learning the practice of explaining this or that via the logic of narrative, there comes a point at which, like our aspiring tennis champion, he understands what factual narrative (or the game of tennis), is in fact all about. That satisfaction he previously took in exercising (as an end-in-itself) his ability to explain why *x* occurred, or how *y* came about, is redirected towards a higher end – namely, the explication of genuine continuities, or 'narrative phenomena'. I call this a higher end not because it is a different activity but because it subsumes, or relies upon, the techniques previously developed.

A distinct shift in emphasis is involved here. Whereas our competent tennis-player formerly played matches so as to enjoy his playing abilities, now his mind is on winning the match, to which aim his stroke-play is now subservient. For instance, he could easily hit the ball harder, or with more flair, but this might not serve his ultimate end of winning the match.

So with our complete historian. Where he might formerly have regarded 'digging into the past' as merely a *means* in order to achieve the *end* of explaining why some particular thing occurred, or how a particular situation came about, he now regards the former as his principal end; namely, the extrication of real, intelligible continuities, or explicatable narrative phenomena.

This is not an entirely different activity since it relies intimately on those learnt techniques of narrative explanation. But these latter now become merely constitutive of it, since their execution is now contributive to a more comprehensive end, and may thus be classed as 'mediate' actions. On the other side of the coin, 'digging into the past' is transformed from a means of answering present enquiries regarding why this or that occurred, into an end-in-itself, whereby phenomena as 'real' as material objects are uncovered to view – namely, 'historical identities'.

This (like becoming a tennis champion), is not an easy achievement. Nor does it correlate with what some philosophers of history appear to think historians should aspire to. However, we are now in a better position to see that many of their prescriptions are addressed, by analogy, not even to accomplished tennis-stroke players (let alone match-winners), but to those learning the basic strokes; and even here, so many of their prescriptions are already off the point albeit, by analogy, 'interesting' to those amongst non-tennis players who have little idea what the game is about but do like to hear it 'discussed'. Similar contortions arise *vis-à-vis* the practice of the sciences and the 'discussions' advanced by a number of philosophers of science.[31]

What we are saying, then, is that an event (such as the outbreak of a war, a scientific discovery, the making of a film), is accounted *for* through the historian's making it part of the story, or account, *of* something – and he has to discover what this 'something' is. It must not be an abstraction nor an invention. Rather, it must constitute an actual, singular identity. To tell the story of something is to explicate the nature of something, and it must be something 'real'. The essence of our argument is that there are some 'things' whose nature can only be exposed by 'telling their story' (via the form of narrative), because their nature *is* that of an intelligible sequence of occurrences – that is, a story. These 'things' I have variously referred to as 'narrative identities', 'narrative phenomena', or 'story-objects', if only to draw attention to the proper correspondence between form and content – in other words, to the appropriateness of the discipline of history to the nature of the object it studies. The ultimate objective of history as a discipline is not, then, to explain why this or that occurred but, *through* that activity, to explicate the nature of 'narrative', 'story', or 'historical' phenomena, a class of phenomena which, although often so complex and/or unique that their constituents defy individuation into universals such as 'wars', 'journeys', or 'tennis matches', are nevertheless as 'real' or 'objective' as other apparently more simply established and understood phenomena such as material objects.

Thus if historians are taken to be involved in explaining why this or that event occurred, or how this or that circumstance came about, such events or circumstances must be subject to narrative explanation – that is, must fall into that class of phenomena whose explanation is treated within the terms of reference of contingent sequences of occurrences. In other words, for an event or circumstance to be a thing subject to narrative explanation it must be involved in something subject to narrative explication. This in turn demands (to revert to Chapter Two's analysis), that the event or circumstance must be an integral episode or outcome of something 'real' which constitutes a *changing identity* – that is to say, a *phenomenon constituted by change*. Thus although the practising historian will refer to numerous kinds of phenomena and engage in diverse subsidiary descriptions, analyses, and explanations for the purposes of clarification, what he is essentially concerned with is changing identities, that is, that class of phenomena constituted by change. In themselves these subsidiary expeditions' only *self-subsistent* rationale relates to the undisciplined interests of antiquarians, whose often meticulous work may on occasions be relevant to that of the historian. This depends upon whether their results impinge upon the historian's essential activity, that of explicating the nature of changing identities. This is what the historian is engaged in, and he can only do this via the narrative form.

He will not, then, be explaining, or accounting for, these phenomena. Rather, he will be exposing their 'reality' to us, or 'explicating their nature', thereby making them intelligible, or 'bringing them into our understanding'. He will not be explaining, or accounting for, them because only if these phenomena, these identities constituted by change, *themselves* changed would the question of explaining or accounting for them arise. And here, the rationale of the historian's approach would again lead him to explicate what are now *new* changing identities, or phenomena constituted by change. Since, however, there are no super/non-human agents responsible for human conduct there can be no such new changing identities. They could only arise if human responses were in fact states of affairs deliberately intended by some non-human agency. And with that possible exception of Marx's notion of 'human history' discussed above, where human beings themselves take on the fashioning of their otherwise spontaneous responses, thereby fulfilling their nature as human precisely through superseding it (a fearsomely interesting but problematic argument), this is exactly a situation implied by determinist theories of history.

Here again we find practising historians' intuitions, which spurn determinism in history, confirming our lines of argument. Determinism implies people do not respond freely to situations but are tools employed by some extra-human agency (for instance, some species of god, or Hegel's 'Idea'), whereby human actions are simply events or manifestations of states of affairs deliberately intended by, and therefore evidencing some 'reason' on behalf of, some extra-human agent. Given this premise, the key to understanding history is therefore not only to identify this agent but also to explain or account for its manipulation of human beings' conduct as *its* response to *its* present 'situation' or 'experience'. This, in turn, would

164

involve an explication of that sequence of occurrences within and by which the conduct of this extra-human agency is explicable.

Such an enterprise is not lunatic in terms of its logic. That, on the contrary, has just been outlined as perfectly coherent. What makes it flawed is that it is faith masquerading as understanding. But cases differ. For example, although they purport to know what their god's responses are *vis-à-vis* its manipulation of human beings, Christian teleologists do not claim to *explain* these responses by reference to an explicatable sequence of occurrences within which their god's conduct constitutes an integral episode or outcome. Rather, those who do attempt to 'explain' their god's conduct do so by reference to speculative propositions regarding its nature or attributes rather than by reference to the (narrative) logic of conduct. Thus it is that, nevertheless, the logic by which Christian determinists explicate past sequences remains lamentably 'half-baked', for they talk only of the *intentions* of their alleged agent, openly professing ignorance (or, indeed, even the absence) of any context whereby the conduct of such an agent may be made intelligible as a response in the first place.

In short, the logic of the discipline of history remains imperturbable, ready to accommodate whatever is said about 'the past' so long as it conforms to the logic of factual narrative (which Christian teleology only half fulfills), *and* so long as it can be inferred from 'evidence' (such as documents, artefacts, or linguistic traits). However, where either logic or evidence, or both, are lacking we are invited into that different world of 'faith' or belief, wherein we hold a proposition to be true not in virtue of the cogency of the arguments advanced to support it but because we trust the source of the proposition.

In numerous instances it is of course by no means unreasonable to rely on faith or belief as a source of knowledge, for if one does not know the answer to a question one consults an authority (that is, a source of allegedly sound information), whereby 'it follows' one can believe the propositions issuing from that source.[32] Historians themselves, indeed, are a potent example of such sources or authorities. Not only, indeed, *can* faith be reasonable; where we encounter it it will often *be* 'reasonable', for most human beings are 'sane' – that is, capable of 'reasoning', or appreciating one thing 'following on' from another. To the normally functioning mind it 'follows' that when an expert on palaeontology proposes a certain fossil is the femur of a brontosaurus we accept this proposition as true.

Nevertheless we must recognise the difference between accepting something as true inasmuch as the arguments supporting it relate to the substantive content of the proposition, and accepting a proposition on the reasonable grounds that its source is reliable. In the former case reason is always involved, whereas in the latter emotion rather than reason can on occasion be involved, whereby one believes what someone says not in virtue of having good reasons for doing so (that is, reasons related immediately to the qualifications, or proven record, of the source), but vicariously (that is, for reasons so distant from the relevant considerations as to render their 'leading toward' the reliability of the source a virtually contingent matter). For example, one might be attracted by an alleged authority's charisma, or because one is in fear of that authority's reprisals for disbelief in its pronouncements. It is not only religions and political movements which are adept in this dual deployment of 'stick and carrot' whereby they achieve belief in their propositions. Family, school, the work-place, and 'public opinion' are also contexts which induce this kind of '*blind*' (that is, *virtually* 'unreasonable') faith or belief.

But in the absence of such unfortunate, sometimes necessary, sometimes appalling, practices, where faith is instead clearly grounded we say that the source of the reasonableness in accepting propositions is nevertheless different from that intelligibility which inheres in arguments directly. The reason I accept what the palaeontologist proposes is not that I understand it as following from previous propositions he has advanced, but that it follows from his expertise that what he proposes is (probably) true. This, in short, is why we have the words 'faith' and 'belief'; not, then, as opposed or contrary to 'reason', but rather as opposed to 'understanding'.

This has been no esoteric philosophical debate, because it does relate directly to the practice of the historian. The upshot of the discussion, still relevant in a world less secular than many suppose, has been that although it can be reasonable to accept an account of the past on faith (because it 'makes sense' to have confidence in the source of the account), this is different from the reasoning involved in constructing an account of the past by inferring, and sometimes proving, the acceptability of propositions based on evidence. Now, it is all the more important to draw attention to this distinction between faith and what I have called 'understanding' because it is one which remains intriguingly blurred in the practice of the discipline of history.

The problem is twofold. Not only is it difficult to differentiate on principle between a proposition about the past based on reasoned acceptance of the reliability of its source as distinct from inferences derived from the immediacy of the evidence – for all we know the two are equated by practising historians more often than we might like to suppose. They frequently cite authorities, as themselves a kind of evidence, to support their propositions about the past. Often, it is true, they do examine the reliability of these sources or 'authorities' before having faith in them; but this is a different exercise from finding evidence to support a proposition. Instead, it supports the alleged truth of a proposition rather than inviting (prior) propositions which, through rendering it intelligible, contribute directly to its validity. (For example, confronted by more advanced extra-terrestrial visitors, and *believing* what they tell us of their technology – 'this spaceship harnesses anti-gravitational energy' – we might understand what they say but not the reasoning supporting their propositions. As such, their technology will be unintelligible to us, although we understand and accept their propositions.)

Now, what we do not know, prima facie, is whether an historian, in citing an authority, does so on 'blind' faith, *or* on reasonable faith, *or* because he has himself studied the material dealt with by the authority and agrees with what it says.

Thus we encounter a distinction, more subtle than often supposed, between 'faith' and its alleged converse, 'reason', as reliable sources of knowledge. Ideally it teaches a hard lesson not only to the historian but to any involved in investigative disciplines; namely, that in their work they should rely solely on those argumentative techniques by which propositions constitutive of the relevant discipline are directly established and supported, rather than argue vicariously by exploiting authorities as if what they propose is itself 'evidence', or part of an intelligible argument. Investigative disciplines should avoid this latter practice – but not, then, because of a mistaken view that it is inherently unreasonable to have belief in what an authority says, but because in interspersing propositions based on belief into a discourse otherwise constituted through reasoning, one thereby interrupts that reasoning, such that the overall argument no longer consists of one thing following from another. In short, one no longer has an authentic 'argument', but a heterogeneous form of discourse which does not correlate one-to-one with the content of what is being explicated.

Thus the historian engaged in research should, where necessary, re-examine the conclusions reached by previous authorities rather than spend time on examining those authorities' credibility. Although there is nothing 'unreasonable' in accepting their accounts in other contexts, the researcher should be prepared to re-work the material to the satisfaction of his own understanding of the matter at hand. To do so preserves the integrity of the discipline as that form appropriate to explicating its content or 'object'. In addition it is precisely this preparedness to re-work previously held, widely respected (hence authoritative), propositions which can be the condition of dramatic break-throughs in knowledge. In short, *understanding* (reason) rather than received wisdom (faith) is the condition of valid knowledge and its extension.

Thus, let children groping in the discipline of geometry, told the angles of any triangle add up to 180°, first be told the figure 180 is purely conventional – that it represents half a circle, which is (only conventionally) divided into 360°. Let it be explained it could just as well be 100° if the arc of a circle were denominated as covering 200 sections. Then let it be explained, or demonstrated, that any triangle drawn, using the line halving the circle as one of its sides, will always be comprised of arcs amounting to the sum of the angles represented by the arc encompassed by that half-circle. In this way we might inspire an understanding of the basics of geometry rather than an understanding merely of the meaning of what authorities have said. The former represents understanding of the content (triangles), because it introduces us to the form of that content. The latter represents merely understanding (and more or less blind acceptance) of the words uttered by an authority on the subject. It does not reveal, through equating the understanding process (the 'form') with the object studied, the manner in which that content is intelligible. The sum of the angles of the triangle thereby appear, as they remain in subsequent years to many a bemused, badly educated youth, 'fabulous' (just as our imagined 'knowledge' of extra-terrestrial technology); and not a lot more can be expected of him in the world of geometry until he abandons faith in authorities, however reasonably founded, in favour of immediate understanding based on arguments intrinsic to the matter in hand. This is not to deny, of course, that common sense dictates that a great deal must initially be taught to children 'by rote', so they can function in a practicable way in the world around them. But it does insist that, at some stage judged by the sensitive intuition of teachers, every child should be given the opportunity to intellectually grasp a subject rather than remain captive to belief.

Just so, then, with the discipline of history. It *is* a discipline. It is a discipline because there are rational parameters to its discourse, ultimately governed by the nature of history as 'object' or 'content'. That 'content', however, is not given, self-sufficient, or autonomous. The rationality which inheres in it as 'content', 'object', or 'subject-matter' is constituted by our propensity to notice, conceive of, and find relevant, one thing following on from, or out of, another. In the case of a natural science this propensity results in the discovery of physical 'laws'; in the case of geometry, in the discovery of the nature of figures; in the case of linguistics, in the discovery of the 'rules' governing languages. In the case of history this propensity is exercised upon what we loosely call 'events', whereby in perceiving continuity in occurrences we conceive of sequences, this in turn generating the explication of the nature of phenomena constituted by change – namely, 'narrative' or 'historical' identities.

Chapter One addressed the issue of isolating the rationale of history as a distinct and intellectually coherent discipline. This led to Chapter Two's close analysis of (factual) *narrative* in general, particularly respecting the logic of its structure, its explanatory potential, and the manner in which it is explicative of 'real' phenomena. Chapter Three pursued those implications of the prior chapter's analysis which relate directly to the practice of construing and presenting 'history', leading into this present chapter's exploration of the 'theory' of the discipline of history, combining more general or abstract principles with the main points they imply for the actual construction of historical accounts.

In the course of these latter two chapters a number of negative injunctions have emerged – for instance, a restricted view of agency; the shunning of specific theories of human conduct in favour of a common-sense, accommodating view, useful and relevant for the historian; a discrete rather than profligate concept of history as 'content' – and it is true such injunctions appear to reduce the possibilities of the study of history, and/ or diminish the scope of its proper compass, beyond the generous limits afforded it not only by the general public but also by some historians themselves, whereby virtually any statement falls under the embrace of 'the discipline of history' so long as it concerns the past. We, however, are content in having argued the correctness of such restrictions, as we are to leave statements about the past as no more nor less than what they are – namely, statements about the past.

In concluding Chapter Two we pointed out that, despite its detailed analysis of narrative in general, it still needed to be seen what the implications were of fitting the historian into his narrative jacket – or, conversely, how the narrative jacket appears when taken from its peg, to be worn by the historian, concerned only with fact, not fiction. Specifically, we asked whether the *narrative* historian is thereby restricted to discoursing on and explaining only certain kinds of things because of the narrative form – and, conversely, whether the explanatory and explicatory powers of narrative are limited or modified in *historical* narrative.

In the course of exploring issues of direct and also alleged relevance to the practising historian, it is hoped these specific questions have been answered, since it has emerged that it is indeed only certain kinds of things whose nature demand explication through the narrative form – or, conversely, that the *factual* narrative form is only appropriate to certain kinds of things. I have called these things 'narrative' or 'historical' identities, meaning phenomena whose nature can only be set out by means of the narrative form. Conversely, I have tried to show the (factual) narrative form is structured on the explication of historical identities. An historical identity is an identity or phenomenon constituted by change (and only in *that* sense a 'changing identity'); and inasmuch as real change rather than mere differentiation, or some unreal abstraction, is present only where we encounter deliberate human actions in the world, then an historical identity is a product of human conduct. Its ingredients, so to speak, are individuals' dealings with the world – for instance, with inanimate objects, other species, each other, ideas, feelings, institutions, and practices. As such, the parameters to the discipline of history, although far tighter than those so loosely encompassed by such phrases as 'the study of the past', remain sufficiently generous to accommodate topics ranging from wine-making, aviation, football, cities, and automobiles, to political constitutions, painting, medicine, and mathematical thinking. This is because what enables aspects of these ingredients to congeal, so to speak, into something specific is the thread of human endeavour weaving discrete lines of continuity, established via intention, through an otherwise randomly differentiated world. It is human intention which creates connectives between states of affairs, which explains why, early in Chapter Three, a largish section was devoted to presenting a (non-specialist) view of human conduct which might assist in disentangling at least those of its features which relate to that concept crucial to the understanding of 'history', namely, continuity.

But an equally crucial, and paradoxically inseparable, concept for our understanding of 'history' is that of *change*. Change is essential to the rationale of narrative (as distinct from mere chronicle); equally, a thing has no history if it never changes. The history of a thing consists of recounting change. Thus narrative is the indispensable life-blood of 'history', both as discipline and 'object'. It cannot make sense to say one recounts the history of the changes 'in' or 'to' a thing, for history *is* the changes in or to a thing. In other words, *some* things are 'historical' by nature – they are constituted by change.

Indeed, there is an intuition harboured by historically minded theorists that there are certain things, otherwise regarded as obscure as to their nature, which only become established as recognisable, singular identities insofar as they have a history replete with change. For example, it is said that to understand what a 'nation' *is* requires one knows its history; that a nation is not truly a real, unique phenomenon until it *has* a history; that a nation, otherwise so difficult a thing to understand, can be defined, then, as the product of a collection of people sharing a common history. The conservative will hence speak in terms of preserving the continuity of a nation precisely through the (careful) acceptance of change, whereas the revolutionary nationalist, employing the same intuition, will speak of promoting the identity of a nation through the shared catharsis of rapid change or dramatic gesture.[33]

Again, some would say the same of the nature of individuals – that they are best understood as 'historical' by nature, whereby to know who someone *is* one needs to know that individual's history (that is, conceive of him or her as an historical phenomenon). And somewhat by analogy with our example of a 'nation', the more conservative regard rapid and drastic change in an individual's life as therefore threatening continuity – and thereby the individual's sense of identity, and hence possibly even his or her sanity. Others, on the contrary, despair of certain individuals ever becoming 'mature', or established as solid identities, until they have been forced to confront significantly varying circumstances.

These, perhaps, are special cases where phenomena which are generally recognised to *be* such (that is, the examples of 'nations' and 'individuals'), are nevertheless regarded as problematic regarding their nature. In the main, however, I have been dealing with what is in a sense their converse – namely, phenomena which are *not* generally recognised as such despite their nature being set out so publicly, ubiquitously, and familiarly, in narrative discourse. In the former case we purport to know the phenomena we are dealing with despite not understanding their nature, whereas in the latter case we are entirely familiar with the kind of discourse explicative of their nature despite not always recognising that we are indeed confronted by distinct phenomena or identities.

Thus I reiterate that 'to do the history' of something is not 'to do the history' of its changes (which, as has been demonstrated, would invite us into a fantastical dimension of explanation simply ruled out in factual narrative), but is to explicate the nature of phenomena constituted *through* change (that is, 'changing identities'). The inexplicability of such phenomena is not a regrettable lacuna to be filled as a last resort by speculative philosophy. Rather, we should note that the very principles which establish them as phenomena in the first place are the same as those which render them 'inexplicable'. This is because, given our analysis of 'change', the conditions under which it can be said to occur are limited to circumstances involving humans' conduct, readily explicable in terms of *its* 'reasons' but stubbornly resistant to any further explanation involving giving 'reasons for' its 'reasons'. In short, a proper understanding of the nature of 'historical' identities (and of the corresponding discipline explicative of their nature), far outweighs any importance attached to those manifold discussions devoted to the nature of historical explanation based only on speculative, unpracticed, or imaginary notions regarding the discipline of history.

In ascertaining the parameters of the discipline of history (whereby Chapter Two's concluding query as to the adequacy of narrative as the framework of the historian's activity is amply met), our tendency has been to comment on the generosity of its compass rather than regret its circumscription – and we have done this not only because of the sheer variety of topics it can embrace but also because of its facility in accommodating the untidiness of human conduct. In talking of human conduct or activity, however, we had occasion to warn against the abstract concept, 'activity in general', arguing instead that one must talk of specific, individual activities. Analogously, no historian would feel comfortable with the description, 'an historian in general'. As with a scientist, of whom the first question asked is, 'scientist of what?', so historians assign themselves to different 'branches' according to what topic or area interests them. These interests are inevitably footloose and correspondingly misleading, for a 'topic' or 'area' may embrace more than one of what we would call a 'branch' of history. For instance, some would be content to identify their branch as Japan, or the seventeenth century, or eighteenth-century France – that is, as a place, a time, or usually both. Others, however, might refer instead to an activity, such as government, science, warfare, or art; and we have seen from our preceding arguments that it is indeed in terms of differing, recognised *activities*, rather than times and/or places,

171

that branches of history properly emerge, since in directing attention to them we are immediately addressing meaningful temporal relationships in human conduct. (I say 'recognised' activities in order to raise a query over the notion of, for example, 'leisure' as 'an activity', and therefore as inviting a distinct branch of history. As in the discussion of 'social' history, where doubts arose as to the specificity of 'social' conduct, so the same might be said of 'leisure' as a specific kind of conduct.)

If, on the other hand, the (alleged) 'branch' of history is Japan or the seventeenth century, one will find the historian, in practice, singling out one or more activities (government, warfare, art), as a condition of presenting coherent narrative rather than a random amalgam of discrete Japanese, or seventeenth-century, happenings.

Against this (merely adumbrated) background to the notion of different 'branches' of history, however, there does appear to be a division of the discipline which is categorially prior to its differentiation into distinct 'branches', and here I refer to what is called 'the history of thought'. Although historians, however diverse their interests, are in the main comfortable in conversing with each other, the historian of thought is either regarded as involved in some markedly different activity or is subject to unrealistic expectations regarding his usefulness or relevance to their enterprises. This is not to say historians are not used to dealing with 'thought'. On the contrary the activities they traditionally deal with (for instance, governing, warfare, religious movements, and economic organisation), cannot but implicate (as does any 'reasoned' activity) the thinking of relevant agents involved – and in dealing with individuals' motivations, reasoning, plans, fears, and strategies, historians incorporate such 'thought' quite readily into their accounts.

But the case would appear to be different where instead of referring when appropriate to the thinking involved in some activity, the activity itself consists solely of 'thinking'. There is, in other words, a conventional distinction between intellectual and other activities. Being conventionally parametered it may not be clear at the edges – for example, is the business of *manifesting* such thinking (for instance, in *writing*) a separate and *non-*intellectual activity? Nevertheless, it is sufficient for our present purposes to call an activity 'intellectual' where thinking is not only involved *in* an activity, but where the activity as a whole is constituted by thinking or 'the production of ideas' – that is, where thinking is solely devoted to producing thoughts.

Yet even this definition remains only approximate. For example, it would seem to equate the activity of designing an aeroplane, or writing a detective novel, with that of enquiring into atomic structure, the nature of justice, or the origins of the French Revolution. On the other hand it could be argued that the activities of designing an aeroplane or writing a detective thriller, although involving a great deal of thinking, are not ultimately concerned with producing ideas but, respectively, with producing actual aeroplanes or intriguing entertainment, whereas the latter examples are concerned to effect an understanding of their topics, and only in that sense to 'produce' something in the real world (namely, a better understanding of a topic).

Even to raise such potential distinctions is to highlight the notion that intellectual activities are more problematic than others, and possibly of a different order, inasmuch as they appear to involve 'thinking' in some different and/or extra ways than do other activities; and yet we can remain unsure as to how. In short, one may be uncertain of the nature of intellectual activity in general, as distinct from some other kind of activity, and consequently unsure as to the nature or even the viability of particular intellectual activities, such as philosophy, mathematics, or, indeed, history. And so long as we lack a clear notion of, for instance, what 'political thinking', 'religious thinking', or 'philosophy' are as activities, then we are correspondingly uncertain as to whether, or how, they can fall under the historian's scrutiny through the attendant form of coherent narrative, with all that that has been shown to imply.

By querying, not the notion, but the nature, of intellectual activity we are, then, implying it is insufficiently understood – and to the extent this is the case it raises questions as to its amenability to historical treatment. In short, can 'thought' (intellectual activity), be an 'object' of the discipline ('form') of history? Or put the other way around, is 'the world of thought' of such a nature that it necessitates the specifically 'historical' explication of its phenomena, thereby generating what is (loosely) called 'the history of thought' as an authentic branch of the discipline of history?[34]

Now, clearly there cannot be a history of thought 'in general' – such a project would be as absurd as a history of non-intellectual activity 'in general'. Rather, we are asking, from the above, whether there can be histories of particular intellectual activities. Certainly, there can be chronicles of them whereby, for instance, the conclusions of one scientist, economist, or political theorist can be set out and then the conclusions of the 'next' are added, and so on. But in asking whether there can be a genuine *history* of scientific, economic, or political thought, and given our explication of the nature of history as a discipline, we are by implication asking whether, or how far, 'intellectual' actions and activities ('intellectual conduct') are amenable to narrative treatment in just the same way as that great variety of other conduct. If so, what are the (otherwise separate) 'actions' which go together to form a 'sequence' of thinking? What *is* 'a sequence of thinking'? – how do the concepts of change and continuity apply? For example, do ideas change? And regarding techniques, is the historian of thought involved in inferring from evidence? If so, what constitutes 'evidence', and what is it that is 'inferred'? If a narrative account of 'thinking' *is* possible, are those same heuristic categories of 'practical', 'mediate', and 'final' actions equally applicable as explanatory aids, or is continuity (and discontinuity) to be somehow differently construed? And if they are applicable, what is it about thinking which is thereby explained? Again, how do we relate an individual's thinking to another's in the form of a properly coherent narrative? – and what are those narrative or historical identities which, as 'content' or 'object', not only vindicate but ultimately *necessitate* the full-blooded (narrative) discipline of history for the recognition and explication of phenomena as 'real' in the 'intellectual' world as we have argued, for example, trees, buildings, wars, and journeys are in the 'worlds' of objects and events?

In short, is the discipline of history (itself a complex, distinct intellectual activity), applicable to 'thought' or 'the intellectual world' (as defined so far)? The very fact histories of the Ford Motor Company, the city of London, the French Revolution, and the rise of Hitler, abound, involve 'thought', and yet are clearly not examples of 'histories of thought', may suggest a categorial distinction between what might be called 'history proper' and the 'history of thought', whereby the latter is merely a *metaphor* for a practice different both in terms of the workings of its discipline and in the nature of its content or 'object'.

If true this would be both a huge and a strange claim, for it would imply that the extensive world of the intellect – encompassing ideas, different intellectual activities, books, disciplines, arguments, intellectual discoveries, 'schools of thought' – is somehow ahistorical, or at least only amenable to historical investigation and treatment in some merely metaphorical sense. If so, it behoves someone to deliver an account of how to handle the 'intellectual' world which makes proper sense of such an alleged distinction. We, however, do not face that challenge since we can see no essential difference between intellectual and non-intellectual activities in the case of history. Where, then, confusion exists regarding the status and/or nature of 'the history of thought', I say it stems as much from a lack of clarity about the nature of history and its corresponding discipline as it does from a lack of clarity about the nature of the world of the intellect.

Having devoted what I have written up to now to clarifying the former, I now turn to the latter topic – not, however, with a view to exploring all its complexities. Rather, I present its analysis both to lend credibility to our anatomy of history from what might otherwise be regarded as an unusual quarter (the history of thought), and to exemplify those arguments I have advanced in explicating the nature of history and its discipline. In other words, and as I hope the concluding chapter will show, not only is the discipline of history literally applicable to 'the history of thought', but 'the history of thought' can only be a coherent undertaking insofar as it conforms exactly to those various principles and observations contained in this preceding analysis of the discipline of history in general.

174

5

THE POSSIBILITY OF THE
HISTORY OF THOUGHT

'THE HISTORY OF THOUGHT'

I concluded Chapter Four by raising the question of whether the world of the intellect is amenable to a properly *historical* treatment – in other words, in what sense do thoughts and ideas 'have a history', or is this merely metaphor? The latter would imply either that 'the history of thought' has no coherent rationale, being instead an amalgam of intellectual biography, philosophical exposition, and the like; or that it does have a coherence, but not that of history. But this is not the only reason why the term, 'the history of thought', might be taken merely metaphorically; if we were to make a conventional distinction between thought and action, no one could take seriously the notion of 'the history of action'. Neither, then, should one take the notion of 'the history of thought' literally.

The term might be unfortunate, then, because of these senses in which it can encourage the belief that whatever 'the history of thought' is, it is not 'history proper' but something different and/or looser in compass. Consequently, the world of the intellect is sometimes treated as not necessitating the strict rigour of historical discipline when exploring its past. The writings of some 'historians of thought' thus variously constitute expositions and clarifications of a thinker's work, or the chronicling of how a particular idea has been differently construed over time, or the ambitious interconnecting of diverse intellectual areas such as art, science, and philosophy, in a certain period. Sheltering under the umbrella term of 'the history of thought' such projects are inevitably informative, often interesting, and in the best of the latter cases, indispensable guide-books and stimulants for students and scholars alike.[1] They are, however, misleading for not only do they purport to exemplify what is a discipline (the history of thought), but in assuming that guise they misrepresent the world of the intellect as 'content', that is, as an 'object' of knowledge.

Rather than submit, however, to metaphorical connotations of the term, 'history of thought', let us recognise the intellectual world is replete with diversity, conventionally differentiated through that same process of abstraction and identification whereby we individualise other things, for example in the world of objects, actions, and qualities. Thus, within the world of 'thought' we distinguish such things as ideas, concepts, arguments; theories, ideologies, philosophies; proofs, disputes, and discoveries. And each of these individuations is subject to further subdivision as we sharpen our discrimination into, for example, political, economic, and sociological theories; idealist and materialist philosophies; or tautological, teleological, and scientific arguments. In short, we find our way amidst the world of thought by differentiating it into discrete 'components', insofar as to do so is relevant to us, workable, and proves reasonably reliable.

Now I take it as read that if 'thought' is genuinely amenable to *historical* treatment we must focus upon those of its components constituted by *change*. In therefore being 'narrative identities' they require the logic of narrative for their apprehension, and thus the form of narrative for their presentation or explication. Our task, then, is to locate within the multi-faceted world of 'thought' where such phenomena pertain – for that is where the formal discipline of the history of thought has its proper place – rather than abandon ourselves to those undisciplined intimations of the term whereby whatever is said about the past world of the intellect is willy-nilly a contribution to the history of thought.

Now clearly, since the world of thought generates *ideas*, such that despite its diversity some would claim they lie at its core, it behoves us to investigate their status – all the more so since some, regarding ideas as changing phenomena, claim they therefore provide the focal point upon which the discipline of history should be brought to bear: in short, that the history of thought is more literally disciplined as the history of *ideas*.

IDEAS

Firstly, an idea has to be *someone's* idea. Ideas are conceived by individual minds and in no other way. However much influenced by other people, 'an idea' cannot but be the product of an individual's mind. There is no such thing as a collective mind or consciousness, whatever the fantasies of some extravagant thinkers may be. 'Mind' is not some general 'pool' in which we all share. For example, if all individuals have up to now divided the human species into male and female this has been because to do so has, in each individual's experience, proved relevant, useful, and reliable. (In addition, we are taught to.) There are of course certain individuals (for instance, trans-sexuals), for whom the distinction is not so relevant, workable, or reliable in their experience, and they have correspondingly different ideas about this aspect of the world they inhabit. They are the exception which proves the rule. Ideas are conceived only by individuals.

Secondly, an idea is a singular thing, in the sense that my idea of what a city 'is', or of what justice 'is', is not a train of thinking or a lengthy argument, but is treated as a singular idea. That it may be the product of an arduous process of thinking does not detract from its status as singular, just as we treat any complex *material* object which has taken a long time to produce and consists of many parts, such as an automobile, as nevertheless a singular thing. For example, then, Spinoza's idea of 'substance' is a singular thing. It has boundaries marking it off from, for instance, his idea of 'modes' of substance. Logically, indeed, it might or might not be appropriate to treat the *whole* of Spinoza's *Ethics* as a single idea. However, that it might prove difficult to do so, and/or to find an employment for it as such, is not a contingent matter; it is precisely the point. In short, an idea's status as a single thing is not so much afforded it by logic but emerges from being treated as singular.

Additionally, in understanding the status of ideas it is worth distinguishing between them and what some would call 'universal ideas', or 'ideas of universals'. For example, in his *Republic* Plato presents us with Thrasymachus' idea of justice. It is not Thrasymachus' idea of 'the idea of justice'; it is his idea of justice. Further, it is his idea of *justice* rather than of something else, or of justice *and* this or that. As, then, a real, singular idea it is a particular concrete identity in the world, analogous in status to this particular ladder or that particular city.

Now it might be objected that this analogy goes too far because, if, as claimed earlier, one can only describe a particular city insofar as one already has an idea of what *any* city is, then how could this apply to Thrasymachus' idea of justice when we have insisted an idea cannot but be an individual's particular idea? In other words, it is reasonable to refer to 'a city in general', or 'any city', whereas we seem to have implied it is not reasonable to refer to 'an idea of justice in general'.

The solution to this, however, merely requires we recognise there are numerous different individual ideas of justice (just as there are numerous individual cities). Indeed, Plato offers us a convenient selection, including that of Cephalus and that of Polemachus. Although different individual ideas, they share the feature of being about what justice is. Consequently, there is as much sense in saying there is such a thing as 'any idea of justice' as in saying there is such a thing as 'any city' – and that there are particular examples of both. If Thrasymachus, Cephalus, Polemachus, and Socrates offer their respective ideas of justice, then to understand them as doing so requires us to identify, or have a 'notion', 'concept', or 'idea', of what *any* idea of justice is. Such notions are often called 'universals', a term relating more to their function than to their status.

Now, because talk of 'having ideas about ideas' can become confusing if only due to language turning back on itself, I propose to refer to a 'universal' such as *any* idea of justice as a 'concept',[2] and reserve the term

177

'idea' for this or that *particular* idea of justice. I say, then, that we can properly refer to Thrasymachus' *idea* of justice. In addition we can point to the generality, namely, *any* idea of justice. But insofar as this latter phenomenon is different from the former it is misleading to call them by the same name, that is, 'ideas'. That both are products of an individual's thinking hardly warrants this for it is to suggest that whatever issues from an individual's thinking should be called 'an idea', whereby the word has no more meaning than precisely that, leaving the world of 'thought' virtually undifferentiated. In short, where things are different from each other, why call them by the same name? For example, when Spinoza refers to 'an idea of an idea'[3] he means that an idea is different from an idea of an idea (for otherwise an idea would be the same as an idea of an idea, which is not what he intends). He should, then, have used a different term for the latter.

Of course, there *is* a point in calling different things by the same name where we wish to classify them into a group of things which share a feature we find it relevant to denote. Sparrows and robins, for example, are both 'birds'. It could only be confusing to call the third term (indicating the group) by the same name as either of the other two, whereby we would be saying there are sparrows, robins, and 'sparrows', by which last term we mean to refer to what sparrows and robins have in common. Just so, then, with ideas and concepts. A concept is not an idea and an idea is not a concept. They are different things. What they share is that they are both 'mental products', or whatever other term is appropriate so long as it is precisely neither 'idea' nor 'concept'.

Thus it is that when we move from identifying different particular ideas of the same thing (for instance, justice), to calling them examples of a generality, such as 'any idea of justice', we might forestall confusion by referring to the latter as concepts rather than ideas. Not only does this avoid linguistic doublethink; it points to a useful distinction within the world of thought whereby we can validly differentiate between Thrasymachus' idea of justice and a concept of justice. Regarding the latter, I have indicated how one arrives at a concept of justice, and will add that only if everyone had the same concept of justice would it be correct to refer to '*the* concept of justice'. Yet it should be clear that any concept, like any idea, can only be the product of individuals' minds, functioning individually.

Concepts, then, like ideas, are real, singular phenomena, such that when we encounter one it can only be *a* (that is, someone's) concept of, for example, justice. There is no such thing as *the* concept of justice, just as there is no such thing, for example, as *the* city. That an idea is an idea of justice rather than of something else is our responsibility, just as is the calling this object 'a city' our responsibility. In both cases it is we who, for those reasons of relevance and workability referred to so often, abstract discrete phenomena from an otherwise undifferentiated world, whereby we respectively perceive this idea of justice or that city. Similarly, then, with concepts. We neither invent whatever our concept of justice, or of a city, is; nor do we find it pre-existing as some kind of disembodied paradigm. Rather, we choose to locate that which is similar in particular ideas and thereby construe a concept, such as 'any idea of justice'. That there is an inextricable dialectic between ideas and concepts should be clear enough. But this is not the place to pursue the matter further, for the principal points stand – namely, that ideas and concepts are different things; that both are individual products of (necessarily) individual minds; and that both are 'real', singular phenomena. Thus, to refer to *the* idea of justice, just as to *the* concept of justice, is to fantasize.

If, then, an idea has the same status as any other real, individual phenomenon, it follows that an idea can be described. As previously argued, this involves saying what is particular about a phenomenon – in this case, what is particular about *this* idea. For example, we describe Thrasymachus' idea of justice by pointing out those of its features which make it different from other ideas of justice. We point, then, not to that which makes it 'essentially' an idea of justice rather than of something else, but to those *contingent* features of it as an idea of justice.

It also follows that '*an* idea of justice' (namely, 'any' idea of justice, or a concept of justice), can be defined. As is clear, this involves seeking that feature we take to be common to otherwise diverse ideas which makes it worthwhile to individuate some of them into ideas of justice rather than ideas of something else. Here we have but to consult a dictionary, for what is it to define the meaning of the *word* 'justice' other than to define 'the' concept of justice? We may take it this is what lexicographers understand themselves to be doing. They do not define 'justice', but tell us the meaning of the word, which they derive not from philosophy but from assessing on what grounds people have found it useful to distinguish ideas as different, including ideas of justice. Thus our definition of 'the concept of justice' (just as the lexicographer's definition of the word 'justice'), will not tell us something about the world insofar as we could claim to have discovered the phenomenon, '(perfect) justice', or *the* concept of justice. We must bear in mind that the definition of the word 'justice' (that is, 'the' concept of justice), is in fact *a* definition (that is, *a* concept) – namely, the particular lexicographer's. But not only do they not all simultaneously agree in their definitions; definitions differ over time, which is to say that 'the' concept of something can differ from one time to another.[4] The most we *can* say of 'the' concept of this or that as set out in dictionary definitions of words' meanings is that it tells us people's thinking revolves around certain recurring axes, and that it has been found to be possible, relevant, and useful to individualise certain products of thinking by generalising them into distinct ideas, such as ideas of justice, love, and sovereignty.

In this effort to find workable parameters to what an 'idea' is, the preceding arguments raise a further aspect of their status – namely, it is clear an idea must be an idea *of something*. For example, of the statement that it is right to benefit one's friends and harm one's enemies we are likely to say it articulates a particular idea of justice. However, of the statement, 'Peter drove to town today', we would be hard-pressed to say it is an 'idea', for of *what* is it an idea? Rather, we would identify the statement as exactly that – a statement, not an idea. This demonstrates that to find this or that idea amongst someone's discourse is *ipso facto* to identify ideas *of* this or that. We cannot do this unless the 'this' or 'that' is generalisable. We say the former statement articulates an 'idea' insofar as we recognise it shares features common to otherwise different statements – namely, they all indicate what is 'just'. We convert the statement into someone's idea of justice. We cannot do the same with the latter statement since it cannot be treated as articulating someone's *idea* of *something*.

We can approach the same point from another direction. Suppose Thrasymachus were to describe his one and only dog. It would be curious to call such discourse his 'idea' of his dog. His dog is a unique thing, incapable of generalisation. To refer to Thrasymachus' 'idea' of his dog is to invite the notion that it is a particular example of 'any' idea of his dog, which is absurd. Thrasymachus' dog is Thrasymachus' dog; we cannot talk of 'Thrasymachus' dog in general'. Just so, we can talk of someone's idea of love, but not of someone's idea of Antony and Cleopatra's love, for this would imply numerous 'Antony and Cleopatra's loves', of which this or that description is a particular example. Thus, of something unique (as is anything with a proper name, such as London), I say there cannot be 'an idea', but what we variously call a perception, an account, an understanding, or a description. Thus if Thrasymachus describes his dog, that is what his discourse amounts to – namely, his description. To claim he is giving his 'idea' of his dog adds nothing but confusion. Similarly, were his dog long dead and he were to offer his recollection, or memory, of his dog, then that is precisely what he would be doing, and we have the requisite terminology to individuate this 'mental product' – namely, a 'memory' or 'recollection'. Why, then, refer to him as giving us his 'idea' of his dog? But we *can* refer to him as having an idea of justice, of love, and of what a dog is. In short, Thrasymachus can have an idea (that is, *his* idea), of what a dog is, but not of his dog in particular. Further, that *we* can refer to Thrasymachus' idea of what a dog is indicates that his idea shares features common to otherwise different statements, such that in identifying his idea of 'a dog', *we* have a *concept*, 'dog', which lexicographers attempt to universalise, not philosophically but through the empirical study of the use of language, when they offer us the meaning of the word 'dog'.

Thus in managing the world of thought, the identification of 'ideas' is merely one amongst numerous differentiations we make – for example, concepts, notions, statements, definitions, perceptions, memories, descriptions, and analyses. All these terms, and more, have been generated as people have tried to render the world of thought manageable and coherent through differentiating its products. Some terms have more exact meanings, and some are more generally agreed upon, than others. Yet on the whole people succeed in making themselves understood without needing clear-cut definitions, just as they do when talking about the world of material objects and the world of actions and events. However (as indicated earlier), for our project of considering whether or in what sense the discipline of history is applicable to the world of 'thought', we *do* need a notion of the nature and status of 'ideas' more precise than that in everyday use, if only because the term 'history of ideas' has a certain currency.[5] But more important is that, when loosely referred to, 'ideas' can be viewed as the very foundation blocks of the variegated intellectual world, or alternatively as its ultimate achievements. Either way ascribes them a role which justifies this closer scrutiny of what they are. Indeed, true to what has been said about lexicographers, we in fact find a wide variety of meanings of 'idea' in dictionary definitions rather than a neat concept derived from philosophy or logic; for example, 'an archetype', 'a conception', 'a plan', 'a notion conceived by the mind', 'a vague belief', and 'a mental perception'. In attempting to give the term more precision, the concept of 'an idea' which I have offered is not meant to be exhaustive, nor persuasive of any particular philosophy other than what is intimated by my setting out what meaning might be given the word to render it more useful, relevant, and exact for our purposes of examining the possibility of applying the discipline of history to the world of thought – hopefully, a meaning not so far removed from common-sense linguistic usage.

What has emerged is that 'ideas' are held by individuals; that they are singular phenomena; that they are 'real', individual things (that is, a particular idea such as Thrasymachus' idea of justice is as 'real' a 'thing' as my dog, or London, insofar as its status as abstracted from, and individuated within, an otherwise undifferentiated world is identical to that of those latter phenomena); that an idea must be an idea *of* something; that the something of which an idea is of must be generalisable; that it is both possible and worthwhile to distinguish between ideas and concepts, and between ideas and the perception, representation, or memory of particular phenomena.

Finally, of special importance to reflections on the 'history of thought', a further characteristic of 'ideas' is implied by the above account – namely, they do not *change*. In insisting an actual idea must be an idea of *something*, we have seen that the status of any particular idea is analogous to that of any particular material object, such as this or that village. Both are real, singular identities which can therefore be described. But just as material objects cannot be said to *change*, neither can ideas. Like the picture of the Mona Lisa, once an idea is conceived, it is given. Numerous things may happen *to* it, of which a chronicle could be produced; but this is far from writing its *history*. In short, it may be stolen (plagiarised), amended, destroyed (shown to be absurd), go unnoticed, or be celebrated. But whatever may happen *to* it, it is fixed for all time as, for example, Thrasymachus' idea of justice or Rousseau's idea of freedom. To claim that 'the idea of freedom' has *changed* because Rousseau has a different idea of freedom from Hobbes is as nonsensical as to claim that since my village is different from yours, 'the village' has changed. We need reminding that *'the'* village does not exist, such that any question of 'its' changing is absurd. Similarly, then, with respect to *the* idea of something. An (that is, someone's) idea of something is akin to this or that painting, of which it may be the case that it is now different from how it was. But, as shown in Chapter Two, this is far from saying it has *changed*. And insofar as ideas are thus not changing identities, or identities constituted by change, they are not historical identities.[6]

In short, given the nature and status of ideas, they have no history. There cannot be a history of the idea of freedom, nor of the idea of anything else. Neither can there be a history of the concept of freedom, nor of the concept of anything else. And if there cannot be a history of this or that idea, then to advance the notion of a 'history of ideas', be they specified as political, economic, or scientific, is to roam even further into the realm of fancy. The most that can be achieved is a combination of what we have called descriptive history (whereby the historian would be restricted to describing various ideas), and an arranging of them according to their dates (namely, what we have called 'chronicling'), and it is difficult to see in what sense either activity, or both taken together, can properly be called 'doing history'.

THINKING

If, then, neither ideas nor concepts provide the focal point for the history of thought, what does? Clearly, our previous arguments demand we concentrate upon *activity*, for only there can *change* properly be said to take place (articulated through narrative). Now, however vague the term is we can at least say that a 'thought' is the product of the activity of thinking, as is a sequence of thoughts. The dictionary further restricts its meaning by suggesting the word not be used to denote *any* mental product, but only 'sober reflection', 'meditation', or 'consideration'. Again, in referring the reader to the term, 'to think', one of its definitions is, 'to exercise the mind otherwise than by passive reception of another's ideas'.[7]

Taking these indications together it is reasonable to urge that 'thought' be understood as the product of a purposive, deliberate, constructive

activity – namely, *thinking*, as distinct from dreaming, imagining, perceiving, or passively reading, listening to, or watching, something. Thus we
can be excused the otherwise empty tautology that 'thinking produces
thoughts', or that 'thought is the product of thinking', and instead note
that thinking, in this sense, is not such a universal activity as might be
supposed. As a question-posing, problem-solving, constructive mental
activity we can see why, for example, historians of political thought have
tended to narrow their focus to contexts where an individual is engaged
in responding to ideas, revising them, following arguments, disputing and
adding to them, in the hope of arriving at satisfactory formulations on a
topic. The explication of what is going on, and the business of explaining
individual moments of this sequential activity, is far removed from the
description of popular notions about politics. Apart from anything else
attracting historians of political thought to the former context (such as the
intrinsic interest of such political thinking), we can see it is only that
former context which requires what I have urged as the properly historical
(that is, narrative) treatment. Where historians of political thought do thus
narrow their focus, this may stem from a happy instinct or conscious
methodology; whichever, it follows from our overall argument regarding
the discipline of history that they *must* restrict their attention to the context
of what we have denoted as the activity of 'thinking', and its environs.

In short, the historian of political thought cannot in practice focus his
interest on a person's political ideas, perceptions, ideals, and prejudices
unless there is evidence they are the product of the activity of thinking.
That this is a restriction imposed by methodology rather than by elitism
is clear, for no one could seriously suppose that, were evidence available
from which to infer that an eighteenth-century barge-man's political views
were the product of careful, independent, constructive thinking, historians
of political thought would not be interested in giving an account of them.

We should only add what was earlier proposed regarding restrictions
on the subject-matter of *any* historian's attention – namely, that inasmuch
as such 'limitations' constitute the prerequisite for the exercise of history
as a discipline, then it would be ill-judged to view them negatively, as if
they interfered with the historian's 'freedom' to study whatever takes his
fancy and in any way it takes him! Just so with the historian of thought.
That there are boundaries to his activity is simply expressive of the fact
that it is a discipline, in both the formal and popular senses of the term.
Rather, then, than (confusedly) regret the restricted focus of the history
of thought at the very outset of investigating its nature as a discipline, let
us proceed to explore its potential within those boundaries; it remains
extensive enough on its own account.

THE COMMUNICATION OF THOUGHT

Clearly, with the exception of one's awareness of one's own mental activity, mental actions are only known inasmuch as they are made manifest. Likes and dislikes, decisions, intentions, opinions, emotions, and ideas, remain hidden in the mind until made manifest either through being deliberately communicated or through explicit physical actions which express them, such as running after a thief or smiling at a joke. We may take it that in the former case, where one *communicates*, the intention is to make manifest what is 'in one's mind', whereas in the latter case that intention is absent; rather, the onlooker infers the agent's mental actions from observing his behaviour. Now, where do 'thoughts' and 'thinking', in the particular sense of the terms urged above, stand in relation to this?

As a species of mental activity, thought is manifested either through *communicating* what one has concluded or conceived – that is, attempting to convey this via language, signs, or art forms such as music and painting – or through that kind of physical activity, such as landing an aeroplane, which clearly invites the inference that 'thinking' is involved, even though the pilot is not engaged in communicating. In this latter case the fact we have to infer the thinking involved is that much clearer, and usually fraught with that necessary feature of any inference, namely, that it can be wrong. Where, however, thought is *communicated*, and particularly where this is done through the apparent immediacy of the use of language rather than through non-linguistic forms which require the mediation of 'interpretation' (for example, music), the need to *infer* the thinking is not so apparent.

In other words, when observing a pilot landing an aeroplane we regard his actions as *evidence* of his thinking. We can do no other, since he is not communicating his thinking to us. On the other hand, when surveying a painting we see it as the communication of thought *if* we are conversant with that mode of communicating. What is required in order to articulate that thinking to those not so conversant is to transpose, or 'trans-form', it into actual language. And when transposing or translating something into recognisable language we do not say we are *inferring* its meaning. Just so, then, with an artist explaining someone's painting to the non–artistic; he 'translates' what it 'means' into language. However, if asked to give an account of the thinking which *produced* the painting he would have to infer it from the finished product.

But if we turn to thought which *is* communicated through language we are likely to say that it neither has to be inferred nor translated (or 'trans-formed'); rather, that the mental actions are immediately expressed through the language employed – in short, that the use of language correlates directly with 'what is in the agent's mind' such that neither inference nor any form of transposition is involved in regarding what

184

someone 'says' as manifesting his thoughts. For example, if Peter says 'I hate Paul' we know immediately what he means without the need either to infer or translate it. (The only *caveat* is whether we doubt his sincerity or linguistic facility, in which case the onus of proof is on the doubter to present evidence of duplicity or illiteracy.)

Nevertheless, however transparent the statement, 'I hate Paul', might be as the manifestation of a mental state, such that it would be wrong to claim it is *evidence* of what is in Peter's mind – rather, it is directly expressive *of* what is in his mind – two questions remain, of intimate relevance to the historian of thought's project. The first is, having produced this 'thought', is it in fact the product of the activity of *thinking* at all? We need reminding that not all one says or writes is the product of thinking. Thus, although Peter's saying 'I hate Paul' is an action which is of course thereby amenable to narrative explanation, only in the event that his statement is the product of thinking will its narrative explanation involve an account *of* his thinking, thereby bringing it (in principle) into the domain of the history of thought.

The second consideration follows closely, for where what is said *is* the product of thinking, then not only can the historian of thought attempt an account of that thinking (which project we have yet to address), but he should also ask why the agent *communicated* this or that thought. In other words, the question arises not only as to why an individual thinks this or that but also as to why he *says* it. In short, if not all that is said is the product of thinking, not all that is thought is *said* – and this is particularly the case where someone is thinking about what he is saying, as when designing a speech or constructing a piece of writing, rather than simply saying or writing everything that comes into his head.

To complete these considerations, and forestall possible confusion, we should add another – namely, that people often think about what they *say* even when what they say is not itself the product of thinking. This takes us back to Peter's saying 'I hate Paul' (assuming this statement does not issue from thinking), which I have already said is amenable to narrative treatment. But we can now see more clearly that what has to be explained is not why Peter hates Paul, but why he *says* so. Here, we treat 'saying' as we do any other kind of action – we account for the *action* of communicating, not for the 'thought' (or emotion, or perception) communicated. Peter may have thought long and hard about *saying* what he said. Thus it is, then, that although *any* historian so frequently deals with what someone said or wrote, possibly involving the recapture of the thinking (where this applies) behind the actual *saying* of this or that, he is by no means thereby engaged in the history of thought. Rather, as will be seen, extra conditions must pertain before any thinking involved in deciding to communicate something becomes, itself, material for the historian of thought.

What is clear from the above is that thinking and the communication of thinking do not merge into a transparent union when thinking is made manifest through the use of language. Thinking and 'saying' are distinct activities. Not all thinking is 'said'; not all that is 'said' derives from thinking. Where it *does* derive from thinking, it does not equate with that thinking, but is *evidence* of it – one has to infer, from what is said, the thinking it evidences. If it is objected that we encounter individuals who simultaneously say everything they think, one can only protest that such individuals are thereby precisely not thinking but babbling or rambling. Moreover, not only are they not thinking; neither are they even thinking about what they are saying.

Sufficient has been said about 'thinking' to summarise a number of propositions relevant to the historian of thought – namely, that thinking can usefully be seen as something specific rather than denoting *any* mental activity; that thinking (other than in the mind of the thinker) is hidden until made manifest; that only parts of thinking are manifested through a medium of communication such as language; that where what someone says is evidence of his actually thinking, that thinking has to be inferred from what he says; that the thinker does not say all that he thinks (otherwise we would not need to infer it); and that in addition to inferring what a thinker thinks (from what he says), we need to explain what he *says* – in other words, why he chose to communicate this or that.

THE HISTORIAN OF THOUGHT AND THE PHILOSOPHER

Having discounted the case where someone says whatever he thinks (on the grounds that he is therefore doing something other than thinking), the nearest we can get to the immediate, transparent manifestation of thinking is where someone expresses an argument (via language). Typically we find him advancing a proposition, defending it by explaining the reasoning which led towards it, suggesting alternative lines of argument, and demonstrating their inadequacies. Alternatively he may lead the reader *towards* the proposition he wishes to proclaim, such that by the time the reader reaches it, it appears incontrovertible. All the 'great' works of political thought, for example, are of this nature, where the author is not only concerned to parade his political ideas but also to show they are the product, not merely of thinking, but of correct thinking.

Confronted by such arguments, the philosopher's business is to assess their cogency. Has the author made a logical mistake? What assumptions are implied in what he says, and are they sound? In short, is what he says 'true'? The historian of thought, on the other hand, is not intimately concerned to assess the truth, adequacy, or consistency of what is said, nor to weigh it against what others have said. Rather, his task is to *explain* or *account for* what is said, which is to treat it as evidence of what was 'going on' in the author's mind – and also to account for the saying of what was actually said. To the extent he succeeds in this dual undertaking we can say he has 'understood' a piece of writing. By 'understand' we do not mean merely that we understand the meaning of the words and sentences used; rather, we mean we can give an account of the piece of writing as a whole, and account *for* any part of it in particular. This amounts to 'understanding' what is before us in terms of what it was the writer was trying to achieve in and by writing what he wrote. By analogy we may observe someone placing a brick here, a tile there, and a joist there. We can correctly identify each action, and discuss it (for instance, in terms of difficulty or clumsiness). But someone observing the same actions can point out that what is *in fact* going on is that the individual is building a house. He will be able to tell us what kind of house and explain why the builder does what he does at any particular point in the process. He will, then, 'understand' what is in front of him.

Just so with controlled pieces of writing. Where what is said is difficult to understand in the simple sense of the term, some readers get no further than identifying the meaning of one sentence to the next. But this by no means implies they therefore 'understand' the piece of writing. Rather, not until recognised as the making of a complex phenomenon (via the medium of argument), can what is in front of one be said to be 'understood'.[8] In short, if one cannot explain or account for something, one has not *understood* what it is. And if one does not even attempt to explain or account for a thing, there is a sense in which one has not properly understood there is 'a thing' there in the first place. The key to the historian of thought's approach lies precisely in adopting a stance at one remove from a piece of writing, to ask 'what is going on?', 'what is it the writer has produced?' And to return to our analogy, if the observer is himself a builder the more likely it is he will understand exactly what is 'going on' as it unfolds. He may, additionally, indulge in criticism or judgement of what is going on. But not only is this a separate project; we can see that such discussion of each action involved may on occasions differ sharply in focus from that offered by other 'interested observers'.

Where a book or some other kind of writing is involved, then, we are confronted by what we might call 'a thought-object'. As a necessarily 'past' phenomenon, its nature might be more or less recondite depending upon its complexity (even in the case of recent works), and/or upon its antiquity. Whichever, the historian of thought's stance, rather than the philosopher's, generates the following sorts of questions: firstly (regarding the thinking evidenced by what the author says), to what arguments, if any, is he responding? To which thinkers is he drawing our attention in support of his views? Which is he hoping to discredit? What are the principal points he wishes to make? What is he trying to achieve by writing this book? Secondly, and more intimately (regarding why he *says* what he says), why is he making this particular point? Why does he change the subject here? What is the point of this chapter, or this part of it? Why does he openly refer to this author but only covertly allude to that one? Why does he avoid countering this obvious objection? Is he deliberately misrepresenting his opponents' arguments, or has he misunderstood them? Why does he intrude this point into his otherwise logical argument?

These and the like questions reflect the stance of the observer, who asks, not what this sentence means and whether what it says is true, but what this piece of writing is meant to be as an artefact, and where has it come from? As with our builder who is obliged to use bricks and mortar to achieve his aims, so our writer or speech-maker is obliged to use language. Can we account for, or explain, what it is that he is doing, both writ large and in detail? If we cannot then we have failed to 'understand' what is before us. Unlike the philosopher, then, the historian of thought is concerned to recapture what was 'going on' in a thinker's mind, treating what he says as evidence rather than as something to be judged. (To be sure, he will be alert, and attend, to where a thinker makes logical and other errors, but only inasmuch as they evidence what the thinker is doing). To the extent he can achieve this he will be reconstructing a unique phenomenon, namely, the thinking activity of a communicating individual. In other words he will be explicating the nature of a narrative identity otherwise lost to us, not because it is lost to our knowledge – the evidence is there – but because we do not know how to recapture it.

GIVING AN ACCOUNT OF THINKING

Having distinguished 'thinking' from 'saying', let us as far as possible deal separately with these activities, however intimately they can be related. Encouraged partly by the dictionary, I have suggested that 'thinking' should be identified not as *any* kind of mental activity but as that which we recognise as the capacity of the mind deliberately either to pose questions of a topic, or to pursue problem-solving formulations to questions put to it, or to combine both by itself setting the questions it then attempts to answer. An example of the first is where one wants to find out something and thus formulates the questions one conceives as relevant. By this I mean to exclude circumstances where, for example, having missed a train the obvious question, 'when is the next one?', springs to mind unsought. It is difficult to construe such a question as the product of deliberate thinking. Rather, this begins when, aware one does not know the time of the next train, one generates the relevant questions to find out. In this sense, then, deliberate question posing is the product of problem solving, for one conceives what questions *follow* from the recognition of the problem.

An example of the second case is where one is asked, 'which is the best train for me, given I do not want to arrive early but still prefer an express train?' The answer does not spring immediately to mind but instead requires the active process of thinking, which involves posing those questions relevant to answering the question. The pursuit of problem-solving formulations is, then, the product of question posing, for one conceives what problem-solutions *follow*, or are implied, in resolving the initial problem.

The third case simply combines the former two, and what emerges is that there is a dialectic between problem solving and question posing whereby they merge into each other. What is common to both activities is the deliberate quest for what does and does not 'follow on' from one stage to the next. This, I suggest, is what constitutes that activity we properly refer to as 'thinking'.

Thus it is that to 'give an account' of thinking, or of a sequence of thought, is to lay bare (as far as possible) how notions follow on from each other in a thinker's mind. In reconstructing thinking we are not dealing with single notions which happen to succeed each other but with a connecting-up of thoughts so that they form an overall sequence. In monitoring this 'following on' we should be able to put the notions into 'prior' and 'subsequent', such that we can say he thinks this because he has just thought that. This, of course, is to follow our model of narrative explanation whereby each successive notion is *explained* or *accounted for* in terms of that which 'preceded' it – in other words, our 'this *then* that' formula. And following our earlier argument we can see that what is achieved is in fact the 'description', or more precisely, the *explication*, of something constituted by change – in this case, what we might call 'a piece of thinking', or if a strongly parametered singular narrative identity, 'an argument'. Unlike 'an association of ideas', the links between notions which pertain in thinking are deliberately sought by the thinker, thereby bringing us squarely into the realm of intentional human activity – that realm where, and only where (as previously argued), history has its rationale, the 'this (then) that' formula being superseded by 'this *then* that'.

Having arrived at these formulations, there are a number of further observations worth making about 'thinking' in order to forestall potential methodological errors regarding what is involved in 'giving an account' of it. Firstly, in talking of notions 'following on' it would be wrong to construe this 'following on' prima facie in terms of its *logical* connotations. This kind of succession characterises only what we call *rational* thinking. But not all thinking is rational. There is the obvious case where, although a thinker aspires to rational thought, he nevertheless makes logical mistakes. But he cannot therefore be said not to be thinking. However, there is also the case where a thinker is not intending his notions to follow on *logically*; rather, their course is determined by the direction he wishes to take to achieve his aims. An obvious context for such thinking is that of the arts. When composing a piece of music, painting a picture, sculpting a figure, or writing a poem, an individual is clearly thinking – posing and solving problems in pursuit of his objective, moving from one notion to the 'next' as he carefully construes how best to advance. For example, in painting one might pursue the implications of using a certain colour, as in 'would using blue here upset the tonal balance I am aiming at?' These are not logical, but aesthetic, implications, such that it is the artist's taste which gives the 'direction' to his thinking rather than any requirement that his notions follow logically. Likewise we could ask a composer why he used the flute to convey the principal theme, and he could proceed to give an account of his thinking, which would similarly be driven by the effect he wished to achieve, and which is nothing to do with logic.

In addition to these examples, drawn from the arts, of contexts where thinking is clearly occurring without its 'following on' being governed by the demands of logic, there is the less obvious case where a thinker believes himself to be pursuing a logical train of thought but where its direction is governed by conclusions he is predisposed towards. This is what some call 'ideological' thinking, where we say of someone's thought that, despite the notions appearing solely to follow on logically from each other, its direction is influenced by, for instance, feminist, racist, or Marxist assumptions, such that it reaches correspondingly feminist, racist, or Marxist conclusions. Although I will return to 'ideology' when examining what is involved in giving an account of 'saying' as distinct from thinking, an important point already emerges here. It would be absurd to undertake critical appraisal of the thinking of our artist or musician in terms of its logical validity. Also it would be difficult, akin to someone attempting to cook a shoe. We would normally claim he has misunderstood the nature of what he is dealing with. Now there is a sense in which the same can be said of 'ideological' thinking, for although it might both purport and appear to be logical, to assess it solely in those terms is to misapprehend what one is dealing with. In short, 'philosophical' critiques of ideological arguments can be exasperating to the historian of, for example, political thought, for they seem premised on the false assumption that all thinking is 'philosophy' under one (dis)guise or another, such that it could be corrected or improved under philosophy's tuition.[9]

If we now turn to what is involved in 'giving an account of' *rational* thinking – that is, a sequence of notions conceived in virtue of their 'following on' logically from each other (sometimes called 'theoretical' as distinct from practical and/or ideological thought) – there is still a measure in which their succession cannot be explained through logic alone. For example, we may suppose someone to be thinking rationally about the

nature of man, trying to reach conclusions by pursuing the logical implications of notions without reference to any particular desired result, and
self-critical of the intrusion of any 'ideological predispositions'. Suppose
him to have reached the notion that man is a machine programmed to
seek what is beneficial to it, and avoid what is harmful; and suppose what
he goes on to derive from this does indeed follow logically. It will
nevertheless not be explicable solely in those terms. For example, his next
thought might be that it therefore follows logically that man deceives
himself when believing he acts freely. But other notions follow equally
logically, such as the notion that man's behaviour can therefore most
effectively be influenced through pain and pleasure. What this shows is
that, even in the case of rational thinking (as we saw earlier even regarding
mathematics), the nextness of the 'next' thought cannot be accounted for
in terms of logic alone. In short, there is more to following a rational
piece of thinking than following its logic unfolding. Rather, the prime
task with *any* thinking is to follow its *direction*, or put another way, its
reasoning, which is not the same as its logic. Thus in the above example,
although it is true the thinker is concerned the 'next' notion follows
logically (because he is deliberately engaged in rational thought), that will
not furnish the explanation for whatever the 'next' notion happens to be
in his thinking. Instead, the most that can be said by way of 'explaining'
why it included this or that notion is that this is what followed (logically)
for this particular thinker. There can be no further explanation or 'reason
for' it. Rather, as with Chapter Four's analysis of 'reason in history', 'the
reason' for it cannot but be the thinker's 'reason', which in this case
amounts to saying there is no reason for what he thinks – his thinking *is*
his 'reasoning'.

EXPLAINING THINKING

The above discussed 'giving an account of' both rational and non-rational
thinking, suggesting it amounts to reconstructing a sequence of notions
which 'follow on' from each other. (I leave the question of *how* to undertake this reconstruction to subsequent sections on 'saying'.) Thus, inasmuch as we construe an intelligible sequence of thoughts or notions, then
any one in particular is explicable, or accounted *for*, in the familiar logic
of narrative explanation – namely, 'he thinks this because he has just
thought that'. We may recall that one of the features of narrative explanation in general is that it does not explain why someone does *x rather
than y*. Just so with the mental actions which combine to form (a sequence
of) thinking. If we can reconstruct someone's thinking into an intelligible
continuity, we are 'explaining' each moment as 'following on' from the
'previous' (either rationally or non-rationally); but this does not explain
why the 'next' notion is this rather than that. This inability to take

explanation further is, however, not the result of some deficiency of narrative logic, but (as argued earlier) is simply to have reached the limits of explanation *per se*.

However, this limit to how far someone's thinking can be explained is one which we are often prone to try overstepping, not only in ordinary conversation but also in academic work. For example, it is often said of a thinker that he thought x because he disagreed with his contemporaries, or shared the aims of a certain group, or was influenced by another thinker. In short, we are prone to say that someone thought in such-and-such a direction *because* of such-and-such a circumstance. We thereby appear to suggest there are causes explaining a person's train of thinking, or even that it is somehow predetermined. But if, as argued earlier, 'reason in history' must be an individual agent's reasoning rather than a set of causes, so with the history of thought, such that where (through narrative logic) we account for what someone thinks we are in effect giving an account *of* his (intellectual) responses.

For example, rather than say someone thought x because he disagreed with his contemporaries, it is more correct to say his thinking x *constitutes* his disagreeing with them. After all, his thinking x is precisely, not evidence, but proof of this disagreeing. In other words, it is wrong to posit two separate things occurring when someone is thinking, as if he first disagrees with his contemporaries and then, as a result, thinks x. Thinking cannot be separated from an individual's *reasons* for how he thinks (although it must be separated from what he *says*). The line his thinking takes is precisely constituted by his reasoning, such that in following the former we follow his reasoning. In short, delineated as an effortful activity, 'thinking' is 'reasoning', whereby we say there is no 'reason' for what someone 'thinks' other than *his* reason, given that he is indeed *thinking*. Thus, just as we earlier claimed the explanation for a man's shutting the window is exhausted by locating the action *as* his response to feeling cold, such that it makes no sense to go on to ask, 'why did he close the window insofar as he felt cold?', so it is absurd to ask of someone whose thinking constitutes a disagreement with his contemporaries, 'but why is he disagreeing with them?' We are making the error either of supposing there is a reason for *his* reason, or that *he* has his reason for his reason! Rather, in accounting for his thinking x we are doing no more than identifying his response to his 'prior' notions. As such, we are exploring his intellectual activity by discovering and 'describing' (narrating) a real identity, namely, his sequence of thinking.

Now it might be objected that to say 'the reason he thought x was because he disagreed with his contemporaries' comes to the same thing as saying 'his reasoning in thinking x was that he disagreed with his contemporaries'. No doubt there is something to this so long as it *is* understood to come to the same thing. But the first formulation more easily invites a false outlook on the nature of thinking, for in suggesting cause and effect it can lead to the erroneous belief that a person's thinking is, in principle, predictable. What is called 'the sociology of knowledge' would appear to derive from this notion, at least to the extent it originates in the view that ideas are determined products rather than human responses. But in purporting to account for what someone thinks by reference to some determining aspects of his sociological context, it is difficult to see how the sociology of knowledge is any more than a sophisticated version of the kind of silliness of which we would accuse someone who claimed, for example, that Marx thought what he thought because he was a communist. Almost as silly would be the claim that Marx was a communist because of what he thought. Both formulations imply a separation between one's thinking and what it constitutes, and in so doing risk inventing unreal agents (such as 'possessive individualism' accounting for Hobbes' thinking), or inviting misunderstandings of the nature of schools or traditions of thought, and ideologies, whereby they are falsely construed as causative forces shaping individuals' thinking.

To argue this further: if, for example, we construe Spinoza to be effortfully *thinking* about an issue, we should not be surprised if in the course of this question-posing, problem-solving activity part of its sequential continuity comprises consideration of relevant notions advanced by Maimonides, since Spinoza was of Jewish upbringing and education. But it would be misleading to propose therefore that such an episode in his thinking occurred because Spinoza was Jewish. Firstly, the relevant thoughts did not 'occur' or 'spring to mind' – they were searched for by him, and *he* regarded this or that as relevant. Secondly, although it might make sense to claim it *was* because Spinoza was Jewish that he was so familiar with Maimonides' ideas, this is far from claiming that where he thinks about Maimonides' ideas he is thinking what he thinks *because* he was Jewish. He might not have included Maimonides in his considerations; equally, non-Jewish thinkers might have included Maimonides in *theirs*. In short, that Spinoza was of Jewish education cannot explain why, in thinking, he conceived such-and-such thoughts.

What we can say, instead, is that since we can only infer what he thinks from what we know of him and from what he *says*, then the fact Spinoza was of a Jewish education provides *our* reason for inferring he was thinking about Maimonides. In other words, Spinoza did not think *x* because he was Jewish. Rather, *we infer* that Spinoza thought *x* because we know he was Jewish; or put another way, because Spinoza was Jewish we are able to infer he thought *x*. Spinoza's being a Jew, then, does not give us 'the reason' he thought *x*. Rather, it explains our inference that he thought *x* – it gives us 'the reason' in or for *our* inference, not 'the reason for' his thinking. And to complete the point; in giving us the 'reason' in our inference, it is not *explaining* the thinking which generated that inference. It simply reveals what *our* thinking was.

This example from Spinoza can be generalised to apply to *all* attempts to explain why someone thinks what he thinks. There are no causes at work, determining what a person thinks, other than the very *modus operandi* of the thinking or reasoning activity itself, which we have analysed in terms of notions 'following on' from each other and whose explanation is thus captive to the logic of narrative explanation and explication and its accompanying 'limitations'. The more the historian of thought knows of a thinker's character, education, upbringing, and social status; of his political, moral, and religious preferences; of the history of his times, the nature of his society, the great contemporary writers and movements – the more he knows of all these factors the better. But when employing such knowledge to give an account *of* an individual's thinking, let him not make the error of claiming he is accounting *for* it. Rather, the knowledge he employs accounts for the inferences *he* makes regarding the character of the thinking he is explicating or revealing.

To conclude this point: in arguing that we cannot explain the course of someone's thinking other than through the nature of its own dynamic as an activity, there being no exterior causes, I say this not only in relation to the historian of thought but to any discipline which deals with thinking. For example, in psychology we might fall into the trap of saying a subject thinks x because he is depressed, whereas it should be clear from the above that depression does not cause him to think x. Rather, we infer from something he says or does, symptomatic of depression, that he thinks x. In referring to depression, then, we are not explaining why he thinks as he does – we are explicating 'the reason in' our inference of what he thinks.

It follows from these arguments about the activity of thinking that, in trying to infer what someone thinks, there is no single methodology tying the historian of thought. Just as in Chapter One where we argued the historian works by inferring from evidence, and, like a detective, should use whatever methodology or discipline is relevant in the particular case, so in the history of thought. There is no single methodology appropriate to inferring what someone thinks from what they say or write. As suggested, the more potentially relevant factors the historian of thought is aware of the better. The only rider to this is the obvious point that it is knowledge of a thinker's *intellectual* context which will normally provide the most immediate and rich source of inferences, unless the thinker is startlingly original. This latter case provides the most difficulty for the historian of thought; but even here, it is his knowledge of the prior history of thought which at least allows him to identify that originality.

THINKING AND LANGUAGE

Before leaving the topic of thinking as an activity (as distinct from 'saying'), one further and sophisticated version of the erroneous notion that thinking can be *explained* other than through reference to its *conatus* requires exposure. This is the notion that the very language one uses is indicative of, or even imposes, a specific world-view, such that we can account for what someone thinks by examining the language in which he expresses himself – in short, that the direction of a person's thinking is influenced, if not 'caused', by the language he uses. Here again we are confronted by the attempt to separate what someone thinks from what his thinking constitutes.

We can begin by making a concession to the above notion, by referring back to our analysis of (material) 'objects' in Chapter One. It is true, for example, that to call something 'a chair' does involve an act of judgement in that we have to decide whether the object is indeed a chair rather than something else. In thinking of something as a chair, one is identifying a certain state of affairs for which there is a given word, 'chair'. In actually *calling* it 'a chair' one is agreeing with that act of abstraction from, and individuation within, states of affairs which originally established the meaning of the word. (I remind the reader that the individualising of states of affairs into discrete things is nothing inherently to do with logic, philosophy, or specific world-views, but derives from the usefulness and relevance of the exercise as borne out by experience.)

Now, we make most identifications or 'perceptions' automatically, such that these two acts of judgement in thinking of calling something 'a chair', although implicit sometime in our past (particularly as we learned to speak), are now closed matters. However, contexts arise which prompt one to renege on the (two) judgements implicit in the choice of language, thereby raising them to explicitness in our experience. Here, we are consciously on the brink of taking a different view of things, such that we may have reservations about continuing to use a certain word. For example, a literary critic may not only have doubts about whether a certain book, commonly called a novel, *is* a novel, but also whether what the word denotes is useful in *any* context. Similarly a political theorist may adopt the same attitude to the term, 'a democracy'.[10] This seems to imply our literary critic or political theorist is conscious of subscribing to a particular view or 'interpretation' of the world when he uses certain terms, such that continuing to use them indicates a particular world-view.

It is along these lines that it can be argued, for example, that to use the word 'alienation' in discussing political society is *ipso facto* to have one's thinking determined in certain directions – and that this is no different in principle from using other political terminology such as 'sovereignty', except that in being a recent innovation its status as evincing a 'judgement' is more explicit. If, however, its currency is maintained long and widely enough, its interpretive, argumentative, or speculative status will recede, 'alienation' becoming as obvious a 'fact of life' as tables, novels, democracies, and sovereignty.

In short, then, this account of language can be taken to imply that it is based on certain presuppositions about reality, and that this must be taken into account when explaining someone's thinking. It is but a short step from this to claim that language determines thinking rather than thinking determining the use of language, as most of us are wont to believe.

Forceful as this argument is, it is not difficult to expose the basis of its errors – namely, the attempt to separate what an individual thinks from his reason for thinking it, as if there is an 'it' which he thinks, rather than 'its' simply constituting his thinking. For example, of the claim that language is based on certain presuppositions about reality, it is somewhat of a schoolboy howler to argue that language therefore determines thinking. We have only to rephrase the premise into the following – 'language is derived from certain thoughts about reality' – to see the illogicality of the conclusion that 'therefore language determines thinking'. But apart from this there is a greater inadequacy at work, for either version of the premise implies separating what an individual thinks from his reasons for thinking it. Language is *not* 'based on certain presuppositions about reality', nor 'derived from certain thoughts about reality'; rather, language *is* the conceptualisation of reality. The language we use is demonstrative of our understanding of reality – and that we use language rather than something else is demonstrative of a *way* in which we understand reality.

This is not to say, then, there are not other ways of 'understanding' reality. We do not say of the artist or the composer that because they do not use language in their work they therefore cannot be said to think! Indeed, our overall point is more easily made by referring to the painter first. He will employ colour in manifesting his 'thinking' or 'understanding'. But the fact he employs colour does not 'determine' what he paints. Again, where he uses this rather than that colour in a particular instance, it would be absurd to claim this determines what he paints. Rather, it is plain his use of colour is *constitutive of* his 'understanding' of (aesthetic) reality.

Just so with language. The very business of using language *is* the conceptualising of reality. To distinguish language and thinking, and make *either* dependent on the other, is to treat a distinction in reason as a distinction in fact. Since language *is* a way of conceptualising reality, it follows that thinking 'in' language is not thinking determined *by* language. Were that so, then in our thinking the question would permanently arise as to whether we simultaneously agree with our thinking; and so on *ad infinitum*, since it could only be answered by means of thinking in language. But thinking is just not like that. It is absurd to raise the question of whether thinking is simultaneously accompanied by one's agreement with one's thinking. Of course, one might agree or disagree with one's thinking *after* one has thought something – there is a sense in which what I have tried to convey as the 'effortful' activity of genuine *thinking* is continually reflexive – but that is not the implication underlying the notion that language determines thinking. In this connection it is worth noting that Marx's formulation of the relation between thinking, language, and reality is not that language is determined by, or the product of, practical consciousness, or 'practice', but that 'language *is* practical consciousness'.[11] Although approaching the issue from another direction, the implication is the same as that advanced here – namely, that when one is thinking 'in' language only one thing is occurring, such that it would be erroneous to separate thinking and language, making the former somehow dependent on the latter. Additionally Marx's approach exemplifies the other side of the coin, for it follows from his formulation that if what an individual thinks is not determined by the language he uses, neither is the language he uses in thinking determined by what he thinks, as we are wont to believe.

The reason we tend to believe the latter is not, then, because it is correct – it is not. Rather, it is because we are used to writings and speeches where we know considerable thought is devoted to the precise use of language when *communicating* with others. *But our present topic is thinking, not its communication*, and one word more about 'thinking' taken in isolation can highlight the difference. As a distinctive activity, we tend to present 'thinking' as the smoothly successive generation of thoughts which follow on from each other, running a unilinear course to a clear conclusion. But *actual* thinking is not like that, particularly where complex issues are being addressed. On the contrary, its course may be likened to that of a turbulent river. Sometimes it runs slowly; at others, quickly. Even in a single stretch the river is rarely a homogeneous volume of water flowing at an even pace in a uniform direction; rather, different currents, surges, swirls, and eddies perpetually intermix. It is true that calm patches are generated, but the overall flow constantly invades them, changing their shape, and sometimes removing them altogether.

Similarly with the course of concentrated thinking. A mêlée of different notions crowd the mind in a constantly changing intermixture. Some are prominent, others weaker; some appear to move forward to one's goal, others appear as hindrances. New ones are generated, whilst others drop out. Yet like the river's course, which despite its turbulence is moving relentlessly forward, so the thinker's effortful managing of the flux of notions which crowd his mind is, hopefully, moving him ever forward to his conclusions. Now, just as the turbulent river generates calm patches of water, so the busy activity of thinking generates discrete thoughts in the form of neatly packaged ideas, concepts, definitions, observations, or assertions. It is these islands of coherence which are likely to be *communicated*, with a corresponding clarity of language. To do so is, so to speak, to hold them *in stasis* from the surrounding turbulence. Is this what prompts some thinkers actually to write down these thoughts, that is, to rescue some apparent calm from their thinking activity before its relentless flow begins the process of revealing the inherent instability of these patches of coherence?

Be that as it may, the point is that behind the apparent lucidity of what a thinker *writes* is the turbulence of the actual thinking process. In reading these rescued patches of calm, expressed through the careful use of language, we are wont to believe we are witnessing his *thinking* as it unfolds. It is this misconception which invites the further one that the language an individual uses 'in' thinking is determined by what he thinks, since his thoughts *as expressed* often evidence a careful *choice* of language. This, however, is not a case of thinking 'in' language being accompanied simultaneously by thinking whether one agrees with the language one is thinking 'in'. Rather, this is that case already noted, where one thinks about whether one agrees with what one has thought *after* the event, and makes corrections and reformulations in what one *writes*, in the interests of truth, clarity, or whatever else one hopes to realise by communicating thoughts to others.

'SAYING' AS EVIDENCE OF THINKING

Having attempted as far as possible to discuss 'thinking' in isolation from 'saying', let us now investigate those aspects of the latter whose comprehension is of intimate relevance to the project of the history of thought.

All the above has been premised on the assumption that we know what an individual thinks. However, we must now return more fully to the point that the activity of thinking is not laid bare to view in what the thinker says or writes – rather, that we need to view what he says or writes as *evidence* of his thinking. We need to do this in two different senses, for firstly no thinker actually *says* all that he thinks; and secondly, what he *does* say is what he has *chosen* to say, this choice being evidence of uncommunicated thinking which therefore has to be inferred.

In the first case we infer from the thought which *is* communicated as much as possible of the thinking that led up to it. As argued earlier, the more we know of the context within which a thinker functions, the more likely we can infer the path his thinking has taken. For example, Bodin opens his *Six Books of the Commonwealth* with a definition of 'a commonwealth', and then says one must begin with the definition because it indicates what 'the final end' of a subject is.[12] We can suspect from the use of this latter term that Bodin has been considering how one penetrates the nature of things and has brought to mind (and found acceptable) the

Aristotelian notion that, in addition to material, formal, and efficient causes determining the nature of a thing, there is its 'final end'. Recognising that part of Bodin's intellectual training occurred in Paris, a bastion of medieval scholasticism, our suspicion can harden into the *inference* that this was what was in his mind. Additionally, that he shortly specifically mentions Aristotle in connection with the 'end' of both the individual and the commonwealth virtually serves as vindication of this inference.[13] (To what extent Bodin's reflection on Aristotle gave both direction and substance to later points he makes, such that we might infer him as thinking about the material, formal, and efficient causes of 'the commonwealth' in subsequent chapters, is worth speculating. Tooley tells us Aristotle's *Politics* 'obviously provided the general model for the *Six Books of the Commonwealth*. The structure is the same'.[14] But he does not pursue our particular speculation.)

The above, then, is an example of approaching what is *said* as evidence of thinking which is *not* said. This process of *inference* is made possible by noting a feature of Bodin's terminology in conjunction with familiarity with aspects of the 'conceptual context' of his education, and by a reference he himself makes later. From this example we may generalise a number of points about viewing what is said as evidence of unstated thinking. Firstly, we are inferring from a thought which *is* expressed (some of) the thinking that led up to it. *We are not, in this procedure, inferring from a thought that is expressed the thinking which led to its expression; that is a separate procedure.* Now, in inferring the thinking which led up to a particular (stated) thought we are rarely afforded sufficient evidence from that thought alone to infer a detailed account of what led to it. Clues vary in their fecundity. (Wolfson, for example, performs a veritable *tour de force* in his sustained account of Spinoza's (unstated) thinking in the *Ethics*, principally and unusually via his remarkably erudite examination of Spinoza's terminology alone.)[15] Yet however modest our inference, whenever we can say an individual thinks x as a consequence of thinking about a or b, we have satisfied the minimal requirement of the narrative form. In short, we have given a (narrative) account of a changing identity – in this case, an episode in an individual's thinking activity. And in giving such an account we are also *explaining* why he thought x (but not why x rather than y), in that narrative sense of 'explanation' set out earlier. Thus from our example we can infer that Bodin was *thinking* about the nature of what we now call 'the State'; it is thus reasonable to infer he was not satisfied with existing understandings (or the lack of them); that he 'therefore then' thought of the Aristotelian approach to the nature of things; that it followed for Bodin that the crux of understanding 'the State' depended upon an initial identification of its 'final end'; and that he 'therefore then' proceeded to reflect on what this is.

It is in this way, then, that we can infer from a thought which is expressed the (likely) sequence of thinking which led up to it. No point in the sequence is determined by 'causes' or other exterior factors – rather, our account is an explication of the way that individual thought. It is the revealing of a real occurrence; namely, a thinker's *response* to an intellectual problem.

In this procedure we should note that not every stated thought invites being viewed as evidence; it depends on the nature of the thought and the terminology used. Also, even where we can infer an individual's thinking, certain parts may be so obvious as not to merit attention. Rather, as in our elementary model of narrative structure, the historian of thought will select those which are 'relevant' and, if appropriate to his project, 'significant'.

The preceding has discussed the unstated thinking leading up to what is actually stated. But there are of course occasions where a thinker *does* express the thinking leading up to a point. Here, all that appears to be required is that we follow the expressed sequence of thoughts – that is, 'understand' what we are reading in the simple sense of the term, which is not, of course, to engage in the historian's activity of inferring something from evidence. We simply follow an expressed argument. For instance, where Bodin says one should start 'with a definition because the final end of any subject must first be understood before the means of attaining it can profitably be considered, and the definition indicates what that end is', he immediately follows by stating; 'If then the definition is not exact and true, all that is deduced from it is valueless'. This latter thought follows from the previous, such that we account for it by saying just that. No inference is involved. His words, 'If then . . .', suggest precisely this. The thought expressed in the next sentence, however, cannot be seen as following on in the same direct (logical) manner, and neither does Bodin's language suggest so, for it continues; 'One can, of course, have an accurate perception of the end, and yet lack the means to attain it, as has the indifferent archer who sees the bull's-eye but cannot hit it'. Although this is an observation which can easily ('. . . of course . . .') be *derived* from the previous sentence, this is different from its following directly. We therefore have to look elsewhere for its explanation, and in this case the terminology offers no clues.

Instead, we are brought to an example of that *second* sense in which what is written is *evidence* of unstated thinking, for we can always ask of anything which is said, 'why is the individual actually *saying* this?' Usually, that is, when one writes something one does not accompany it with an account of why – and if one did, the question would still arise as to why one did! Yet in any controlled piece of writing which articulates thinking in our strict sense of the term, we can assume that in addition to thinking about the topic in hand the writer also thinks what to actually communicate, how to express it, and in what order. If we can recover this unstated thinking we can offer an account of the thinking which leads up, not to the thought as stated (as in our first sense of the term, 'evidence'), but to the choice to actually state the thought. In short, we can explain why the individual *says* this or that – and there is a point in this, for there is a strong sense in which we do not know what a writer or speaker means by a sentence if we do not know what he means by either writing or speaking it. For example, we may overhear a person say to someone, 'What a lovely day it is!' We understand the meaning of the sentence, but this is different from understanding the meaning of saying it.[16] He may be trying to break the ice with a neighbour, make an approach to someone who attracts him, or conform to conversational convention.

We have, then, two different senses of the term, 'meaning'; the meaning of what is said, and the meaning of (the action of) saying it.[17] If we fail to recognise this, or confuse the two, we risk either believing that insofar as we understand the meaning of what someone has written we have also understood his writing it – or of believing that all we have to do to understand someone's writings is to understand what he writes. Rather, we must recognise the need to treat saying or writing as any other intentional human activity, whereby we convert 'neutral'[18] actions into meaningful human conduct, such as when we comprehend someone's kicking a ball as making a pass, exercising, or removing an obstacle from his path. Thus regarding the activity of saying or writing something, we must of course first understand what is written, but we can also proceed to infer the meaning of writing it.

We have seen, then, the two senses in which what is said or written can be treated as *evidence* from which to infer unstated thinking.[19] The historian of thought is concerned with both senses despite their difference. By analogy, suppose an archaeologist discovers a coin, and that he does not have to *infer* it is a coin, just as the historian of thought does not have to infer what one of Bodin's sentences *means* in the simple sense of the term. Now, the coin may offer itself as evidence in two senses. Firstly, we may infer something about a past culture from an aspect of the nature of the coin itself – for instance, its markings or metallurgical composition. This is akin to the historian of thought inferring from a thought which *is* expressed some of the unstated thinking which led up to it – our first kind of evidence. But secondly, the archaeologist may infer something about a past culture not from the nature of the coin itself but from its location. This is akin to the historian of thought inferring from a stated thought something about the writer's thinking by considering why he stated it. What preceded the sentence? What succeeded it? In short, like the archaeologist paying attention to the *location* of the coin, the historian of thought attends to the 'location' of what is said in order to infer the thinking behind *saying* it – and this can be done with respect to individual sentences, paragraphs, or the ordering of entire sections or chapters, whereby in the latter case we attempt to understand not merely what a book 'says', but what the author was trying to achieve by constructing it.

We have already exemplified the former kind of inference where, from Bodin's terminology, we could infer the thinking leading to the thought he wrote. Using the same passage, we may now exemplify the latter kind of inference. I claimed that where Bodin writes, 'One can, of course, have an accurate perception of the end, and yet lack the means to attain it, as has the indifferent archer who sees the bull's-eye but cannot hit it', the thought this sentence contains cannot be accounted for in terms of its following on *logically* from the previous sentence. But in asking, then, *why* he wrote this sentence, attention to those surrounding it enables the inference that he wished to make two points regarding his having opened with a definition; firstly, that it *is* worth striving for a true understanding of things – 'With care and attention, however, he may come very near it, and provided he uses his best endeavours, he will not be without honour, even if he cannot find the exact centre of the target'; secondly, that if one does not understand the nature of what one is dealing with, then all one proposes regarding it will be useless – 'But the man who does not comprehend the end, and cannot rightly define his subject, has no hope of finding the means of attaining it, any more than the man who shoots at random into the air can hope to hit the mark'.[20]

It is because he *wishes* to make these two latter points that Bodin introduced the thought expressed in his analogy of the indifferent archer; that is, he wrote that thought in order to facilitate the two subsequent points, for they *do* follow logically from his analogy. He did not, then, express the thought contained in the analogy 'for its own sake', but to bring the reader to see the reasoning behind, and hence the correctness of, the two subsequent points he makes – and, provisionally, I have suggested he made these two latter points simply because he wanted to. Unlike the stating of the archer analogy they are not preparatory to some subsequent argument, even though he does later allude to their gist, as quoted below. (Indeed, Tooley has Bodin begin a new paragraph after these two points.)

Now, in claiming he made these two latter points for their own sake we are thus dealing with what I have called 'final' actions (whereas his articulating the archer analogy is a 'mediate' action), and although we will shortly examine these species of 'saying-actions', we may immediately recall that our analysis of *any* 'final' actions suggests their resistance to being 'explained' any further than through what their 'finality' already indicates.

In this example from Bodin, however, we do not have to leave these two 'final' points to that extent inexplicable, for even if we can say no more about why he *stated* them, we can return to examine them in our *first* sense of 'evidence', to infer the thinking which led up to what they articulate. Familiarity with the history of political thought affords the knowledge that many a theorist reflects on the rationale of theoretical, philosophical, or abstract thinking and writing about politics, society, and government – in other words, questions their own activity, or its rationale as undertaken by others (for example, Plato in his cave analogy, Cicero in Book One of his *The Republic*, Machiavelli in his *Discourses*, More in Book One of *Utopia*, Hegel in his Preface to *The Philosophy of Right*, Marx in his *Theses on Feuerbach*, and Oakeshott in his *Rationalism in Politics*).

Now it is certain Bodin encountered this theme in his extensive reading (which included Plato, More, and Machiavelli), and it is therefore reasonable to infer from these two 'final' points that this is what he had in mind, and that what he wrote is his (remarkably succinct) response to it. This inference is strengthened by his later in the same chapter specifically mentioning both Plato and More on the theme of utopianism, or what might now be called the theory/practice problematic: 'We aim . . . to attain, or at least approximate, to the true image of a rightly ordered government. Not that we intend to describe a purely ideal and unrealisable commonwealth, such as that imagined by Plato or Thomas More. . . . We intend to confine ourselves as far as possible to those political forms that are practicable'.[21]

In thus reverting to that first sense of 'evidence' in which one infers the thinking which led to what is actually expressed, I will only add that it is, in theory, an eclectic procedure. To see something in an expressed thought as a clue regarding its origins can depend upon the character of the thought itself, which may yield nothing even to the most scrupulous, or on one's alertness, knowledge, and imagination, whereby sundry aspects of a writer's context may afford clues. In practice, however, we reiterate that where the historian of thought studies more abstract writings, attention to terminology and/or a familiarity with preceding themes will normally provide the richest sources of inferences. (This approach can even bear fruit in a negative sense, since where a writer ignores themes altogether – as, for example, Hobbes' lack of reference to history in *Leviathan*'s argumentation, or Locke's avoidance of the term 'sovereignty' in his second *Treatise of Civil Government* – we can draw inferences where we suspect it was deliberate.) To the extent these practical likelihoods dominate what is otherwise an eclectic methodology, we can see why this approach of viewing what is written as evidence of unstated thinking affords the discipline of the history of thought a more *cumulative* character than some other branches of history.

The case is different, however, where we view a thinker's choice to *state* this or that as evidence of his thinking process. We have already given examples of this from Bodin's opening passage; but unlike the former methodology which is (in principle) eclectic, this latter is not, and thus lends itself to formal analysis. We thus need to demonstrate how the saying or writing of something, as any other deliberate human action, is only rendered explicable through narrative logic. But before doing this we should confront a potential objection to following this course; namely, it might be argued that insofar as one is treating of, for example, the history of *political* thought, then to account for why a thinker *writes* what he writes is to explain how he constructs and presents arguments – and that the exposition of the thinking involved in these activities is nothing to do with specifically *political* thinking. Rather, the proposed methodology will apply to *any* argumentative writer, be his interest in, for example, politics, economics, or philosophy. In short, then, it might be objected that the historian of political thought should not explore why, for instance, Bodin *wrote* this or that sentence, paragraph, or chapter, because to do so is not to expose his *political* thinking but simply his 'argumentative' thinking.

To this I reply, firstly, that there is no such thing as 'political thinking' if this is meant to denote a species of thinking different from that exemplified in, for example, economic thinking. Rather, there is thinking about politics, and thinking about economics. There can never be thinking *per se*. Secondly, I say that one cannot construct an argument *per se* – it has to be an argument about this or that, just as one cannot, for instance, build *per se*, but must build this or that. The most we can say of arguing 'in general' is that 'to argue', in this context, is 'to maintain by reasons', 'to make clear', 'to prove'.[22] But when it comes to thinking out any *actual* argument – for instance, what follows from what, what needs to be shown first, how to make a point clear, how to forestall objections – then I say that just as one cannot think about building in the abstract but only about how to build this wall or that house, so one cannot think about arguing in the abstract but only about this argument about politics or that argument about economics.

Thus I claim it is incorrect (because in practice impossible), to separate someone's thinking about, for instance, politics from his thinking about how to argue his case. Rather, the most that can be said is that his thinking how to argue is not so much 'thinking about politics' as 'thinking about the thinking about politics' which has occurred in the privacy of the mind, with a view to articulating the latter in a manner which makes clear one's conclusions and demonstrates their soundness by constructing convincing chains of reasoning from which they follow. And as is clear, *if* such 'thinking about thinking about politics' is done in good faith rather than simply to offer seemingly convincing argument for appearance's sake – an exercise in casuistry – then in addition to improving the *presentation* of the argument it will also fulfil that demand of 'reflexive' thought whereby one checks one's thinking for mistakes. In the light of this it is not surprising that reflexive thinking can be at its most intense and effective in the actual process of *writing* (for others).

To summarise, and offer an analogy, I say then that just as it would be absurd to claim the thought a poet puts into the actual *writing* of a poem is nothing to do with him as a poet, but only as a 'writer', so it would be absurd to suggest the historian of, for example, political thought should not attend to the thought involved in what a thinker on politics chooses to actually write, on the grounds that it is nothing to do with his thinking about politics.[23] If there is no such thing as 'thinking *per se*', nor 'arguing *per se*', neither is there such a thing as 'writing *per se*'.

'SAYING' AS A FINAL ACTION

Having defended the historian of thought's need to explain why a thinker actually *writes* what he does, on the grounds that the thought involved is contributive to the thinking about the subject in hand, we can now proceed with that formal analysis of what is involved in explaining why people 'say' things. (I mean 'say' in the general sense, under which writing is subsumed; and in the first instance I refer to *any* kind of 'saying', leaving until subsequently the application of general principles to that kind which constitutes *argumentation*.) Now we have claimed that in giving a narrative account of (and thereby 'explaining') *any* actions, including 'saying' things, the broad framework within which we must work involves characterising the saying of things in each instance as either final, practical, or mediate actions. Let us consider each in turn.

For the saying of something to constitute a 'final' action, an individual has to be saying what he says for the sake of it. It might be objected that people do not do this, but a little reflection will show this often to be the case, and sometimes exasperatingly so. Saying things for the sake of saying them is simply a particular and unexceptional case of doing something for the sake of it, and was analysed in Chapter Three as doing something for the experience *of* doing it – that is, one 'enjoys oneself' doing it. Regarding 'saying' things, this implies it is possible to say something for the experience accompanying saying it. For example, the saying of 'what a lovely day it is!' can be a final action. Now it is difficult not to see that expressing a thought for the sake of doing so is *ipso facto* to believe oneself to be saying something *true*, and to enjoy doing so.

To argue this *a posteriori*, why should anyone knowingly say something false for the sake of saying it? No one misleads or lies for the sake of it. Rather, one must have an objective in lying, deceiving, or misleading people, such that to knowingly say something false is surely an example of a *practical* action; one would be trying to achieve some purpose, for which the falsehood is a means to that end. We may also show the point *a priori*, for we can claim that when someone engages in an action for its own sake there is nothing prompting him to do less than justice to it – that is, execute the action according to the criteria demanded by it. What follows from this Platonic sense of 'doing a thing justice' is that to say something for the sake of saying it is to intend to say something true, and that there is thus something in human beings which makes the expounding of true statements pleasurable in itself. We do not need to limit this to intellectual or rational discourse; rather, it would appear to be a universal phenomenon accounting for much of human communication, from academic theses to trivial bus-stop conversations. It is, then, not going too far to claim that to say something for the sake of saying it is to attempt to do justice to the truth, for what is it to say something (of a propositional nature) other than to say what is the case?

Now, where we can characterise someone's saying something as a final action, it follows from our earlier analysis that no further questions remain regarding why the individual said it. It is true that identifying it as a final action involves seeing it as the 'free' response of the individual *to* some aspect of his circumstances – for example, to this idea or that event. But having given an account of the action as a final action, one has thereby accounted *for* it, and no further explanation is possible. Thus, having attended to the context, we claimed that Bodin's writing the thoughts expressed in the last two sentences of his first (Tooley) paragraph constitutes a 'final' action. They are the conclusions he reached to the problem of the rationale of political theory, and stated 'for the sake of it' – that is, for the sake of expressing what he took to be true propositions, and for no further reason. They do not prepare the way for some subsequent points he either wishes or needs to make, nor are they an integral part of some larger argument (respectively, 'practical' and 'mediate' actions, as will emerge below). It also follows from our analysis of beginnings and endings that we should be open to the possibility of there being several points even within one chapter where an author's writing something constitutes a final action, implying that the reader may encounter a number of discrete points which at the least interrupt the overall continuity of discourse, or reveal its absence altogether. This is far more likely in everyday 'saying', and all we need reminding of is that, in his search for 'what was really going on', the rationale of the (narrative) historian's activity is to discover real continui*ties* in conduct, not 'continuity in general'.

Having claimed, then, that the explanation for why anyone 'says' something is exhausted where we can identify the action as a final action, it might nevertheless be objected that this does *not* exhaust the explanation because, in 'saying' something, one is *communicating*, and thereby intending to achieve some objective *vis-à-vis* the audience; that therefore the action must be practically motivated. Seen in this light our notion of 'saying' as a 'final' action is fallacious, for if all acts of communication are necessarily directed to some exterior objective, then where someone has a thought he believes to be true, *and* communicates it, our notion fails to address what it is he is trying to achieve, thus stopping short of a full explanation of what is going on. In short, even where someone does appear to say something 'for the sake of it', the question *does* remain, 'why does he bother to *say* it?' Why, for example, do individuals trouble to construct complex books of argument in such a manner as to render their notions and ideas *communicable*? If one has no practical objectives, such as money, career, fame, or political persuasion, why write a book?

In response let us recall our footballer who enjoys tying his boot-laces 'for the sake of it'. That the action has a purpose – to secure the boot to the foot – does not thereby resolve it into a *practical* action, for this is the *intrinsic rationale* of the action. Only if it is performed for some 'exterior' objective – for example, in order to play football – is it a practical action. We added that all (deliberate) actions are *intrinsically* purposeful but that this does not mean they are necessarily performed for the sake of achieving their rationale, never mind any exterior objective. Rather, where they are final actions they are undertaken for the sake of experiencing doing those things involved in the action – as, for example, in what we call 'playing at' something.

The same holds for 'saying' things construed as final actions. That in saying something the purpose is to be heard and understood, constitutes the intrinsic rationale of the action. Thus although an act of communication is always undertaken 'in order to' achieve the general object of being heard and understood by others, this is not to say it necessarily must be performed for the sake of achieving that object. Rather, where it is a final action, it is undertaken for the sake of experiencing what is intrinsically involved, and there *is*, then, no further explanation for it.

These observations do, however, raise a further question of such intimate relevance to the activity of writing as to warrant some speculation; namely, given that people often enjoy 'saying' things for its own sake, what does this tell us about human beings? If the above might offer relief to some writers' existential doubts about why they struggle on (the 'secret' is that, like our suffering footballer gasping for breath, they enjoy themselves/their activity) it does not tell us *why*, as a general phenomenon, saying things for the sake of it is enjoyable.

The question may be unanswerable. We may simply be content to say human beings are like that. However, the following possibilities might be proposed: perhaps there is something in people which craves the consent of others to their thoughts, suggestive of a need to be able to say, 'you are just like me'. Alternatively, we have all encountered the bore of whom we say, 'he likes the sound of his own voice', suggestive of a need for self-affirmation, or maybe even dominance over others. Again, some may relate the phenomenon to the urge towards creativity, a point which could be persuasive but for the fact that we are not only referring to the painstaking construction of books but also to fleeting and trivially voiced observations. For my part, I regard the phenomenon of communication 'for its own sake' as evidence of the inherent sociability of man, for it can most realistically be construed as a form of *sharing* – in this case, of thought rather than food or shelter. I say this because where one 'says' something in order to achieve a *practical* purpose, this must be a self-interested action inasmuch as one aims to achieve some ultimately self-related objective in relation to others' conduct or attitudes. Although therefore concerned with the *efficacy* of one's communication, one has further objectives, and this is different from wanting to communicate efficiently simply because one enjoys doing what that intrinsically involves – namely, being heard and understood. This latter is communicating as a *final* action, and in the absence of any (necessarily) self-directed practical motivation it is difficult to see how the enjoyment of being heard and understood does not equate with an innate urge to share what can only otherwise remain uniquely one's own – namely, one's thoughts.

One more point emerges from this speculation about innate sociability, once again proffering solace to some writers. Some of the most intensive and sustained cases of communication for the sake of it are those exemplified by carefully thought-out and painstakingly written books, undertaken for no 'exterior' purpose. It is well known that such writing is a solitary business, such that where we encounter individuals who devote most of their attention (if not time) to it, it is difficult to conceive of a more unsociable activity. Indeed, so much is this the case that one might wish to reverse entirely our notion of the innate sociability of man, and instead point to these writers as evidence that man is essentially a *solitary* being who only associates with others when it is in his own interest to do so.

We see, however, that the writer is exonerated from the accusation of being radically unsociable. On the contrary, it is neither the lively communication of the market-place nor the buzzing conversation in the crowded pub which proclaims the inherent sociability of mankind. The former is self-motivated, practical communication, whilst where the latter might be communication for the sake of it, the value of what is shared is poor testimony indeed to the significance of 'sociability'. Rather, the most fulsomely *social* conduct is manifested instead in the reclusive solitude of the selfless writer's struggling activity!

'SAYING' AS A PRACTICAL ACTION

As has already emerged, for the saying of something to constitute a *practical* action it is necessary it is said in order to achieve some objective. Such communication is a means to an end. It would be wrong to argue that the objective of communicating is to be heard and understood, for that is what one is doing *in* communicating. In short, where an act of communication is a practical action its objective cannot be to communicate; rather, it must be directed, *through* communicating, to achieving some objective *vis-à-vis* the audience whereby they will do, or believe, this or that.

Turning specifically to the history of thought, where we are confronted by complex and argumentative books and (in addition to the thoughts they express) seek to account for what is *written*, we encounter saying as a practical action wherever it is clear a writer says something *in order to* be in a position to propose an argument. For example, prior to actually arguing a case it may be necessary to define some terms, locate the debate one is contributing to, or indicate one is moving from one argument to another. These are all instances where one is saying something out of necessity, in order to render the ensuing argument intelligible. As with any purely practical actions, they are burdensome. An extreme instance occurs in the version of *The Philosophy of Right* Hegel prepared for publication, where he tells us near the beginning, 'the concept of right, so far as its coming to be is concerned, falls outside the science of right; it is taken up here as given and its deduction is presupposed'.[24] His writing this is itself a practical action, for he is saying he does not intend to undertake the necessary business of making numerous preliminary points before he even starts the book, since they had already been made in his *Encyclopaedia*! In this sentence, then, he is either advertising the latter book (a practical action), or he at least deemed it necessary to indicate where an understanding of the derivation of the concept of right, as necessary to make *The Philosophy of Right* fully intelligible, can be found – again, a practical action.

The only other point I will observe here regarding 'saying' as a practical action is that where it occurs there will be a tendency to present what is said with a degree of conviction rather than tentatively. As noted, all practical actions bear the mark of commitment on the part of the agent, and what this implies regarding saying things which are necessary to enable one to proceed to arguing a case is that one precisely does not want to argue *these* points. Concerned they are accepted, one presents them forthrightly, whereas the argument they *enable* may itself be intentionally hesitant or controversial. Thus, for example, in that more formal manner of writing Spinoza employed in his *Ethics*, where the rationale for saying what is said is that much more explicit, we find him beginning with a number of definitions and axioms, thereby indicating that these points (although of course not unarguable in themselves) are not to be argued, but are necessary to understand in order to make the succeeding Propositions (which *are* argued) intelligible. The didactic nature of such 'saying' as a practical action is at its most extreme in the above quote from Hegel, for there the reader is asked to accept as 'given' a matter which is not even touched upon, and whose adequacy is 'presupposed'!

'SAYING' AS A TASK

In Chapter Three we drew a distinction between discrete practical actions and a *sequence* of practical actions devoted to an overall objective. We called the latter a 'task' or 'chore', recognising the difference between a task and single practical action is, ultimately, conventional. The same applies to 'saying' things. The issuing of a command could in theory be seen as a 'task' where it involves saying more than one thing, whilst an entire speech, such as an election address, could be viewed as a single action. But conventionally we would distinguish between them. Thus, examples of 'saying' as a task (rather than as a single action) are instruction leaflets, or manuals on how to effect something, such as a television repair, a political revolution, or moral perfection. Just as with discrete practical actions, the crux of the matter is efficiency – what is said is said because the sayer deems it *necessary* in order to achieve his desired result.

Specifically regarding the history of thought, we encounter 'saying' as a task in those *argumentative* writings aimed at *persuading* the reader to a certain course of *action* through getting his assent to the soundness of what is argued. They are frequently met with in the history of, for example, political, religious, and economic thought, and it is clearly important to recognise them where they occur since this greatly facilitates accounting for the thinking behind what is said.

Such writings are often called 'ideological', and since so much has been written on that concept it is as well to make clear the kind of writing I am referring to. Firstly, I mean writings of an argumentative, or propositional, nature. Not all writings which seek to persuade to a course of action are of this kind; rather, one can earnestly implore someone to do something without adducing any arguments or seeking assent to any propositions. Secondly, in *any* argumentative writing the author is of course hoping to gain the reader's assent to propositions he advances. But that is not the same as trying to persuade him to a course of *action*. Rather, where a writer is arguing the adequacy of propositions (for instance, about the nature of justice, the relationship between capital and liquid assets, or the motivation behind a painter's work), he does not do so *in order to persuade* the reader that what he says is true, as if this were an exterior objective. Rather, the demonstrating of the adequacy of propositions is *intrinsic* to the very nature of arguing. However, as in our example of tying laces, one need not undertake this activity of arguing 'in order to' achieve its intrinsic 'objective'. Instead, it can be undertaken for the sake of performing what the activity involves. The difference is clear, for if one argues a case solely *in order to* secure assent, one might achieve this more easily by lying, distorting, or exaggerating. Where, on the other hand, one argues a case because one enjoys the activity, there is nothing influencing one to do less than justice to the truth as one sees it. In this case, to describe someone as engaged in *persuasion* sits uncomfortably with the spirit of the activity, whereas in the former case it *does* add to our understanding of what is happening to say that someone's arguing is devoted to persuasion. And the question arises as to why one should wish to *persuade* someone of the truth of what one says 'just for the sake of it'. Clearly, one must have some exterior objective, and it is difficult to see what else this could be than getting him to *do* something (for instance, buy a painting, vote for that party, or support this church).

I say, then, that all arguing of an analytic, propositional, or explanatory nature seeks the reader's assent by its very nature, but this is different from arguing *prescriptively*, where the object is to *persuade* the reader to a course of *action* by gaining his assent to analytic or explanatory propositions. It is this latter which is often called 'ideological' writing, although the term is also used to denote *thinking* allegedly constrained by 'unconscious' adherence to certain values. We have already exposed this perspective on 'thinking' as erroneous. (For example, we cannot explain that someone thinks x because he is, for example, a male chauvinist. Rather, it is because he is a male chauvinist that *we* infer he thinks x. And even where we are correct – he does indeed think x – the most that can be said is that his thinking x precisely *constitutes* his male chauvinism rather than being caused by 'it'.) Additionally, of course, the term 'ideology' is used popularly to refer to a political programme.

In meaning rather different things, then, at least one of which invites a misleading view on 'thinking', the term has maybe outlived its usefulness. It is preferable to refer to practically motivated, or prescriptive, argument as distinct from arguing 'for its own sake', or 'theoretical' argument. Although it is often easy to recognise the former – where a writer lies, exaggerates, misrepresents opponents, ignores counter-arguments, or employs polemics, rather than arguing for the sake of conveying (or 'sharing') what he takes to be the truth of a matter – there are cases where what is 'going on' in someone's arguings is not so evident, making it correspondingly difficult to account for what he says. These can occur for two different reasons.

Firstly, we encounter thinkers who see themselves as simply arguing what they take to be the truth of a matter and yet *are* engaged in prescription. Their writings exhibit few of the above tell-tale signs of bias, being moderately worded and cogently argued. Yet the overall effect is persuasive of a course of action (or, what comes to the same thing, of a *commitment* to a particular moral, political, or religious view). In such cases some might appeal to the 'unconscious' influence of the thinker's values causing him to construct a piece of persuasion, although I prefer to describe him as *deluded* about what he is doing (that is, mistaken, through ignorance), rather than appeal to such a curiosity as 'unconscious thinking'. An interesting example of such writings is Rousseau's famous *Discourse on the Origins of Inequality*, where we may suppose he understands himself to be doing his best to achieve and share a truthful answer to the question posed by the Dijon Academy – namely, 'What are the origins of inequality amongst men, and is it authorised by natural law?' In his writing, so severe is Rousseau's indictment of the institution of private property that we can suspect he is not only concerned to demonstrate the adequacy of his analysis, but *through* this, to *persuade* his readers to do something about it. I call this an interesting example because the ever-enigmatic Rousseau himself later recognised either that this was what he had unintentionally (?) done, or at least that his readers would assume this is what he had (deliberately) done – for as it was going to print he added an exasperatingly equivocal paragraph in which he not only denies his *Discourse* was intended as a call to abolish private property, but denies also that it was intended as a call to *any* course of action.[25]

The second case where it is difficult to determine what a thinker is doing arises from writings solely devoted to demonstrating the truth of a matter, yet which in sum or in part are persuasive of a course of action despite evidently not being designed as such. In short, akin to 'pure science', or 'science for science's sake', which can generate by-products of practical use, so a non-practically motivated, or 'theoretical', enquiry into the nature of something can involve arguments which bear prescriptive implications. An interesting example is Hegel's *Philosophy of Right*. Unless he 'protesteth too much', we may take him at his word where he devotes considerable space towards the end of his Preface to insisting that 'science' or 'philosophy' cannot prescribe, and points out that since his book is philosophical it is radically non-prescriptive. According to Hegel, the only *effect* philosophy can have upon a recipient is the solace offered by understanding that matters are as they should be – and this is merely a by-product, for the philosopher does not engage in his activity *in order to* achieve this, as if it were an objective. Since, perhaps unlike Rousseau, Hegel has clearly thought about and explained the issue, he is unlikely to be deluded about what he is doing in the ensuing book. Yet it bristles with prescriptions, down to some of the finer details of social, economic, and political life. Also, indeed, we might say his arguings regarding philosophy itself are prescriptive, for in addition to offering an understanding of what philosophy is, they constitute a view which is *persuasive* of a course of action – in this case, forbearance from attempting to alter affairs so they accord with one's own 'philosophy'.

The above are peculiarly complex examples of the difficulty in determining prima facie what someone is doing in his writing, and thus in giving an account of the thinking behind what he chooses to write. But where straightforwardly engaged in a practical project (that is, 'saying as a task'), we can account for what he chooses to say (that is, explain why he says *x* 'next'), in terms of that narrative logic inherent in the carrying out of a sequence of actions devoted to the achievement of an overall exterior objective. The only rider to what might otherwise therefore be a simple matter is that deliberately *prescriptive* argument, precisely because designed as such, can be literally tricky, as is recognised, for example, of passages in Locke's *Two Treatises of Civil Government* where he employs sleight-of-hand techniques. But apart from such tricks as deliberate ambiguity, linguistic game-playing, and sleight-of-hand, where cases are still not straightforward the way to explore an author's thinking in what he writes is precisely to employ that analytic framework now being elaborated, whereby we examine each successive thing said in order to determine whether it constitutes a single practical action, part of a 'task', or a final action; or whether it falls into that (yet to be explicated) intermediate category of 'mediate' actions.

Here, I refer back to the example of gardening, where we said it can often be difficult to determine whether it is undertaken for its own sake or as a (practical) task. If it appears that all the actions are directed towards the objective of a tidy, fertile garden, then we can identify them as part of an overall task. But we have warned of that untidy ambivalence in human conduct whereby both final and practical actions intermix, such that in practical gardening one might nevertheless do a thing for the sake of it despite constraints of time and efficiency – or vice versa, where gardening for the sake of it one can come across and do things which need to be done for practical purposes.

We have suggested that close attention to what is done can usually sort out such ambiguities. The same applies to giving an account of what a writer is doing – that is, to inferring the thinking governing what someone *writes*. In the case of argumentative writings undertaken solely for the sake of demonstrating the truth of a matter, the temptation to intersperse prescriptive points can be acceded to. Given their wider and more enduring audience, books offer this temptation far more than do (academic) articles. Conversely, writings undertaken as practical tasks can include reflections where the thinker indulges in saying things for the sake of (sharing) the truth of a matter, thereby interrupting the otherwise practical discourse. Commissioned by The League of the Just to argumentatively persuade readers towards a political commitment, *The Communist Manifesto* is such an example, for it includes passages where Marx and Engels make observations and propose arguments solely for the sake of communicating what they take to be true.

Given, then, that it is not always straightforward to determine what a writer is doing from one point to the next, we should observe that writings most likely to exhibit ambivalence are those argumentative works

213

whose subject-matter touches on moral conduct – in other words, which purport to explain political, sociological, economic, and various 'philosophical' matters, rather than works on pure and applied science, technology, or, for example, animal behaviour. (Certain areas which might otherwise fall into the latter grouping, such as psychology and ecology, can nevertheless touch on moral conduct, and be correspondingly less straightforward in their construction.) This is simply because *persuasion*, as I have used the term, is concerned with getting people to follow a course of action and thus relates particularly to moral conduct, if by 'moral' we mean what people 'ought' to do. Thus, for instance, we are far more likely to find writings which exhibit a complex intermixture of intentions within political thought than in mathematics, although even in the latter case, if theories are perceived to have 'philosophical' or theological implications (as in the seventeenth-century 'scientific revolution'), we need to be alert to a possible variety of intentions and motivations in what a thinker writes.[26]

We cannot yet, however, summarise the techniques of investigation involved in giving an account of the thinking governing the actual 'saying' of this or that – that is, in sorting out what a thinker is *doing* in what he writes – until we have analysed the remaining kind of action as it relates to 'saying'; namely, mediate actions.

'SAYING' AS A MEDIATE ACTION

In Chapter Three I used the term 'mediate' to denote any action undertaken as part of a (final) activity, as distinct from successive *practical* actions involved in the execution of a task. I referred to the former kind of actions as intrinsic to, or constitutive of, those instances where individuals engage in recognisably parametered (sometimes literally rule-bound), structures of related actions, which when undertaken for the sake of undertaking them I called 'activities' as distinct from tasks or chores. We also suggested that what would normally be regarded as tasks *can* be executed for their own sake – and vice versa, what normally are regarded as (in our terms) final activities *can* be performed in order to achieve a practical objective. Additionally, we noted both kinds of orientation may be interspersed during the same undertaking.

How does 'saying things' fit into this general context of mediate actions and final activities? We have already characterised 'saying' where it comprises single final actions – namely, saying something for the sake of communicating something one takes to be true – and noted that the distinction between an action and an activity (understood as comprising a number of constitutive actions), is conventional.

Now with respect to the history of *thought* I suggest that 'saying' as a (final) activity occurs wherever we encounter someone explaining a thing or arguing a case (for its own sake). Either involves saying more than one thing, for they consist of showing how one thing follows from another through a chain of reasoning. One attempts to show one's conclusions are correct inasmuch as they derive from observations which correspond with reality and reasonings which are consistent; in short, one is exhibiting that one's conclusions make sense.

We have said the intrinsic rationale of 'saying' in general is to be heard and understood, and that in the case of arguing or explaining, the additional rationale is that of demonstrating the adequacy or truth of one's principal points. Where one argues or explains for the sake of it, I have already shown why I prefer to view this activity as an exercise in sharing understanding (which some might equate with 'educating'), rather than as a task of *persuasion*. Now, in 'saying' as a final activity, particularly saying things of a propositional nature, a good deal of what a thinker writes is devoted to contributing to the *coherence* of the argument. I use this formulation in preference to 'things a thinker writes in order to render his argument coherent', for if we took this literally, of what would the argument itself consist? Nothing. In 'saying' as a (final) activity, then, mediate actions are those things said in the course of arguing a case. They *comprise* the arguing, their function being to clarify and substantiate the overall point(s) the thinker wishes to make. None of the particular things said as mediate actions are in themselves *necessary* to the activity of arguing this or that case (despite scholastic attempts to standardise modes of argument); but they are *intrinsic* to it. Doubtless we can say of a poor argument that the author should have dealt with this or that objection, or should have shown how this or that point follows, and in that sense claim a particular argument *necessitates* saying this or that. But as in tennis, where the actions *comprising* the actual playing are mediate actions, categorially different from those *practical* actions which are *necessarily* undertaken (such as retrieving the ball), so with arguing.

For example, in arguing a case it may be *necessary* to first define some terms in order to be subsequently intelligible. Such actions are practical, not mediate, actions. But where what the thinker writes contributes to the coherence, consistency, and overall adequacy of a point (as in stating premises, drawing implications, and countering alternative arguments), he is performing mediate actions. Thus where the saying of something is a mediate action, whatever point is being made is not expressed for its own sake – a final action – nor because it is *necessary* in order to undertake some activity – a discrete practical action. Neither, finally, is it made as simply one part of a sequence of practical actions comprising an overall task. Rather, it is being said as part of the ongoing activity of arguing. Now of course, arguing may itself be carried out for either practical or theoretical purposes, just as one can play tennis in order to keep fit rather than for its own sake. But this simply reminds us of the potentially ambiguous status of mediate actions. Where arguing is employed as part of an overall (practical) task (that is, *prescriptive* argument), they might be viewed simply as part of the sequence of practical actions the task involves. On the other hand, arguing has its own rationale which must be minimally conceded to irrespective of whether it is practically inspired or engaged in for the sake of the truth. Just so with playing tennis. If one does it as an exercise task, to keep fit, one's actions are still to an extent captive to the rationale of the game. In these cases, then, the (mediate) actions comprising playing tennis or arguing a case are in that no man's land between being on the one hand straightforwardly practical actions contributing to an overall task, and on the other being non-practically motivated actions governed by the nature of the activity they are part of.

EXPLAINING WHAT IS 'SAID'

We have claimed the history of thought focuses upon the activity of thinking; that thinking has to be inferred from what is 'said'; that what is 'said' is therefore to be treated as *evidence* of thinking, although in two different ways – firstly, as evidence of the thinking leading up to whatever thought is made manifest in being 'said' – and secondly, as evidence of the thinking behind the actual 'saying' of what is said. Regarding the latter, this amounts to giving an account of what an individual is *doing* by saying this or that, and to facilitate this I have tried to show, in principle, in what ways 'saying' things can be characterised (like any other kind of action) as practical, final, and mediate actions – and how the distinction between tasks and final activities is also relevant. As with Chapter Three's treatment of actions in general, then, where we drew up this common-sense framework as a way of analysing those sovereign twin demands of narrative logic, namely, continuity and change, so here with respect to 'saying' things. It now remains to see how the historian of thought can apply this formal heuristic to infer the thinking which accounts for what is actually written.

Although the discriminations I am proposing will in practice often be made in an untidy order dictated by the particular text in question, it seems logical to first identify any major 'final' points which (by definition) the thinker wants to make for the sake of making them. This involves distinguishing between such points and things said in the course of arguing them – namely, mediate actions. Accounting for a thinker's making a final point involves characterising it as his response to some aspect of his intellectual world. As shown, this rules out his making it in order to effect anything, such as persuade the reader to a course of action or help him follow the argument. Rather, it should be presented as his saying a thing for the sake of saying something true. This spelling out of the making of a point as a final action in response to such-and-such, and in this or that way, exhausts the possibility of any further explanation. As a 'free' response we cannot know either *why* he responded in this instance or *why* he responded in the way he did, because neither have any 'reason' other than precisely his agency. As with any final action, his doing what he did *constitutes* his 'reasoning' at that moment and in those circumstances.

But to characterise what is 'said' in this manner is not to achieve little. To monitor a thinker's 'free' responses to his intellectual world tells us much about that individual. Even more important, where our characterisation of the 'saying' of something is correct we will have extracted a species of genuine 'happenings' from an otherwise undifferentiated scenario of intellectual occurrences. In short, we will have begun to perceive authentic narrative or 'historical' identities in the world of thinking, as distinct from merely chronicling (and perhaps criticising) what a writer means from one point to the next.

Having identified and characterised a 'final' point a thinker is concerned to voice, the next undertaking is to locate, and characterise as such, things said in the course of arguing a final point – in other words, associated 'mediate' actions – and to distinguish them from any associated 'practical' actions. This, then, amounts to distinguishing what is said as *part of* the arguing of a final point from what is said *in order to be in a position to* advance the argument in the first place. The form these latter 'practical' actions take with respect to *argumentative* writings are those things said in order to render the succeeding argument *intelligible*, whereas mediate actions take the form of things said as contributive to, or constitutive of, its *coherence*. It is in this manner that the two criteria of argument for argument's sake – namely, intelligibility and coherence – find their places in the activity of arguing.

Regarding *practical* actions associated with argument for argument's sake, they are thus analogous to retrieving the tennis ball, where what is said is done not as part of the activity, but *in order to* continue it. Correspondingly, their explanation falls under that straightforward formula of doing a thing in order to achieve the objective of continuing the activity in question (or, in the case of tasks or chores, in order to press on with achieving the overall objective). In this circumstance I have suggested practical actions are thus the saying of things *in order to* render the succeeding point(s) intelligible. Included in such actions are those passages, themselves of no substantive importance, whose purpose is to link succeeding argumentation with what has preceded, particularly where a new theme is being introduced. The objective is to demonstrate the relevance of the proceedings to the overall argument. Brief résumés, reminding one what has gone on before, are also examples of 'practical' actions, undertaken in order to put the reader in a position to follow the argument. Akin, then, to retrieving the tennis ball, they are not themselves part of the argumentation, but necessary in order to facilitate it.

217

It is tempting to view their explanation as of little further interest, for as with any practical action it is knowledge of their objective which furnishes their explanation. However, there is a circumstance in the case of *communicating* in general, and in argumentative writings in particular, which should extend our interest in them. We have noted that practical actions are 'cursed' with the hallmark of *necessity;* further, that in many contexts what is necessary is objectively established, in this sense doubly imposing upon the agent. For example, in order to make a fire I must fetch the coal. When arguing a case, however, the determination of what is necessary for the reader to follow the argument is more subjective for the thinker. He includes what *he* thinks is necessary rather than having to submit to established, objective necessities. Thus, unlike in fetching the coal, we are brought back to an aspect of an individual's thinking which may invite further insights into 'what is going on' in his mind. Although not the sole consideration in a thinker's estimation of what he needs to say to render his points intelligible, I suggest the principal, and potentially most revealing, is the audience he hopes to reach. For example, if writing for professionals in an established discipline (as in academic articles), much that might otherwise be necessary to assist their following the argument is taken for granted. At the other extreme, if he wants to make himself understood to an audience unfamiliar with his subject, or whose presuppositions (political, moral, religious), would impede their following him, these circumstances will involve his careful construction of numerous passages of a practical orientation.

Thus, attentive consideration of practically motivated passages within argument for argument's sake may furnish clues regarding the thinker's desired audience, and thus offer further insights into 'what he is doing' in what he says. For example, unlike in his *Tractatus Theologico-Politicus*, in his *Ethics* Spinoza says nothing to assist non-intellectuals to follow his argument; nor anything to encourage religious intellectuals. On the contrary, the marked absence of passages motivated by any practical objective other than facilitating unbiased, intellectual understanding bears witness to his intentions in writing the book – namely, to address what in the seventeenth century were called 'free-thinkers', who by definition, however, are neither chronologically nor culturally bound. That this was his thinking is further evidenced by his caution over the circulation of his earlier version, namely, the *Short Treatise*, and by his correspondence regarding the publication of the *Ethics* itself.[27] Although circumspect in an age of passionate religious sensibilities (not for fear of persecution, but in order to procure a fair reception for his long-worked masterpiece), that he nevertheless thought it worthwhile to publish the *Ethics* at some point – his death intervened – is testimony of his optimism, at least regarding future generations.

PRACTICAL AND THEORETICAL ARGUMENT

If, then, the way we explain practical actions associated with arguing differs from how we explain the making of final points, so the way we explain *mediate* actions differs from both. As already urged, the rationale of what we call 'argument in general' is that of 'making a case' for a point one wishes to state. By arguing rather than merely stating the point, one hopes to show it to be sound, and this involves demonstrating it is derived from a consistent chain of reasoning based on reasonable assumptions and/or accurate observations. One thereby invites agreement to the point being made. I say 'invites agreement' in order to leave open the writer's motivation. Where arguing a point which is *not* a final point, but propounded in order to persuade people to do this or that or to adopt certain values, then it is more accurate to say that, in doing those things involved in arguing, one is *courting* agreement – and in that eventuality the only intrinsic constraint on how one executes the rationale of this activity is one's estimation of the audience's gullibility. Exaggerations and distortions of fact, casuistic reasonings, the seductive allure of mystifying terminology, straightforward untruths – all these and more are used in such arguing, and there seems neither reason to expect any less, nor deplore the practice, if we view the matter with clear minds. Such conduct is intrinsic to 'courting agreement' (or practical/prescriptive argument), and is itself morally neutral. Hitler, we might say, did not argue 'badly' in parts of *Mein Kampf* – rather, one might disapprove of the points to which he wished to court agreement. However, the only concern of the historian of thought is to distinguish things said in the course of arguing points both from the points themselves and from things said in order to make the argument intelligible in the first place; and to an extent, such mediate actions are explicable both in their occurrence and content simply by identifying them as such. I say 'to an extent' because, where engaged in *practical* arguing, the fact that there is an overall (exterior) objective can influence the manner in which the arguing is carried out, such that awareness of its practical motivation can enable insights into why it was performed in a particular way. Here we are brought back to that ambiguity in those mediate actions constitutive of carrying out a task or chore, whereby they might easily be viewed as simply part of an ongoing sequence of practical actions but for the added ingredient that their rationale is, in this case, argumentative rather than merely assertive.

The case is different, however, where one argues a *final* point or points. As already claimed, to make a point for the sake of doing so cannot but equate with saying something one takes to be true. Now, in *arguing* such points one is assuredly 'inviting agreement', for that is the rationale of *all* arguing. However, in inviting agreement to a *final* point an author is doing no more than inviting the reader to see that the point is true. He is not trying to affect the reader's conduct; nothing 'hangs' on whether his argument is successful. His sole 'interest' in arguing the adequacy of his points is to establish a common perception of what is (hopefully) true. I say, then, that in arguing a final point one is not 'courting agreement' (whereby efficiency in achieving that objective is the dominant criterion for how it is performed), but *sharing an insight* into the truth of a matter (whereby the intellectual adequacy of the arguing process itself is the sole criterion for how it is performed). In thus referring again to that essentially *social* nature of the theorist's work, it is clear that in such arguings there is not only no need to lie, distort, or in some other way deceive – it would be absurd. Equally (although vanity might intervene), nothing should deter the arguer from conceding where he has made an error.

Such arguing (devoted to establishing a shared perception of what is true), I call 'theoretical' argument. Frequently encountered in numerous disciplines, it is not to be confused with 'philosophy'. On the contrary, much philosophical writing is intended to persuade the reader to this or that mode of conduct, is correspondingly 'disingenuous', but is still called 'philosophy' simply inasmuch as it addresses matters outside the competence of established disciplines. Theoretical argument, on the other hand, is essentially disinterested, despite the paradox that it can generate impassioned disputes. However, rather than take this as undermining the impartial nature of theoretic arguing (and thus of 'theory' itself), we should instead observe that such passion can arise from *concern* for truth for its own sake. Irrespective of what might *hang* on whether such-and-such is true (a prison sentence, a good investment, or moral salvation), occasions arise and temperaments are displayed where it is clear that 'the truth' is valued on its own account. That this is not a feature exclusive to obscure academic debate, nor to the 'academic' personality, is clear from those numerous contexts where individuals hotly dispute the most trivial of truths ('We went there in June, dear, not July' . . . 'You're wrong, it *was* July!'). Where such disputes occur, lies or other deliberate tricks are precisely *not* employed, despite the passions engendered. The Hobbesian notion that where untruth offends, as frequently occurs, then this is a species of (intellectual) pain demanding redress, may be correct; moreover, where truth is valued on its own account we might consider Spinoza's notion that true or 'adequate' understandings bear witness to the proper ('active') functioning of the mind, necessarily accompanied by pleasure – particularly, we might add, where the truth about a matter is actively thought out, resulting in the pleasure of 'enlightenment'.

Such notions may help answer an obvious question regarding 'theoretical' argument; namely, what is the *use*, or point, of truth for its own sake? On the face of it, truth can of course matter for *practical* purposes. For example, the bridge builder needs to argue 'the truth' about stresses and materials with the reluctant architect, just as parents need to argue 'the truth' about electric shocks with their meddlesome children. But in these cases where one argues what is true in order to achieve a practical objective, it is not truth itself which matters; it is the achieving of the objective (respectively, a safe bridge, a child out of danger). Because of this, I reiterate that where arguing something to be true in order to achieve a practical purpose, the point is not so much to establish what is true as to engender the listener's *belief* that what one says is true, whereby we are brought back to the perfectly respectable 'threat' of disingenuous arguings. Thus we must conclude that although it seems obvious truth can matter for *practical* purposes, this is far from necessarily the case; the urge to argue that such-and-such is true does not derive from valuing truth for its own sake. In short, what *is* true does not matter – paradoxically, for practical purposes it has no inherent use.

The reverse is the case with respect to arguing the truth of a matter for the sake of the truth. On the face of it such an activity would appear to have no point and thus seem 'useless'. It is in this sense that arguments are dismissed as 'merely academic' or 'purely theoretical' in contexts where workable solutions are sought to practical problems. Now, if by 'useful' we mean 'useful in practice', such a dismissive attitude towards 'theoreti-cal' arguing is justified. When confronted by a situation demanding effec-tive action, stubbornly arguing over the truth of this or that for its own sake is rightly condemned as irrelevant – indeed, 'useless'. This merely confirms, from another direction, that for practical purposes what *is* true does not matter; or to put it precisely, that what is true *is* true does not matter. All that counts is that the listener accepts what is argued and acts accordingly. So long, then, as we mean 'useful in practice', the notion that truth for its *own* sake is 'useless' holds.

However, we can broaden the meaning of 'useful' in the manner utili-tarians conceived of it, whereby anything conducive to happiness is con-strued as useful, and anything doing the opposite is construed as *not* useful. In other words, something may be 'useful' even though it does not contribute towards the execution of this or that project. To thus release the notion of 'usefulness' from the sole realm of practical conduct gives it a more generous compass, and avoids the tautology otherwise threatened in the claim that 'truth is useful for practical purposes, but not for its own sake'. Thus, following the observation that *un*truth offends, it is then a species of intellectual *pain*. Counterproductive of happiness, it is thus distinctly *not* 'useful'. On the other hand, working towards a truth through proper observation and correct reasoning has rightly been viewed as a species of intellectual pleasure, and can therefore be described as 'useful' in our broader sense of the term. Further, to *share* that process of enlighten-ment (as when we argue the truth of a matter to others, for the sake of it), is to offer that same pleasure to others – an inherently social act which is thereby an additional source of 'usefulness' insofar as *any* species of genuine (that is, non-self-seeking), sociality is valued as contributive to human happiness.

It is for these reasons that to pursue the truth for the sake of it, and through argument to share this enlightening activity with others, are neither of them 'useless' or pointless activities. Neither, however, are they *practical* activities.

Within argument for argument's sake, then, we have already located *mediate* actions as those things said which, in contributing to the coherence, consistency, and overall adequacy of final points the thinker wishes to demonstrate, *constitute* the actual activity of arguing. Now, if mediate actions constitutive of *practical* arguing are, as I qualified it, 'to an extent' explicable simply by identifying them as such, this qualification is entirely removed in the case of *theoretical* argument. Where we can identify mediate actions constitutive of arguing something for the sake of the truth, we can *explain* why the thinker is saying such-and-such simply by stating he is doing so 'because' he is arguing this or that (final) point. If it is objected that this does not explain why he *says* what he says in the course of his arguing, nor why he does not argue the point in some different way, we can only reply that these are questions which cannot be answered through the narrative form – nor, as suggested in analogous contexts, in any other way. Rather, we have to rest content with saying this happens to be the way the thinker argues this particular point. Different individuals do things in different ways. The point is to sort out *what* it is that they are doing at any one time. For example, this person is playing tennis, and appears to be doing so for the sake of it. Given this latter, it is not possible to explain why he plays in the particular manner he displays – 'the action is the man', as tennis player. Just so with the activity of arguing. This person is engaged in the activity of arguing a point, and appears to be doing so solely for the sake of it (the *rationale* being to demonstrate the truth about a matter, just as the rationale of playing tennis is, as in all sport, to win). Given this, it is not possible to explain why he argues in this or that manner. The (intellectual) action is the man, as arguer.

One further point remains to be addressed within this analysis of 'mediate' actions as they relate to 'theoretical' argument. The issue arises from the controversial topic of the relation between 'theory and practice', and although much of the above has contained clear implications about this, until resolved it leaves all that we have said regarding 'arguing for the sake of it' hanging in the air.

Simply put, the issue is whether what I have called 'theoretical' thinking and arguing are *possible* undertakings in the first place. Some for simple reasons – for instance, 'all human conduct is interest-inspired' – and others for complex reasons – for instance, 'thinking is determined by ideologically weighted language' – claim that 'theoretical' thinking, or the urge disinterestedly to understand something for the sake of understanding it, is impossible. A consequential claim is that objectivity or impartiality is a myth. Each of us cannot but 'have an interest' in how we understand aspects of our world because each of us, for example, cannot but have a gender, a country, a class status, a place in a family, and a unique life experience; any one or more of these features 'matters' to us, such that certain understandings of our world will be more 'convenient' to us than others; thus our thinking is always subjective, partial, and even prejudiced, rather than being capable of objectivity and impartiality.

To refute this claim (not only for the sake of what is true, but also to guard the coherence of what I have said regarding 'mediate' actions in relation to 'theoretical' argument), I revert to what many otherwise contrary thinkers have straightforwardly urged; namely, that some things are done in order to achieve a practical objective whilst others are done for the sake of doing them – further, that actions which appear the same may nonetheless be differentiated along these lines. Thus, for example, one may have a cup of tea in order to wake oneself up, *or* 'for the sake of it' (that is, as a way of enjoying oneself). One may play football in order to earn money, or for its own sake. One may engage in sexual intercourse in order to produce offspring, or for the sake of it. One may analyse a country's politics in order to advise on how to win an election, or for the sake of analysing them. One may seek to understand, explain, or account for something in order to assist in the execution of some project, or for the sake of understanding, explaining, or accounting for it. In short, to do something for the sake of doing it, as distinct from doing something as a means to an end, is not only a possible but a general phenomenon. All we need to reiterate is that thinking, explaining, arguing, and understanding are no exceptions to this straightforward observation. If they were, then what is exceptional about them? And if their exception cannot be explained it follows that those who play football, have a cup of tea, or 'make love' are deluded when they believe themselves to be doing these things simply because they enjoy doing them, which is absurd.

So far in this chapter, all that we have argued has concerned the thinking of discrete individuals as evidenced in and by what they 'say' in this or that piece of writing. In other words, akin to our earlier analysis of the extraction of genuine continuities in individuals' (non-intellectual) actions, thereby uncovering real 'happenings' and 'occurrences', we have restricted our analysis so far to intellectual 'happenings' and 'occurrences' constituted by the activity of discrete individual thinkers in single pieces of writing. We have said that in reconstructing these intellectual 'happenings' we are in fact recovering the thinking this or that individual engaged in and for which his writing provides evidence in two different senses. The discriminatory processes I have suggested, whereby we infer something thought from what is 'said' and/or infer the thought in actually '*saying*' what is said, enable us to answer such (typically disinterested – that is, 'historical') questions as 'what is on the author's mind here?', 'who is he arguing against?', 'why does he include these points?', 'why is this chapter so brief?', and 'what does he hope to achieve by writing this book?' Regarding the last three questions, where I have proposed a heuristic centred on inferring the thinking evidenced by the actual *stating* of this or that (via the notions of final, practical, and mediate intellectual actions), I do not mean the historian of thought should examine every clause in a piece of writing, just as he will not need to examine every term employed in that *first* sense of viewing what is 'said' as evidence of what is on the thinker's mind. Rather, in understanding in the simple sense what a writer means from one clause to the next, I suggest the historian of thought will also 'instinctively' be following what the writer is *doing* from one moment to the next in something like the terms I have set out. Only where he finds passages problematic from this point of view will he feel the need to scrutinise them for clues, and here he may need to make more explicit to himself the interpretive techniques which, as an historian of thought, he implicitly applies in his normal course of reading something.

As such, I have not presented the above proposals (on how to interpret the actual *saying* of things) prescriptively, as somehow intended to alter the practice of historians of thought. Rather, as in theorising the discipline of history in general, I only hope to have made that practice more explicit and, through displaying its integrity, shown in what sense it is worthwhile. Better explanations, and differently articulated heuristics, may be possible, but only so long as they explicate the same activity – namely, that of the practising historian of thought, which is to uncover 'what happened' and 'why', thereby explicating *actual* 'occurrences' and 'events' in that history (of which the discrete writings of individuals are but a part, as will shortly emerge). He achieves this by giving an account *of* an individual's thinking, a procedure which is itself *explanatory* of that thinking in just the way we have argued *any* narrative account bears formidable explanatory potential in virtue of its logic or form.

It is true the course of our analysis has revealed limits to what can be explained – for instance, we cannot explain *why* a thinker responds as he does to this or that argument; nor, in theoretical argument, why he argues a point in the way he does – but rather than complain of this and thus go in search of some illusory alternative 'history' of thought centred on, for example, philosophical interest in what is *said*, or on its ideological interpretation (both of which risk intricate discussion and analysis of thoughts the writer never conceived, and of intentions he never had in saying what he said – in short, a 'history' of much that never happened!), it is more constructive to recognise that, in leading *up to* the limits of 'explaining thinking', the historian of thought's approach is revealing *of* those limits. In other words, he uncovers that ineradicable basis of all other or further 'history of thought', namely, the ultimate uniqueness of individual intellectual conduct – as inherently unpredictable and untidily 'inexplicable' a phenomenon as other species of human conduct, and for which the narrative form is peculiarly appropriate.

'INTELLECTUAL DEVELOPMENTS'

Having explored what is involved in uncovering the thinking evidenced in the discrete writings of individuals – that unsurpassable reality from which whatever subsequent 'historical identities' are uncovered must be derived – let us now progress to an examination of precisely those further aspects of the historian of thought's work of which I have already given notice. Here, I revert to Chapter Four's concluding observation that, as a discipline, the history of thought is no different in principle from the history of anything else. All history derives from individuals' actions ('thinking' being an intellectual action), but is not exhausted by them in their discreteness. Rather, we theorised what we variously called 'narrative identities' or 'story-objects' in Chapter Two, meaning thereby the linking of otherwise discrete occurrences into *sequences*. I called these sequences of occurrences *events*, and noted that some are strongly paradigmed, thereby attracting individuation through such 'event-nouns' as weddings, boxing matches, and journeys, whilst others are left as unique. These latter are constituted by the 'stories' they form, and Chapter Three examined the principal problems the practising historian encounters in dealing with them – for instance, where they begin and end, and what to include in their telling.

In theorising the nature of 'events', then, we were no longer dealing solely with the actions and activities of this or that individual, but with contexts where genuine narrative identities emerge from the interplay between numbers of individuals. As we put it, the historian is not merely the biographer of individuals' conduct; he deals with more expansive phenomena, namely, events or 'story-objects' such as wars, revolutions, and the rise and fall of empires. Chapter Four concluded with the assertion that the discipline of history (construed in both form and content in terms of the logic of narrative), is *literally* applicable to the history of thought – and vice versa, that the history of thought only forms a coherent discipline if it conforms exactly to those principles of 'history in general' set out in Chapter Four. Thus, in speculating upon the possibility of 'the history of thought' we were led to ask: what, in that history, constitute those (trans-individual) narrative identities or 'story-objects' which not only vindicate, but ultimately necessitate, the full-blooded (narrative) discipline of history for the recognition or explication of phenomena as 'real' in the intellectual world, as are, for instance, cities and political crises in the respective worlds of objects and (non-intellectual) events?

The first case where the historian of thought transcends the study of a particular piece of writing pertains where he remains with the same thinker, but looks at others of his writings to see if they are connected. By 'connected', of course, I refer to that seminal distinction between meaningful narrative and mere chronicle which informs history proper. Here, then, the concepts of change, continuity, and difference are crucial. Where one piece of an author's writing differs from another we must be wary of assuming the later work constitutes some change (that is, development), in his thinking. He may simply be thinking about something else, in which case it would be as futile to claim he is developing his thinking as to claim of someone who yesterday played chess and today cleans his car that he is thereby 'developing his activity'. Since there is no such thing as 'activity in general' nor 'thinking in general', they cannot be developed. Rather, thinking must always be thinking about this or that, and it is only where a piece of writing evidences that an author is thinking about the same matters as in his earlier work that the potential arises of constructing a genuine changing identity – that is, where we can properly refer to his thinking this *then* that. I say 'the potential' because we should be alert to the possibility that although a later work deals with similar matters, the author may have forgotten his earlier piece or, despite *our* seeing the topics as similar, may not do so himself. In short, where reconstructing this kind of 'narrative identity', 'story-object', or 'event' which abounds in the intellectual world – namely, someone's 'intellectual development' – we must guard against searching for an unending continuity. As urged frequently up to now, the historian is in search of real continuities, not 'continuity in general'.

This said, let us examine some instances of this species of event – namely, someone's 'intellectual development'. By this we do not necessarily mean to refer to complete 'changes of mind', even though, as we shall see, these can be involved. Rather, an intellectual development may consist of a refining of certain ideas, an elaboration upon others, or additional thinking devoted to answering objections. But at the least, something must have changed in the writer's thinking since otherwise there is no genuine 'changing identity' to reconstruct, bringing us back to the truism that without change there is no history. An instance of this kind of intellectual development is afforded by some of Spinoza's purely 'philosophical' writings, where his *Ethics* can be studied as a substantial development of the thinking he put into his earlier *Short Treatise on God, Man, and his Well-being*. None of the ideas in the earlier work are contradicted in the later; there are no dramatic changes of mind. What *is* to be found is that the later work evidences that Spinoza neither abandoned nor forgot his earlier ideas on God, man, and the human good, but rather that he greatly elaborated upon them. Additionally, he integrated his thinking on epistemology as set out in *On the Improvement of the Understanding*, and added new ideas regarding what we now call psychology and the philosophy of mind. As such, we can see the *Ethics* as the creative synthesis of a long-continuing process of thinking about certain matters – in other words, as evidence of an 'intellectual development'.

Of course, such phenomena are not rare in the world of thought. For example, in the history of political thought we frequently encounter the 'early' writings of 'matured' thinkers (such as Hobbes, Rousseau, Hegel, and Marx), and it is not surprising the attention of historians of thought is drawn to them, for their study holds out the promise of uncovering genuine historical identities or 'narrative phenomena' of which we would otherwise be ignorant. For instance, so much did Marx write, and so meticulously are his early writings now documented, it is not surprising a number of excellent accounts of his 'intellectual development' are extant. What, however, is perhaps not always clearly perceived is that such works, in explaining how someone's thinking evolved, not only 'tell a story' but, in my more technical terms, explicate the nature of an 'event'. Viewed in this light, those issues raised in Chapter Three regarding beginnings and endings, selection, relevance, and significance should play a part in such accounts. For example, rather than include all an individual's writings in an account of his intellectual development, we should only include those relevant to the 'story-object' we are explicating. This implies a need to locate a beginning, a content focused on a changing identity, and an ending – and without a clear idea of what the 'changing identity' in question is, one is likely to lose one's bearings. For instance, in an account of Spinoza's intellectual development, should one incorporate his *Treatise on the Reckoning of Chance*? And what of his correspondence? Or in the case of Marx, is it valid to give an account of his intellectual development which ends with *The German Ideology*? Should we include, even begin, an account of Hobbes' intellectual development towards *Leviathan* with a survey of his *Thomas White's De Mundo*? Should we continue our account into Hobbes' post-*Leviathan* writings?

The answers to these questions revert us to the notion that the historian of thought must focus on someone's thinking about this or that, rather than include all his writings in the futile search for someone's 'thought as a whole'. The latter is an abstraction, not a genuine narrative identity, and is thus not an object of the historian of thought's study. In the example of Spinoza, then, we need a clear view of what it was he was thinking about which culminates in the *Ethics* before we can ascertain whether his work on chance is relevant. Just so, does the development of what Spinoza was thinking about in the *Ethics* and some earlier writings in fact culminate there, or should we include his subsequent (unfinished) *Tractatus Politicus* on the grounds that it continues this development? In the case of Marx, what is the thinking he develops in such a manner as to persuade many historians of thought they can extract a coherent story which eventuates in the 'mature' Marx? Most locate it as that complex

227

problematic involving philosophic idealism and materialism, social deprivation, and the relation between theory and practice – which Marx appeared to resolve to his own satisfaction by the summer of 1846, after which his thinking was directed to other matters (possibly constitutive of a separate intellectual development or 'story-object'). Whether this is the correct parametering of a discrete historical identity may be open to dispute, particularly regarding its alleged ending in 1846. It is not to our purpose here to enter the controversy, but rather to highlight the nature of those 'events' I have called 'intellectual developments' by asserting that the solution to it must focus, not on Marx's thinking, but on his thinking *about this or that*.

This locating of 'what it is that a thinker was thinking about' as the key to identifying intellectual developments is often a difficult enterprise where writings are complex and multi-thematic. In the example of Hobbes, moreover, it is rendered impossible if one relies on those unfortunate editions of *Leviathan* which variously abridge or even omit Chapters Three and Four on the (mistaken) grounds that they add 'little or nothing to Hobbes's philosophy of man and government'.[28] The publication of *Thomas White's De Mundo* in 1976 should increasingly reveal the irresponsibility of such truncations of Hobbes' masterpiece.[29] No historian of thought can function properly with abridged writings, for he is being presented with evidence which has been tampered with.[30]

INCONSISTENCIES AND MISTAKES

In this process of linking a thinker's different works by extracting genuine (changing) continuities, or strands of 'intellectual development', we sometimes encounter inconsistencies in someone's thinking, or even a change of mind. The historian of thought's attention is gripped on either occasion since both are examples of the unusual, itself a somewhat surprising encounter in any history. Although I have earlier given good reasons why fact is stranger than fiction – elementary narrative structure's signposts are those happenings which are *not* 'conventionally contiguous' – this does not mean history is replete with surprises. Indeed, the rationale of the narrative reconstruction of occurrences and events is precisely to render them intelligible and therefore, if not unexpected, at least not constantly surprising. For instance, if after Hitler's invasion of Poland Britain had declared war on the USA, this would have been surprising, by which we mean it would appear inexplicable; and if there is one motive driving the historian, it is to *explain* 'what happened'. In short, the apparently inexplicable is the ultimate challenge, such that the historian as much deplores surprise occurrences as he welcomes them (a love/hate attitude typical of any intellectual).[31] Coincidences are a particularly unsettling species of 'surprise', and are consequently rarely suggested in historical writings.[32]

Accidents and shocks such as assassinations cannot, however, be wished away, and there is a sense in which their rude intrusion into narrative sequences which were intelligible up to their occurrence is precisely what makes them 'surprising', for where they are inconsequential such misfortunes may cause regret, but not astonishment.

In the history of thought, then, inconsistencies and outright changes of mind are of particular interest. The former can, of course, suggest the latter (as in, 'does the apparent contradiction between Machiavelli's republicanism in the *Discourses* and his enthusiasm for princely virtue in *The Prince* mean he changed this aspect of his political thinking?'), but not necessarily so. For example, many have suggested a contradiction between the innate moral laws in Locke's second *Treatise of Civil Government* and his analogy of the mind as a blank sheet of paper awaiting experience's inscriptions in his *Essay Concerning Human Understanding*, but do not construe this as evidence that Locke changed his mind on the subject of the origin of ideas. In short, a change of mind always involves a contradiction between one work and another, but not necessarily vice versa. Let us first address that kind of inconsistency which does not evidence a change of mind.

We should first note that a thinker can of course contradict himself within the same work; but here we are simply likely to say he has made a mistake. In itself this may be important (that is, 'relevant'), if it has implications for subsequent points a writer makes, and thus invites an explanation of why he made the error. However, we should not regard such contradictions as moments of a thinker's intellectual development since a carefully constructed piece of writing is not a place where someone *develops* his thinking, but one where he *states* his present thinking. That it may be confused, contradictory, or in some other way mistaken, tells us something about his present thinking, but not about how or whether it has developed from thinking set out, and evidenced in, his previous writings. Exceptions to this are where, in the course of writing something, a thinker is in fact 'thinking out loud', exploring the implications of his ideas rather than crafting an exposition of his present thinking. However, such writings – for instance, Marx's *Economic and Philosophical Manuscripts of 1844* – are precisely not 'books' or 'essays' in the sense of constituting unified monoscripts; and where a writer nevertheless presents them as such, the deficiencies in both their structure and content will be manifest. (We can be sure that, had Marx intended to publish the *1844 Manuscripts* as a monoscript, they would exhibit differences from their extant form and content.)

A particularly interesting example of the difference between an intellectual development (necessarily spanning more than one of an author's writings) and inconsistencies within a single work, returns us to Rousseau's *Discourse on the Origins of Inequality*, for when we include a later addition, it exemplifies both phenomena. Firstly, in the original essay which included a number of 'Notes',[33] one of the principal topics Rousseau introduces is that of private property, particularly in land: 'The first man who, having enclosed a piece of ground, bethought himself of saying "This is mine", and found people simple enough to believe him, was the real founder of civil society'.[34] Yet in the remainder of the *Discourse* he does not use this denunciation as part of an argument for some kind of communal exploitation of resources. So obvious would this conclusion be that its omission appears as an interesting example of an inconsistency – that is, as in other contexts of human conduct, the *failure* to do this or that can on occasions be seen as contradictory. However, we should note that not only does Rousseau not draw this obvious consequence; *nothing* materially further regarding property 'follows' from his point. Instead, then, of being what I have called a 'mediate' point constitutive of some larger argument, it appears he made this point regarding the link between private property, inequality, and civil society, as a 'final' point. And we can view it as such by identifying it as one of the principal *answers* he gave to the question posed by the Dijon Academy (for one of the clearest examples of a final point is where, in the interests of truth as one sees it, one gives an answer to a question).

So far, then, we are either faced by an interesting example of an inconsistency in Rousseau's thinking in the *Discourse*, or by an alternative centred on the notion that he was sticking to his Dijon brief – namely, to explain the origins of inequality, say whether it is vindicated by Natural Law, and to do no more, such as propose solutions.

However, we now encounter an instance of what I have called an 'intellectual development', and it is one of intimate relevance to the above query. Rousseau subsequently appended a paragraph to the Note referred to above, in which he *adds* to the thinking expressed in (and possibly also that evidenced by) the *Discourse*.[35] The gist of the paragraph is that the author is aware some kind of communism could be construed as following from his argument regarding property in the *Discourse*, and he denies he intends any such inference. Instead, he equates absence of private property with that idyllic state of 'pre-civilised' natural man outlined in the first chapter of the *Discourse*, and appears to argue it is impossible to return to that primitive state; that one should therefore reconcile oneself to 'civilis-ation', adopting an attitude that is as grateful for virtue, where it can be found, as it remains contemptuous of vices. (Although it is misleading of the Everyman edition to close the *Discourse* with this paragraph – Rousseau had it inserted quite near the beginning of Part One! – to nevertheless end a version of it on this note of resigned pessimism may be viewed as an appropriate 'gloss'.)

I say this is a development of Rousseau's thinking because, after having conceived those thoughts on private property expressed in the *Discourse*,

230

not only did he think again about the topic, but he thought some *more* about it – that is, he *added* to what he said earlier. Although on principle (as I have urged) we cannot explain why his thinking on property developed in this rather than some other way, we can explain what *prompted* him to develop his thinking, and what prompted him to *communicate* this development. Not only was he anticipating attack as a 'back to Nature' oddity, he had already encountered such satire in response to his earlier *Discourse on the Arts and Sciences*. He *communicated* his additional thinking in order to disabuse his critics; that is, in his own interest, to make them think differently of him – a practical action.

This episodic relation between the *Discourse* and the later paragraph is interesting, then, not only as a concrete example of an 'intellectual development', but also because it might help determine whether the 'failure' to draw some kind of communistic conclusion in the former writing was an inconsistency or not – in short, help sort out 'what actually happened' in an account of aspects of Rousseau's thinking in the *Discourse*.

CHANGES OF MIND

The most dramatic instances of 'intellectual developments' are those where a thinker actually changes his mind about notions he proposed earlier, as evidenced by his saying things we can be sure he knows contradict what he said earlier. A well-known example is Marx's distinct change of mind, between 1844 and 1846, about the nature of human beings. In the *1844 Manuscripts* he defines them as essentially and uniquely self-conscious, and elaborates upon their consequent propensity for self-fulfilment and its converse, 'alienation'. In *The German Ideology* (1846), however, 'man' as essentially self-conscious is replaced by 'men' as essentially producers. That Marx was aware of his change of mind is shown by his scathing reference to 'consciousness' and 'alienation' a few passages further on. (We should note that in turning his scorn upon his earlier notions he did not understand himself to be publicly castigating himself, for he had not published the *1844 Manuscripts*, and did not intend to. As far as his readers were supposed to know – for he *did* originally intend to publish *The German Ideology* – he was satirising a premise of German idealist philosophy.)

Another well-known instance of a change of mind returns us to Rousseau's *Discourse on the Origins of Inequality*, with its familiar theme of the 'noble savage'. Some five years later this being whose humanness is authenticated only through his independent self-reliance is referred to in *The Social Contract* as 'a stupid and unimaginative animal' rather than 'an intelligent being and a man'.[36] What now authenticates an individual's humanness is no longer self-reliance but an (idealised) citizenship where 'each citizen is nothing and can do nothing without the rest', where 'his own resources' are taken away and replaced by 'new ones alien to him, and incapable of being made use of without the help of other men'.[37] That Rousseau was aware of this change of mind is evident enough from the very emphasis he puts on the distinction between 'natural' and 'citizenised' man in the above passages – unless we are to believe, against overwhelming evidence, that he had somehow forgotten his earlier *Discourse*!

Now if, as we have claimed, inconsistencies between a thinker's writings arouse the twin instincts of curiosity and a desire for 'tidiness' in the historian of thought, these are at their most intense when he is confronted by a distinct change of mind. It is not surprising, then, that many have explored such examples with a view to 'explaining' them; and in that fashion I have urged as characteristic of any 'historical explanation', the best do so by giving an account *of* the change of mind. In other words, they do not speculate upon some mysterious 'cause' suddenly provoking it, but instead carefully reconstruct the sequence of thinking that 'eventuates' in those ideas which are now so disconsonant from their origins as to warrant the claim that the thinker actually 'changed his mind'. Regarding the two cases cited above, historians of thought have the advantage of numerous of the thinkers' writings interspersed between the points of final disconsonance, plus detailed biographies and extensive information about contemporary events and circumstances – and what we find in both cases is not so much a sudden conversion to an alternative point of view as a development of thinking which 'happens' to eventuate in one which is not only different from, but contradictory of, the earlier (and in Rousseau's case, actually *opposite* to it). If such developments seem peculiar, one can only observe that in any 'developing' situation matters often conclude differently, if not contrarily, to how they began (and, I will add, in neither of the above cases would it be convincing to argue, as with Hegelian dialectics, that the earlier thinking precisely *generated* the later contrary thinking, as will be clear from below).

Thus: in our example of a 'change of mind' by Rousseau, we have already encountered a passage demonstrative of his beginning to develop the *Discourse on the Origins of Inequality*'s viewpoint on 'natural man' as early as spring 1755, and have inferred he added the relevant paragraph in response to contemporary and anticipated satire. In it he is already indicating that some kind of return to primeval nature does *not* necessarily follow from his admiration of 'natural man'. Yet the satire continued, as well as praise from other quarters, on the theme that Rousseau was recommending, or at least implying, some utopian 'return to nature'. It is conceivable that at some stage in the *Discourse* he was, but he always denied the inference. Whether, as could be his wont, he was disingenuous about this, or whether he intuited that there remained room in the way he thought about things to properly accommodate 'civilised' man once he put his mind to the political writing he had toyed with producing, we cannot be sure. What does seem clear is that by the time he came to construct *The Social Contract* there was sufficient scope in the complex of his thinking about individuals' moral predicament to permit him an idealised view of 'citizenised' man which to his mind solved the dilemma he left us with in the paragraph referred to. (Vaughan draws attention to a further development of this dialectic between 'natural' and 'social' man in Rousseau's subsequent *Émile*.)[38] We might even suppose Rousseau took particular pleasure in writing those passages I have quoted from *The Social Contract*, for of the two possibilities they raise – either that he was mistaken in his famous *Discourse* or that his critics had shamefully and persistently misrepresented him – the latter is obviously the message, the more so since his language is so unequivocal. In short, he gives the lie to his critics by contemptuously penning the very words which they could only regard either as his deliberate and reckless admission of inconsistency, or as incontrovertible proof of their having wronged him. (We should recall that Rousseau was as versed in the wiles and nuances of allusion as any of the *philosophes* he by then regarded as his enemies.)

Similar lessons can be learnt from our example of that 'change of mind' we referred to in Marx's thinking. In the *1844 Manuscripts*, 'conscious life activity distinguishes man immediately from animal life activity',[39] whereas some two years later, in *The German Ideology*, 'men can be distinguished from animals by consciousness, religion, or anything else you like. They themselves begin to distinguish themselves from animals as soon as they begin to *produce* their means of subsistence.[40] There can be no doubt his thinking regarding 'the definition' of the essentially human has changed from passages in the *1844 Manuscripts*, where his exposition of self-consciousness as the essence of being human is almost impassioned. However, this is merely symptomatic of a more general shift constituted by the intensive development of Marx's thinking between 1844 and 1846, sometimes (controversially) referred to as the shift from the 'young' to the 'mature' Marx, and subjected to much examination, perhaps nowhere more damagingly than in Tucker's *Philosophy and Myth in Karl Marx*.[41]

What does seem clear is that far from Marx suddenly changing his mind (about self-consciousness) in 1846, he was already responding to aspects of Feuerbach's ideas, in the very same section of the *1844 Manuscripts* where he expounds upon self-consciousness, in such a manner as to leave room for a subsequent development of his thinking towards the eventually contrary point reached in *The German Ideology*. The relevant proposition is 'every relationship in which man stands to himself is realised and expressed only in the relationship in which a man stands to other men'.[42] He then argues that in his alienated productive activity 'man' engenders the worker-capitalist relationship; that 'private property is thus the product, the result, the necessary consequence, of alienated labour', rather than its cause.[43] He then poses a key question: 'How . . . does man [*der Mensch*] come to alienate . . . his labour?' and adumbrates the answer (which he intends to elaborate upon, but does not – the manuscript breaks off a few passages later) in the following way:

> We have already gone a long way to the solution . . . by transform-
> ing the question of the origin of private property into the question
> of the relation of alienated labour to the course of humanity's devel-
> opment. For when one speaks of private property, one thinks of
> dealing with something external to man. When one speaks of labour,
> one is directly dealing with man [*der Mensch*] himself. This new
> formulation of the question already contains its solution.[44]

The fact is, Marx had argued himself into a bind, for it is difficult to talk convincingly about 'man', 'humanity', 'the essence of being human', and at the same time of actual men being *essentially* (ontologically?) divided into opposed groups.

The symptoms of this problematic are manifest in some passages preced-ing those just quoted, where Marx uses the term 'man' and the pronoun 'he', intimating 'mankind in general', but also refers to *other* 'men' and 'strangers', apparently forgetting he has already universalised 'man', thereby leaving no room for 'other men' or 'strangers' also to belong to 'mankind'. Thus:

> through estranged labour man [*der Mensch*] . . . creates the relation-
> ship in which other men [*andere Menschen*] stand to his production
> and to his product, and the relationship in which he stands to these
> other men. Just as he creates his own production as the loss of his
> reality . . . so he creates the domination of the person who does not
> produce over production. . . . Just as he estranges his own activity
> from himself, so he confers upon the stranger an activity which is
> not his own.[45]

Here, Marx confuses the particular and the universal. 'Mankind', rather than actual men, appears as an agent, and then becomes confused with actual men. It is as if one argued that 'mankind' generated women as part of 'itself'. Either there are actual men and women who together comprise 'mankind', or there is mankind comprising only men, and however women are 'engendered', they are nothing to do with 'mankind'. In short, there may be capitalists and workers who together comprise 'mankind', but it is as difficult to see how 'mankind' can generate workers as it is to see how workers, solely comprising mankind, can generate capitalists as, presumably, part of 'mankind'.

It is thus not surprising that when Marx's thinking generates the ques-tion, 'how . . . does man come to alienate . . . his labour?', he apparently abandoned the attempt to answer it further than the adumbration already quoted, for the problem is intractable whilst he continues to try to combine actual (divided) men with the abstract universal, 'man', in the same sequence of thinking. He came to recognise this error by the writing of *The German Ideology*, where he levels precisely this accusation against Feuerbach; 'As far as Feuerbach is a materialist he does not deal with history, and as far as he considers history he is not a materialist'.[46]

Tucker nicely sets out this dilemma in Marx's thinking, but then makes a case as extraordinary as it is mischievous. He tells us,

> Marx was at least obscurely aware of the shakiness of his position, for he made a note in the manuscript saying: 'We must think over the previously made statement that the relation of man to himself first becomes *objective* and *real* through his relation to another man'. Evidently, he never did so.[47]

Dramatically, Tucker closes the chapter with this 'proof' of his thesis that Marx irresponsibly lapsed into 'mythology' when he unthinkingly transferred individual alienation, a valid psychological phenomenon, into a social phenomenon, namely, class-division.

Now although it may be true that Marx was 'aware of the shakiness of his position', Tucker's reference to the so-called note is thoroughly misleading. Firstly, he gives the impression that Marx, 'obscurely aware' of his difficulties, added a 'note' indicating self-doubt. In fact, the passage he quotes does not appear towards the abortive breaking-off of the manuscript. Secondly, it is not a 'note'. It simply continues a line of thinking, advancing an uninterrupted argument. Thirdly, and perhaps most tellingly, only Tucker translates Marx as saying, 'We must think over . . .'. Subsequent authoritative versions of '*Man bedenke noch...*' translate him as saying 'We must bear in mind . . .',[48] or, as Marx saying to his *reader*, in the course of arguing his point, 'Consider further . . .'.[49] Fourthly, that this is the sense of what Marx is saying is clear from the ensuing sentence which begins 'Thus', or 'Therefore', indicative of the uninterrupted flow of discourse. In short, Tucker has seriously misrepresented the text.

Finally, in misrepresenting Marx as 'adding a note' to himself to 'think over' the point in question, Tucker then has the temerity to say, 'Evidently, he never did so'. In fact, it is clear that Marx precisely *did* 'think over' the question of man's nature and the role of self-consciousness. It played a crucial role in the ensuing development of his thinking towards that point (in *The German Ideology*) where we can justly claim he has 'changed his mind' on the matter – morever, that this was an integral part of that more general shift from the 'early' to the 'mature' Marx. (In his subsequent *Marx-Engels Reader* Tucker reproduces the widely used Milligan translation which appears in the *Collected Works* version I have quoted, so it would appear he was prepared to abandon, if not his overall thesis, at least the damaging insinuation incorporated in his textual gloss.)[50]

The subsequent development of Marx's thinking is well-known, and it is only relevant here to indicate his developing position on 'human nature'. By March of the year following his writing the *1844 Manuscripts* we find Marx criticising Feuerbach's notion of 'the essentially human'; 'the essence of man is no abstraction inherent in each single individual. In its reality it is the ensemble of the social relations'. Rather than conceive of actual human beings characterised by the social relations historically pertaining, Feuerbach 'abstract[s] from the historical process', and the human essence 'therefore can be regarded only as "species", as an inner, mute, general character'.[51] This is close to the notion that it is pointless to attempt a definition of 'the essence of mankind'. Shortly after these *Theses* Marx was joined by Engels, who had recently completed his *The Condition of the Working-class in England* (an obvious encouragement for Marx's thinking to continue in the 'historical-materialist' direction), and from late autumn into the following year they wrote *The German Ideology*. In his own opening section Marx further developed his thinking on 'the essence of man' to the point where he now talks only of 'men', being persistently dismissive of the term 'Man'. Feuerbach, he complains, 'never arrives at the actually existing, active men, but stops at the abstraction "man" '. He 'relapse[s] into idealism'.[52] In contrast to what Marx had argued in the *1844 Manuscripts*, now 'Men can be distinguished from animals by consciousness, religion, or anything else you like. They themselves begin to distinguish themselves from animals as soon as they begin to *produce* their means of subsistence'.[53] Irrespective of any philosophical notion of 'Man' and his 'self-consciousness', actual men need to satisfy their material needs, reproduce their kind, and engage in social cooperation better to achieve these ends. Only after these considerations 'do we find that man also possesses "consciousness". But even from the outset this is not "pure" consciousness', and Marx proceeds to argue that 'consciousness is . . . from the very beginning a social product', specific to the natural and social environment historically pertaining.[54]

That these two examples of a change of mind do not centre on some sudden (mysterious) conversion, but rather are explicable through our following the revising and amending process undertaken by Rousseau and Marx, is typical of thinkers studied in the history of thought. For example, of another famous 'change of mind', Eduard Bernstein's abandonment of Orthodox Marxism, Tudor's analysis culminates in; '[Bernstein's] conversion did not come from a book or from any other identifiable source, nor was it a sudden event occasioned by some striking experience. It was a gradual change which passed unnoticed by everyone (including Bernstein himself), until November 1896'.[55] I suggest two related reasons for this. Firstly, akin to other historians' interest in 'important' events, historians of thought focus on 'important' thinkers in their respective areas – and at least one of their features is that they are competent at thinking. Of someone whose thinking displays many and sudden changes of mind we are justified in saying he is confused, and correspondingly unworthy of being taken seriously. Secondly, then, even where an historian of thought's attention is drawn to lesser known thinkers, if he encounters one who displays the above source of confusion he will probably have helped account for his obscurity, and also find the project of 'following' that writer's thinking and its development not only difficult – competent thinkers can, after all, be difficult to follow – but frustrating to the point of being futile. In short, he would be trying to reconstruct a story from radically discontinuous occurrences and events.

Good thinkers, then, neither suddenly nor frequently change their minds (and where, as occasionally, they nevertheless do, they are likely to be as embarrassed as any political or religious apostate usually is, and express this by voicing the typical convert's extremism regarding his previous position: for example, in *The German Ideology* Marx's and Engels' invective against those ideas constitutive of their own earlier 'idealism' is scathing.) Rather, where thinkers develop their thoughts about this or that in successive writings, a point can be reached where their present viewpoint is contrary to, or even the reverse of, their earlier. In accounting for this 'change of mind', the historian of thought retraces the evolution of his subject's thinking. As already argued, at no stage will he be able to say *why* his subject thought this or that. Instead, he *is* able to infer what *prompted* him to think this or that *next*. In other words, he attempts to reconstruct an intelligible continuity, whereby we say he is accounting *for* this change of mind by giving an account *of* the sequence of (intellectual) occurrences culminating in the changed viewpoint. In short, his 'historical explanation' consists of a narrative explication of a real (narrative) phenomenon or 'event'; namely, a special case of what I have called an 'intellectual development'.

DISPUTES

The next category of 'event' in the history of thought further supersedes the study of one individual's single piece of writing, for amongst the variegated world of intellectual 'happenings' is a class of 'historical identities' or 'narrative continuities' constituted by the interplay between at least two thinkers. I refer here to what are commonly called intellectual disputes between individuals. Akin to their physical counterparts, they have their beginnings and endings, necessarily involve at least two contending individuals, can be more or less protracted, bitter, or pointless, can end indeterminately or with clear victory and defeat, and can peter out of their own accord or be stopped by the intervention of another party, or by some intrusive new circumstance. I draw these parallels with physical disputes not only to focus attention on the diverse possibilities which pertain in intellectual disputes but also to enliven their actuality. As real events they centre on actual individuals who intentionally contend with each other over distinct issues. In other words, we are not talking loosely of, for example, 'the' argument between idealism and materialism, Protestantism and Catholicism, or fascism and liberalism. As set out at the beginning of Chapter Three, this would be to people the intellectual world with disembodied agents busily contesting each other – a fantasy world of idealists' imaginings. (If it be objected that, in line with Chapter One's analysis of the 'reality' of things, 'materialism' *etc.* are as real as any other differentiated phenomena so long as the terms prove relevant and workable – as, for instance, those things denoted by the words 'skyscraper', 'teenager', and 'commuter' – I say firstly they are not terms either relevant or workable if denotive of *agency;* and secondly that the extent to, and sense in which, such terms *do* denote 'real' things will be explored further below.)

By a dispute, then, I mean an actual, deliberate exchange of conflicting views conducted by two individuals. The history of (religious, scientific, philosophical, political) thought is replete with such disputes – for example, the famous one between Luther and Erasmus over free-will, or that between Marx and Bakunin over a range of issues – and for our purposes of exploring their *disciplinary* implications for the historian of thought, it is important to guard against inventing disputes which never occurred. For instance, whether much of Locke's argumentation in his second *Treatise of Civil Government* was directed against Hobbes or not,[56] it is clear the two did not engage in disputation. Likewise, even where two thinkers are contemporaneously propounding contrary views, we need additional evidence before inferring they are disputing with each other. Where real disputes *are* found their explication can only be achieved through the narrative form, since their content is a genuine continuity constituted by change. In tracing such narrative identities, then, all the disciplinary implications of factual narrative apply, as also its corresponding achievements and 'limitations'. For example, we should supersede mere chronicle, and instead unravel a narrative identity with a beginning and an end. Also, we may need to exploit the heuristic of 'practical', 'mediate', and 'final' actions; for instance, is a contender out to destroy his opponent or persuade him to change his mind? And in either case, does he have some purpose or does he do it for the sake of it? Might he be disputing not so much in order to change his opponent's mind as to educate him via gentle correction, in the manner Spinoza corresponded with Tschirnhaus? Where a dispute is centred on a particular topic, as in Erasmus and Luther over free-will, is that topic merely symptomatic of a broader dispute (as, for example, salvation through faith alone or through works, thereby involving the dogmatics behind disputed practices in the Catholic Church)? Or again, where a dispute ranges over a number of

238

topics, are they separate issues or merely a means whereby a power-struggle is played out (as, for example, with Marx and Bakunin)?

A further feature of intellectual disputes important in 'explaining' them is whether the disputants deliberately published them. If not, as was the case with Spinoza's (increasingly exasperated) correspondence with Tschirnhaus, that somewhat special possibility of disputation for purely educative purposes applies (at least respecting one of the participants). Where, however, contenders do deliberately publish their disputes (as, for instance, did so many of the early Protestant reformers), the likelihood of their being practically inspired, and thus symptomatic of broader issues, is almost overwhelming. Clearly the intention is to address an audience as much as, if not more than, the opponent, and we can expect that this urge to reach others stems from the desire to *persuade* them to believe this or that because something of practical importance underlies the issue. Alternatively, a disputant may wish to intimidate, or impress, his audience, whereby respectively power or hubris are his practical objectives.

But not all deliberately published disputes *ipso facto* invite interpretation as practically inspired. There remains the theoretical possibility of parties 'sharing' their dispute with a public, not in order to persuade it one way or another for some practical purpose, but for the (social) sake of it. In practice, however, we may look in vain for such enlightened instances except in academic journals where, occasionally, this possibility is practised.

Finally, insofar as we are treating of *disputes*, and given exaggerated concerns over the issue of objectivity as it affects the historian, this is an appropriate place to reiterate that clear implication of his position as 'observer' – namely, that he does not take sides. Given the very nature of intellectual disputes, perhaps the temptation to comment on who is right (whereby one vicariously participates in them), is highlighted. It is clear, however, that not only are such comments irrelevant to the historian of thought's project; it is quite possible to do without them. A worse temptation, out of partiality towards one side, would be to distort one's account of a dispute so as to seduce one's audience into taking the side one approves of. Politicians and others with axes to grind do this all the while. But *as observers* we can, and do, precisely recognise this, and our ability to expose where it occurs validates the possibility of objectivity. It also invites us to employ that same ability upon our *own* accounts. Although I have earlier discounted the claims of those who imply this is impossible – that all thinking is in some sense value-laden or 'ideological' – this is perhaps the point at which to appeal that if the historian of thought can vet others' thinking for partiality, then what is special about his *own* thinking that makes it impossible for him to undertake the same process?

In fact, of course, practising historians and historians of thought are as aware of the temptation towards partiality as they are of how to deal with it. Here we can do no better than cite the closing passage from F. Wendel's Foreword to his study of the thought of one of the most disputatious and contentious thinkers of the sixteenth century, Jean Calvin:

> Need it be added that in this exposition I have tried to conform to as strictly historical a method as possible? My intention was to present Calvin's thought just as it emerges from the documents and the historical surroundings, and not according to any ideological preferences. Such an effort requires a certain effort of adaptation, perhaps even of sympathy, but it does not necessarily imply adherence without reservations. If it did, we should end by having to condemn all history of philosophical or religious ideas'.[57]

CONTROVERSIES

A further respect in which intellectual disputes are usefully analogous to physical ones is that when fisticuffs break out between two individuals, others sometimes join the fray. They may do so sooner rather than later, have diverse motivations, opt out again before the contest is over, or even change sides during it. Just so with intellectual disputes. Others may be drawn, or invited, into a dispute, whereby it expands into a more complex trans-individual event. In short, if physical fights between two can escalate into general brawls, so intellectual disputes can escalate into what are general debates or *controversies* in the world of thought. As with disputes, these more complex phenomena are narrative identities, thereby requiring the form of narrative for their apprehension as real rather than artificially constructed events. Because numerous individuals may be involved, the historian of thought's project in giving an account of a controversy increases in complexity. What prompted this individual to join in? How does that newcomer complicate the arguments of the opposition? Why is the controversy expanding into this area of debate? It is clear that since these are the kind of questions generated by the narrative form, then insofar as the historian of thought is able to answer them he will be engaged on an undertaking of considerable analytic stature, this giving the lie to those claims that narrative lacks not only explanatory but also analytic insight.

This becomes clearer if we extend our notion of trans-individual events in the world of *physical* conflict from general brawls into those ultimately complex (narrative) phenomena we call *wars*, particularly those involving numerous countries divided into (sometimes shifting) alliances. Analogous escalations occur within the world of intellectual controversies, and where this has taken place the two worlds share features sufficiently similar to be of heuristic aid to the historian of thought's imagination. Let us therefore expose these similarities, and cite some examples, in order to provide some familiar signposts to what, when theorised, are the potential intricacies of diverse 'trans-individual narrative identities' in the intellectual world.

Firstly, I have suggested a distinction between intellectual disputes and controversies on the grounds that 'following' the argumentative interplay between several participants introduces a dimensional complexity absent where there are merely two opponents. I have called the former 'disputes' and the latter 'controversies'. The semantics are not important – as with physical conflicts, 'fights', 'scuffles', 'brawls', 'battles', and 'wars' are just some examples denoting either different nuances or substantial distinctions, and it is not always clear which. Most, however, would mean by 'a war' something substantially different from 'a fight'. But whichever terms are used, both for physical and intellectual conflicts, they have been generated to denote real phenomena of such familiarity as to warrant their individuation from an otherwise teeming kaleidoscope of 'happenings'. 'Disputes' and 'controversies' are, then, as real and as different in the intellectual world as are fisticuffs and wars in the world of physical conflict.

Secondly, not only can we find a language expressive of the objective reality of, and difference between, definite classes of intellectual event – namely, disputes and controversies – but where the latter have been especially noticeable at the time, or for their subsequent significance, they have been awarded proper names. Analogously, although physical conflicts of one kind or another are a permanent feature of human affairs, only the most important are given their own name. Most *wars*, however, were by their nature important in their time, and some remain so because of their subsequent significance; they are thus named – for example, the First World War, the Vietnam War. Other so-called 'grubby little wars' remain anonymous, at least to the 'outside' world. Similar situations regarding the naming of disputes and controversies pertain in the world of intellectual conflicts. It is replete with disputes between two individuals – one can identify any number of them in today's plethora of academic journals alone, as well as in past periods of exceptional intellectual turmoil exemplified, for instance, in the incessant religio-political pamphleteering during the English Civil War, or in the countless theological tracts of Reformation Europe a century earlier. As with physical fights between two individuals, so ubiquitous are intellectual disputes that few are singled out to the extent of conferring proper names on them. Rather, only those *significant* insofar as they changed an intellectual climate, or are now viewed as peculiarly expressive *of* a climate, are mentioned in intellectual histories, and sometimes even (re)published.[58]

The case is different with those 'larger' phenomena, namely, controversies. They are far fewer because they only occur when a number of individuals (and organisations 'sponsoring' their own contestants) become sufficiently exercised over an issue to become embroiled. The issue, then, was more or less important at the time; the 'larger' the controversy in terms of its longevity and the number and importance of the participants, the more it presses itself on the historian of thought's attention as an obvious phenomenon, and the likelier its significance in later intellectual episodes. Thus many controversies are awarded proper names, such as The Investiture Controversy, the Conciliar Dispute, and the Revisionist Debate, whilst others, albeit not named, are set out by historians of thought as a result of their efforts to extract discrete, intelligible (narrative) phenomena from the permanent flux of intellectual activity.

A third similarity between intellectual and physical conflicts is that, just as many of the latter are understood as *revolutions* against established powers, so are many intellectual controversies.[59] For example, to the extent we can view the Reformation as one huge controversy rather than as a series of related controversies and disputes, it can be seen (in its intellectual ramifications) as a revolution against the established doctrinal orthodoxy of Roman Catholicism – and like most revolutions, it had been brewing for some time, began as an effort to achieve reform, needed strong if not fanatical leaders to (sometimes reluctantly) turn it into a revolution, had its waverers, spawned 'extremists' amongst those in the rank and file who took seriously all their leaders said, and ended by replacing the previous orthodoxy by new ones more disciplined than that which they rebelled against.

A fourth similarity between intellectual controversies and particularly wars and revolutions is the capacity of those on one side to fall out amongst themselves, thereby engendering a controversy in their own ranks. The Revisionist Debate is one such example, and more are to be found in, for instance, religious and scientific intellectual history, where adherents to new theories begin to squabble amongst themselves. In short, just as we understand some wars to be *civil* wars, so we can find larger and smaller analogies in the world of intellectual activity.

This capacity for internecine strife invites a fifth similarity between physical and intellectual conflicts, for where such struggles occur, organised efforts are sometimes made to regroup into a united front. The Council of Trent was a famous example, where, under pressure from Emperor Charles V, the papacy summoned a council in 1545, which sat intermittently until 1563, to promote reform of the Catholic Church and establish a clarified theology – in short, a mammoth effort by the Catholic Church to 'get its act together' to counter the Protestant Reformation.[60] Another example, though of lesser proportions and notably less success, was the effort made by the German Social-Democratic Party at its 1898 Stuttgart Conference, and even more determinedly at its Hanover Conference the following year, to tackle the schism in its ranks and in the broader socialist movement threatened by Bernstein's apparent unorthodoxy.[61]

Mention of internecine strife leads to a further similarity which can

242

pertain between physical and intellectual conflicts – namely, what we call a 'cold war'. Just as in the archetypal Cold War between Nato and the Warsaw Pact where head-on war was avoided, so occasions arise in the world of intellectual controversies where opposed parties deliberately refrain from direct engagement, and instead devote their activity to getting, or keeping, their own 'act' together. Bred of a combination of mutual respect, hostility, and indifference, this situation has its counterpart in those intellectual contexts where opposed groupings do not engage in overt controversy but instead display a *de facto* recognition of the status quo. As in international relations, such (Hobbesian) stand-offs only pertain where the opposed groupings are well-established powers, such that what might be lost by the risk of all-out conflict is judged to be more than what could be gained. Thus an uncomfortable 'peace' reigns – that is, until or unless something transpires to make one party believe it can make significant inroads on its opponent's position with little risk of loss.

The clearest examples of this must surely be those long periods the great religions go through when they refrain from intellectual controversy with each other; given their respective strengths there would appear to be no point. Yet should one of them sense that circumstances (for instance, an overall moral decline in 'the West'), favour a successful outcome, then we might witness the ending of this or that 'cold war' and the beginnings of a head-on religious controversy prompted by one religion's revived evangelism in the heart of the enemy camp. Actual examples of this scenario can be found to have punctuated the 'cold war' usually pertaining between atheists and religious believers, for occasions have arisen where the former judge it worthwhile to engage the latter in direct controversy – as, for example, did some seventeenth-century 'free thinkers' (albeit in guarded language), as the influence of the 'new science' and new techniques of Biblical criticism took hold; or again, for example, as a result of feeling the odds tipped substantially in their favour by Darwin's theory of evolution. (Nowadays, such is the truth-esteem of the physical sciences in particular, it is difficult to envisage circumstances where religious believers would welcome open controversy with atheists over the 'factual' aspect of their beliefs. Rather, when they cannot adopt the 'cold war' stance of evading controversy they had best continue their retreat from both historical and scientific matters and hope instead for new circumstances wherein they might gain some important new *moral* advantage by actively engaging with atheists.)

There might be more to explore occasioned by these similarities between large-scale physical conflicts and intellectual controversies but for the fact that few of either occur in a vacuum. Rather, particularly where they are more or less orchestrated, the latter involve organisations – religious denominations, political movements, commercial interests, professional lobbies – concerned to defend and promote their interests. In short, it matters in a practical way which side triumphs. Thus it is, for instance, that over political matters one rarely encounters the equivalent of a 'cold war' in intellectual circles; controversy is endless. Similarly, for instance, regarding theories of education. Because vested interests and practices are at stake, controversies are frequent and are not engaged in to argue the truth of a matter but in order to secure ground. In other words, where vested interests have a stake in the outcome, as is so often the case with large-scale controversies in the intellectual world, the thinking manifested during them is purely practical. As such (unless confronting new situations – for instance, political thinkers grappling with the emergence, and now the possible decline, of 'the State'), it is unlikely to be intrinsically interesting, creative, or innovative, and there is little more to be done in 'following' such controversies than identifying the practical objectives underlying the participants' arguments.

Is it going too far to suggest such a study would constitute not so much a history of *thought* as a history of how groups argued in order to assert their interests – that is, a history of rhetorical confrontation, of 'saying as a task'? Whilst it is true the history of thought must include unravelling where and how practical interests impinge upon the expression and direction of both 'saying' and thinking – contexts theorised earlier in this chapter, originating in the observation that people often think about what they say even when it is not the product of thinking – there can be so much more involved in the discipline, primarily because of what I have called 'theoretical' thinking manifested in discrete books, intellectual developments, disputes, and other controversies.

To emphasise this we can draw one final analogy between physical and intellectual conflict. Fisticuffs between two individuals are *sometimes* engaged in not in order to achieve any self-interested objective in beating one's opponent (for instance, self-defence), but solely to achieve the *intrinsic* objective in any fight – namely, to win. Now, why should anyone engage in a physical fight 'for its own sake' unless as a way of establishing fairness between individuals? In other words, we may identify a species of (physical) conduct, necessarily involving relations between individuals, we call 'moral'; that is, the active pursuit of 'right'. Where this involves one in a fight (of course, 'in order to' win), the logic of one's actions is not self-directed but devoted to 'right action' itself. Just so, I have urged, with 'theoretical' thinking, where, in dispute or controversy, the *intrinsic* objective is of course to win, but the logic of engaging in argument is not self-directed. Rather, it is devoted to demonstrating the truth to the opposition – another case of that social activity of 'sharing' or 'educating'. In both cases – fighting for the right in conduct and disputing the truth – one of the signs that such is what a contender understands himself to be doing is that he will 'do justice' to the rationale of the activity; respectively, fight morally (for example, not exploiting innocent parties, avoiding unnecessary cruelty), and dispute with intellectual integrity (for example, not deliberately misrepresenting arguments, avoiding unnecessary insults) – in short, in both cases to refrain from the use of 'dirty tricks'.

Now, in relation to large-scale intellectual controversies in particular, we may be sure that just as justice is rarely if ever the issue in warfare and other physical conflicts involving numerous participants – rather, they are interest-inspired collisions – so in intellectual controversies. They are rarely if ever engaged in by any faction solely as a way of enlightening the opposition regarding what is true. Rather, they are engaged in in order to achieve practical objectives; and so I revert to what I said – namely, that where the historian of thought can identify the kind of narrative identity constituted by large-scale interest-inspired intellectual controversies, the degree to which he will need to exploit that variety of explicatory and explanatory techniques I have suggested as composing his arsenal is limited. He will be restricted primarily to exposing the logic of 'saying' as a practical task, and will find himself, albeit an historian of thought, somewhat isolated from the activity of intimately following and accounting for the thinking evidenced in and by individuals' writings.

Further (although only a by-product of his study), just as the historian is unlikely to gain much *moral* instruction by restricting his work to the study of wars – rather, it is more likely to be gained from the study of *individual* conduct – so the historian of thought is unlikely to gain much *intellectual* benefit from the reconstruction of the thinking constitutive of controversies. He is more likely to acquire it from the study of individual writings and disputes, where *theoretical* thinking is so much more prevalent.

'SCHOOLS' OR 'TRADITIONS' OF THOUGHT, AND 'ISMS'

In this exposition of those kinds of (real) phenomena in the world of thought analogous to what were theorised as 'events' in the world of actions – that is, intellectual phenomena transcending single works – we have extracted what I have called 'intellectual developments', 'disputes' (between two individuals), and 'controversies' (multi-partied arguments), from an otherwise bewildering complex of ceaseless intellectual 'activity in general'. Our penultimate category comprises what are variously called 'schools of thought', 'traditions of thought', or this or that 'ism' – provisionally, for example, 'the Aristotelian school of thought', 'the liberal-democratic tradition of thought', 'socialism'. In the absence of strict semantic conventions these phenomena might also be called (intellectual) 'movements', but I propose to restrict that term to what I take to be a different class of phenomena referring to such as 'the Renaissance', and which constitutes our final category considered below.

Regarding the former three terms as interchangeable, then (whereby we can refer, for instance, to 'the socialist school of thought', or 'the socialist tradition of thought', or 'socialism'), it is as well at the outset to clarify in what sense this classification denotes *real* phenomena at all rather than mere 'things of reason', since its compass ranges ostensibly from the markedly imprecise, such as 'materialism', to the reasonably precise, such as 'Marxism'. Now it is clear that if, for example, by 'materialism' and 'idealism' we mean to denote 'schools' or 'traditions' of philosophy represented respectively by all those who explain reality as matter in motion and by all those who explain it as the manifestation of mind, then we denote nothing *real*. Rather, they denote abstract universals which identify classes of otherwise different things in virtue of something they have in common, just as the terms 'man', 'woman', 'land', and 'sea'. Only by pointing to *this* materialist, idealist, man, woman, piece of land, or stretch of sea, do we denote anything *real*. Thus, where referred to in this manner we must be clear that schools or traditions of thought are not actual phenomena. They neither effect nor affect anything in the intellectual world, nor can be affected by it. Rather, as classificatory terms their function is descriptive, whereby in saying someone 'belonged' to, for instance, 'the Thomist school of theology', all we mean is his thinking shared a combination of premises sufficiently prevalent, unusual, or in some other way noticeable, as to warrant its abstraction from the generality of theological ideas by naming it – that is, Thomism.

In short, where used in this manner it adds nothing to the description of someone as a Thomist to say he belonged to 'the Thomist school of thought', for in this sense Thomism, or the Thomist school or tradition of thought, is not an actual existent. As such, Thomism can therefore make no gains, nor suffer setbacks. Neither can there be 'good' or 'bad' Thomists in the sense that they can benefit or harm 'it'. Just so in political thought, for example regarding Marxism, socialism, and liberalism, where the suffix, 'ism', is used as equivalent to the suffix, 'ness', in words such as 'yellowness' or 'manliness'. This banana may be yellow; it may be more or less yellow; an aspect of its appearance is that it partakes in 'yellowness'. But 'yellowness' itself is a fixed, unchanging abstraction, not a 'real', 'actual', 'existing' phenomenon.

Where, then, there is no indication that anything other than abstract universals are being denoted, it follows that any discussion of the world of thought, and particularly any account of its *history*, which inhabits that world with the presence (even worse, the activity), of these 'isms', or schools or traditions of thought, is entirely fantastical. Yet it is not an infrequent occurrence, and may even not be called an error – for example, the notion that 'utilitarianism' influenced J. S. Mill, or that Lenin changed 'Marxism' – so long as those who use such formulae are clear they are employing a kind of shorthand and are correspondingly sure-footed regarding how far they extend such metaphorical usage. Just as there comes a point at which to stop talking (metaphorically) of states and governments doing this or that, and instead apprehend the reality of this or that individual's actions within whatever complex context he operates, so in the history of thought. Better to apprehend *actuality*, a point is reached indicative of the need to abandon simplifying metaphor and refer instead to direct realities, such as intellectual developments, changes of mind, disputes and controversies, all ultimately grounded on the specific thinking of concrete individuals. Otherwise, we are threatened with an intellectual world peopled by 'isms', or schools or traditions of thought, busily engaged in expanding their influence, determining individuals' thinking, contesting disputed areas of intellectual territory, making progress, and fighting off decline.

The worst case is where this tendency gets so out of control that new 'isms', not even valid as abstract universals, are paraded as players on the stage of intellectual history. For instance, although we might be sufficiently persuaded of the usefulness, relevance, and scope of applicability of Macpherson's syndrome, 'possessive individualism', to justify its inclusion amongst other established descriptive universals generated by the study of the history of political thought, this is far removed from the practice of willy-nilly converting not only every thinker but also every conceivable position (whether actually conceived or not!) into an 'ism', *and* metamorphising these already wraith-like apparitions into actors in the intellectual drama of the history of thought. The result of such double conjuring is to invite the unwary into a phantasmagorical world (and history) of thought from which it is doubtful, if seduced, they will emerge with their senses.[62]

Let us instead return to the real world of genuine intellectual phenomena to see in what sense schools or traditions of thought, or 'isms', *can* be as 'real' or 'actual' as are large-scale *events* in non-intellectual history. I have argued that what makes any event a 'real' phenomenon (as distinct from an artificial juxtapositioning of separate occurrences and actions), is that one is able to establish a genuine continuity between otherwise discrete happenings, such that an authentic sequence emerges into view rather than a mere chronology imposed on disconnected occurrences by the observer. I have referred to such sequences as 'story-objects' or 'narrative identities', and have pointed to their parametering in terms of their having beginnings, a 'content' constituted by *change*, and (at least, potentially) endings. I insisted the corresponding form in which they are apprehended or explicated is that of narrative, which (when factual) circumscribes the boundaries to history as a *discipline*.

Thus if, for example, the First World War was *an* event, the test of the 'reality' or 'actuality' of this event is that its story can be told as a coherent narrative. This implies it must have parameters to its compass – in other words, a beginning, a 'middle' constituted by the ('relevant') selection of happenings which were 'next', and (since it is past), an ending. These parameters may be more or less precise, or more or less arguable. Just as we may be unsure where this field ends and that meadow begins, and argue whether the pond is part of the field, so we may be unsure whether the Easter Rising in Ireland in 1916 was 'part of' the First World War, and argue whether the latter ended in 1918 or, as some claim, continued with what we call the Second World War. In short, our apprehension of events as singular varies in exactitude, either because 'the event' in question is itself so extensive in time and occurrences, or because of our own failures in definitional clarity (for instance, is that economy suffering a recession, depression, or a slump?). But however difficult it might be to establish when an event began and ended, and exactly which occurrences constitute its (narrative) structure, the *first* condition of its actuality is that we are at least examining those phenomena of which, if it is to be a real event at all, it must be composed – namely, occurrences.

These observations should suffice as pointers to where and in what sense schools or traditions of thought, and the ubiquitous 'isms', are phenomena in the history of thought as real or actual as the thinking of an individual, or as intellectual developments, disputes, and controversies, rather than mere abstract universals. Any 'ism' or school or tradition of thought only constitutes a concrete, empirical phenomenon insofar as its story can be told – in other words, insofar as it is a narrative identity. *If* there is such a *real* (intellectual) phenomenon as, for example, Marxism, then it must be a 'story-object' rather than a set of ideas many thinkers happen to share. It must have had its origins, and be constituted by a subsequent sequence of (different) occurrences which follow on from each other '*next*', (that is, have a content or development comprised of *change*). In addition one must be alert to the possibility of its ending at some future point, or to its having already ended as a *single* story-object by virtue, for example, of splits too severe to be mended (as happened to 'socialism' after 1918) – or of its being so broadly dissipated as to lose an identity sufficiently viable for genuine narrative treatment (in the way we might say 'liberalism' has long disappeared into the ether through ceaseless loose rhetoric).

If, then, this is the only sense in which schools or traditions of thought, or 'isms', are *real* phenomena, certain implications follow for students and practitioners of the history of thought, the first of which must surely be to exercise caution over that profusion of 'isms' which abound, particularly in some philosophical writings. For example, 'materialism' can probably be said never to have 'existed', because there has not been one more or less continuous, developing (that is, changing) debate over their position by those who have called themselves 'materialists'. However, the case is different *vis-à-vis*, for instance, Marxism, socialism, and liberalism. Here, precisely in virtue of each having a *history*, these schools or traditions of thought can be displayed as genuine narrative identities,[63] whereas the most one could do with those many thinkers correctly described as 'materialists' is produce a chronicle of their appearances over time, not a 'history of materialism'.

This leads to another implication regarding 'isms' as *real* phenomena, for if Marxism, for example, is only a genuine school of thought inasmuch as its history can be told – in other words, inasmuch as it 'has a history' – this amounts to saying that as a real, individual phenomenon, Marxism *is* its history. Arriving at this formulation demonstrates just how different Marxism as a real phenomenon is from Marxism as an abstract universal. The latter rightly implies 'an essence' of Marxism, for it denotes precisely that which otherwise different sets of ideas have in common. The former, however, exactly expunges any 'essence of', or 'essential', Marxism, for in meaning to denote it as a real, individual phenomenon, then Marxism is unique to its own (necessarily changing) history. Conceived thus, at any one time 'Marxism' is no more nor less than what those who call themselves Marxists mean by it, and it is only insofar as this *changes* (as evidenced by arguments amongst themselves) that 'Marxism' is established as an overall narrative identity, outstripping any one individual's version of it. Viewed in this light, there can be no 'good' or 'bad' Marxists, nor equally, for instance, 'good' or 'bad' Christians, if this implies that individual Marxists or Christians are obliged to bring their thinking into accord with some 'essential' Marxism or Christianity. However, this is not to say individuals cannot contribute to either Marxist or Christian thought – on the contrary, the very existence of these 'schools' as real phenomena depends precisely upon, not having members *per se*, but upon the innovative contributions of those adherents who revise, amend, dispute, expand, and in other ways *develop* the existing understandings. Doubtless there is a sense in which such contributions can be judged as 'productive' or the reverse, but individuals cannot be said to 'betray' Marxism or Christianity, for such a notion implies an unchanging orthodoxy, the very reverse of that which makes a school of thought a genuine (historical) identity.

It can only be an irony of intellectual life that a principal technique nevertheless exploited by innovative contributors to a school of thought, in persuading otherwise sceptical colleagues of the value of their innovations, is to insist upon their own orthodoxy and brand fellow-members who oppose them as betrayers and renegades. This curiosity regarding the argumentative techniques at the heart of schools of thought as real, 'living' phenomena, whereby they are only sustained by a continuous superseding of 'orthodoxy' defended precisely in the *name* of that orthodoxy, makes them strange, almost contradictory phenomena. In short, it is just those whose contributions salvage an 'ism' from being no more than an abstract universal who, in achieving this, exploit their 'ism' as if it *were* an abstract universal! It is therefore not surprising that some believe them, and correspondingly misunderstand the nature of (real) schools or traditions of thought, for it is the latter themselves which not only encourage this error but seem to *need* to in order to exist. Strange phenomena indeed, which can only flourish by denying their nature!

INTELLECTUAL 'MOVEMENTS'

In establishing the sense in which schools or traditions of thought, or 'isms', are empirically real phenomena rather than either mere 'things of reason' or artificial constructs, their status as *individual* phenomena was crucial in that latter determination. In other words, if salvaging them from being no more than abstract universals involved construing them (where possible) as *narrative* identities, salvaging them from being artificial juxta-positionings of occurrences was equally important, and involved construing them (where possible) as genuine sequences or continuities – that is, authentically parametered as *individual*, singular, or unitary phenomena. In short, for a school or tradition of thought or 'ism' to be empirically real it is as important that it offer itself as a narrative *identity* as that it offer itself as a *narrative* identity. 'Its' singularity as an 'identity' must be objective rather than the product of juxtaposing *separate* occurrences into an artificial sequence.

In moving now to explore that kind of phenomenon at furthest remove from the thinking evidenced in a writer's single work – namely, those 'things' we call intellectual '*movements*', such as the Enlightenment, the Renaissance, and the 'scientific revolution' – we are exactly confronted by phenomena whose status as 'real' is equivocal precisely inasmuch as their status as *individual*, or singular, appears open to question. In short, if by 'real' as applied to happenings we mean they actually occurred, then the question arises as to whether, for instance, the Enlightenment was a *real* phenomenon of which it can be said 'it' actually occurred, since the principles underlying its individuation are not so accessible as those underlying the previous phenomena we have examined.

The parallel to this situation can be exemplified in 'the Industrial Revolution'. Given the manner in which this is variously discussed, some imply that 'it' did occur – that is, it was a real event. Others, that 'it' is merely a term denoting a number of otherwise discrete events which *we* juxtapose in virtue of their sharing certain common features. The former may retort that it had a beginning, a development whereby aspects of its happenings are narratively sequenced (namely, a 'this *then* that' structure), and an end. The sceptic can reply that by 'the Industrial Revolution' we mean to denote, not *an event*, but a period within which a panorama of features – for example, housing, work practices, social structure, and economic organisation – was variously affected by new sources of power, scientific discoveries, and technological innovations. Both may agree the Industrial Revolution was indeed multi-faceted, but the former viewpoint is that 'it' was a real (overall) event despite this, whereas the latter is that it was *not* a real event *because* of this. Insofar as both have something to recommend them, we can say that in talking of 'the Industrial Revolution' as a real phenomenon we straddle the border between invention and fact – that is, its status as a 'real' phenomenon is equivocal.

Just so with intellectual 'movements'. The Enlightenment, for instance, is sometimes referred to as if it was an (admittedly complex, multi-faceted) event, of which 'the story' can be told. Others use the term purely descriptively to denote a period (not an overall event) in which a variety of intellectual undertakings and activities shared the characteristic of emanating from an enthusiasm for the critical application of 'reason' to established wisdoms, institutions, and practices. The same ambiguity characterises talk of 'the Renaissance' and other such multi-faceted movements, and it as well to make clear why it is necessary to confront this ambiguity rather than let it be.

If intellectual movements are *real* phenomena, their status cannot but be that of narrative identities or 'story-objects'. Only as such can they be objects of the historian of thought's attention in the sense that he can proceed to explicate what this or that movement was by means of reconstructing it as a narrative identity. Historians study *real* actions and events, not inventions of the imagination nor constructs of reason. If, then, 'the Enlightenment', or that denoting any other movement, is a collective term for that which otherwise discrete phenomena have in common, then 'the Enlightenment' is a construct of reason, akin in status to 'yellowness'. As such, however useful, relevant, and workable the term is for the historian of thought (such that we can say we are pointing to something real *about someone* in describing him as 'an Enlightenment thinker'), the Enlightenment itself is not an object of his study because 'it' was not something which *happened*.

Thus this ambiguity regarding the status of intellectual movements is not a trifle. On the contrary, we seem confronted by a threateningly equivocal class of phenomena whose status we need to theorise in order to determine either how to approach them, or even whether they are approachable at all through the discipline of history. As indicated, the problematic aspect of these phenomena stems from an obvious ambiguity regarding their status as *individual*, singular, or unitary, and hence as coherently parametered. Unlike many other phenomena, these are palpably composite; and it is this which directs further attention to the connection between the 'reality' of 'things' or 'phenomena' and both the logic and praxis of their individuation.

Logically, if by 'a thing' (or 'phenomenon') we mean a single thing –

251

this as distinct from *that* – then if something is not a single unit it cannot be 'a thing'. Thus a part of a thing is not itself a thing, nor is a collection of things. This is why we have the terms, 'a part' and 'a collection', whereby we distinguish between a thing, a part of a thing, and a collection of things: otherwise we would be reduced to talking of, respectively, a thing of a thing and a thing of things.

Now, if by calling a thing '*real*' I mean it actually exists – or if the 'thing' is an event, that it actually occurred – then a thing can be real, a part of a thing can be real (but is not itself a real thing), and a collection of things can be real (but is not itself a real thing). In this way, by sticking to our terms, we avoid the conundrum, 'is part of a thing itself a thing?', or, 'is a collection of things itself a thing?'

The praxis of individuation, however, eludes this logic, for 'things' are extracted and individuated from an otherwise undifferentiated mêlée of objects (and happenings) only insofar as we find it useful, relevant, and workable (rather than *logical*) to do so. A consequence is that, logic notwithstanding, parts and collections of things are individuated and denoted, and thereby presented as single units – that is, as things in their own right; moreover, as *real* things. For example, this garden can be understood as a (single) thing, or as a collection of things, or as part of a (larger) thing – for example, an estate. The rosebed is part of the garden; but it can also be understood as a single thing in its own right, or as a collection of things. Thus, the praxis of individuation often glosses over the status of 'things' in a dialectic between things, parts of things, and collections of things, since the very praxis of denoting a phenomenon – 'this is a garden' – implies it is both singular ('this is *a* garden'), and real ('this *is* a garden').

In this sense, then, the 'reality' of 'things' we denote is only ever a potential, albeit one constantly realised in the praxis of identifying them. There is thus nothing wrong in talking of the garden as a real (single) thing, despite its also being both a collection of things and part of a thing, so long as to do so 'works'. Indeed, many 'things' are denoted ('noticed') as such precisely *because* they are collections of things (for instance, a wolf-pack, a crowd of people), or parts of things (for instance, a handle, a palm of a hand).

So far, then, there appears a possible (and frequent) disconsonance between the logic and the praxis of individuating things. But let us return to our initial premise in logic in order to explore another of its implications, one of particular relevance to those (composite) phenomena whose status I have suggested is equivocal. Thus: logically, if by 'a thing' we mean a single thing – *this* as distinct from *that* – then if something is not a single unit it cannot be 'a thing'. Thus, a *piece* of a thing is not itself a thing, nor is a *number* of things. Now, if by calling a thing 'real' I mean it actually exists – or if 'the thing' is an event, that it actually occurred –

then a thing can be real, but a piece of a thing is not real; rather, it is a mental construct. Likewise, a number of things is not real, but a mental construct.

Thus I am positing a distinction between 'parts' and 'pieces', and between 'collections' and 'numbers', which is both logically defensible (if appropriately defined) *and* is a way of expressing a distinction in the praxis of individuation. For example, I can point to a cow and say it is a thing which exists; I can point to its tail and either say it is part of the cow or a thing in itself. Either way, I mean the tail is *real*. If, however, I point to five cows and say 'there is a number of cows', neither in logic *nor* in practice do I mean this 'number' is 'a thing' which exists or is real. Rather, 'it' is the abstract product of a mental operation – namely, the counting of things selected for something they have in common. Any amount of real things can in this way be added up into 'a number'; for instance, there are a number of balding blue-eyed fifty-year-old male Members of Parliament. It is true that those numbered are 'real things', but 'the number' itself does not refer to a real single identity. The case is different when we treat of a *collection* of things which in practice we treat as a (singular) actual or real thing. For instance, a wolf is a real thing; a collection of wolves is a real thing (that is, a wolf-pack); but five wolf-packs, or 'a number' of wolf-packs, is not. This is a distinction intimated in the ordinary use of language, where we say 'there *is* a wolf-pack in that area', or 'there *is* a collection of people around that shop window', but 'there *are* a number of cows in that field', or 'there *are* a number of people carrying umbrellas'.

Likewise in the other direction. Suppose I encounter something I call a 'piece' or 'fraction' of a cow. Neither in logic nor in practice do I mean this 'piece' is 'a thing' which exists in its own right. On its own it is anonymous. Unlike a *part* of a cow (its tail, its hoof), a 'piece' of a cow is only meaningful as 'a piece' – that is, as an (abstract) mental construct. This becomes clear if we conceive of the cow sliced into a thousand pieces. All things can (theoretically) be divided into 'pieces' (but not necessarily into 'parts'), and as many as one wishes. Each piece is denoted as such precisely in virtue of what it has in common with the others – namely, and solely, that they are pieces of a cow. The cow's tail, however, is *part* of the cow, and is thereby individuated (named) and denoted as a real thing; it escapes the abstract anonymity of being merely a 'piece' of the cow.

I say, then, that neither 'a piece' of a thing nor 'a number' of things are themselves real phenomena, whereas in the praxis of individuation 'a part' of a thing and 'a collection' of things are both construed as real, singular identities. To conclude this exposition we can observe that some 'things', 'phenomena', or 'identities' are regarded, in their individuation, as neither parts of other things nor as themselves consisting of parts. Others, as noted, are individuated precisely in virtue of being regarded as parts of other things or as collections of things. Yet others leave these options in abeyance. Finally, some 'things', despite being articulated in the manner we individuate real, singular phenomena, are merely mental constructs; universals such as 'mankind' are an obvious case, but so are 'things' which are 'pieces' of real things, and 'things' which are 'numbers' of real things.

Having thus extended our analysis of the individuation of 'things' or 'phenomena' beyond that already proffered in Chapters One and Two, we have derived a kind of typology of 'thinghood' of sufficient scope to address the equivocal status of intellectual 'movements'. What kind of 'thing', then, was that referred to as 'the Enlightenment', or that called 'the Renaissance'? In the above terms, if 'materialism' is neither 'a thing', a part of a thing, a piece of a thing, a collection of things, nor a number of things, but an abstract universal, does the Enlightenment have the same status? If so, 'it' never happened. Or if, for example, the intellectual school called Marxism is a 'real thing' precisely in virtue of being a (sequenced) collection of real things – books, arguments, disputes, controversies – does the Enlightenment share this status? If so, we should include 'movements' along with schools or traditions of thought and 'isms', as objects of the same techniques of historical reconstruction rather than insist they form a separate (problematic) class.

In fact, I suggest intellectual movements fall between these alternatives. On the one hand they are not (mere) abstract universals, for they are clearly time and place-bound. In addition, where we refer, for instance, to a Renaissance work of art such as Michelangelo's *Pietà*, we are not denoting 'a piece' of the Renaissance, implying that abstract connotation I have outlined. Rather, the *Pietà* is an individual real thing. Can we thus say, on the other hand, that the *Pietà* is *part* of the Renaissance, thereby conceiving the latter as a genuine identity composed of different parts which form a single (sequenced) collection of things? The difficulty here is that whatever else 'it' was, the Renaissance was neither an ongoing controversy (and thus not the same kind of thing as the Reformation), nor a self-conscious school or tradition of thought (or 'ism') constituted by ongoing internal debate regarding its doctrine and/or direction. Rather, since Burckhardt's *Civilisation of the Renaissance in Italy* (1860), there has been substantial debate over *what* the Renaissance was. For example, was it restricted to Italy? When did it begin? When did it end? Was it forward or backward-looking? What areas and activities did it embrace? Kristeller, for instance, refers to the 'diversified and even chaotic efforts' of Renaissance thought,[64] and Bronowski and Mazlish, after confessing 'the idea of the Renaissance is a singularly complicated one', conclude, 'Obviously, one's decision as to what the Renaissance *was* affects one's idea of when it *occurred*'.[65] Whatever else, here we at least encounter the notion that the Renaissance was, in our terms, 'a thing' which occurred (or 'a real occurrence'). Yet Kristeller seems uneasy over this notion, at least with respect to Renaissance humanism, for he qualifies his introductory remarks on Petrarch thus: 'Petrarch . . . has often been called the initiator of Renaissance humanism, but I should prefer to call him its first great representative'.[66]

What seems clear is that historians' equivocation over what the Renaissance *was* is unresolvable until they settle the prior question of what *kind* of 'thing' it was. That the latter is unspecified surely accounts for much of the equivocation in the first place, vindicating our claim that intellectual movements form an ambiguous class of 'objects' for historical study. We do not, that is, find historians asking what *was* the First World War, despite its complexities; neither asking what *was* the Reformation, whatever other questions they may pose about it – and this, I suggest, is because they instinctively know what *kind* of 'thing' they are studying.

I propose that intellectual movements are, in fact, most nearly what I have explained as 'numbers' of things. As such, they are not 'real things' (unlike *collections* of things), but more 'things of reason'. But they are not mere abstract universals, for a movement is not 'an idea' but a number (of things) – that is, if a movement's status if that of a number of things noticed for what they have in common, it is nevertheless a finite number restricted in time and place. As such there seems little to distinguish a movement such as the Renaissance from a 'period' designated for something noteworthily common regarding its features, such as 'the Elizabethan period'. This latter term intimates that a particular 'style' characterised a variety of aspects of life in Elizabethan England, from dress to architecture, from manners to drama; that this 'style' formed a common base, so to speak, which was manifested in many different ways. Another way of putting this, more approximating to the actual semantics of 'a movement', is that this style was *transmitted* into many different areas.

It is just this intimation of a *process* of *transmission* which most clearly salvages a movement as 'a number of things collated for what they have in common' from being no more than an abstract universal. Indeed, it goes further, for in intimating some kind of *sequence* of actions and events it also suggests this particular 'number of things' is more than merely a construct of reason. It is in this sense that, although the Renaissance can be seen as 'a number' of things collated for what they have in common (in art, literature, philosophy, and politics), this 'number' is intimated as being, not the product of *our* interest in selecting the principle of commonality, but as the product of a real, objective process of 'spreading' some common base outwards into diverse areas – that is, as composed of a sequence of actions and events which actually occurred. A suitable analogy is the gradually dissipating turbulence caused by a passing boat. As we notice this and that bobbing up and down and being displaced, we relate these otherwise disparate incidents together into a continuing sequence of 'this *then* that' – and we do this because they *are* interrelated. Thus, although identifying 'a number' of otherwise separate 'things' occurring, in this case it is not we who are choosing which to pick in virtue of some common feature *we* select (unlike, for instance, 'there are a number of yellow objects in this room').

We should note the analogy requires a moving boat as the *originator* of *consequences* which eventually *cease*; in other words, we are approaching the logic of a narrative identity. However, it is not a full-blown, developed narrative identity (or 'story-object') because we do not pursue 'what happened next' with regard to any one consequence of the initiating occurrence, as would be the case if we pursued the story in which a particular ripple wet this man's shoes, such that he then took them off, then went in search of his towel, then argued with his child who had drenched it, and then stormed off in a huff. Instead, in restricting ourselves to the common consequences of the initiating occurrence (that is, in perceiving 'the number' of happenings occasioned by the passing boat as 'a phenomenon'), we are denoting a kind of aborted, repetitive narrative identity – a quasi-event – which rather than proceeding from *a* to *b* to *c* . . . , proceeds from *a* to *b*1, to *b*2, to *b*3. . . .

To the extent this analogy is instructive of the nature and status of intellectual movements, we may see more clearly what *kind* of 'thing' they are, such that in better understanding their form we can be more confident about their content – in other words, say what, for example, the Renaissance *was*. An intellectual 'movement' is a term denoting 'a number' of (real) things included in 'it' by virtue of their manifesting common features attributable to some single source. In being 'a number' of things, any movement may thus be said not to be a 'real thing' but merely a 'thing of reason'. On the other hand, although falling short of constituting a genuinely collective thing made of interacting parts, a 'movement' can be said to partake of aspects of a 'real (single) thing' insofar as the various things which make up 'the number' derive from an actual, common originating source rather than from some quality abstracted by us. It is true the status of these quasi-real phenomena is less clear than that of other 'real things' and 'things of reason', but I trust this is more because of their peculiarity than of my limitations in clarifying their nature.

In addition to posing the question of whether such 'quasi-real' phenomena are appropriate objects of his discipline, the above definition imposes a number of conditions upon the practising historian of thought. Firstly, in 'noticing' the common features, they must be new. Secondly, they must be attributable to a common source grounded in actual happenings. Thirdly, then, this common source has to be identified. Fourthly, some account of the process or mechanisms of *transmission* needs to be given. Where these conditions look capable of being met, then the historian of thought has uncovered a phenomenon potentially explicable through the discipline of (narrative) history – namely, an intellectual movement – however innovatory he might have to be *within* the logic of that discipline (for example, in giving evidence of the process of transmission which at least approximates to the conventional narrative logic of 'this happened, *then* that'). Where these conditions appear incapable of being met due to the nature of the topic, I suggest the historian of thought leave well alone – for instance, leave 'post-modernism' as merely an abstraction, a descriptive term, not indicative of any narrative identity which ('really') occurred.

It is as much outside the scope of this book as it is of my competence to now proceed to ascertain how 'real' a phenomenon was either the Renaissance or the Enlightenment, classical examples of what we call intellectual 'movements'. Regarding them, I will restrict myself to the suggestion that the former, although lacking the parametered (narrative) identity of a school or tradition of thought, more nearly approximates to a real phenomenon than does the Enlightenment, for it could be argued it better meets those conditions I have proposed as implicit in the notion of 'a movement' as more than a mere 'thing of reason'. Firstly, although there has been considerable debate regarding when the Renaissance began, the newness of its common features appears indisputable – namely, the emergence of a culture alert to, appreciative of, and inquisitive about the natural and human (and classical) world, as distinct from one dominated by the formalisms of abstract theology. By comparison, what is generally proposed as the common feature of the Enlightenment – the critical application of reason to traditional beliefs, practices, and institutions – appears to me as both less time and place-bound. For example, what of the seventeenth-century rationalists' extensive reasoned enquiry into astronomy, Biblical criticism, political order, and morality? Secondly, because of the debate over when the Renaissance began, there has been no shortage of persuasive suggestions as to *what* began it, from the fall of Constantinople, to the discovery of the New World, to the development of a specifically Italian commercial culture – that is, various notions of a common source grounded in actual circumstances and/or events. By comparison, where not offered as simply occurring without explanation, the Enlightenment is less convincingly presented as grounded on, for instance, the admixturing of 'French rationalism' with 'English empiricism', or Voltaire's visit to England between 1726–29. Finally, regarding the *transmission* of the respective features of the Renaissance and the Enlightenment, one might query whether the personal and literary contacts of *salon* figures such as D'Alembert, Diderot, and Voltaire (and the sporadic patronage of 'enlightened despots'), albeit efficacious, formed as all-pervasive a mechanism as the curricular changes Renaissance humanists introduced into Italian universities?

The foregoing are difficult judgements to make, and I have proffered my suggestions more as sketches of how the criteria determining the relative authenticity of intellectual movements as (at least, quasi-) real phenomena might be applied in particular cases rather than as considered conclusions from the extensive researches such judgements would require.

In this enquiry into what phenomena properly offer themselves to the discipline of the history of thought, I have suggested a gradation of 'objects' moving ever further from the base-point of an individual's thinking evidenced in a single piece of writing – that is, to intellectual developments; disputes; controversies; and schools or traditions of thought (or various 'isms'). Now – in being the kind of 'objects' they are – in treating of intellectual 'movements' I suggest we have reached the limits of this gradation, for we have already intimated that the discipline through which they are apprehended begins to depart from that of history. In short, it is difficult to conceive of any 'larger' intellectual phenomena which would not be entirely amorphous in character (a fate from which it has been difficult enough to salvage 'movements' themselves, and to which some should doubtless be consigned), and which thus require a form of discourse altogether outside the discipline of history (and perhaps outside *any* coherent discipline). As argued in Chapter Four, in any study form and content must correspond dialectically: that we apprehend 'events' is just as much because there are, 'out there', narrative identities, as because we have the ability to construe things narratively. Now, if 'a movement' is essentially 'a number of things', then the manner in which 'it' is apprehended is multiform rather than solely that of the (narrative) discipline of history whereby one explicates an identity constituted by change (and in so doing, explains why this and that happened). Although aspects of narrative logic *are* involved in apprehending an intellectual movement – that is, identifying origins, mechanisms of transmission, and its ending – it is not the only form appropriate to the 'object', since in being 'a number of things' the form in which this kind of phenomenon is apprehended is a mixture of narrative, analytic, and descriptive 'history'.

For instance, in giving an account of the Renaissance one might show how a particular work of literature is 'an example' of it. The work is neither caused by nor 'part' of the Renaissance. Rather, as Kristeller on Petrarch, it 'represents' it. One then moves to another 'example' or 'representation', for instance, from painting. In each case one might be able to trace the process of transmission of the common features from the original source, or find cases of cross-transmission between the different examples – that is, engage in narrative. But the primary form of apprehension is analytic – namely, perceiving the common features as exemplified in *this* and *that* – building up to an account or *description* of something. This 'something' is not an event (which can only be 'described' by employing the narrative form), but a *number* (of things); and the way one conveys the apprehending of 'a number' of things (unlike a collective thing), is simply to give an account of each one in turn, centred on how it exemplifies the core common features in its own *particular* way – that is, one employs the logic of *description*.

By analogy, one may be told that 'an interesting thing' is going on; namely, a number of grisly murders. When one asks to know more about this phenomenon, one is told about each murder in turn in respect of its particular gruesomeness. One now has a (chronological and descriptive) account of this phenomenon, this 'number of grisly murders'. Their occurrences may be coincidental – or some may be copy-cat killings, in which case their connectedness through this process of transmission confers on this phenomenon of 'a number of grisly murders' more of the status of a 'real' identity in its own right. This would be even more the case if they were all committed by the same serial-killer, whereby we would say this 'number of grisly murders' is, in effect, one single real thing occurring – a 'serial' thing, so to speak. Our account of this phenomenon would then shift its centre of gravity from descriptive accounts of each murder towards a far greater input of narrative reconstructing of a 'story-object'.

In like manner I suggest intellectual 'movements' are in the first instance 'numbers of things' exhibiting a common feature, and in the worst cases a particular alleged movement may be no more than a coincidence and thus entirely a 'thing of reason' – that is, a product of analytic 'history' rather than an historical identity requiring the discipline of factual narrative for its apprehension and presentation. But the working supposition of historians of thought who talk of intellectual 'movements' is that at the very least there is some degree of actual interconnectedness between the different things which, in exhibiting a set of common features, comprise 'the number' of things constitutive of any 'movement'. Just how far any movement can further escape from being an amorphous phenomenon, and instead more closely approach the structured, parametered status of a genuine narrative or historical identity, must depend on each particular case. But none can entirely escape a degree of amorphism, for if one did we would be apprehending something different – most likely, either a school or tradition of thought, or a controversy. For example, Marxism is sometimes referred to, and treated as, an (intellectual) movement, and sometimes as a school of thought; the Reformation, either as a controversy or a movement. Where these phenomena are seen as 'movements', then to the extent 'they' are therefore amorphous in status, the form or 'discipline' appropriate to their apprehension is correspondingly an admixture of analytic, descriptive, and narrative logic. Where, on the other hand, they are seen as controversies or as schools of thought, their status as 'story-objects' requires the uniform discipline of narrative history for their explication.

CONCLUSION

It is perhaps appropriate that the logic of this enquiry into the possibility of the history of thought – itself offered as both an exemplar and a test-case of what the preceding chapters of this book proposed regarding the discipline of history in general – should culminate in the examination of intellectual 'movements' (paralleled, of course, in all kinds of non-intellectual history where 'movements' are identified). Their equivocal status as 'real things' is necessarily matched by the correspondingly equivocal nature of the discipline(s) through which they are explicated – namely, an intermixture of analytic, descriptive, and narrative logic. Our opening exploration of 'what is history?' precisely began by differentiating between these three approaches, and we now conclude at a point where we are confronted by phenomena which require their coalescence for their reconstruction and articulation. We have, then, turned full-circle. It must be left to the reader to determine whether this point at which we conclude is appropriate because this intermixing of forms leads to that slippery slope where the discipline of history encompasses anything said about the past – or appropriate, conversely, because in arriving at phenomena requiring a complex of approaches, we have reached the pinnacle of what the discipline can achieve when emancipated (if not wholly) from the narrative form.

Ultimately, however, the fate of history as a discipline cannot be determined by attempts to theorise its nature. Rather, it is daily determined by a combination of what those who call themselves 'historians' actually do, with what those who identify a subject called 'history' mean by the term. They need not always correspond. Rather, we should expect an interplay between what practitioners of the discipline and what ordinary observers understand by it. On the sidelines stands the theorist, relatively powerless to influence the fate of what emerges in this praxis of individuating a thing called 'history'. What *is* clear is that, as with any other designated activity, what we mean by 'history' affects how we undertake the discipline, just as how we find ourselves actually undertaking it affects what we mean by the term. Whatever emerges as the current understanding does not need the sharp outlines and complex internal finesse aspired to by theorists – but it does need to 'work'; that is, as an identification of a specific activity it must be relevant, workable, and reliable. Marx, ultimately, attempted to treat 'capitalism' as a story-object rather than as a 'movement', thereby making his explication of the phenomenon captive to the logic of (narrative) history. Yet his story-object had an ending predicted on the basis of analysis – not, of course, an empirical ending grounded on what actually happened. In short, his 'history' became intermixed with a variety of other approaches in addition to factual narrative, and whatever else it achieved, simply did not 'work' as 'history'. Whether current attempts increasingly to broaden the scope of the discipline (away from narrative explanation and explication of 'what happened') will 'work' has yet, I believe, to become clear. What *is* stubbornly clear is that there remains 'out there' a teeming, restless scenario of human actions and events deserving of being identified, understood, and explained; and if we wish to perceive this dimension of life aright, then there are any number of stories waiting to be told.

NOTES AND REFERENCES

1 WHAT IS HISTORY?

1 E.g. for a considered version of this, see G. Graham, *Historical Explanation Reconsidered*, Aberdeen University Press, 1983, p. 9 (see below, p. 144, Chapter Four, plus accompanying note 15, for a fuller reference to this monograph).

2 Cf. J. H. Hexter, *The History Primer*, London, Allen Lane/The Penguin Press, 1972, pp. 67, 329, 368.

3 E.g. see Chapter Five below, pp. 182–183; 188–191; 197–198.

4 Noteworthy for the purposes of the arguments in this book, see *The Oxford English Dictionary* (2nd edn, Vol. VII, 1989, p. 261), entry, 'History . . . ad.L.*historia*, narrative of past events, account, tale, story'. See also R. Koselleck, *Futures Past – On The Semantics of Historical Time*, trans. K. Tribe, Massachusetts, MIT Press Cambridge, 1985, pp. 27–38, for an interesting account of the difference, in German semantics, between '*Historie*' and '*Geschichte*'.

5 Cf. Hexter, op. cit., pp. 388–399, for a panegyric on 'common sense' and the historian.

6 I. Asimov, *Foundation*, London, Panther, 1972, pp. 7–28.

7 Albeit, not *entirely* in vain; despite M. G. Murphy's observation that 'in recent years there has been a marked increase in the number of non-narrative historical studies. One may, I think, confidently predict that this trend will continue in the future' (M. G. Murphy, *Our Knowledge of the Historical Past*, Indianapolis & New York, Bobbs-Merrill, 1973, p. 124). In a *Guardian* article (22 November 1980) entitled 'The New Art of Narrative History', Lawrence Stone wrote approvingly of 'new historians' reverting to narrative (albeit a new, 'non-naive' type), because disillusioned with economic determinist models – but he detected five differences between the old and new narratives; 1 an interest in the poor and obscure rather than the rich and powerful; 2 the inclusion of explicit analysis (although it interrupts the narrative flow); 3 the exploitation of new sources such as trial records; 4 the use of pyschological and anthropological theories in telling their stories; 5 the telling of stories not for their own sake but to illuminate past cultures.

8 E.g. the topic of narrative in historiography frequently appeared between 1962–1971 in the journal, *History and Theory*, culminating in W. H. Dray's article, 'On the Nature and Role of Narrative in Historiography' (Vol. 10, No. 1, 1971, pp. 153–171), a full and sound survey of an ongoing debate perhaps encouraged by Gallie's complaint, 'I find it astonishing that no critical philosopher of history has as yet offered us a clear account of what it is to follow or construct an historical narrative' (W. B. Gallie, *Philosophy and the Historical*

Understanding, London, Chatto & Windus, 1964, p. 12): after a lapse, the topic reappeared regularly in *History and Theory* throughout the 1980s, H. White observing that 'In contemporary historical theory the topic of narrative has been the subject of extraordinarily intense debate' ('The Question of Narrative in Contemporary Historical Theory', *History and Theory*, Vol. 23, No. 1, 1984, p. 1); and if we are to believe A. P. Norman's account of contemporary positions on narrative in history, the topic should continue to warrant the journal's attention in the present decade; 'Something is rotten in state-of-the-art narrative theory. Time has done nothing to correct it, and philosophers have managed even less' (A. P. Norman, 'Telling it like it was: historical narratives on their own terms', ibid., Vol. 30, No. 2, 1991, p. 119).

9 Cf. chapters 1–5 of W. B. Gallie, op. cit.; but also, more recently, P. A. Roth's attempt to counter '*a priori* objections to the notion of a narrative explanation', in P. A. Roth, 'Narrative Explanations: The Case of History', *History and Theory*, Vol. 27, No. 1, 1988, p. 12.

2 THE STRUCTURE OF NARRATIVE

1 *Pace*, apparently, R. F. Atkinson, *Knowledge and Explanation in History*, London, Macmillan, 1978: 'One way of exercising control over facts is to arrange them in chronological order, another is to bring them under general classifications. The former is the procedure of narrative history, the latter that of analytic history' (p. 21); and again later, where he attempts to give some credence to 'narrative explanation' even where it *is* based on a mistaken (in my view) idea of narrative – 'since it is universally allowed that *mere* narrative (chronicle) can fail to be explanatory, it may be asked what conditions have to be satisfied before it becomes so' (p. 130). Quite so, but the answer must remain 'never' whilst narrative and chronicle are equated.

2 E.g. see Plato, *The Republic*, Parts III and X.

3 See H. Tudor, *Political Myth*, London, Pall Mall, 1972, pp. 123ff.

4 See R. Koselleck, *Futures Past – On The Semantics of Historical Time*, trans. K. Tribe, Massachusetts, MIT Press Cambridge, 1985, p. 95, for an alleged distinction between 'natural' and 'historical' time-sequencing.

5 Cf. R. Martin, 'Other Periods, Other Cultures', ch. 11 of his *Historical Explanation: Re-enactment and Practical Inference*, London, Cornell University Press, 1977 (an extended and principally sympathetic examination and development of Collingwood's idea of 're-enactment').

6 I say, 'construed as', to take account of those scientists now attempting to integrate elements of chance/arbitrariness into their explanations of natural processes.

7 B. de Spinoza, *A Theologico-Political Treatise*, in *The Chief Works of Benedict de Spinoza*, trans. R. H. M. Elwes, New York, Dover Publications, 1955, Vol. 1, p. 86.

8 *The Concise Oxford Dictionary*, Oxford, Oxford University Press, 1952, p. 65.

9 *Karl Marx/Frederick Engels: Collected Works*, London, Lawrence & Wishart, 1976–, Vol. 5, p. 3.

10 See G. A. Reich, 'Chaos, History, and Narrative', and D. N. McCloskey, 'History, Differential Equations, and the Problem of Narration', both in *History and Theory*, Vol. 30, No. 1, 1991, for intriguing intimations of the relevance of narrative logic to 'chaos theory'.

11 *The Concise Oxford Dictionary*, p. 76.

12 Cf. T. Kuhn, *The Structure of Scientific Revolutions*, University of Chicago Press,

1967, p. 117, where, in discussing 'transformations of vision', Kuhn observes that 'Lavoisier . . . saw oxygen where Priestley had seen dephlogisticated air and where others had seen nothing at all'; also see note 18 to Chapter Five below.

13 See G. Graham, *Historical Explanation Reconsidered*, Aberdeen University Press, 1983, pp. 57–62, for the consequences of a mistaken (in my view) notion of narrative which leads its author to claim that 'the history in which . . . historical explanation consists comprises a single event whereas narrative typically is the story of a sequence of events' (p. 57), and involves his repeating earlier claims (ibid., pp. 30–34) that, *pace* Collingwood and Dray, 'there is a clear, obvious, and intelligible criterion of historical explanation which we can adopt without having to assert or deny any distinction . . . between the human and the natural worlds' (ibid., p. 36). Where he reiterates this, he adds that 'an allied distinction, equally untenable and useless, is that between scientific and historical explanation' (ibid., p. 76).

14 E.g. see T. Hobbes, *Leviathan*, ed. J. Tuck, Cambridge University Press, 1991, p. 111 (ch. 9, Pt 1).

3 THE PRACTISING HISTORIAN

1 E.g. see note 63 to Chapter Five below.

2 K. Marx, *Economic and Philosophical Manuscripts*, in *Karl Marx – Early Texts*, trans. & ed. D. McLellan, Oxford, Blackwell, 1971, p. 168.

3 *Karl Marx/Frederick Engels: Collected Works*, London, Lawrence & Wishart, 1976–, Vol. 5., p. 3.

4 E.g. ibid., Vol. 3, pp. 276–277.

5 T. Hobbes, *Leviathan*, ed. J. Tuck, Cambridge University Press, 1991, pp. 146–147 (ch. 21, Pt 2).

6 J. Bodin, *Six Books of the Commonwealth*, ed. M. J. Tooley, Oxford, Blackwell, 1967, p. 5.

7 E.g. see B. de Spinoza, *Ethics*, in *The Chief Works of Benedict de Spinoza*, trans. by R. H. M. Elwes, New York, Dover Publications, 1955, Vol. II, closing paragraphs to 'Note' to Prop. XLIX, Pt II.

8 E.g. see *Karl Marx/Frederick Engels: Collected Works*, London, Lawrence & Wishart, 1976–, Vol. 5, pp. 87–88.

9 E.g. see M. Oakeshott, 'On Being Conservative', in *Rationalism in Politics*, London, Methuen, 1962, pp. l68ff.; also M. Oakeshott, *On Human Conduct*, Oxford, Clarendon Press, 1975, pp. 73–74.

10 E.g. see *Karl Marx/Frederick Engels: Collected Works*, London, Lawrence & Wishart, 1976–, Vol. 3, pp. 274–275.

11 See R. Martin, *Historical Explanation: Re-enactment and Practical Inference*, London, Cornell University Press, 1977, pp. 71–74, for a treatment of the problem of 'alternative courses of action' in explaining human conduct.

12 Cf. Martin's (ibid., p. 45) gloss on Collingwood's assertion that, once 'an historical fact has been . . . ascertained, grasped by the . . . re-enactment of the agent's thought in his mind', then 'there is no such thing as the supposed further stage of . . . scientific history, which discovers their causes or laws or in general explains them' (Martin quoting from R. Collingwood's *The Idea of History*, Oxford University Press, 1946, pp. 176–177).

13 E.g. see B. de Spinoza, op. cit., Prop. XI, Pt II; Prop. IX, Pt III; Prop. XXVI, Pt IV.

14 A question addressed by E. Hobsbawm in 'From Social History to the History

of Society' in *Daedalus*, Vol. 100, No. 1, 1971, pp. 20–45, and again (somewhat more hesitantly) in 'Economic and Social History Divided', *New Society*, 11 July 1974, pp. 74–76, where he confesses, of social historians, 'we are far from clear what "society" (whose structure and development is to be historically studied) actually means'.

15 For a longer list, see Hobsbawm's 1971 article (op. cit.), and H. Perkin, 'Social History in Britain', *Journal of Social History*, Vol. 10, No. 2, 1976, pp. 129–143.

16 E.g. see R. Holt, *Sport and the British, A Modern History*, Oxford, Clarendon Press, 1989, p. 358, where he says, 'when the social historians find that sociologists quite reasonably disagree profoundly about what it is they are trying to explain . . . the historian retreats into the 'facts' and constructs his 'stories' based frequently upon the sequence of what seem to be significant events in a chosen individual activity'; yet of the criterion of *significance* (in our terms, 'relevance' – see Chapter Four), Holt adds, 'this is without doubt the major obstacle for anyone writing a general [social] history'.

17 Meanwhile, the debate on 'social history' continues, as evidenced by A. Briggs' review essay of C. Lloyd's *Explanation in Social History* (1986), in *History and Theory*, Vol. 29, No. 1, 1990, pp. 95–99, and C. Lloyd's claim (in 'The Methodologies of Social History', *History and Theory*, Vol. 30, No. 2, 1991), that 'The most fundamental of the . . . main philosophical issues pertaining to the study of the history of society concerns the nature of the object of inquiry. What is society?' (p. 189).

18 *Pace* G. Graham, *Historical Explanation Reconsidered*, Aberdeen University Press, 1983, p. 70: 'deciding between different explanations just is a matter of settling the facts'.

4 HISTORY AND THEORY

1 Cf. G. Graham, *Historical Explanation Reconsidered*, Aberdeen University Press, 1983, p. 45.

2 See R. Koselleck, *Futures Past – On The Semantics of Historical Time*, trans. K. Tribe, Massachusetts, MIT Press Cambridge, 1985, pp. 116–129, for a markedly different notion of 'chance'.

3 T. Hobbes, *Leviathan*, ed. J. Tuck, Cambridge University Press, 1991, pp. 31–33 (ch. 5, Pt 1).

4 E.g. see *Karl Marx/Frederick Engels: Collected Works*, London, Lawrence & Wishart, 1976–, Vol. 3, pp. 341–342.

5 Ibid., Vol. 6, p. 482.

6 E.g. see ibid., Vol. 5, p. 3.

7 E.g. see ibid., pp. 35–36.

8 Ibid., p. 24.

9 E.g. see *Karl Marx & Frederick Engels: Selected Works*, London, Lawrence & Wishart, 1968, p. 182; also S. Avineri, *The Social and Political Thought of Karl Marx*, Cambridge, Cambridge University Press, 1968, pp. 149, 227.

10 See G. Lichtheim, *Marxism*, London, Routledge, Kegan, & Paul, 1964, pp. 234–258; also R. Bhaskar, *Reclaiming Reality – A Critical Introduction to Contemporary Philosophy*, London, Verso, 1989, pp. 125–134.

11 E.g. see *Karl Marx/Frederick Engels: Collected Works*, London, Lawrence & Wishart, 1976–, Vol. 3, pp. 303–304.

12 Ibid., Vol. 5, p. 41.

13 H. Tudor, *Political Myth*, London, Pall Mall, 1972, pp. 114–120.

14 R. Tucker, *Philosophy and Myth in Karl Marx*, Cambridge, Cambridge University Press, 1964, pp. 144–149.

15 Graham, op. cit., p. 24: although giving divergent views to many proposed here and elsewhere in this book (and not addressing the history of *thought*), this monograph poses a number of similar questions, and is a good (nonexhaustive) critical bibliographical source for the topic of 'historical explanation', which it is fair to say has dominated most recent analytic philosophy of history in general.

16 Ibid., p. 43.

17 Ibid., p. 63.

18 E.g. see B. de Spinoza, *Ethics*, in *The Chief Works of Benedict de Spinoza*, trans. R. H. M. Elwes, New York, Dover Publications, 1955, Vol. II, Prop. XXXV, Pt II.

19 Cf. Graham, op. cit., p. 11.

20 Cf. ibid., p. 13.

21 Cf. ibid., p. 6.

22 *The Concise Oxford Dictionary of Current English*, Oxford, Clarendon Press, 1990.

23 K. Marx & F. Engels, *The German Ideology*, London, Lawrence & Wishart, 1965, p. 38.

24 Cf. Kuhn's observation that, where 'confronted with anomaly or with crisis' regarding existing scientific paradigms, one of the common responses of scientists themselves is 'recourse to philosophy', T. Kuhn, *The Structure of Scientific Revolutions*, University of Chicago Press, 1967, p. 90.

25 E.g. see R. Martin, *Historical Explanation: Re-enactment and Practical Inference*, London, Cornell University Press, 1977, p. 14.

26 E.g. the *Begriffsgeschichte* group of German scholars, including Koselleck, of whose essays Tribe says, 'What will strike . . . the Anglo-American reader at once is the range of intellectual interests and capacities that these essays display. It would be hard to imagine work of such depth and theoretical diversity being produced today by a senior, English-speaking professor of history'; Koselleck, op. cit., p. viii.

27 P. Gardiner, *The Philosophy of History*, London, Oxford University Press, 1982, p. 2.

28 Portentously, Graham concluded his monograph by claiming that 'the mistaken notions about historical explanation I have been examining constitute only one aspect of a more general misunderstanding of the nature of history as a whole' (op. cit., p. 77); also cf. J. H. Hexter, *The History Primer*, London, Allen Lane/The Penguin Press, 1972, p. 10, for an early statement of the same complaint (this time by a practising historian), of which the remainder of his book is, to an extent, an elaboration.

29 E.g. see L. Feuerbach, *Principles of the Philosophy of the Future*, New York, Bobbs-Merrill, 1966, pp. 8–10.

30 *Karl Marx/Frederick Engels: Collected Works*, London, Lawrence & Wishart, 1976–, Vol. 5, p. 3.

31 E.g. see the survey in chapters 2, 3, and 4 of Bhaskar, op. cit.

32 E.g. see G. Friedrich, *Tradition and Authority*, London, Pall Mall, 1972, ch. 4.

33 As was said, for example, of the 1916 Easter Rising in Ireland; e.g. see J. C. Beckett, *A Short History of Ireland*, London, Hutchinson, 1979, p. 151.

34 According to Kvestad, in 1977, 'On the whole, the methodology of the history of ideas is in its infancy' (N. B. Kvestad, 'Semantics in the Methodology of the History of Ideas', *Journal of the History of Ideas*, Vol. 38, No. 1, 1977,

p. 174). That some historians of thought themselves continued to be concerned about their activity is adduced by D. F. Lindenfield, in 'On Systems and Embodiments as Categories for Intellectual History', *History and Theory*, Vol. 27, No. 1, 1988; he tells us that 'The unsettled state of intellectual history will be evident to anyone familiar with the literature of recent years', and that he will attempt to 'make a contribution to calming the queasiness that is currently besetting the field' of intellectual history (p. 30); he proceeds to give examples of this 'queasiness'.

5 THE POSSIBILITY OF THE HISTORY OF THOUGHT

1 See D. Boucher's useful review of the most recent examples of such projects in the field of the history of *political* thought, in 'Histories of Political Thought in the Post-methodological Age', *History of Political Thought*, Vol. 14, No. 2, 1993, pp. 301–316, where he discusses G. Williams, *Political Theory in Retrospect* (1991), J. Plamenatz, *Man and Society* (revised by J. Plamenatz and R. Wokler, 1992), and I. Hampsher-Monk, *A History of Modern Political Thought* (1992).

2 For a markedly different (contemporary) approach to 'what is a concept', see ch. 2 of P. Thagard, *Conceptual Revolutions*, New Jersey, Princeton University Press, 1992, which, despite equating 'concepts' with 'ideas', includes a useful brief summary of both the history of, and present approaches to, the general problematic regarding the status of ideas/concepts.

3 E.g. B. de Spinoza, *Ethics*, in *The Chief Works of Benedict de Spinoza*, trans. R. H. M. Elwes, New York, Dover Publications, 1955, Vol. II, Prop. XXIX, Pt II.

4 See K. Tribe's Introduction to R. Koselleck, *Futures Past – On The Semantics of Historical Time*, Massachusetts, MIT Press Cambridge, 1985, pp. xi ff., for an account of the centrality of the historicity of concepts in the development of '*Begriffsgeschichte*' as a distinctive feature of German historiography; see also M. Richter, '*Begriffsgeschichte* and the History of Ideas', *Journal of the History of Ideas*, Vol. 48, No. 2, 1987, pp. 247–263.

5 Indeed, the book described on its jacket as 'the first collection of essays on problems of method in the history of ideas to be assembled' is called *The History of Ideas* (ed. P. King, London & Canberra, Croom Helm, 1983).

6 *Pace* D. L. Hull, 'Central Subjects and Narrative Identities', *History and Theory*, Vol. 14, 1975; discussing intellectual history, he observes, 'Histories of ideas are one of the most interesting and certainly the most problematic type of history produced by historians . . . The low opinion which many contemporary historians have of histories of ideas . . . stems from the peculiar nature of ideas as central subjects' – that is, they lack 'sufficient unity and continuity to support an historical narrative' (p. 271). After a brief discussion, Hull concludes, 'Whether ideas can be interpreted so that they are legitimate central subjects is a disputed question. I am predisposed to the opinion that they can be' (p. 273).

7 *The Concise Oxford Dictionary*, Oxford, Oxford University Press, 1952.

8 See I. Shapiro, 'Realism in the Study of the History of Ideas', *History of Political Thought*, Vol. 3, No. 3, 1982, for a comprehensive critical survey of those (for instance, Q. Skinner, J. G. Pocock, and J. Dunn), who have variously argued 'that writing a text is performing a linguistic action', and therefore, that 'to understand the meaning of a text . . . we must understand the linguistic action performed by the author in writing it' (p. 535).

9 *Pace* King, op. cit., p. 55, where he says 'any history of ideas, in its most

significant dimensions, is effectively reducible to a history of some branch or aspect of the history of philosophy'.

10 E.g. see B. Crick, *Basic Forms of Government*, London & Basingstoke, Macmillan, 1973, pp. 55–57.
11 K. Marx & F. Engels, *The German Ideology*, London, Lawrence & Wishart, 1965, p. 42 (Marx's emphasis).
12 J. Bodin, *Six Books of the Commonwealth*, ed. M. J. Tooley, Oxford, Blackwell, 1967, p. 1.
13 Ibid., p. 3.
14 Ibid., p. xvi.
15 H. A. Wolfson, *The Philosophy of Spinoza*, New York, Meridian, 1965.
16 Cf. P. Hardy's review essay of M. R. Waldman's, *Toward a Theory of Historical Narrative – A Case Study in Perso-Islamicate Historiography*, in *History and Theory*, Vol. 20, No. 3, 1981, pp. 337–338.
17 A point made to philosophers by Q. Skinner, in 'Conventions and the Understanding of Speech Acts', *Philosophical Quarterly*, Vol. 20, No. 78, 1970; regarding 'understanding speech acts' and 'the subject of statements and their understanding', Skinner concluded his article by saying, 'this might well seem a genuinely fruitful direction in which to step out – though the ice over there is undoubtedly very thin' (p. 138); nevertheless, this has not stopped him from stepping out further on a substantial number of occasions (see King, op. cit., pp. 322–323, for bibliography merely up to 1979), and it must partly be to his credit that the ice is no longer so thin.
18 See T. Kuhn, *The Structure of Scientific Revolutions*, University of Chicago Press, 1967, pp. 124–126, for Kuhn's interesting speculations regarding the problematic of 'some neutral observation-language'.
19 *Pace* G. Graham, 'Can There Be History of Philosophy?', *History and Theory*, Vol. 21, No. 1, 1982; 'what a man writes or says is not evidence for his thought, it *is* his thought' (p. 46).
20 Bodin, op. cit., p. 1.
21 Ibid., p. 2.
22 *The Concise Oxford Dictionary*.
23 Cf. Kuhn's claim that 'to discover how scientific revolutions are effected, we shall . . . have to examine not only the impact of nature and of logic, but also the techniques of persuasive argumentation effective within the quite special groups that constitute the community of scientists'; Kuhn, op. cit., p. 93; although not a point he goes on to explore, he appears to be suggesting that the manner in which scientists argue their ideas is part of their (scientific) thinking.
24 G. Hegel's *Philosophy of Right*, trans. T. M. Knox, Oxford, Clarendon Press, 1962, pp. 14–15.
25 See pp. 229–231 (and note 35), below.
26 E.g. see L. Strauss, *Persecution and the Art of Writing*, University of Chicago Press, 1988.
27 See Spinoza, *Correspondence*, op. cit., Vol. II, Letter XIX (pp. 296–297).
28 J. Plamenatz's editorial note to his edition of Hobbes' *Leviathan*, London, Fontana, 1962.
29 E.g. see E. E. Cooper, 'Hobbes and God: a re-assessment of Hobbes' "real" views on religion, from the fresh perspective of the recently published "Thomas White's *De Mundo* examined" ', an unpublished MA (with Distinction) dissertation, January 1991, University of Ulster at Coleraine.
30 E.g. Tooley's edition of Bodin, op. cit.

31 See Kuhn, op. cit., p. 38, where, talking of *scientific* work, he observes that whatever originally attracted someone to a problem, e.g. usefulness, 'Once engaged, his motivation is of a rather different order. What then challenges him is the conviction that, if only he is skilful enough, he will succeed in solving a puzzle that no one before has solved or solved so well. Many of the greatest scientific minds have devoted all their professional attention to demanding puzzles of this sort'.

32 See note 2 to Chapter Four above.

33 *The Political Writings of Jean-Jacques Rousseau*, ed. & trans. C. E. Vaughan, Oxford, Blackwell, 1962, Vol. 1, pp. 150, 202.

34 J.-J. Rousseau, *Discourse on the Origin of Inequality*, in *The Social Contract and Discourses*, trans. G. D. H. Cole, London, Everyman, Dent, 1966, p. 192.

35 That it was definitely added after the *Discourse* (including its 'Notes') was completed is verified by both Vaughan, op. cit., p. 207, and the editors of the 1964 Gallimard edition of *Jean-Jacques Rousseau – Oevres Completes*, Vol. III, p. 1367, who claim it was sent to Rey, Rousseau's Amsterdam publisher, whilst the *Discourse* was already in the press – that is, sometime in Feb./March 1755: see *Correspondence Complete de Jean-Jacques Rousseau*, ed. R. A. Leigh, Geneva, Institut et Musée Voltaire, 1966, Vol.III, pp. 275ff. (The *Discourse* had been written during 1753–4.)

36 J.-J. Rousseau, *The Social Contract*, in *The Social Contract and Discourses*, trans. G. D. H. Cole, London, Everyman, Dent, 1966, p. 16.

37 Ibid., pp. 32–33.

38 Vaughan, op. cit., Vol. II, pp. 137–142.

39 *Karl Marx/Frederick Engels: Collected Works*, London, Lawrence & Wishart, 1976–, Vol. 3, p. 276.

40 Ibid., Vol. 5, p. 31.

41 R. Tucker, *Philosophy and Myth in Karl Marx*, Cambridge, Cambridge University Press, 1964.

42 *Karl Marx/Frederick Engels: Collected Works*, London, Lawrence & Wishart, 1976–, Vol. 3, p. 277.

43 Ibid., p. 279.

44 Ibid., p. 281.

45 Ibid., p. 279.

46 Ibid., Vol. 5, p. 41.

47 Tucker, op. cit., p. 149.

48 *Karl Marx/Frederick Engels: Collected Works*, London, Lawrence & Wishart, 1976–, Vol. 3, p. 278.

49 *Karl Marx – Early Texts*, trans. & ed. D. McLellan, Oxford, Blackwell, 1971, p. 142; also (for 'consider', rather than 'consider further'), *Karl Marx – Early Writings*, trans. & ed. T. B. Bottomore, London, C. A. Watts & Co., 1963, p. 130.

50 *The Marx-Engels Reader*, ed. R. C. Tucker, New York, W. W. Norton & Co., 1972, p. 64.

51 *Karl Marx/Frederick Engels: Collected Works*, London, Lawrence & Wishart, 1976–, Vol. 5, p. 4.

52 Ibid., p. 41.

53 Ibid., p. 31.

54 Ibid., pp. 41–44.

55 H. Tudor and J. M. Tudor, *Marxism and Social Democracy*, Cambridge, Cambridge University Press, 1988, p. ll.

56 E.g. see J. Dunn, *The Political Thought of John Locke*, Cambridge, Cambridge University Press, 1969, pp. 77–83.

57 F. Wendel, *Calvin – The Origins and Development of his Religious Thought*, London, Fontana, 1978, p. 12.

58 E.g. *Erasmus – Luther; Discourse on Free Will*, trans. & ed. E. F. Winter, New York, Frederick Ungar Publishing Co., 1961.

59 Cf. Kuhn, op. cit., pp. 91–93, for his treatment of the parallels between intellectual (in this case, scientific) revolutions and political revolutions.

60 E.g. see B. Reardon, *Religious Thought in the Reformation*, London & New York, Longman, 1981, pp. 302ff.

61 See H. Tudor's 'Introduction' to *Marxism and Social Democracy*', op. cit., somewhat of an exemplar in the historical presentation of a 'real', parametered intellectual controversy – in this case, a crucial phase in the Revisionist Debate.

62 E.g. see my review of R. Bhaskar's *Reclaiming Reality – A Critical Introduction to Contemporary Philosophy* (London, Verso, 1989), in *History of European Ideas*, Vol. 14, No. 3, 1992, pp. 436–438.

63 E.g. see G. Lichtheim, *A Short History of Socialism*, Glasgow, Fontana/Collins, 1977; also, the same author's *Marxism*, London, Routledge, Kegan & Paul, 1964, and contrast with R. Berki's approach to 'what is socialism?' in R. N. Berki, *Socialism*, London, J. M. Dent & Sons, 1975, where, in calling socialism 'not a single thing, but a range, an area, an open texture, a self-contradiction' (p.16), Berki appears to recognise he is close to denoting 'socialism' as (speculatively, idealistically?), a thing which determines itself, for after pointing out that 'this approach has had many an illustrious advocate' (ibid.), he adds a note saying, 'It would no doubt be presumptuous to call our approach 'dialectical', though it carries the influence of such works as Hegel's *Phenomenology*' (note 6, p. 157).

64 P. Kristeller, *Eight Philosophers of the Italian Renaissance*, Stanford, California, Stanford University Press, 1964, p. 143.

65 J. Bronowski & B. Mazlish, *The Western Intellectual Tradition*, London, Hutchinson, 1960, p. 3.

66 Kristeller, op. cit., p. 5.

BIBLIOGRAPHY

ABBREVIATIONS

HPT   *History of Political Thought*
HT   *History and Theory*
JHI   *Journal of the History of Ideas*

1 WORKS CITED

Aristotle, *The Politics* (trans. T. A. Sinclair), Harmondsworth, Penguin, 1964.

Asimov, I. *Foundation*, London, Panther, 1972.

Atkinson, R. F. *Knowledge and Explanation in History*, London, Macmillan, 1978.

Avineri, S. *The Social and Political Thought of Karl Marx*, Cambridge, Cambridge University Press, 1968.

Beckett, J. C. *A Short History of Ireland*, London, Hutchinson, 1979.

Berki, R. N. *Socialism*, London, J. M. Dent & Sons, 1975.

Bhaskar, R. *Reclaiming Reality – A Critical Introduction to Contemporary Philosophy*, London, Verso, 1989.

Bodin, J. *Six Books of the Commonwealth*, ed. M. J. Tooley, Oxford, Blackwell, 1967.

Boucher, D. 'Histories of Political Thought in the Post–methodological Age', *HPT*, Vol. 14, No. 2, 1993, pp. 301–316.

Briggs, A. Review essay of C. Lloyd's *Explanation in Social History* (1986), in *HT*, Vol. 29, No. 1, 1990, pp. 95–99.

Bronowski, J. & Mazlish, B. *The Western Intellectual Tradition*, London, Hutchinson, 1960.

Cervantes, M. de *The Adventures of Don Quixote*, (trans. J. M. Cohen), Harmondsworth, Penguin, 1968.

Cicero, *The Republic* (trans. C. W. Keyes), London, Heinemann, 1966.

Collingwood, R. *The Idea of History*, Oxford University Press, 1946.

The Concise Oxford Dictionary, Oxford, Oxford University Press, 1952.

The Concise Oxford Dictionary of Current English, Oxford, Clarendon Press, 1990.

Cooper, E. E. 'Hobbes and God: a re-assessment of Hobbes' "real" views on religion, from the fresh perspective of the recently published "Thomas White's *De Mundo* Examined" ', unpublished MA (with Distinction) dissertation, University of Ulster at Coleraine, 1991.

Crick, B. *Basic Forms of Government*, London & Basingstoke, Macmillan, 1973.

Dray, W. H. 'On the Nature and Role of Narrative in Historiography', *HT*, Vol. 10, No. 1, 1971, pp. 153–171.

271

Dunn, J. *The Political Thought of John Locke*, Cambridge, Cambridge University Press, 1969.

Erasmus – Luther; Discourse on Free Will (trans. & ed. E. F. Winter), New York, Frederick Ungar Publishing Co., 1961.

Feuerbach, L. *Principles of the Philosophy of the Future*, New York, Bobbs-Merrill, 1966.

Friedrich, G. *Tradition and Authority*, London, Pall Mall, 1972.

Gallie, W. B. *Philosophy and the Historical Understanding*, London, Chatto & Windus, 1964.

Gardiner, P. *The Philosophy of History*, London, Oxford University Press, 1974.

Graham, G. *Historical Explanation Reconsidered*, Aberdeen University Press, 1983.

——'Can There Be History of Philosophy?', *HT*, Vol. 21, No. 1, 1982, pp. 37–52.

Hampsher-Monk, I. *A History of Modern Political Thought*, Oxford, Blackwell, 1992.

Hardy, P. Review essay of M. R. Waldman's, *Toward a Theory of Historical Narrative – A Case Study in Perso-Islamicate Historiography*, in *HT*, Vol. 20, No. 3, 1981, pp. 337–338.

Hegel, G. *Philosophy of Right*, trans. T. M. Knox, Oxford, Clarendon Press, 1962.

Hexter, J. H. *The History Primer*, London, Allen Lane/ The Penguin Press, 1972.

Hobbes, T. *Leviathan* (ed. J. Plamenatz), London, Fontana, 1962.

——*Thomas White's 'De Mundo' Examined* (trans. H. W. Jones), London, Bradford University Press, 1976.

——*Leviathan* (ed. J. Tuck), Cambridge University Press, 1991.

Hobsbawm, E. 'From Social History to the History of Society', *Daedalus*, Vol. 100, No. 1, 1971, pp. 20–45.

——'Economic and Social History Divided', *New Society*, 11 July 1974, pp. 74–76.

Holt, R. *Sport and the British, A Modern History*, Oxford, Clarendon Press, 1989.

Hull, D. L. 'Central Subjects and Narrative Identities', *HT*, Vol. 14, 1975, pp. 253–274.

King, P. (ed.) *The History of Ideas*, London & Canberra, Croom Helm, 1983.

Koselleck, R. *Futures Past – On The Semantics of Historical Time* (trans. K. Tribe), Massachusetts, MIT Press Cambridge, 1985.

Kristeller, P. *Eight Philosophers of the Italian Renaissance*, Stanford, California, Stanford University Press, 1964.

Kuhn, T. *The Structure of Scientific Revolutions*, University of Chicago Press, 1967.

Kvestad, N. B. 'Semantics in the Methodology of the History of Ideas', *JHI*, Vol. 38, No. 1, 1977, pp. 157–174.

Lemon, M. C. Review of R. Bhaskar's *Reclaiming Reality – A Critical Introduction to Contemporary Philosophy* (1989), in *History of European Ideas*, Vol. 14, No. 3, 1992, pp. 436–438.

Lichtheim, G. *Marxism*, London, Routledge, Kegan & Paul, 1964.

——*A Short History of Socialism*, Glasgow, Fontana/Collins, 1977.

Lindenfield, D. F. 'On Systems and Embodiments as Categories for Intellectual History', *HT*, Vol. 27, No. 1, 1988, pp. 30–50.

Lloyd, C. 'The Methodologies of Social History', *HT*, Vol. 30, No. 2, 1991.

Locke, J. *Two Treatises of Civil Government*, London, J. M. Dent & Sons, 1962.

——*Essay Concerning Human Understanding*, (ed. M. Cranston), London, Collier-Macmillan, 1965.

Machiavelli, N. *The Prince & the Discourses*, New York, The Modern Library, 1950.

Martin, R. *Historical Explanation: Re-enactment and Practical Inference*, London, Cornell University Press, 1977.

Karl Marx – Early Writings (trans. & ed. T. B. Bottomore), London, C. A. Watts & Co., 1963.

Karl Marx – Early Texts, (trans. & ed. D. McLellan), Oxford, Blackwell, 1971.

Marx, K. & Engels, F. *The German Ideology*, London, Lawrence & Wishart, 1965.

Karl Marx & Frederick Engels: Selected Works, London, Lawrence & Wishart, 1968.

The Marx-Engels Reader, (ed. R. C. Tucker), New York, W. W. Norton & Co., 1972.

Karl Marx/Frederick Engels: Collected Works, London, Lawrence & Wishart, 1976– .

McCloskey, D. N. 'History, Differential Equations, and the Problem of Narration', *HT*, Vol. 30. No. 1, 1991, pp. 21–36.

More, T. *Utopia*, (trans. P. Turner), Harmondsworth, Penguin, 1965.

Murphy, M. G. *Our Knowledge of the Historical Past*, Indianapolis & New York, Bobbs-Merrill, 1973.

Norman, A. P. 'Telling it like it was: historical narratives on their own terms', *HT*, Vol. 30, No. 2, 1991, pp. 119–135.

Oakeshott, M. 'On Being Conservative', in *Rationalism in Politics*, London, Methuen, 1962.

——*On Human Conduct*, Oxford, Clarendon Press, 1975.

The Oxford English Dictionary (second edn), Oxford, Clarendon Press, 1989.

Perkin, H. 'Social History in Britain', *Journal of Social History*, Vol. 10, No. 2, 1976, pp. 129–143.

Plamenatz, J. *Man and Society* (revised by J. Plamenatz and R. Wokler), Harlow, Longman, 1992.

Plato, *The Republic* (trans. D. Lee), Harmondsworth, Penguin, 1974.

Reardon, B. *Religious Thought in the Reformation*, London & New York, Longman, 1981.

Reich, G. A. 'Chaos, History, and Narrative', *HT*, Vol. 30, No. 1, 1991, pp. 1–20.

Richter, M. '*Begriffsgeschichte* and the History of Ideas', *JHI*, Vol. 48, No. 2, 1987, pp. 247–263.

Roth, P. A. 'Narrative Explanations: the case of history', *HT*, Vol. 27, No. 1, 1988, pp. 1–13.

The Political Writings of Jean-Jacques Rousseau (ed. & trans. C. E. Vaughan), Oxford, Blackwell, 1962.

Jean-Jacques Rousseau – Œvres Completes, Gallimard edition, 1964.

Rousseau, J.-J. *The Social Contract and Discourses* (trans. G. D. H. Cole), London, Everyman, Dent, 1966.

Correspondence Complete de Jean-Jacques Rousseau (ed. R. A. Leigh), Geneva, Institut et Museé Voltaire, 1966.

Shapiro, I. 'Realism in the Study of the History of Ideas', *HPT*, Vol. 3, No. 3, 1982, pp. 535–578.

Spinoza, B. de *The Chief Works of Benedict de Spinoza* (trans. R. H. M. Elwes), New York, Dover Publications, 1955.

——*Short Treatise on God, Man, and his Well-being*, (trans. A. Wolf), New York, Russell & Russell, 1963.

Skinner, Q. 'Conventions and the Understanding of Speech Acts', *Philosophical Quarterly*, Vol. 20, No. 78, 1970, pp. 118–138.

Stone, L. 'The New Art of Narrative History', in the *Guardian*, 22 November 1980.

Strauss, L. *Persecution and the Art of Writing*, University of Chicago Press, 1988.

Thagard, P. *Conceptual Revolutions*, New Jersey, Princeton University Press, 1992.

Tucker, R. *Philosophy and Myth in Karl Marx*, Cambridge, Cambridge University Press, 1964.

Tudor, H. *Political Myth*, London, Pall Mall, 1972.
Tudor, H. & Tudor, J. M. *Marxism and Social Democracy*, Cambridge, Cambridge University Press, 1988.
Waugh, E. *Sword of Honour*, London, Eyre Methuen, 1965.
Wendel, F. *Calvin – The Origins and Development of his Religious Thought*, London, Fontana, 1978.
White, H. 'The Question of Narrative in Contemporary Historical Theory', *HT*, Vol. 23, No. 1, 1984, pp. 1–33.
Williams, G. *Political Theory in Retrospect*, Aldershot, Elgar, 1991.
Wolfson, H. A. *The Philosophy of Spinoza*, New York, Meridian, 1965.

SELECTIVE READING

Historical methodology, and narrative

Atkinson, R. F. *Knowledge and Explanation in History*, London, Macmillan, 1978.
Briggs, A. Review essay of C. Lloyd's *Explanation in Social History*, (1986), in *HT*, Vol. 29, No. 1, 1990, pp. 95–99.
Cebik, L. B. 'Understanding Narrative Theory', *HT*, Vol. 25, (Beiheft 25), 1986, pp. 58–81.
Dray, W. H. 'On the Nature and Role of Narrative in Historiography', *HT*, Vol. 10, No. 1, 1971, pp. 153–171.
Gallie, W. B. *Philosophy and the Historical Understanding*, London, Chatto & Windus, 1964.
Gardiner, P. *The Philosophy of History*, Oxford, 1982.
Graham, G. *Historical Explanation Reconsidered*, Aberdeen University Press, 1983.
Hardy, P. Review essay of M. R. Waldman's *Towards a Theory of Historical Narrative: A Case Study in Perso-Islamicate Historiography*', in *HT*, Vol. 20, No. 3, 1981, pp. 337–338.
Hexter, J. H. *The History Primer*, London, Allen Lane/ The Penguin Press, 1972.
Hobsbawm, E. 'From Social History to the History of Society', *Daedalus*, Vol. 100, No. 1, 1971, pp. 20–45.
——'Economic and Social History Divided', *New Society*, 11 July 1974, pp. 74–76.
Hull, D. L. 'Central Subjects and Narrative Identities', *HT*, Vol. 14, 1975, pp. 253–274.
Kellner, H. 'Narrativity in History: Post-structuralism and since', *HT*, Vol. 26 (Beiheft 26), 1987, pp. 1–29.
Koselleck, R. *Futures Past – On The Semantics of Historical Time* (trans. K. Tribe), Massachusetts, MIT Press Cambridge, 1985.
Kuklick, B. Review essay of J. H. Hexter's *The History Primer*, in *HT*, Vol. 11, 1972, pp. 352–359.
Lloyd, C. 'The Methodologies of Social History', *HT*, Vol. 30, No. 2, 1991, pp. 180–219.
McCloskey, D. N. 'History, Differential Equations, and the Problem of Narration', *HT*, Vol. 30, No. 1, 1991, pp. 21–36.
McCullagh, C. B. 'The Truth of Historical Narratives', *HT*, Vol. 26 (Beiheft 26), 1987, pp. 30–46.
Martin, R. *Historical Explanation: Re-enactment and Practical Inference*, London, Cornell University Press, 1977.
Murphy, M. G. *Our Knowledge of the Historical Past*, Indianapolis & New York, Bobbs-Merrill, 1973.

Norman, A. P. 'Telling it like it was: historical narratives on their own terms', *HT*, Vol. 30, No. 2, 1991, pp. 119–135.

Olafson, F. A. 'Narrative History and the Concept of Action', *HT*, Vol. 9, 1970, pp. 265–289.

Passmore, J. 'Narratives and Events', *HT*, Vol. 26, (Beiheft 26), 1987, pp. 68–74.

Perkin, H. 'Social History in Britain', *Journal of Social History*, Vol. 10, No. 2, 1976, pp. 129–143.

Reich, G. A. 'Chaos, History, and Narrative', *HT*, Vol. 30, No. 1, 1991, pp. 1–20.

Roth, P. A. 'Narrative Explanations: the case of history', *HT*, Vol. 27, No. 1, 1988, pp. 1–13.

Stone, L. 'The New Art of Narrative History', in the *Guardian*, 22 November 1980.

Topolski, J. 'Conditions of Truth of Historical Narratives', *HT*, Vol. 20, No. 1, 1981, pp. 47–60.

——'Historical Narrative: Towards a Coherent Structure', *HT*, Vol. 26 (Beiheft 26), 1987, pp. 75–86.

White, H. 'The Question of Narrative in Contemporary Historical Theory', *HT*, Vol. 23, No. 1, 1984, pp. 1–33.

Methodology in the history of thought

Boucher, D. 'Histories of Political Thought in the Post-methodological Age', *HPT*, Vol. 14, No. 2, 1993, pp. 301–316.

Femia, J. V. 'An Historicist Critique of "Revisionist" Methods for Studying the History of Ideas', *HT*, Vol. 20, No. 2, 1981, pp. 113–134.

Graham, G. 'Can there be History of Philosophy?', *HT*, Vol. 21, No. 1, 1982, pp. 37–52.

Hardy, P. Review essay of M. R. Waldman's *Toward a Theory of Historical Narrative – A Case Study in Perso-Islamicate Historiography*, in *HT*, Vol. 20, No. 3, 1981, pp. 337–338.

Janssen, P. L. 'Political Thought as Traditionary Action: the critical response to Skinner and Pocock', *HT*, Vol. 24, No. 2, 1985, pp. 115–146.

Kelley, D. R. 'What is Happening to the History of Ideas?', *JHI*, Vol. 51, No. 1, 1990, pp. 3–25.

King, P. (ed) *'The History of Ideas'*, London & Canberra, Croom Helm, 1983.

Koselleck, R. *Futures Past – On the Semantics of Historical Time*, (trans. K. Tribe), Massachusetts, MIT Press Cambridge, 1985.

Krieger, L. 'The Autonomy of Intellectual History', *JHI*, Vol. 34, No. 4, 1973, pp. 499–516.

Kuhn, T. *The Structure of Scientific Revolutions*, University of Chicago Press, 1967.

Kvestad, N. B. 'Semantics in the Methodology of the History of Ideas', *JHI*, Vol. 38, No. 1, 1977, pp. 157–174.

Lacapra, D. 'Rethinking Intellectual History and Reading Texts', *HT*, Vol. 19, No. 3, 1980, pp. 245–276.

Lindenfield, D. F. 'On Systems and Embodiments as Categories for Intellectual History', *HT*, Vol. 27, No. 1, 1988, pp. 30–50.

Mash, R. 'How Important for Philosophers is the History of Philosophy?', *HT*, Vol. 26, No. 3, 1987, pp. 287–299.

Pagden, A. 'Rethinking the Linguistic Turn: current anxieties in intellectual history', *JHI*, Vol. 49, No. 3, 1988, pp. 519–529.

Parekh, B. & Berki, R. N. 'The History of Political Ideas: a critique of Q. Skinner's methodology', *JHI*, Vol. 34, No. 2, 1973, pp. 163–184.

Ree, J. Review essay of *Philosophy in History*, ed. R. Rorty, J. B. Schneewind, & Q. Skinner, in *HT*, Vol. 25, No. 2, 1986, pp. 205–215.

Richter, M. '*Begriffsgeschichte* and the History of Ideas', *JHI*, Vol. 48, No. 2, 1987, pp. 247–263.

Shapiro, I. 'Realism in the Study of the History of Ideas', *HPT*, Vol. 3, No. 3, 1982, pp. 535–578.

Skinner, Q. 'Conventions and the Understanding of Speech Acts', *Philosophical Quarterly*, Vol. 20, No. 78, 1970, pp. 118–138.

Stern, L. 'Hermeneutics and Intellectual History', *JHI*, Vol. 46, No. 2, 1985, pp. 287–296.

Strauss, L. *Persecution and the Art of Writing*, University of Chicago Press, 1988.

Thagard, P. *Conceptual Revolutions*, New Jersey, Princeton University Press, 1992.

INDEX